INSTRUCTOR'S MANUAL with VIDEO GUIDE

Tony L. Henthorne
University of Southern Mississippi

MARKETING: AN INTRODUCTION

9th edition

Gary Armstrong
Philip Kotler

PEARSON
Prentice Hall

Upper Saddle River, New Jersey 07458

AVP/Executive Editor: Melissa Sabella
Editorial Project Manager: Melissa Pellerano
Project Manager, Production: Kerri Tomasso
Operations Specialist: Arnold Vila
Printer/Binder: OPM Digital Print Services
Cover Printer: OPM Digital Print Services

Credits and acknowledgments borrowed from other sources and reproduced, with permission, in this textbook appear on appropriate page within text.

Pearson Education Ltd., London
Pearson Education Singapore, Pte. Ltd
Pearson Education, Canada, Inc.
Pearson Education–Japan
Pearson Education Australia PTY, Limited
Pearson Education North Asia, Ltd., Hong Kong
Pearson Educación de Mexico, S.A. de C.V.
Pearson Education Malaysia, Pte. Ltd
Pearson Education Upper Saddle River, New Jersey

PEARSON
Prentice Hall

10 9 8 7 6 5 4 3 2 1

ISBN-13-978-0-13-602114-8
ISBN-10-0-13-602114-X

Contents

PREFACE

How to Use

The Ninth Edition of Armstrong/Kotler's *Marketing: An Introduction* has a complete set of supplemental learning and teaching aids. The *Instructor's Manual* plays a central role in organizing this package. This manual has been designed so the instructor can plan lectures, discussions, online learning activities, and written assignments in a coordinated and efficient manner.

All 16 chapters of the text have been carefully reviewed in order to develop the most logical and helpful manual for you, the instructor. Primary features of the *Instructor's Manual* are described below.

Professors on the Go

This section is designed with the busy professor in mind. It serves to bring key material upfront in the manual, where an instructor who is short on time can take a quick look and find key concepts, activities, and exercises that he/she can incorporate into the lecture, without having to page through all the material provided for each chapter.

Previewing the Concepts: Chapter Objectives

Each chapter of the text contains a list of important objectives. These objectives are also listed at the beginning of each chapter of the *Instructor's Manual*. In addition, each objective is tied to the specific section of the text in the **Chapter Outline** section of this manual.

Just the Basics

In this Ninth Edition, there are two sections to each chapter in the ***Instructor's Manual***. The first section, **Just the Basics**, provides several sections that summarize the textbook chapter and end-of-chapter materials. The second section, entitled **Great Ideas**, provides additional student projects and other material that will help you present the material and manage your time effectively.

Chapter Overview

Each chapter of the textbook is summarized in the **Chapter Overview**. This section provides the instructor with a condensed version of the information included in the chapter. This condensation of material is especially helpful in planning chapter sequence presentation and any desired chapter combinations. In addition, this section may help the instructor plan introductory lecture and/or summary remarks.

Annotated Chapter Notes/Outline

This section is the core of the *Instructor's Manual*. This teaching outline is a thorough condensation (specifically tied to the actual phrases and definitions used in the textbook) of the material included in the textbook chapters. This outline includes major and minor headings from the textbook. The instructor will notice that special information sections appear periodically in the body of the outline. This material is highlighted in text boxes throughout the text. The purpose of the boxes is to indicate to the instructor where key material appears in the book, and to offer suggestions for the proper use of the various teaching aids. These blocks contain the following items of information: **Key Terms, Figures, Tables, Linking the Concepts, Chapter Objectives,** and the end-of-chapter material, including **Discussing the Issues, Application Questions, Under the Hood/Focus on Technology**, and **Focus on Ethics**.

In this edition, there are also some blocks that give additional questions you can ask the class as you are going through the material. **Let's Discuss This** generally focuses on thinking about what was presented and expanding on it. **Applying the Concept** attempts to take the information presented and bring it to life in a real marketing situation.

Travel Log—Discussing the Issues and Application Questions

Discussing the Issues and **Application Questions** along with associated comments appear in this section. The questions appear in the textbook (so assignments can be made from textbook chapters); however, comments and answers to the questions only appear in the *Instructor's Manual*. Note that proper placement of the **Discussing the Issues** and **Application Questions** is up to the instructor, although placement suggestions do appear in the **Chapter Outline** section.

Under the Hood/Focus on Technology

This section is included in the end-of-chapter materials in the textbook. In the *Instructor's Manual*, the comments and answers are given. This section is intended to give the students a greater understanding of how technology has impacted companies in their marketing efforts.

Focus on Ethics

Much has been noted in the press recently about the failure of corporate ethics as it relates to accounting and executive compensation. Yet marketing has always been questioned about its ethics, and there have been several consumer movements as a result. Therefore, **Focus on Ethics** was developed to enable students to think through the various issues that frequently come up in making marketing decisions. These questions will force the students to think like marketing managers in order to tackle some of the tough issues facing companies today.

Great Ideas

This section provides additional information to aid in the instructor's development of the material for presentation to class.

Barriers to Effective Learning

This section has been developed to aid the instructor in understanding which of the concepts or activities contained in the textbook chapters may be difficult learning assignments for the average student. By reviewing this section, the instructor may be able to direct preparation toward those topics that are perceived as being more difficult. In addition, this section provides suggestions for dealing with difficult learning concepts.

Student Projects

Three to five additional projects are listed for effective student learning. These can be done individually or in groups, and can be done in class or as homework assignments. These projects could also provide a rich source of extra credit projects, if desired.

Classroom Exercise/Homework Assignment

This is an additional assignment to help relate the textbook material to real-world situations. As the majority of these projects depend on access to the Internet, they can be assigned as homework when there is no network connection in the classroom.

Classroom Management Strategies

This section provides a timetable for individual chapter lectures. The timetables are based on a 60-minute class; you will need to increase or decrease the amount of time for each section of the chapter to account for shorter or longer class periods. The time table provided normally has from four to six sections (time segments are suggested) which give guidance to the instructor on what topics to cover, how to coordinate these topics with text features (i.e., *Figures*, *Tables*, *Marketing at Work* and other material as appropriate) and in-class discussions.

Company Case Notes

This section of the *Instructor's Manual* offers a synopsis, teaching objectives, answers to discussion questions, and suggestions on how to teach the case. It also indicates additional chapters in which the case can be used.

Video Case Notes

The last section in the *Instructor's Manual* contains teaching notes to accompany the video cases found in the appendix of the textbook, consisting of an Executive Summary, Questions, and Teaching Ideas for each case. Please contact your Prentice Hall sales representative for access to the DVD containing the video segments noted.

Annotated Instructor's Notes

These notes are found **online only** and serve as a quick reference for the entire supplements package. Suggestions for using materials from the Instructor's Manual, PowerPoint slides, Test Item File, Video Library, and online material are offered for each section within every chapter. Visit www.prenhall.com/kotler to access these **Annotated Instructor's Notes**.

RECOMMENDED SYLLABUS

Week	Readings
1	Chapters 1
2	Chapters 2
3	Chapter 3
4	Chapter 4
5	Chapter 5
6	Chapter 6 Appendix 3
7	Chapters 7
8	Chapters 8
9	Chapters 9 Appendix 2
10	Chapter 10
11	Chapter 11
12	Chapter 12
13	Chapter 13
14	Chapter 14
15	Chapter 15
16	Chapter 16

Professors on the Go!

Chapter 1
Marketing: Creating and Capturing Customer Value

Key Concepts

Needs, wants, and demands
Marketing offers
Customer value and satisfaction

- Copy or clip three advertisements from newspapers or magazines. What customer needs are the advertisers trying to meet?
- Many people have purchased products through Amazon.com. Certainly, the product purchased is important, but describe the complete marketing offer of Amazon.com. What services, information, or experiences are included?
- This chapter discusses the concepts of customer value and satisfaction. Building on this knowledge, is it logical to assume that if you increase the perceived customer value for a product that there is a corresponding increase in customer satisfaction? Under what conditions might this not occur?

Key Concepts

Choosing a value proposition
Marketing management orientations

- Contrast the following marketing management orientations: "The Selling Concept" and "The Marketing Concept." Can you name a market or market category where "The Selling Concept" is still the most popular marketing management orientation?
- How is your college positioned in the marketplace?

Key Concepts

Relating to customers
Relating to partners
Creating customer loyalty and retention

- Customer loyalty and retention programs are important in building customer relationships and customer equity. Discuss why a national grocery chain such as Von's or Kroger's would choose a "club" program over a "frequency" program.
- "Today, most marketers realize that they don't want to connect with just *any* customers." Do you agree with this statement? Why? Which company would be more likely to follow this creed, Wal-Mart or Porsche?
- Think of a company or brand that you buy over and over. What might your customer lifetime value be, assuming they continue to delight you?

Chapter 2
Company and Marketing Strategy:
Partnering to Build Customer Relationships

Key Concepts

Market-oriented mission statements
Setting goals and objectives
Designing and analyzing a business portfolio

- In a small group, discuss whether the following statement from Burton Snowboards North America, manufacturer and marketer of a leading snowboard brand, meets the five criteria of a good mission statement: "Burton Snowboards is a rider-driven company solely dedicated to creating the best snowboarding equipment on the planet."
- Which of the following two terms do you think best describes the process of developing and maintaining a fit between the organization's goals and capabilities and its changing marketing opportunities: strategic planning or corporate planning. Why?
- The BCG growth-share matrix identifies four classifications of SBUs: Stars, Cash Cows, Question Marks, and Dogs. Briefly discuss why management may find it difficult to dispose of a "Question Mark."

Key Concepts

Market segmentation, target marketing, and market positioning
The 4 Ps of marketing

- Discuss each of the three steps that a company must perform in choosing the best market segments and designing strategies to maximize profitability in selected segments.
- Nordstrom's and Kohl's are two department stores. Visit their Web sites (www.nordstroms.com and www.kohls.com) to familiarize yourself with each. Who do you think each is targeting? How might they be trying to position themselves in the marketplace?
- Do you think that the "4 Ps" marketing mix framework does an adequate job of describing marketer responsibilities in preparing and managing marketing programs? Why? Do you see any issues with this framework in relation to service products?
- Why would a focus on the 4 Cs be more important than the 4 Ps?

Chapter 3
Analyzing the Marketing Environment

Key Concepts
Microenvironmental forces

- List the six actors in the company's microenvironment. Next, go to the Wal-Mart Web site (www.walmart.com), scroll down to Investor Relations section, and click on the most recent annual report. How many of the six microenvironment actors can you find? Briefly describe each.
- Get in groups in class and role-play bringing a new product to market that the R&D department has just developed. There should be a person for each of these roles: R&D, Marketing, Finance, Purchasing, Suppliers, and a Marketing Intermediary. Each should argue from their point of view and for the needs of each of their organizations. Report your findings and your impressions to the class.
- What does a marketing intermediary do?
- How many publics can you name for your college or university?

Key Concepts
Macroenvironmental forces

- A writer once observed, "You can watch the size of the Cadillac market shrink by just reading the obituaries." In the context of the external environmental forces discussed in the chapter, what did this person mean? What has Cadillac done to counter this trend? From an environmental management perspective would you consider Cadillac's actions to be reactive or proactive? Why?
- There's an old saying that, "two good marketing people can make up for one bad technology decision." Is it a certainty that a company will lose out on new opportunities if it does not keep up with new technology? Explain your position. Can you think of an industry segment where technology may not play an important role?
- Collect ten advertisements and comment on how they apply to the cultural environment (use the areas suggested by the chapter as a place to begin). What effect do cultural values and beliefs have on consumption? Relate this approach to what you learned about the marketing concept and value delivery in the previous chapters.
- Do you think the Internet should be regulated? Why or why not? Do you buy online? Why or why not?

Chapter 4
Managing Marketing Information to Gain Customer Insights

Key Concepts

Where to get marketing information
Marketing research

- Assume that you are a regional marketing manager for a cellular phone company. List at least three potential sources of internal data and discuss how these data would help you create cellular services that provide greater customer value and satisfaction.
- In this chapter we define primary data and secondary data. Once secondary data, such as customer usage, is gathered and analyzed with the express purpose of making a pricing decision, is it still called secondary data or is it primary data?
- Imagine you are an owner of a small children's clothing store that specializes in upscale girl's fashion from size 2 to 6. You have found a potential clothing line, but you are unsure whether or not the line will generate the sales needed to be profitable. Which type of research methodology (exploratory, descriptive, or causal) is best suited to solve your research objective. Why?
- Discuss why you would use a focus group to gather information, rather than interviewing the same people individually.

Key Concepts

Analyzing marketing information and customer relationship marketing
Marketing research for small businesses and nonprofits
Ethics in marketing research

- Small businesses and nonprofit organizations often lack the resources to conduct extensive market research. Assume that you are the director of fundraising for a small nonprofit that is focused on a social issue. List three ways, using limited resources, that you could gather information about your primary donor group.
- Find an example of a company that you believe uses customer relationship management. Describe the process. Outline the "connections" created with customers, suppliers, and publics.
- Talk to students on campus from other countries about the uses of market research in their countries. Is there a focus on market research there? How is it conducted? Are their any taboos or social norms that need to be taken into consideration? Compare answers in class from the different countries represented.
- What do you think is the greatest problem today with respect to ethical business practices on the Internet? What solution would you offer?

Chapter 5
Understanding Consumer and Business Buyer Behavior

Key Concepts

Consumer behavior model
Cultural, social, personal, and psychological factors

- A bank used Consulting Business Intelligence Values and Lifestyles (VALS) research to profile a customer segment that did not use any automated or electronic services. Based on your knowledge of this lifestyle classification system, speculate what might be the primary and secondary VALS type for this customer segment.
- In general, how are decisions and the decision processes for business markets similar to those of consumer markets? How are they different?
- List four primary characteristics of the business market.

Key Concepts

Complex, dissonance-reducing, habitual, and variety-seeking behavior
The stages of the buyer decision process
New product adoption process
Environmental, organizational, interpersonal, and individual influences
The business buying process

- In a small group, discuss how the buyer decision process for a college student would differ from that of a snowboarder in purchasing a backpack. How would you use this knowledge to develop an advertising plan?
- The vice president of marketing for a regional doughnut retailer says, "We believe our customers exhibit high involvement buying behaviors." Do you agree? Why or why not?
- Assume that while you were vacationing in Australia, you ran across a book published there that you believed would do well in the United States market. You negotiate U.S. distribution rights with the Australian publisher, and set about getting it into the major U.S. outlets—Amazon.com, Barnes & Noble, and Borders. Go to the Web sites for these companies and find out how you list books with them. How have they used the Internet to simplify their buying process? Do their procedures meet the needs of small businesses that want to sell to these giants? Why or why not

Chapter 6
Customer Driven Marketing Strategy: Creating Value for Target Customers

Key Concepts

Segmenting consumer markets
Requirements for effective segmentation

- Briefly define the four sets of primary segmentation variables. If you could only use one set of variables to segment prospective students for the "part-time" MBA Program at your university or college, which would it be? Why?
- The chapter discusses requirements for effective segmentation. Suppose you are a product manager in a regional fast-food restaurant company. You are listening to a presentation on a new sandwich wrap idea (chicken breast and okra), and it is your turn to ask questions. Write five questions that you would ask the person presenting this product idea. Each question should be directed at one of the five segmentation requirements.
- Go to a retail bookstore and survey the magazine section. What unique market segments appear to be the target of specialty magazines? How did you determine the segments?
- Find ads for several different types of cars. For instance, select one mini-van, one SUV, one sports car, and one sedan. What market is each trying to reach? What type of segmentation is the advertiser using?

Key Concepts

Evaluating marketing segments
Selecting target market segments
Identifying and choosing competitive advantages

- Is it a good idea for a small company to adopt a differentiated segmentation strategy? Explain.
- You've gone to work for a shoe designer who is just launching her business. Suggest a way to segment the market for her. Then, select a target market to go after, keeping in mind segment size and growth, structural attractiveness, and probable company resources.
- What is the best way to evaluate a target market?
- How is competitive advantage obtained?
- How does a company choose the right competitive advantage to promote?

Chapter 7
Products, Services, and Brands: Building Customer Value

Key Concepts

Products, services, and experiences
Levels and classifications of products
Product and service decisions

- Is Microsoft's Vista operating software a product or a service? Describe the core, actual, and augmented levels of this software offering.
- What is a brand? Describe the value of branding for both the buyer and seller.
- Take a product of your choice and analyze it using the diagram found in Figure 7.1. Be sure to carefully outline each of the three major levels.

Key Concepts

Brand equity
Building strong brands
Managing brands

- List ten of your favorite brand names. What do you like about the product and/or brand name? What do you dislike? What image does the brand have in your mind? When was the last time you abandoned a brand you had used for some time in favor of a new brand? Why did this happen?
- Go to the supermarket and list five examples of products/brands that have been brand extended. Do you think this makes sense or not?
- What is brand equity?

Key Concepts

Nature and characteristics of a service
Marketing strategies for service firms

- Merrill Lynch is one of the world's leading financial management and advisory companies (see www.ml.com).Do ML's financial advising activities meet the four special characteristics of a service? Explain.
- What are the five links in the service-chain?
- List a service that you use that you think is very good. Why is the service good? Review the service using the material from the chapter. What specifics about the service make it very good from a marketing standpoint? Now, do the same thing with a service that you don't like. After comparing them separately, compare them against each other. What could you do to improve the negative service? If you were a competitor, how could you attack the positive service?
- What are the four characteristics of a service? Apply these to a dentist's office.

Chapter 8
New-Product Development and Product Life-Cycle Strategies

Key Concepts

The steps in the new product development strategy

- Under what conditions would you consider not test marketing a product?
- You are a new-product manager and have been asked to design an idea screening process for your company. Prepare a five-step process for screening consumer convenience good ideas.
- Take a product that has failed. Analyze why this happened. What suggestions could you offer that might have prevented the failure?
- What are the different types of test markets?

Key Concepts

Product life-cycle strategies

- What is a fad? Take a fad product and show how it could be maintained on the market past its fad stage. Describe your strategies for doing so. How could the Internet be used to aid your strategy?
- Collect and describe ten advertisements that show products in different phases of a product life-cycle. What did you use to determine which stage the products were in?
- What is the difference between a style, fashion, and fad?
- What are the different strategies for modifying a product in the maturity stage?
- What are the strategies for dealing with products in the decline stage?

Chapter 9
Pricing: Understanding and Capturing Customer Value

Key Concepts

Internal factors affecting pricing
External factors affecting pricing
Cost-based pricing
Value-based pricing
Competition-based pricing

- The chapter points out that many companies do not handle pricing well. Beyond focusing too much on cost, what are some of the other difficulties that marketers have in setting prices?
- Interview a local business about their pricing philosophy and/or strategy. Use their terms and then apply what you have learned from them to assess their approach to those described in the text. What are the similarities and differences? How successful do the strategies appear to be? How did you make this judgment?
- Explain why the elasticity of demand is such an important concept to marketers who market a "commodity-type" product?
- Cost-plus-pricing and target-profit-pricing are two different types of cost-based pricing. Which of these methods is a better tool for marketers?
- According to the text, the pricing challenge for many businesses is to find ways to maintain the company's pricing power. What does this mean?
- What are the primary methods of competition-based pricing?

Key Concepts

Market-skimming and penetration pricing
Product mix pricing strategies

- What market conditions would discourage a company from using a penetration-pricing strategy to enter a market?
- Cell phone companies use a two-part pricing strategy. From a consumer's perspective, is there a better pricing strategy? What is it? Explain.

Key Concepts

Pricing within channel levels
Pricing across channel levels

- Lawful price discrimination by sellers is a common practice. Discuss the conditions under which this price discrimination practice becomes unlawful.
- Find several examples where a retail outlet charges less than the manufacturer's suggested price. Why would they do that? Can you find any examples of retailers charging more than the suggested price? How would a manufacturer react to each of these scenarios?

Chapter 10
Marketing Channels: Delivering Customer Value

Key Concepts

Value delivery network
Channel members add value
Channel behavior
Vertical and horizontal marketing systems

- Describe at least three different distribution channels a new textbook might take to get from the publisher to the student-consumer?
- Take a product or service of your choice and draw a diagram of the channel of distribution that is used to bring the product or service to the marketplace.
- Why are marketing intermediaries used?

Key Concepts

Making channel design decisions
Making channel management decisions

- What are some of the methods companies use to motivate channel partners?
- College students frequently want food late at night, You are going to launch a business that picks up and delivers food to on-campus dormitories. Using the information in the text, design your channel of distribution. What are the needs of the consumer? What are your channel objectives? Do you want to use any intermediaries?

Key Concepts

Marketing logistics and its functions
Integrated logistics management

- Why would a company consider outsourcing its own logistics functions?
- What are the overall goals of integrated supply chain management? What can a company do to achieve the close working relationships necessary for effective supply chain management?
- What do you think is the most critical function performed in logistics? Explain why and describe how the field is changing and what you think will happen in the future.

Chapter 11
Retailing and Wholesaling

Key Concepts

Types of retailers
Marketing decisions retailers make
The future of retailing

- What are the four characteristics used in the chapter to classify retailers? What are the seven major store retailer types? Give an example of each type.
- Explain why it is important for retailers to define their target markets and to decide how they will position themselves in these markets. Give an example of a national specialty retailer who has done this well.
- Consider this statement made by a retailing insider: "The mall represents a point in time in the evolution of retailing….We are reaching the end of one era and entering something new." What is the "something new" that is being suggested? Where will Americans be shopping if not at the malls?
- Considering the increased use of the Internet, what are the ramifications that you think will affect retailing?
- What is a category killer? What is a hypermarket?

Key Concepts

Types of wholesalers
Marketing decisions made by wholesalers
Trends in wholesaling

- Suppose that you are a manufacturer's agent for three lines of complementary women's apparel. Discuss what types of marketing mix decisions you will be making.
- How can wholesalers use the Internet to increase their business? Provide an example of how wholesalers can use the Internet to compete.
- What are the functions of wholesalers? Can these be replaced? If so, how?
- What do you think is the most dramatic trend in wholesaling?

Chapter 12
Communicating Customer Value: Advertising and Public Relations

Key Concepts

The promotion mix
The need for integrated marketing communications
The communications process

- Many companies are adopting the integrated marketing communication concept. Discuss two major problems that this marketing communications philosophy is designed to remedy.
- Find an example of the communication process shown in Figure 12.1. Illustrate and explain each component part.
- What is integrated marketing communications? Why has a shift in this direction occurred?

Key Concepts

Steps in developing effective communications
Setting the total promotion budget
Setting the overall communication mix and integrating the mix
The role of public relations

- Compare and contrast personal and non-personal communication channels.
- How do you determine communications objectives?
- Find at least five different forms of appeals in magazine advertisements. Compare and contrast the effectiveness of each. How were the appeals communicated to you?
- Find at least two examples each of push and pull strategies used by marketers.
- What is the major advantage of the objective-and-task method for setting the promotional budget? What is the major drawback?
- Describe the six roles that public relations can perform. Which do you believe to be the most crucial to the success of a business?

Chapter 13
Communicating Customer Value: Personal Selling and Sales Promotion

Key Concepts

The nature of personal selling and the role of the sales force
Designing the sales force strategy and structure
Managing the sales force

- According to the chapter, salespeople serve "two masters." What does this mean? Is it a good or bad thing?
- The ability to build relationships with customers is the most important of a salesperson's key talents. Do you agree with this statement? Explain.
- What is the role of the sales force in modern business?

Key Concepts

Seven steps in the personal selling process
Customer relationship management

- The text emphasizes the link between personal selling and customer relationship management. Why is this link such an important concept?
- Suppose your grade in one of your classes is hovering between an A and B. How would you apply the seven steps in the personal selling process to convince your professor that you deserve an A?
- Demonstrate how a salesperson could prospect for sales customers via the Internet. Which search sites seemed to be the most effective in your search effort? Try to be as specific as possible with the illustration you chose.
- How should salespeople strive to build relationships? What is relationship marketing?

Key Concepts

The different types of sales promotion objectives
Customer promotions

- Sales promotion objectives vary greatly. Suppose you are the interested in spurring short-term customer buying of your product. What type of sales promotion do you believe would be the most appropriate? Why?
- Go to your local department of discount store. List and describe four examples of customer promotions you see. Which do you believe to be the most effective?

Chapter 14
Direct and Online Marketing: Building Direct Customer Relationships

Key Concepts

Benefits of direct marketing
Customer databases
Forms of direct marketing
Integrated direct marketing
Public policy and ethical issues in direct marketing

- Write a description of the most irritating, unfair, deceptive, or fraudulent experience you've had with a direct marketing company.
- Using your university or college as an example, describe three different databases that would be useful for recruiting efforts. How could these databases be obtained?
- Write a position paper on privacy and security issues in direct marketing. Where are the industry's strengths and weaknesses? What would you recommend to solve problems facing the industry?
- What are the benefits to buyers of direct marketing?
- What are the benefits to sellers from direct marketing?

Key Concepts

Click-only companies and click-and-mortar companies
Setting up an e-marketing presence
The promise and the problems of e-commerce

- Many traditional brick-and-mortar companies have now become click-and-mortar companies. Has the reverse been true (can you name many click-only companies that are now click-and-mortar companies)?
- What is a blog? Are blogs usually social or work-related? How are blogs different from Web communities? Explain.
- Visit two Internet sites, one you like and one you don't like. Evaluate and compare each site using the 7 Cs of effective Web design. Based on the evaluation, which site is better designed?
- As marketing director of a small urban sportswear company, you have been given the assignment to spread the word to 18–25 year-old Internet users that your company has some great products. One of the ways you intend to communicate this message is via Web communities. Outline a plan for doing so. What Web communities might you choose? How would you use viral marketing to aid your effort?
- What are the basic Internet security fears of consumers? Are these fears justified?

Chapter 15
The Global Marketplace

Key Concepts

The international trade system
Economic, political-legal, and cultural environments

- Explain how the addition of the World Trade Organization as a functioning body has changed the nature of international commerce.
- The United States has a trade restriction on Cuba. Is this restriction a tariff, quota, or embargo? To what extent does this trade restriction allow U.S. businesses to export their products to Cuba?
- Find five examples of international products that you regularly buy. Have these products been customized for sale here in the U.S.? Is the producing company following standardization or adaptation in each case?
- Define the following terms: *tariff, quota, embargo, exchange controls,* and *nontariff trade barriers*. Explain the role played by these terms in international trade.

Key Concepts

Deciding whether to go international
Deciding which markets to enter and how to enter them

- Assume your boss has asked you for your opinion on how your company should enter the Japanese, South Korean, and Vietnamese markets with a new line of women's athletic shoes. Would you recommend entering with a standardized marketing mix or an adapted marketing mix? Explain.
- Assess the joint-venture opportunities a software manufacturer would have available if it were looking to market to the European Union?
- Discuss the three market entry strategies shown in Figure 15.2. Which of these strategies is the riskiest? Why?

Key Concepts

The 4 Ps internationally
Global marketing organization

- Write a brief position paper on why you would like to "be in" or "work for" an international firm. What would you see as advantages and disadvantages to working for an international firm? You are free to pick any firm you wish (such as BMW, Sony, Honda, Shell Oil, etc.) to use as an illustration for your comments.
- List and briefly discuss each of the five international product and promotion strategies shown in Figure 15.3.
- What is dumping? Is it a sound strategy?

Chapter 16
Marketing Ethics and Social Responsibility

Key Concepts

The impact of marketing on individuals, society, and business

- Review the claims made by consumers, consumer advocates, public policy makers, and others that the marketers are harming consumers through planned obsolescence, shoddy or unsafe products, and poor service to disadvantaged consumers. Do you agree with these claims?
- Review the responses offered by marketers to claims that high distribution costs, high advertising and promotional costs, and excessive markups lead to high prices that are harmful to the consumer. Do you agree with the marketers' responses?
- Bring an example of a firm that you do not think is being socially-responsible to class. How did you determine this? What were the firm's negative actions? What could the firm do to remove the negative social image?

Key Concepts

Consumerism
Environmentalism

- Can an organization be focused on both consumerism and environmentalism at the same time? Explain.
- Find five examples of products or marketer practices that you perceive to be environmentally-sensitive. How can you tell that this is a policy that is being stressed?
- What is environmental sustainability? List and describe the four parts of Figure 16.1.

Key Concepts

Enlightened marketing
Marketing ethics

- Find an example of a company that you perceive is practicing enlightened marketing. Describe why you feel the company qualifies. Is its practice publicized? Should it be?
- List and describe the forms of products shown in Figure 16.3. Which of these are desirable, and which are not?
- How do firms meet their social responsibility function?

Chapter-by-Chapter Material

CHAPTER 1
Marketing: Creating and Capturing Customer Value

Previewing the Concepts: Chapter Objectives

1. Define marketing and outline the steps in the marketing process.
2. Explain the importance of understanding customers and the marketplace, and identify the five core marketplace concepts.
3. Identify the key elements of a customer-driven marketing strategy and discuss the marketing management orientations that guide marketing strategy.
4. Discuss customer relationship management and strategies for creating value *for* customers and capturing value *from* customers in return.
5. Describe the major trends and forces that are changing the marketing landscape in this age of relationships.

JUST THE BASICS

Chapter Overview

Marketing is managing profitable customer relationships.

The goal of marketing is to create value for customers and to capture value in return.

Marketing is defined as a social and managerial process by which individuals and groups obtain what they need and want through creating and exchanging value with others.

Chapter 1 is organized around five steps in the marketing process (see Figure 1.1) – from understanding customer needs, to designing customer-driven marketing strategies and programs, to building customer relationships and capturing value for the firm.

Annotated Chapter Notes/Outline

Introduction

Procter & Gamble (the makers of Tide) is a great marketing organization. Tide controls 43 percent of the detergent market.

To keep Tide competitive in the market it became important to determine how Tide "speaks" to customers.

Tide was viewed as getting clothes clean, but also as being an "arrogant, masculine" brand.

P&G was successful in repositioning the product as being more relevant in the day-to-day existence of its largely female clientele.

Today's successful companies have one thing in common: they are strongly customer focused and heavily committed to marketing.

What is Marketing?

A simple definition of marketing is *managing profitable customer relationships.*

Marketing must both attract new customers and grow the current customers.

Every organization must perform marketing functions, not just for-profit companies.

Non-profits (colleges, hospitals, churches, etc.) also must also perform marketing.

Marketing Defined

Most people think of marketing as selling and/or advertising—"telling and selling."

Marketing must focus on satisfying customer needs.

We define **marketing** as the process by which companies create value for customers and build strong customer relationships in order to capture value from customers in return.

Use **Key Term** *Marketing* here Use **Chapter Objective** 1 here

The Marketing Process

Use **Figure** 1-1 here

Figure 1-1 (viewed earlier) shows the five-step marketing process.

1. Understand the marketplace and customer needs and wants.
2. Design a customer-driven marketing strategy.
3. Construct a marketing program that delivers superior value.
4. Build profitable relationships and create customer delight.
5. Capture value from customers to create profits and customer quality.

In the first four steps, companies work to understand consumers, create customer value, and build strong customer relationships.

In the final step, companies reap the rewards of creating superior customer value. By creating value *for* consumers, they in turn capture value *from* consumers in the form of sales, profits, and long-term customer equity.

Let's Discuss This

At this point, stop and ask students if the marketing process just described was what they had in mind when they signed up for this class. Did they understand the full extent of marketing? What was their idea of marketing when they first walked through the door?

Understanding the Marketplace and Customer Needs

Five core customer and marketplace concepts are critical: (1) *needs, wants, and demands*; (2) *marketing offers (products, services, and experiences)*; (3) *value and satisfaction*; (4) *exchanges and relationships*; and (5) *markets.*

Customer Needs, Wants, and Demands

The most basic concept underlying marketing is that of **human needs.**

Human **needs** are states of felt deprivation. They include *physical, social, and individuals* needs. These needs were not created by marketers; they are a basic part of the human makeup.

Wants are the form human needs take as they are shaped by culture and individual personality. An American *needs* food but *wants* a Big Mac.

When backed by buying power, wants become **demands.**

The best marketing companies go to great lengths to learn and understand their customers' needs, wants, and demands.

Use **Key Terms** *Needs*, *Wants*, and *Demands* here.
Use **Discussing the Issues** 1 here
Use **Application Question** 1 here

Applying the Concepts

If time permits, have the students break into groups to discuss the concepts of needs, wants, and demands as they were applied to their decision-making process for applying to college, and accepting the offer from the University they are attending. Have them discuss their groups' responses in terms of the needs, wants, and demands, rather than how they might describe it to their friends or family.

Market Offerings—Products, Services, and Experiences

Needs and wants are fulfilled through **market offerings**—some combination of products, services, information, or experiences offered to a market to satisfy a need or want.

Market offerings include *products* and *services*—activities or benefits offered for sale that are essentially intangible and do not result in the ownership of anything.

Marketing myopia occurs when a company becomes so taken with their own products that they lose sight of underlying customer needs.

Use **Key Term** *Market Offering* here

Customer Value and Satisfaction

Customers form expectations about the value and satisfaction that various market offerings will deliver and buy accordingly.

Satisfied customers buy again and tell others about their good experiences.

Dissatisfied customers switch to competitors and disparage the product to others.

Customer value and customer satisfaction are key building blocks for developing and managing customer relationships.

Exchanges and Relationships

Exchange is the act of obtaining a desired object from someone by offering something in return.

Marketing consists of actions taken to build and maintain desirable exchange *relationships* with target audiences.

Use **Key Term** *Exchange* here Use **Chapter Objective** 2 here

Markets

A **market** is the set of actual and potential buyers of a product.

Marketing means managing markets to bring about profitable customer relationships.

Figure 1.2 shows the main elements in a modern marketing system.

Use **Figure** 1-2 here Use **Discussing the Issues** 2 here

Designing a Customer-Drive Marketing Strategy

Marketing management is defined as the art and science of choosing target markets and building profitable relationships with them.

Use **Key Term** *Marketing Management* here

The marketing manager must answer two important questions:

1. What customers will we serve (what's our target market)?
2. How can we serve these customers best (what's our value proposition)?

Selecting Customers to Serve

A company must decide *who* it will serve.

It does this by dividing the market into segments of customers (*market segmentation*) and selecting which segments it will go after (*target marketing*).

Marketing managers know they cannot serve all customers. By trying to do so, they end up not serving any well.

Demarketing is the act of purposefully reducing the number of customers or to shift their demand temporarily or permanently.

Use **Key Term** *Demarketing* here Use **Discussing the Issues** 3 here

Marketing management is *customer management* and *demand management.*

Choosing a Value Proposition

A company's *value proposition* is the set of benefits or values it promises to deliver to consumers to satisfy their needs. (BMW promises "the ultimate driving machine.")

Such value propositions *differentiate* one brand from another.

Marketing Management Orientations

Marketing management wants to design strategies that will build profitable relationships with target consumers. But what *philosophy* should guide these marketing strategies?

There are five alternative concepts under which organizations design and carry out their marketing strategies:

1) The Production Concept

The **production concept** holds that consumers will favor products that are available and highly affordable.

Management should focus on improving production and distribution efficiency.

2) The Product Concept

The **product concept** holds that consumers will favor products that offer the most in quality, performance, and innovative features.

Under this concept, marketing strategy focuses on making continuous product improvements.

3) The Selling Concept

The **selling concept** holds that consumers will not buy enough of the firm's products unless it undertakes a large-scale selling and promotion effort.

The concept is typically practiced with unsought goods—those that buyers do not normally think of buying, such as insurance or blood donations.

These industries must be good at tracking down prospects and selling them on product benefits.

4) The Marketing Concept

The **marketing concept** holds that achieving organizational goals depends on knowing the needs and wants of target markets and delivering the desired satisfactions better than competitors do.

Under the marketing concept, customer focus and value are the *paths* to sales and profits.

It views marketing not as "hunting," but as "gardening."

The job is not to find the right customers for your product but to find the right products for your customers.

Customer-driven companies research current customers deeply to learn about their desires, gather new product and service ideas, and test proposed product improvements.

Customer-driving marketing is understanding customer needs even better than customers themselves do and creating products and services that meet existing and latent needs.

5) The Societal Marketing Concept

The **societal marketing concept** questions whether the pure marketing concept overlooks possible conflicts between consumer *short-run wants* and consumer *long-run welfare*.

The societal marketing concept holds that marketing strategy should deliver value to customers in a way that maintains or improves both the consumer's *and the society's* well-being.

Use **Key Terms** *Production Concept, Product Concept, Selling Concept, Marketing Concept,* and *Societal Marketing Concept* here Use **Figures** 1-3 and 1-4 here Use **Chapter Objective** 3 here Use **Discussing the Issues** 4 here

Preparing an Integrated Marketing Plan and Program

The company's marketing strategy outlines which customers the company will serve and how it will create value for these customers.

Next, the marketer develops an integrated marketing program that will actually deliver the intended value to target customers.

The marketing program consists of the firm's *marketing mix*, the set of marketing tools the firm uses to implement its marketing strategy.

The marketing mix tools are classified into the *four Ps* of marketing: product, price, place, and promotion.

The firm blends all of these marketing mix tools into a comprehensive *integrated marketing program* that communicates and delivers the intended value to chosen customers.

Use **Linking the Concepts** here

Building Customer Relationships

Customer Relationship Management

Customer relationship management is the most important concept of modern marketing.

Customer relationship management is the overall process of building and maintaining profitable customer relationships by delivering superior customer value and satisfaction.

It deals with all aspects of acquiring, keeping, and growing customers.

Relationship Building Blocks: Customer Value and Satisfaction

The key to building lasting customer relationships is to create superior customer value and satisfaction.

Customer Value

This is the customer's evaluation of the difference between all the benefits and all the costs of a market offering relative to those of competing offers.

Customers often do not judge values and costs "accurately" or "objectively."

They act on *perceived* value.

Customer Satisfaction

Customer satisfaction depends on the product's perceived performance relative to a buyer's expectations.

If the product's performance falls short of expectations, the customer is dissatisfied. If performance matches expectations, the customer is satisfied. If performance exceeds expectations, the customer is highly satisfied or delighted.

Although the customer-centered firm seeks to deliver high customer satisfaction relative to competitors, it does not attempt to ***maximize*** customer satisfaction.

A company can always increase customer satisfaction by lowering its price or increasing its services. But this may result in lower profits.

The purpose of marketing is to generate customer value profitably.

Customer Relationship Levels and Tools

Companies can build customer relationships at many levels.

At one extreme, a company with many low-margin customers may seek to develop *basic relationships* with them.

At the other extreme, in markets with few customers and high margins, sellers want to create *full partnerships* with customers.

Many companies offer *frequency marketing programs* that reward customers who buy frequently or in large amounts.

Companies sponsor *club marketing programs* that offer members special benefits and create member communities. (For example, Harley-Davidson sponsors the Harley Owners Group [H.O.G.].)

Use **Key Terms** *Customer Relationship Management, Customer Satisfaction,* and *Customer Perceived Value* here
Use **Marketing at Work** 1-1 here
Use **Application Questions** 2 here

The Changing Nature of Customer Relationships

Yesterday's big companies focused on mass marketing to all customers at arm's length.

Today's companies are building deeper, more direct, and more lasting relationships with carefully selected customers.

Relating with More Carefully Selected Customers

Called *selective relationship management*, many companies now use customer profitability analysis to weed out losing customers and to target winning ones for pampering.

Relating More Deeply and Interactively

Today's marketers are incorporating interactive approaches that help build targeted, two-way customer relationships.

Increasingly, marketers are using new communications approaches in building closer customer relationships.

Consumers have more information about brands than ever before.

Companies can no longer rely on marketing by *intrusion.*

Companies must practice marketing by *attraction*—creating market offerings and messages that **involve** consumers rather than interrupt them.

Consumer-generated marketing has become a significant marketing force.

Partner Relationship Management

Partners inside the Company

Every employee must be customer focused.

David Packard, late co-founder of Hewlett-Packard, said, "Marketing is far too important to be left only to the marketing department."

Today, firms are linking all departments in the cause of creating customer value.

Rather than assigning only sales and marketing people to customers, they are forming cross-functional customer teams.

Marketing Partners outside the Firm

Marketing channels consist of distributors, retailers, and others who connect the company to its buyers.

The *supply chain* describes a longer channel, stretching from raw materials to components to final products that are carried to final buyers.

Through *supply chain management*, many companies today are strengthening their connections with partners all along the supply chain.

Use **Key Term** *Partnership Relationship Management* here. Use **Discussing the Issues** 5 here.

Capturing Value from Customers

The first four steps in the marketing process outlined in Figure 1.1 involve building customer relationships. The final step involves capturing value in return.

By creating superior customer value, the firm creates highly satisfied customers who stay loyal and buy more.

Creating Customer Loyalty and Retention

The aim of customer relationship management is to create not just customer satisfaction, but customer delight.

This means that companies must aim high in building customer relationships.

Customer delight creates an emotional relationship with a product or service, not just a rational preference.

Use **Key Term** *Customer Lifetime Value* here Use **Chapter Objective** 4 here Use **Application Questions** 3 here

Let's Discuss This Have the students discuss brands with which they have an emotional bond. For some students, this could be Abercrombie & Fitch. For others it could be a brand of beer. At a major university, it could be the university itself. Then ask them to discuss how they would react if another brand made them an interesting offer: would they be willing to switch brands under that circumstance? Why or why not?

Growing Share of Customer

Share of customer is defined as the share the company gets of customers purchasing in their product categories. (Thus, banks want to increase "share of wallet.")

Use **Key Term** *Share of Customer* here

Building Customer Equity

Companies want not only to create profitable customers, but to "own" them for life, capture their customer lifetime value, and earn a greater share of their purchases.

What Is Customer Equity?

Customer equity is the total combined customer lifetime values of all of the company's current and potential customers.

Clearly, the more loyal the firm's profitable customers, the higher the firm's customer equity.

Customer equity may be a better measure of a firm's performance than current sales or market share.

Building the Right Relationships with the Right Customers

Not all customers, not even all loyal customers, are good investments.

Figure 1.5 classifies customers into one of four relationship groups, according to their profitability and projected loyalty.

"Strangers" show low potential profitability and little projected loyalty. The relationship management strategy for these customers is simple: Don't invest anything in them.

"Butterflies" are potentially profitable but not loyal. The company should use promotional blitzes to attract them, create satisfying and profitable transactions with them, and then cease investing in them until the next time around.

"True friends" are both profitable and loyal. There is a strong fit between their needs and the company's offerings. The firm wants to make continuous relationship investments to delight these customers and retain and grow them.

"Barnacles" are highly loyal but not very profitable. There is a limited fit between their needs and the company's offerings.

Important point: Different types of customer require different relationship management strategies.

The goal is to build the *right relationships* with the *right customers.*

Use **Key Term** *Customer Equity* here
Use **Figure** 1-5 here
Use **Marketing at Work** 1-2 here
Use **Linking the Concepts** here

The Changing Marketing Landscape

This section looks at four major developments: the new digital age, rapid globalization, the call for more ethics and social responsibility, and the growth in not-for-profit marketing.

The Digital Age

The recent technology boom has created a digital age.

The most dramatic new technology is the **Internet**.

Beyond competing in traditional market*places*, companies now have access to exciting new market*spaces*.

The Internet has now become a global phenomenon.

The number of Internet users worldwide now stands at almost 1.2 billion and will reach an estimated 1.8 billion by 2010.

Online marketing is now the fastest growing form of marketing.

In addition to the "click-only" dot-coms, most traditional "brick-and-mortar" companies have now become "click-and-mortar" companies.

Some 65 percent of American online users now use the Internet to shop.

Use **Key Term** *Internet* here
Use **Discussing the Issues** 6 here
Use **Under the Hood/Focus on Technology** here

Rapid Globalization

Marketers are now connected *globally* with their customers and marketing partners.

Almost every company, large or small, is touched in some way by global competition.

American firms have been challenged at home by the skillful marketing of European and Asian multinationals.

McDonald's now serves 52 million customers daily in 31,600 restaurants worldwide—some 65 percent of its revenues come from outside the United States.

Today, companies are buying more supplies and components abroad.

The Call for More Ethics and Social Responsibility

Marketers are being called upon to take greater responsibility for the social and environmental impact of their actions.

Corporate ethics and social responsibility have become hot topics for almost every business.

Forward-looking companies view socially responsible actions as an opportunity to do well by doing good.

Use **Focus on Ethics** here

The Growth of Not-for-Profit Marketing

The nation's nonprofits face stiff competition for support and membership. Sound marketing can help them to attract membership and support.

So, What Is Marketing? Pulling It All Together

Marketing is the process of building profitable customer relationships by creating value for customers and capturing value in return.

The first four steps in the marketing process create value *for* customers.

The final step in the process allows the company to capture value *from* customers.

After the marketing strategy is defined, the marketing program is developed, which consists of the four Ps.

When building value for customers, companies must utilize marketing technology, go global in both selling and sourcing, and act in an ethical and socially responsible way.

Figure 1.6 shows a model of the marketing process.

Use **Chapter Objective** 5 here Use **Figure** 1-6 here

Travel Log

Discussing the Issues

1. Explain the goal of marketing and how companies achieve it. (AASCB: Communication)

   Answer:

   The goal of marketing is to *create profitable relationships* by *satisfying customer needs.* **Marketing** is the process by which companies create value for customers and build strong customer relationships in order to capture value from customers in return. Marketing consists of actions taken to build and maintain desirable exchange relationships with target audiences involving a product, service, idea, or other object. If the marketer understands consumer needs; develops products and services that provide superior customer value; and prices, distributes, and promotes them effectively, this goal will be achieved easily. Beyond simply attracting new customers and creating transactions, the goal is to retain customers and grow their business with the company. Marketers want to build strong relationships by consistently delivering superior customer value.

2. Compare and contrast customer needs, wants, and demands. (AACSB: Communication)

   Answer:

   The most basic concept underlying marketing is that of human needs. Human **needs** are states of felt deprivation. They include basic *physical* needs for food, clothing, warmth, and safety; *social* needs for belonging and affection; and *individual* needs for knowledge and self-expression. These needs were not created by marketers; they are a basic part of the human makeup. **Wants** are the form human needs take as they are shaped by culture and individual personality. Wants are shaped by one's society and are described in terms of objects that will satisfy needs. When backed by buying power, wants become **demands**. Given their wants and resources, people demand products with benefits that add up to the most value and satisfaction.

3. Why is target market selection important for a customer-driven marketing strategy? How might target market selection impact customer satisfaction? (AACSB: Communication)

   Answer:

   To design a winning marketing strategy, the marketing manager must answer two important questions: *What customers will we serve (what's our target market)?* and *How can we serve these customers best (what's our value proposition)?* The company must first decide *who* it will serve—that is, the target market. It does this by dividing the market into segments of customers (*market segmentation*) and selecting which segments it will go after (*target marketing*). Some people think of marketing management as finding as many customers as possible and increasing demand. But marketing managers know that they cannot serve all customers in every way. By trying to serve all customers, they may not serve any customers well. Instead, the company wants to select only customers that it can serve well and profitably. Ultimately, marketing managers must decide which customers they want to target and on the level, timing, and nature of their demand. Simply put, marketing management is *customer management* and *demand management*.

4. Name and describe the five different marketing management orientations. Which orientation do you believe your school follows when marketing its undergraduate program? (AACSB: Communication; Reflective Thinking)

   Answer:

   There are five alternative concepts under which organizations design and carry out their marketing strategies: the production, product, selling, marketing, and societal marketing concepts. The **production concept** holds that consumers will favor products that are available and highly affordable. Therefore, management should focus on improving production and distribution efficiency. The **product concept** holds that consumers will favor products that offer the most in quality, performance, and innovative features. Under this concept, marketing strategy focuses on making continuous product improvements. The **selling concept** holds that consumers will not buy enough of the firm's products unless it undertakes a large-scale selling and promotion effort. The **marketing concept** holds that achieving organizational goals depends on knowing the needs and wants of target markets and delivering the desired satisfactions better than competitors do. Under the marketing concept, customer focus and value are the *paths* to sales and profits. Instead of a product-centered "make and sell" philosophy, the marketing concept is a customer-centered "sense and respond" philosophy. The **societal marketing concept** questions whether the pure marketing concept overlooks possible conflicts between consumer *short-run wants* and consumer *long-run welfare*. The societal marketing concept holds that marketing strategy should deliver value to customers in a way that maintains or improves both the consumer's *and the society's* well-being.

   Students' responses will vary when discussing their school's marketing. Many students at a large state school might feel a bit of the production concept, since the school provides affordable education for a large number of students. If a school tends to market very innovative programs and markets itself on its high standings and selectivity, students might see their college as following the product concept. The selling concept might come through if students feel their school has a strong recruitment program which reaches many high school students. Students might mention the marketing concept if they feel the school is customer driven and bases its programs and offerings on student feedback. A few students might mention the societal marketing concept if their schools offer programs or research that really helps society.

5. Explain the difference between *share of customer* and *customer equity*. How does an understanding of share of customer help marketers attain higher customer equity? (AACSB: Communication; Reflective Thinking)

   Answer:

   Share of customer is the share a business gets of the customer's purchasing in their product categories. For example, consumers purchase financial services from banks and other financial institutions such as insurance companies. Many insurance companies now offer banking and investment services to capture a greater share of an individual consumer's purchases of these offerings. Increasing share of customer is one way to increase a customer's lifetime value—the value to a company of a satisfied, loyal customer over his or her lifetime. **Customer equity** is the total combined customer lifetime values of all of the company's current and potential customers. Clearly, the more loyal the firm's profitable customers (that is, high share of customer), the higher the firm's customer equity. Customer equity may be a better measure of a firm's performance than current sales or market share. Whereas sales and market share reflect the past, customer equity suggests the future.

6. Discuss how the Internet impacts marketing. (AACSB: Communication)

   Answer:

   Today, the Internet links individuals and businesses of all types to each other and to information all around the world. It allows anytime, anywhere connections to information, entertainment, and communication. Companies are using the Internet to build closer relationships with customers and marketing partners. Beyond competing in traditional market*places*, they now have access to exciting new market*spaces*. The Internet has now become a truly a global phenomenon, and the growing and diverse Internet population means that all kinds of people are now going to the Web for information and to buy products and services.

   The phenomenal surge and meltdown of the "dot-coms" has resulted in a new version of the Internet—a "second coming" of the Web often referred to as *Web 2.0*. Web 2.0 involves a more reasoned and balanced approach to marketing online. It also offers a fast-growing set of new Web technologies for connecting with customers, such as Weblogs (blogs) and vlogs (video-based blogs), social networking sites, and video-sharing sites. The interactive, community-building nature of these new technologies makes them ideal for relating with customers.

Application Questions

1. Estimate how much you might be worth to an automobile manufacturer if you purchased a model offered by that manufacturer for every automobile purchase you make for the rest of your life. What factors should you consider when deriving an estimate of your lifetime value to that manufacturer? (AACSB: Communication; Reflective Thinking)

   Answer:

   Students' responses will vary, but they should consider the number of years they expect to live, how frequently they will purchase a new automobile, the sales price of the automobile and whether they will "trade up" as they get older, purchases they make for others (such as children), and others they may influence to purchase that manufacturer's brand. For example, students that are currently 21 years old could live for another 60 years or more. If they purchase a new automobile every five to 10 years, they will purchase 6-12 automobiles for themselves in that time. They may purchase an automobile for one or more children and might influence friends or family members to switch to this manufacturer. Students might also add in service revenues. In their calculations, students should consider that there are costs for acquiring them as a customer, but that those costs decrease as they become loyal customers.

2. In a small group, develop an after-school child care service targeted toward working mothers. How will you enable them to get the best value? Define what you mean by value and develop the value proposition of your offering for this target market. (AACSB: Communication; Reflective Thinking)

   Answer:

   Students' responses will vary. One key variable is how their target market defines "value." Some mothers might want enriching experiences for their children, while others may merely want a "babysitter." Regardless, the groups must decide how it will serve targeted customers to achieve the value expected—how it will *differentiate and position* itself in the marketplace. Their *value proposition* is the set of benefits or values it promises to deliver to consumers to satisfy their needs.

3. Ask five consumers to describe an instance when they were dissatisfied with a marketing exchange, one in which they were satisfied, and one in which they were delighted. Ask them why they were or weren't satisfied and why they were delighted instead of merely satisfied. Also ask about the impact of these experiences on their long-term relationships with a company and loyalty to the brand. Report on what you learned. (AACSB: Communication; Reflective Thinking)

Answer:

Customer satisfaction depends on the product's perceived performance relative to a buyer's expectations. If the product's performance falls short of expectations, the customer is dissatisfied. If performance matches expectations, the customer is satisfied. If performance exceeds expectations, the customer is highly satisfied or delighted. Students will probably find that consumers can more easily recall instances when they were dissatisfied or delighted.

Under the Hood: Focus on Technology

Cutting-edge technology is now being used to improve customer service in the food service industry. The person taking your order at a fast-food drive-thru may not be in the restaurant—in fact, he or she may not even be in the state and could possibly be in another country. Several McDonald's restaurants in Colorado, Minnesota, and Missouri process orders through a centralized facility in Colorado, and other fast-feeders such as Hardee's and Carl's Jr. are joining in. High-speed data connections and voice-over-Internet Protocol technology, or VoIP, enable businesses to outsource this task so that workers can concentrate on preparing the food and filling orders accurately. Some systems take temporary digital images of customers or cars placing orders so that workers can avoid mix-ups and speed up service. Domino's Pizza uses Internet technology for order placements and is launching a text-message ordering system for registered customers. Sit-down restaurants are also experimenting with tableside phone ordering and are placing credit/debit swipes at customers' fingertips. In Asia, customers routinely use their smart phones or palm computers to place an order from anywhere, and we will see this technology in the United States in the near future. Customers must be careful, however, because professional order-takers are better at up selling (that is, getting customers to order more expensive options) and increasing the average order size.

1. What are the advantages and disadvantages of such technologies for marketers? How does this technology add value for customers? (AACSB: Communication; Reflective Thinking)

   Answer:

   Students' responses will vary, but there are several advantages for marketers:
   - reduced costs—typical ordering costs of 25-30 cents can be reduced down to 20-24 cents.
   - more accurate order fulfillment
   - higher average orders
   - greater profits
   - more satisfied customers

Some disadvantages include:

- problems if the system is down and there are not enough employees in the restaurant to meet demand
- privacy concerns if photos of customers are taken
- smart phone ordering technology pushes the ordering costs on to customers
- back-lash if outsourcing order-taking takes jobs from local workers
- customers feeling pressured to spend more

The value to customers is that orders are filled more quickly and accurately. One of the reasons customers patronize fast-food restaurants is because they want their food quickly. Food quality may improve as well because employees can concentrate more fully on food preparation.

2. While such technology is being used in restaurant service applications, discuss other areas where it can add value for customers. (AACSB: Communication; Reflective)

   Answer:

   Students' responses will vary, but other areas include customer service outsourcing, customers scanning items when placing them in shopping carts, delivery of promotional offers directly to customers' phones, and using smart phone technology to not only order products/services but also pay for them.

Focus on Ethics

Marketing to children has always been controversial. Indeed, in the 1970s, the Federal Trade Commission considered prohibiting all advertising to children, and in some other countries it is illegal to advertise to children. Now, with the child obesity rate in the United States greater than 18 percent and predicted to exceed 20 percent in just a few years, there is pressure on marketers, in general, and food marketers, in particular, to curb their marketing practices to children. Studies report that children view more than 20 food ads each day with over 90 percent of them promoting high-fat, high-sugar products. The marketing concept focuses on satisfying customers' needs and wants, but are marketers crossing the line when they cater to younger consumers' wants for products that may counter parental wishes or that may be unhealthy?

1. What ethical responsibilities do companies that market products having potentially adverse health effects have to consumers? (AACSB: Communication; Ethical Reasoning)

   Answer:

   Students' responses will vary, but this is a good question to emphasize the societal marketing concept. The **societal marketing concept** questions whether the pure marketing concept overlooks possible conflicts between consumer *short-run wants* and consumer *long-run welfare*. Is a firm that satisfies the immediate needs and wants of target markets always doing what's best for consumers in the long run? The societal marketing concept holds that marketing strategy should deliver value to customers in a way that maintains or improves both the consumer's *and the society's* well-being. As Figure 1.4 shows, companies should balance three considerations in setting their marketing strategies: company profits, consumer wants, *and* society's interests. One aspect that may encourage marketers to be more socially responsible is the threat of regulation and lawsuits. For example, marketers must now list the amount of transfat on product nutrition labels, New York City has banned transfat in all restaurants, and McDonald's has been sued by plaintiffs for obesity-related damages to children.

2. What actions are marketers taking to market their products to children more ethically? Discuss industry initiatives that help marketers market to children more responsibly. (AACSB: Communication; Ethical Reasoning)

   Answer:

   Students' responses will vary, but they should be able to discuss several examples of how marketers are responding. Marketers are doing several things to market to children more ethically. For example, companies including McDonald's, Kraft Foods, and General Mills are re-evaluating their products and making more healthful options. Kids can get sliced fruit instead of french fries and many breakfast cereals now use whole grains. Industry initiatives include codes of ethics by groups such as the American Marketing Association, and there are several guidelines for advertising to children. One strong force in industry is the Children's Advertising Review Unit, which is a part of the Council of Better Business Bureau's National Advertising Division (see www.bbb.org for more information).

GREAT IDEAS

Barriers to Effective Learning

1. For most students, this will be their first introduction to marketing and all its ramifications. To most of them, marketing is nothing more than selling and/or advertising, and this gets reinforced daily when they see "marketing" job ads that are really sales positions. It helps to get students talking about what marketing is, and to give examples of what they think is really good marketing. Try to bring in contemporary examples that the students can relate to.
2. Building relationships can sometimes be easy to understand in a business-to-business transaction, but it can be much more difficult to comprehend in consumer businesses. Use examples such as Amazon.com that do a wonderful job of developing one-on-one relationships with millions of customers through their tracking of customer purchases and analysis of these purchases to recommend additional items. Ask students to discuss how they feel about the companies they

buy from. Have any developed relationships with them that have made them loyal to the brand or store?

3. Demarketing is always a problem for students. Most of them have not yet encountered anything like it. The light bulb seems to go on, though, when you talk about National Parks and how crowded they get, and efforts to get people to go see them during off-peak travel times. Again, having students come up with their own examples will increase the level of understanding.
4. Societal marketing is also something that can be a little unclear to students. Why should fast food chains, for instance, be responsible for the nation's obesity (just one very topical discussion point)? Understanding how one should balance the need for profits with what some might consider being "soft" issues can be difficult at times. And that can be made even more difficult among the politically-astute students, as they can easily lead the class into a left versus right discussion on individual versus corporate versus governmental responsibility. Try to not let that happen, instead focusing on how companies can actually increase their revenue and profits by showing that they care about their customers and their communities. Newman's Own is a brand that could be discussed, as most profits are donated to charities, and they have moved strongly into ensuring a sustainable environment.
5. Traditional-age undergraduates have spent their entire lives with technology, and so some of them can actually snicker when the discussion turns to how technology has changed business in general and marketing more specifically. A discussion of the difficulties of connecting to consumers without the Internet is warranted. How would the students approach a one-on-one relationship with millions of customers if they didn't have email or the Internet or blast faxes?
6. At this stage, students are very apprehensive about the course. When they walked into class, they thought they might learn about selling and advertising, and now they've discovered that there is much more to marketing than just those two subjects. Talking about how much fun it is to be the center of the company, and knowing more about customers than any other functional area in the company, can sometimes ease their minds and make them look forward to learning more. Emphasizing that marketing combines both the analytical and the creative can also ease some tension. The accounting and finance majors will find that there is something in it to suit their more analytical frame of reference, and the artists and designers who hope to become fashion mavens can also rest assured that although they will need to understand the more logical areas of the subject, their intuition can still reign supreme.

Student Projects

1. What does the term "marketing" mean to you? Think about an automobile you would like to have (realistically) when you graduate. Write about how each phase of the marketing process is addressed by that vehicle
2. Why is it important to truly understand the customer? Make a list of 10 "wants" that you have. What would have to occur to move each of these from "wants" to "needs?"

3. Not everyone can be part of your market. Go take a look at ABC online (www.abc.com). Who would you say is their market? Why?
4. Review the five alternative concepts under which organizations design and carry out their marketing strategies. Now, take a look at one of the auto dealers in your town. Which one of these five concepts do you believe they are typically employing? Why?
5. Think of a product or retailer to which you are loyal. What has caused this loyalty? What could a competing product/retailer do to break this loyalty?

Small Group Assignment

Form students into groups of three to five. Each group should read the opening vignette to the chapter on Procter & Gamble. Each group should answer the following questions:

1. Can you develop a relationship with a laundry detergent brand?
2. How does P&G create lasting customer value?

Each group should then share its findings with the class.

Individual Assignment

Companies are realizing that losing a customer means more than losing a single sale. It means losing a stream of revenue from that customer over their lifetime. Reread the story of Stew Leonard (under Capturing Value from Customers).

Is it possible to take his idea of "the customer is always right" too far so that it becomes a negative on the company? Why or why not?

Think-Pair-Share

Consider the following questions, formulate an answer, pair with the student on your right, share your thoughts with one another, and respond to the questions from the instructor. These questions could also be given as out-of-class assignments.

1. Do marketers create needs?
2. What is Lexus' value proposition?
3. How is marketing different from selling?
4. What are two companies with which you have an emotional bond? Describe that bond.

Classroom Exercise/Homework Assignment

Five core customer and marketplace concepts are critical to success: (1) *needs, wants, and demands*; (2) *marketing offers (products, services, and experiences)*; (3) *value and satisfaction*; (4) *exchanges and relationships*; and (5) *markets.*

Take a look at Sea Ray boats (www.searay.com). Answer the following questions:

1. What needs, wants, and/or demands is Sea Ray attempting to fill?
2. Describe their marketing offers.
3. How are they providing value?
4. Describe the relationships they have with their customers.
5. What are their markets?

Classroom Management Strategies

The first chapter of this textbook sets the stage for the rest of the content. It outlines the major topics and principles that will be discussed in each of the following chapters, and gives the student a good grounding in what to expect in their journey into the world of marketing.

First classes are always difficult, both for the instructor and for the student. Therefore, using examples that students can relate to easily is always a good idea when starting out.

In reviewing the material in class, a good way to break it down follows. This assumes a typical one-hour structure; if the class is longer, you can work through the Marketing Application in class. If shorter, you can either break the chapter over two sessions, or shorten each topic's allotted discussion time.

1. Ten minutes should be spent on discussing what marketing really is. Many students will come into class thinking they are going to be learning all about advertising, or all about selling. Ask students to talk about what they think marketing is, and to use examples of what they've encountered in their own lives.
2. Ten minutes can also be spent on the second major topic of the chapter, understanding the marketplace and consumer needs. Discussing the differences of needs, wants, and demands, and how they relate to marketing, can greatly enhance the students' understanding of the basis of marketing. Also included in this section are the notions of marketing offers, satisfaction, and relationships. You can discuss the various ways companies develop relationships with their customers. Using Amazon.com, the company discussed in the opening pages of the chapter, can really help the students understand that a company with millions of customers can still easily develop relationships with each and every one of them.
3. Another 10 minutes can be spent on designing customer-driven marketing strategies. Many students will still not understand how needs, wants, and demands can drive companies' product development, but this section of the chapter will help them see it a little more clearly.
4. Preparing a marketing plan and program can be covered in 5 minutes. This section shows how everything they learn in marketing will be pulled together, but it is too soon in the semester to be spending a lot of time on the topic.
5. Customer relationships are the heart of the chapter and the entire text. Spend 15 minutes discussing this topic, and use examples that the students will appreciate.

Discussing the difference in the relationships they have with their hairdresser or barber and that of www.bn.com or another one of the Internet merchants can drive home the importance of holding on to good customers. Students will also be well aware of frequency marketing programs, and examples of those will also be beneficial.

6. The final 10 minutes can be spent discussing the future of marketing and the development of customer relationships. The majority of students will never have known an era without the Internet. Asking them how they would have developed relationships with their customers without the assistance of technology is a good way to get a discussion started on how marketing programs are developed. Then you can talk about how the advent of email and the Internet has opened the entire world for even a small retailer, as well as raised some ethical issues, such as the marketing of the American culture to the entire world, regardless of their societies' mores and culture.

If time permits, revisit the question of "what is marketing?" The students should now have a greater appreciation of the science behind marketing, as well as the creativity necessary to develop successful marketing programs.

CHAPTER 2
Company and Marketing Strategy: Partnering to Build Customer Relationships

Previewing the Concepts: Chapter Objectives

1. Explain companywide strategic planning and its four steps
2. Discuss how to design business portfolios and develop growth strategies
3. Explain marketing's role in strategic planning and how marketing works with its partners to create and deliver customer value
4. Describe the elements of a customer-driven marketing strategy and mix, and the forces that influence it
5. List the marketing management functions, including the elements of a marketing plan, and discuss the importance of measuring and managing return on marketing investment.

JUST THE BASICS

Chapter Overview

In this chapter, we dig deeper into steps two and three of the marketing process—designing customer-driven marketing strategies and constructing marketing programs.

First, we look at the organization's overall strategic planning.

Next, we discuss how marketers partner closely with others inside and outside the firm to serve customers.

We then examine marketing strategy and planning—how marketers choose target markets, position their market offerings, develop a marketing mix, and manage their marketing programs.

Finally, we look at measuring and managing return on marketing investment.

Annotated Chapter Notes/Outline

Introduction

NASCAR has grown swiftly from a pastime for beer-guzzling Bubbas into a national marketing phenomenon.

How? Through customer-driven marketing strategy.

NASCAR creates high-octane experiences that result in strong relationships with its tens of millions of fans. In return, NASCAR captures value from these fans, both for itself and for its many sponsors.

Like NASCAR, outstanding marketing organizations employ strongly customer-driven marketing strategies and programs that create customer value and relationships.

Companywide Strategic Planning: Defining Marketing's Role

Strategic planning is the process of developing and maintaining a strategic fit between the organization's goals and capabilities and its changing marketing opportunities.

Strategic planning sets the stage for the rest of the planning in the firm.

Companies usually prepare annual plans, long-range plans, and strategic plans.

The annual and long-range plans deal with the company's current businesses and how to keep them going.

In contrast, the **strategic plan** involves adapting the firm to take advantage of opportunities in its constantly changing environment.

The strategic planning process begins with the company defining its overall purpose and mission.

Applying the Concept
Have students break into groups of four to six to discuss what a likely strategy would be for attracting new students to their university. Have them develop a brief statement that describes the university's fit between their goal of attracting the best students and their capabilities for then educating those students.

The stages of the strategic planning process are outlined in Figure 2.1.

This mission is turned into objectives that guide the whole company.

Marketing planning occurs at the business-unit, product, and market levels.

Use **Key Term** *Strategic Planning* here. Use **Chapter Objective** 1 here. Use **Discussing the Issues** 1 here. Use **Figure** 2-1 here.

Defining a Market-Oriented Mission

When management senses that the organization is drifting, it must renew its search for purpose.

A **mission statement** is a statement of the organization's purpose—what it wants to accomplish in the larger environment.

A clear mission statement acts as an "invisible hand" that guides people in the organization.

Mission statements should be ***market oriented*** and defined in terms of customer needs.

A market-oriented mission statement defines the business in terms of satisfying basic customer needs.

Management should avoid making its mission too narrow or too broad.

Mission statements should be
- ***realistic.***
- ***specific.***
- ***market environment.***
- based on ***distinctive competencies.***
- ***motivating.***

Use **Key Term** *Mission Statement* here. Use **Application Question** 2 here. Use **Table** 2-1 here.

Setting Company Objectives and Goals

The company turns its mission into detailed supporting objectives for each level of management.

Each manager should have objectives and be responsible for reaching them.

Marketing strategies and programs must be developed to support these marketing objectives.

Each broad marketing strategy must then be defined in greater detail.

Designing the Business Portfolio

A **Business portfolio** is the collection of businesses and products that make up the company.

The best business portfolio is the one that best fits the company's strengths and weaknesses to opportunities in the environment.

Business portfolio planning involves two steps:

1. The company must analyze its ***current*** business portfolio and decide which businesses should receive more, less, or no investment.
2. It must shape the ***future*** portfolio by developing strategies for growth and downsizing.

Analyzing the Current Business Portfolio

The major activity in strategic planning is business **portfolio analysis.**

Use **Key Term** *Business Portfolio* here. Use **Chapter Objective** 2 here.

Portfolio analysis is where management evaluates the products and businesses making up the company.

The steps in portfolio analysis are:

1. To identify the *strategic business units* (SBU). The SBU is a unit of the company that has a separate mission and objectives and that can be planned independently from other company businesses.
2. To assess the attractiveness of its various SBUs and decide how much support each deserves. Most companies are well advised to "stick to their knitting" when designing their business portfolios.

The purpose of strategic planning is to find ways in which the company can best use its strengths to take advantage of attractive opportunities in the environment.

Most standard portfolio-analysis methods evaluate SBUs on two dimensions:

1. The attractiveness of the market or industry
2. The strength of the position in that market or industry.

The Boston Consulting Group Approach

A company classifies all its SBUs according to the **growth-share matrix** (see Figure 2.2).

The vertical axis: ***market growth rate*** provides a measure of market attractiveness.

The horizontal axis: ***relative market share*** provides a measure of company strength in the market.

Use **Key Terms** *Portfolio Analysis* and *Growth-Share Matrix* here.
Use **Figure** 2-2 here.
Use **Discussing the Issues** 2 here.

The growth-share matrix defines four types of SBUs:

Stars. High-growth, high-share businesses or products. They will turn into cash cows.

Cash cows. Low-growth, high-share businesses or products. They produce a lot of cash that the company.

Question marks. Low-share business units in high-growth markets. They require a lot of cash to hold their position.

Dogs. Low-growth, low-share businesses and products.

One of four strategies can be pursued for each SBU.

1. The company can invest to *build* its share.
2. It can invest just enough to *hold* its share.
3. It can milk its short-term cash flow, or *harvest*.
4. It can *divest* by selling it or phasing out.

As time passes, SBUs change their positions in the growth-share matrix. Each SBU has a life cycle.

Problems with Matrix Approaches

Difficult, time consuming, and costly to implement.

These approaches focus on classifying *current* businesses but provide little advice for *future* planning.

Many companies have dropped matrix methods in favor of customized approaches better suited to their specific situations.

Developing Strategies for Growth and Downsizing

A company's objective must be "profitable growth."

Marketing has the main responsibility for achieving profitable growth for the company.

The **product/market expansion grid** is used in identifying growth opportunities (see Figure 2.3).

- **Market penetration**—making more sales to current customers without changing its products.
- **Market development**—identifying and developing new markets for its current products.
- **Product development**—offering modified or new products to current markets.
- **Diversification**—starting up or buying businesses outside of its current products and markets.

Use **Key Terms** *Product/Market Expansion Grid, Market Penetration, Market Development, Product Development* and *Diversification* here. Use **Figure** 2-3 here.

Companies must also develop strategies for **downsizing**.

When a firm finds brands/businesses that are unprofitable or no longer fit the overall strategy, it may prune, harvest, or divest them.

Use **Key Term** *Downsizing* here.

Planning Marketing: Partnering to Build Customer Relationships

Marketing plays a key role in the company's strategic planning.

1. Marketing provides a guiding *philosophy*—the marketing concept.
2. Marketing provides *inputs* to strategic planners.
3. Marketing designs *strategies* for reaching the unit's objectives.

Customer value is the key ingredient in the marketer's formula for success.

In addition to ***customer relationship management***, marketers must also practice ***partner relationship management.***

Use **Chapter Objective** 3 here.

Partnering with Other Company Departments

Each company department is a link in the company's **value chain**.

Use **Key Term** *Value Chain* here.

Use **Discussing the Issues** 3 here.

Success depends on how well the various departments coordinate their activities.

A company's value chain is only as strong as its weakest link.

Ideally, a company's different functions should work in harmony to produce value for consumers.

Other departments may resist the marketing's efforts because their actions can increase purchasing costs, disrupt production schedules, increase inventories, and create budget headaches.

Yet marketers must find ways to get all departments to "think consumer."

Partnering with Others in the Marketing System

Firms need to look beyond its own value chain and into the value chains of its suppliers, distributors, and customers.

Companies today are partnering with the other members of the supply chain to improve the performance of the customer **value-delivery network**.

Competition takes place between the entire value-delivery networks created by competitors.

Use **Key Term** *Value-Delivery Network* here.
Use **Linking the Concepts** here.
Use **Under the Hood: Focus on Technology** here.

Let's Discuss This
Have the students describe the possible Value-Delivery Network for their favorite coffee shop or bar.

Marketing Strategy and the Marketing Mix

Figure 2-4 shows the major activities in managing marketing strategy and the marketing mix.

Consumers are in the center. Profitable customer relationships are the goal.

Marketing strategy is next—this is the broad logic under which the company attempts to develop profitable relationships.

Guided by the strategy, the company develops its marketing mix—product, price, place, and promotion.

Use **Key Term** *Marketing Strategy* here. Use **Figure** 2-4 here.

Customer-Driven Marketing Strategy

Marketing requires a deep understanding of customers.

There are many different kinds of consumers, and they exhibit many different kinds of needs.

Companies cannot profitably serve them all.

Companies must divide up the total market, choose the best segments, and design strategies for profitably serving chosen segments.

This process involves ***market segmentation***, ***market targeting***, ***differentiation***, and ***positioning***.

Market Segmentation

Market segmentation is the process of dividing a market into distinct groups of buyers who have different needs, characteristics, or behavior who might require separate products or marketing programs.

Every market has segments, but not all ways of segmenting a market are equally useful.

A **market segment** consists of consumers who respond in a similar way to a given set of marketing efforts.

Use **Key Terms** *Market Segment, Market Segmentation, Market Targeting, Differentiation,* and *Positioning* here. Use **Chapter Objective** 4 here. Use **Focus on Ethics** here.

Market Targeting

Market targeting is evaluating each market segment's attractiveness and selecting one or more segments to enter.

A company with limited resources might serve only a few "market niches."

Market niches are segments that major competitors overlook or ignore.

Most companies enter a new market by serving a single segment. If this proves successful, they add segments.

Market Differentiation and Positioning

Product ***position*** is the place the product occupies relative to competitors in consumers' minds.

Positioning is arranging for a product to occupy a clear, distinctive, and desirable place relative to competing products in the minds of target consumers.

Positioning begins with **differentiation**—*differentiating* the company's market offering so that it gives consumers more value.

Developing an Integrated Marketing Mix

Use **Key Term** *Marketing Mix* here. Use **Figure** 2-5 here. Use **Discussing the Issues** 4 here.

The **marketing mix** is the set of controllable, tactical marketing tools that the firm blends to produce the response it wants in the target market.

The marketing mix consists of the "four *Ps*": ***product, price, place***, and ***promotion***. (Figure 2.5).

- ***Product:*** the goods-and-services combination the company offers to the target market.
- ***Price:*** the amount of money customers have to pay to obtain the product.
- ***Place:*** the company activities that make the product available to target consumers.
- ***Promotion:*** the activities that communicate the merits of the product.

From the buyer's viewpoint, the four Ps might be better described as the four Cs:

- ***Product = Customer solution***
- ***Price = Customer cost***
- ***Place = Convenience***
- ***Promotion = Communication***

Managing the Marketing Effort

Managing the marketing process requires the four marketing management functions of ***analysis, planning, implementation***, and ***control***.

Use **Figure** 2-6 here. Use **Discussing the Issues** 5 here.

Marketing Analysis

Analysis should be performed to understand the markets and marketing environment the company faces.

Use **Key Term** *SWOT Analysis* here. Use **Application Question** 1 here.

SWOT analysis is used to evaluate the company's strengths (S), weaknesses (W), opportunities (O), and threats (T).

- Strengths include capabilities, resources, and positive situational factors.
- Weaknesses include negative internal factors and negative situational factors.
- Opportunities are favorable external factors.
- Threats are unfavorable external factors.

Use **Figure** 2-7 here. Use **Application Question** 3 here.

Marketing Planning

A detailed marketing plan has to be developed for each business, product or brand.

Table 2-2 shows the major sections of a marketing plan for a product or a brand.

Use **Table** 2-2 here. Use **Chapter Objective** 5 here.

Marketing Implementation

Marketing implementation turns ***plans*** into ***actions***.

Use **Key Term** *Marketing Implementation* here.

Implementation requires the company to blend its people, organizational structure, decision and reward systems, and company culture in a way that supports its strategies.

Marketing Department Organization

The marketing organization must be designed so it can carry out the strategies/plans that are developed.
In small companies, one person may perform all the marketing functions. In large companies, many specialists are found.

The ***functional*** organization is the most common form. This organizational form has the different activities headed by a functional specialist, such as sales, advertising, marketing research, etc.

A ***geographic*** organization might be utilized in a company that sells nationally or internationally.

A ***product management*** organization can be found in companies with many different products or brands.

A ***market*** or ***customer management*** organization is used in companies that sell one product to many different kinds of markets and customers.

Very large companies might utilize a ***combination*** of all these forms.

Marketing Control

Use **Key Term** *Marketing Control* here.

The control process includes the following:

- ***Operating control*** checks the ongoing performance of the marketing programs against the annual plan.
- ***Strategic control*** looks at whether the company's basic strategies are matched to its opportunities.

A major tool to use here is a ***marketing audit,*** which is a comprehensive examination of a company's environment, objectives, strategies, and activities.

Use **Key Term** *Marketing Control* here. Use **Video Case: Mayo Clinic** here.

Measuring and Managing Return on Marketing Investment

Marketing managers must ensure that their marketing dollars are being well spent.

Return on marketing investment (or ***marketing ROI***) is the net return from a marketing investment divided by the costs of the marketing investment.

Use **Key Term** *Return on Marketing Investment* here. Use **Discussing the Issues** 6 here. Use **Chapter Objective** 5 here.

It measures the profits generated by investments in marketing activities.

A company can assess return on marketing in terms of standard marketing performance measures, such as brand awareness, sales, or market share.

Marketing dashboards—meaningful sets of marketing performance measures in a single display used to monitor strategic marketing performance.

Marketers are using customer-centered measures of marketing impact, such as customer acquisition, customer retention, and customer lifetime value.

Travel Log

Discussing the Issues

1. Define strategic planning. List and briefly describe the four steps that lead managers and the firm through the strategic planning process. What role does marketing play in strategic planning? (AASCB: Communication)

   Answer:

   Strategic planning is the process of developing and maintaining a strategic fit between the organization's goals and capabilities and its changing marketing opportunities. At the corporate level, the company starts the strategic planning process by defining its overall purpose and mission (see Figure 2.1). This mission then is turned into detailed supporting objectives that guide the whole company. Next, headquarters decides what portfolio of businesses and products is best for the company and how much support to give each one. In turn, each business and product develops detailed marketing and other departmental plans that support the companywide plan. Marketing planning occurs at the business-unit, product, and market levels. It supports company strategic planning with more detailed plans for specific marketing opportunities.

2. Describe the Boston Consulting Group's approach to portfolio analysis and identify the problems associated with it. (AACSB: Communications)

   Answer:

   Using the Boston Consulting Group (BCG) approach, a company classifies all its SBUs according to the **growth-share matrix** shown in Figure 2.2. On the vertical axis, *market growth rate* provides a measure of market attractiveness. On the horizontal axis, *relative market share* serves as a measure of company strength in the market. The growth-share matrix defines four types of SBUs:

   Stars. Stars are high-growth, high-share businesses or products. They often need heavy investment to finance their rapid growth. Eventually their growth will slow down, and they will turn into cash cows.

Cash cows. Cash cows are low-growth, high-share businesses or products. These established and successful SBUs need less investment to hold their market share. Thus, they produce a lot of cash that the company uses to pay its bills and to support other SBUs that need investment.

Question marks. Question marks are low-share business units in high-growth markets. They require a lot of cash to hold their share, let alone increase it. Management has to think hard about which question marks it should try to build into stars and which should be phased out.

Dogs. Dogs are low-growth, low-share businesses and products. They may generate enough cash to maintain themselves but do not promise to be large sources of cash.

The circles in the growth-share matrix represent a company's current SBUs. Once it has classified its SBUs, the company must determine what role each will play in the future. One of four strategies can be pursued for each SBU. The company can invest more in the business unit in order to **build** its share. Or it can invest just enough to **hold** the SBU's share at the current level. It can **harvest** the SBU, milking its short-term cash flow regardless of the long-term effect. Finally, the company can **divest** the SBU by selling it or phasing it out and using the resources elsewhere. As time passes, SBUs change their positions in the growth-share matrix.

The major problems associated with matrix approaches are that they can be difficult, time consuming, and costly to implement. Management may find it difficult to define SBUs and measure market share and growth. In addition, these approaches focus on classifying *current* businesses but provide little advice for *future* planning.

3. Compare and contrast the four product/market expansion grid strategies and provide an example of each. (AACSB: Communications)

Answer:

The four product/market expansion strategies are: market penetration, market development, product development, and diversification. **Market penetration** involves identifying and developing new markets for its current products. An example is marketers of a brand encouraging current users to purchase more of the brand. **Market development** strategy involves identifying and developing new markets for its current products. New markets could be new geographic markets or other markets defined by demographics, lifestyle, or product use. Management could consider **product development** offering modified or new products to current markets. For example, Procter & Gamble may attempt to get current users of its Crest toothpaste to purchase a new offering, Crest mouthwash. Finally, a company may consider **diversification** by starting up or buying businesses outside of its current products and markets. In this strategy, the marketer offers an entirely different product to a completely different market than currently served.

4. Discuss the differences between market segmentation, targeting, differentiation, and positioning. (AACSB: Communication)

   Answer:

   Market segmentation is the process of dividing a market into distinct groups of buyers who have different needs, characteristics, or behavior who might require separate products or marketing programs. **Targeting** involves evaluating each market segment's attractiveness and selecting one or more segments to enter. **Positioning** is arranging for a product to occupy a clear, distinctive, and desirable place relative to competing products in the minds of target consumers. Effective positioning begins with **differentiation**—actually *differentiating* the company's market offering so that it gives consumers more value.

5. Define each of the four Ps. What insights might a firm gain by considering the four Cs rather than the four Ps? (AACSB: Communication; Reflective Thinking)

   Answer:

   The four Ps of marketing are: product, price, place, and promotion. **Product** means the goods-and-services combination the company offers to the target market. **Price** is the amount of money customers have to pay to obtain the product. **Place** includes company activities that make the product available to target consumers. **Promotion** means activities that communicate the merits of the product and persuade target customers to buy it. The four Cs—customer solution, customer cost, convenience, and communication—describe the four Ps from the customer's viewpoint. By examining products and services using the four Cs, marketers may be better equipped to build customer relationships and offer true value.

6. What is return on marketing investment? Why is it difficult to measure? (AACSB: Communication; Reflective Thinking)

   Answer:

   Return on marketing investment (or marketing ROI) is the net return from a marketing investment divided by the costs of the marketing investment. It is difficult to measure due to lack of measurement tools. In addition, many performance measures other than sales are important, including brand awareness, advertising impact, and customer lifetime value.

Application Questions

1. Explain what a SWOT analysis involves. Develop a SWOT analysis for a bank in your community. (AACSB: Communication; Reflective Thinking)

   Answer:

   A **SWOT analysis** evaluates an organization's overall strengths (S), weaknesses (W), opportunities (O), and threats (T) (see Figure 2.7). Strengths include internal capabilities, resources, and positive situational factors that may help the company or organization to serve its customers and achieve its objectives. Weaknesses include internal limitations and negative situational factors that may interfere with the organization's performance. Opportunities are favorable factors or trends in the external environment that the organization may be able to exploit to its advantage. And threats are unfavorable external factors or trends that may present challenges to performance.

   Students' responses will vary regarding the SWOT analysis of a local bank. Relevant strengths and weaknesses for a bank include factors such as reputation, human resources, financial resources, and so on. Opportunities and threats involve changes in the demographic, economic, and technological environments. For example, a growing population is an opportunity, whereas a declining one is a threat.

2. In a small group, visit Web sites of familiar companies (such as Nike, Kraft, or Caterpillar) until you find a company with a good mission statement. Evaluate this statement using the five attributes of a good mission statement outlined in the chapter. (AACSB: Communication; Reflective Thinking; Use of IT)

   Answer:

   Students' answers will vary, but they should explain and apply the five criteria of a good mission statement: (1) realistic, (2) specific, (3) fits the market environment, (4) based on distinctive competencies, and (5) motivating.

3. Unlike other advertising awards, Effie awards are not granted solely for creative execution. They are given for "Ideas that Work." Visit www.effie.org to learn about these awards and to read published case studies about winners. Present one case study to the class. (AACSB: Communication; Use of IT)

   Answer:

   Students can click on "About Effie" on the left side of this Web site to learn more about this award. Clicking on "Winners Showcase" allows students to read case studies of winners from several categories over several years. It is suggested that instructors assign specific case studies for students to present to the rest of the class to get a good cross-section of topics and marketing problems addressed.

Under the Hood: Focus on Technology

Visit the Web sites of several car manufacturers and you will see the technological innovations offered with today's vehicles. From GPS navigation systems to audio and DVD entertainment systems, advanced technologies are enhancing today's car-owning experience. Microsoft, known mostly for its computer operating systems, has been working with Fiat to develop a new "infotainment" system known as Blue&Me. Currently offered only in limited Fiat models, the system integrates mobile phones, MP3 players, and an Internet connection through controls mounted on the steering wheel. The new technology will also contain a navigation system, weather and traffic forecasts, and antitheft devices.

1. According to the product/expansion grid, which strategy best describes Microsoft's expansion into automobile applications? (AACSB: Communication; Use of IT; Reflective Thinking)

   Answer:

   This is a nice example of market development. Microsoft has applied its existing software in developing systems for automobile manufacturers. Some students might argue this is diversification, since these "new" products have been designed for the new market. This can be turned into a healthy debate about whether these are truly new products or if they constitute changes in the technology that adapt the existing products for new uses.

2. How is Fiat an important member of Microsoft's value-delivery network? (AACSB: Communication; Reflective Thinking)

   Answer:

   Fiat is very important to Microsoft. The two companies are working together in the development of the software. Fiat has a good understanding of what the customer wants in its vehicles. It is giving Microsoft the opportunity to build its automobile strategic business unit. Microsoft will later be able to market the system to other automobile manufacturers.

Focus on Ethics

You've learned that a customer-driven marketing strategy incorporates market segmentation, targeting, differentiation, and positioning. Procter & Gamble (P&G) excels at developing offerings based on customer-driven marketing. It markets more than 100 different brands in more than 20 consumer product categories. For example, P&G offers seven brands of body wash and soaps, six brands of laundry detergent, and three brands of dish soap. Each brand is targeted to satisfy the needs of a specific market segment. But are consumers' needs really that different when it comes to cleaning our bodies, clothes, or dishes? Or is the company simply creating meaningless product differences to hype in its advertising to consumers?

1. Go to www.pg.com to learn about the brands offered by P&G. Select one product category in which P&G offers multiple brands. What is P&G's positioning for each brand in that product category? Then, visit a store and record the prices of each brand, using a common basis such as price per ounce. Write a brief report on what you learn. Are there meaningful positioning differences between the brands? Are any price differences you find justified? (AACSB: Communication; Reflective Thinking)

   Answer:

   Students' responses will vary depending on the product category selected and store visited. Students can easily find the positioning of each brand from the company's Web site. For example, the positioning for each brand of P&G's laundry detergents is:

Cheer:	"Dirt goes, color stays"
Dreft:	"For a clean you can trust"—detergent for baby clothes
Era:	"Powerful laundry detergent that is tough on stains"
Gain:	"The smell says clean"
Ivory:	"Mild cleansing"
Tide:	"Knows fabrics best"

   Prices for each brand will vary depending on the store visited but students will likely find differences in price per ounce. This should spark a lively debate about whether the brands themselves are really different.

2. Some marketing critics argue that many such products are simply commodities and no one brand is better than another. Are their real differences in the actual formulations of the P&G brands you investigated? Is it right for P&G to position brands in a way that consumers perceive them to be different and then price them accordingly? (AACSB: Communication; Ethical Reasoning)

   Answer:

   Students' responses will vary. However, they should demonstrate an understanding that in positioning its product, the company first identifies possible customer value differences that provide competitive advantages upon which to build the position. The company can offer greater customer value either by charging lower prices than competitors do or by offering more benefits to justify higher prices. But if the company *promises* greater value, it must then *deliver* that greater value. Thus, effective positioning begins with **differentiation**—actually *differentiating* the company's market offering so that it gives consumers more value. Once the company has chosen a desired position, it must take strong steps to deliver and communicate that position to target consumers.

P&G's laundry detergents are not all the same. It's true that they satisfy the basic functional need of getting clothes clean, but each brand's formulation offers something else beyond basic cleaning. For example, Gain has a fragrance that lasts, differentiating it from the other brands offered.

Great Ideas

Barriers to Effective Learning

1. Students will largely be unfamiliar with strategic planning and its concepts and objectives. Making this come alive with the examples in the textbook, or your own examples from your own experience, will help them deal with the complex issues in this section.
2. Working through a mission statement for the marketing department of your university, or for the business college within which it exists, may give the students a greater appreciation for the difficulty and importance of defining a mission that lives and breathes life into the objectives that follow.
3. The Boston Consulting Group's portfolio analysis tool can also be difficult to understand. Again, working through examples with companies the students should be familiar with will aid understanding.
4. University business courses rarely talk about cross-functional team work, so this may come as a surprise to students. If they have worked in internships with large companies, they may well have seen functional silos at work, and their coursework only serves to reinforce that mentality. Examples of companies failing because of a lack of team work—which can happen frequently at small companies in particular—will open many students' eyes to the importance of ensuring that all functions work in concert to make the company a success.
5. Value chains and supply chains are important concepts that also are typically not discussed in other courses. Getting students to understand these concepts is important for their understanding of the remainder of the course. Showing how sloppy quality in a component purchased from a vendor ultimately affects customer satisfaction will help.
6. Market segmentation and targeting is universally a new concept to students, unless they happen to have a parent who works in marketing. Although this is discussed in detail in a future chapter, showing how a large, amorphous market can be broken down in more and more detailed groups of buyers will help.
7. Market positioning can be difficult to understand as well. Students will normally think of a product in terms of its features, and although positioning includes the features, it also spans the concepts of benefits and perceptions. Using examples of brands at opposite ends of a price continuum, such as Rolex versus Timex watches, helps drive home what positioning means.

Student Projects

1. Look at the mission statements of five companies in the same industry. How do their mission statements differ and how are they alike? Which ones do you believe are good?
2. A business portfolio is the collection of businesses or products that make up the company. Take a look at Ford (www.ford.com). Describe Ford's business portfolio in terms of both businesses and products.
3. Using the Boston Consulting Group's growth-share matrix, place Ford's vehicles on the grid. Which are the stars, the cash cows, the question marks, and the dogs?
4. Still using Ford as our example, discuss the product positioning of their SUVs and trucks.

Small Group Assignment

Form students into groups of three to five. Each group should read the opening vignette to the chapter on NASCAR. Each group should answer the following questions:

1. What has caused NASCAR's wild popularity?
2. What has been the company's primary strategy?
3. What is NASCAR doing to ensure its future growth and success?
4. What "connections" is NASCAR attempting?

Each group should then share its findings with the class.

Individual Assignment

Consider Dillard's Department Stores (www.dillards.com) and Macy's (www.macys.com). What is the positioning strategy of each? How are they similar? How are they different?

Think-Pair-Share

Consider the following questions, formulate and answer, pair with the student on your right, share your thoughts with one another, and respond to questions from the instructor.

1. Design a mission statement for your college/university.
2. What are some of the problems with using a matrix approach (such as the BCG matrix)?
3. What is the difference between market development and product development?
4. Under what conditions might downsizing be a usable strategy?

Classroom Exercise/Homework Assignment

Develop a strategy for attracting new students to your college or university. Write a statement that describes your college/university's fit between the goal of attracting the best students and their capabilities for then educating those students

Classroom Management Strategies

This chapter starts outlining some fairly difficult subjects for students. Strategic planning, growth-share matrices, and even the development of the marketing mix are relatively tough concepts for a second chapter in a beginning marketing text. Therefore, when planning how to present the material, be sure to leave plenty of time to go through at least some of the Applying the Concepts, as well as defining what the Key Terms really mean in the everyday working world. Several of the concepts presented in this chapter become important later in the text, and if the students come away understanding this chapter, they will have an easier time later in the semester.

1. Companywide Strategic Planning can be covered in about 15 minutes. Focus on the "thread" that ties together the corporate strategic plan, corporate and business unit objectives, and the business or product portfolio. This last topic should be prominent in the discussion, as it sets the stage for later discussions of new product development.
2. The second major section of the chapter, Planning Marketing, can be covered in 5 minutes. Although this section is important and touches on issues that will come up later in the text, it does not need to have the same level of focus as the other topics in this chapter.
3. The next section, Marketing Strategy, is extremely important; 20 minutes should be devoted to this topic. In particular, ensuring the students understand the true meaning of developing an intelligent marketing mix will set the stage for such later topics as integrated marketing communications, because they will already have thought about how different components of a plan should work together.
4. Finally, 20 minutes should also be devoted to Managing the Marketing Effort. This section should really drive home the notion that marketing isn't just a creative endeavor. For instance, under marketing analysis as well as understanding the marketing environment, you can point out how these topics are a big part of what market research is all about.

CHAPTER 3
Analyzing the Marketing Environment

Previewing the Concepts: Chapter Objectives

1. Describe the environmental forces that affect the company's ability to serve its customers
2. Explain how changes in the demographic and economic environments affect marketing decisions
3. Identify the major trends in the firm's natural and technological environments
4. Explain the key changes in the political and cultural environments
5. Discuss how companies can react to the marketing environment

JUST THE BASICS

Chapter Overview

This chapter shows that marketing does not operate in a vacuum but rather in a complex and changing environment.

Other *actors* in this environment—suppliers, intermediaries, customers, competitors, publics, and others—may work with or against the company.

Major environmental *forces*—demographic, economic, natural, technological, political, and cultural—shape marketing opportunities, pose threats, and affect the company's ability to serve customers and develop lasting relationships with them.

To understand marketing, and to develop effective marketing strategies, you must first understand the environment in which marketing operates.

Annotated Chapter Notes/Outline

Introduction

McDonald's has been losing share to "fast-casual" restaurants because consumers today want more choices.

As the market leader, McDonald's often bears the brunt of criticism.

McDonald's has strived to realign itself with the changing marketing environment, and it appears to be paying off.

Marketers need to be good at building relationships with customers, others in the company, and external partners.

The marketing environment consists of the actors and forces outside marketing that affect marketing management's ability to build and maintain successful relationships with target customers.

More than any other group in the company, marketers must be the trend trackers and opportunity seekers.

A company's ***marketing environment*** consists of the actors and forces outside marketing that affect marketing management's ability to build and maintain successful relationships with target customers.

Use **Key Term** *Marketing Environment* here. Use **Chapter Objective** 1 here.

The ***microenvironment*** consists of the actors close to the company that affect its ability to service its customers.

The ***macroenvironment*** consists of larger societal forces that affect the microenvironment.

Use **Key Terms** *Microenvironment* and *Macroenvironment* here.

The Company's Microenvironement

Marketing management's job is to build relationships with customers by creating customer value and satisfaction.

Figure 3.1 shows the major actors in the marketer's microenvironment.

Use **Figure** 3-1 here.

The Company

All the interrelated groups form the internal environment.

All groups should work in harmony to provide superior customer value and relationships.

Suppliers

Suppliers provide the resources needed by the company to produce its goods and services.

Marketing managers must watch supply availability—supply shortages or delays, labor strikes, and other events can cost sales in the short run and damage customer satisfaction in the long run.

Marketing managers monitor the price trends of their key inputs.

Marketing Intermediaries

Marketing intermediaries help the company to promote, sell, and distribute its products to final buyers.

Use **Key Term** *Marketing Intermediaries* here.

- ***Resellers*** are distribution channel firms that help the company find customers or make sales to them. These include wholesalers and retailers.

- ***Physical distribution firms*** help the company to stock and move goods from their points of origin to their destinations.

- ***Marketing services agencies*** are the marketing research firms, advertising agencies, media firms, and marketing consulting firms that help the company target and promote its products to the right markets.

- ***Financial intermediaries*** include banks, credit companies, insurance companies, and other businesses that help finance transactions or insure against the risks associated with the buying and selling of goods.

Marketers recognize the importance of working with their intermediaries as partners rather than simply as channels through which they sell their products.

Customers

Five types of customer markets:

1. *Consumer markets:* individuals and households that buy goods and services for personal consumption.
2. *Business markets:* buy goods and services for further processing or for use in their production process.
3. *Reseller markets:* buy goods and services to resell at a profit.
4. *Government markets:* made up of government agencies that buy goods and services to produce public services.
5. *International markets:* buyers in other countries, including consumers, producers, resellers, and governments.

Competitors

Marketers must gain strategic advantage by positioning their offerings strongly against competitors' offerings in the minds of consumers.

No single competitive marketing strategy is best for all companies.

Publics

Use **Key Term** *Public* here. Use **Discussing the Issues** 1 here.

A **public** is any group that has an actual or potential interest in or impact on an organization's ability to achieve its objectives.

- *Financial publics* influence the company's ability to obtain funds.
- *Media publics* carry news, features, and editorial opinion.
- *Government publics.* Management must take government developments into account.
- *Citizen-action publics.* A company's marketing decisions may be questioned by consumer organizations, environmental groups, etc.
- *Local publics* include neighborhood residents and community organizations.
- *General public.* The general public's image of the company affects its buying.
- *Internal publics* include workers, managers, volunteers, and the board of directors.

Use **Video Case** here.

Applying the Concept
Describe the microenvironment for the School of Business at your university. What internal departments must the school interact with? Who are the customers and competitors? Do you know if there are any marketing intermediaries? What publics might be interested in what the School of Business is doing?

The Company's Macroenvironment

Figure 3.2 shows the six major forces in the company's macroenvironment.

Use **Figure** 3-2 here.

Demographic Environment

Use **Key Term** *Demography* here. Use **Chapter Objective** 2 here. Use **Discussing the Issues** 2 here.

Demography is the study of human populations in terms of size, density, location, age, gender, race, occupation, and other statistics.

Changes in the world demographic environment have major implications for business.

Thus, marketers keep close track of demographic trends and developments in their markets, both at home and abroad.

Changing Age Structure of the Population

The U.S. population stood at over 302 million in 2007 and may reach almost 364 million by the year 2030.

The single most important demographic trend in the United States is the changing age structure of the population.

Baby Boomers. The post-World War II baby boom produced 78 million **baby boomers**, born between 1946 and 1964.

Baby boomers account for nearly 30 percent of the population, spend about $2.3 trillion annually, and hold three-quarters of the nation's financial assets.

The youngest boomers are now in their early-to-mid forties; the oldest are entering their sixties.

Boomers are spending $30 billion a year on *anti*aging products and services.

Generation X. The baby boom was followed by a "birth dearth," creating another generation of 49 million people born between 1965 and 1976.

Author Douglas Coupland calls them **Generation X.**

Others call them the "baby busters."

Increasing parental divorce rates and higher employment for their mothers made them the first generation of latchkey kids.

They developed a more cautious economic outlook.

The GenXers are a more skeptical bunch.

Millennials (also called Generation Y or the echo boomers). Born between 1977 and 2000, these children of the baby boomers number 83 million.

This group includes several age cohorts:

- *tweens* (aged 8-12),
- *teens* (13-18); and
- *young adults* (the twenty-somethings).

45 percent of Millennials describe their race as something other than white.

Use **Key Terms** *Baby Boomers, Generation X,* and *Millennials/Generation Y* here. Use **Marketing at Work** 3-1 here. Use **Under the Hood: Focus on Technology** here.

Generational Marketing. Defining people by their birth date may be less effective than segmenting them by their lifestyle, life stage, or the commons values they seek in the products they buy.

The Changing American Family

The "traditional household" consists of a husband, wife, and children (and sometimes grandparents).

In the U.S.:

- Married couples with children make up 23 percent of the households;
- Married couples without children make up 29 percent;
- Single parents comprise 16 percent.
- Nonfamily households make up 32 percent.

Both husband and wife work in 57 percent of all married-couple families.

Let's Discuss This Most of the students' parents will be from the Baby Boom generation. Discuss how the students' upbringing and daily lives may have differed from what their parents experienced in their own upbringing, and what those differences mean for marketers.

Geographic Shifts in Population

About 14 percent of all U.S. residents move each year.

The U.S. population has shifted toward the Sunbelt states.

Americans have been moving from rural to metropolitan areas.

A Better-Educated, More White-Collar, More Professional Population

The U.S. population is becoming better educated.

In 2004, 86 percent of the U.S. population over age 25 had completed high school.

Between 2004 and 2014 the number of professional workers is expected to increase 21 percent and manufacturing is expected to decline 5 percent.

Increasing Diversity

The United States has become more of a "salad bowl" in which various groups have mixed together but have maintained their diversity by retaining important ethnic and cultural differences.

The U.S. population is about 66 percent white, 15 percent Hispanics and 13 percent African Americans.

The Asian American population now totals about 5 percent of the population.

By 2050, Hispanics will comprise an estimated 24 percent of the U.S. population.

Many companies have begun to target gay and lesbian consumers.

They are twice as likely as the general population to have a household income over $250,000.

Another attractive segment is the nearly 54 million adults with disabilities.

Use **Linking the Concepts** here. Use **Application Questions** 1 here.

Economic Environment

Use **Key Term** *Economic Environment* here.

The **economic environment** consists of factors that affect consumer purchasing power and spending patterns.

Subsistence economies – consume most of their own agricultural and industrial output.

Industrial economies – constitute rich markets for many different kinds of goods.

Changes in Income

Throughout the 1990s, American consumers fell into a consumption frenzy.

Consumers now face repaying debts acquired during earlier spending splurges.

Value marketing—just the right combination of product quality and service at a fair price.

Income distribution in the United States is very skewed.

- *Upper-class* consumers: spending patterns are not affected by current economic events and who are a major market for luxury goods.

- *Middle class:* somewhat careful about its spending but can still afford the good life some of the time.

- *Working class:* must stick close to the basics of food, clothing, and shelter and must try hard to save.

- *Underclass:* must count their pennies when making even the most basic purchases.

Changing Consumer Spending Patterns

Food, housing, and transportation use up the most household income.

Engel's law states that as family income rises, the percentage spent on food declines.

Changes in major economic variables have a large impact on the marketplace.

Use **Key Term** *Engel's Laws* here. Use **Discussing the Issues** 3 here.

Natural Environment

The **natural environment** involves the natural resources that are needed as inputs by marketers or that are affected by marketing activities.

Trends in the natural environment:

1. *Shortages of raw materials.*
2. *Increased pollution.*
3. Increased government intervention.

Companies are developing *environmentally sustainable* strategies.

Use **Key Term** *Natural Environment* here. Use **Chapter Objective** 3 herre. Use **Discussing the Issues** 4 here.

Technological Environment

The **technological environment** is the most dramatic force now shaping our destiny.

Use **Key Term** *Technological Environment* here.

Technology has released such wonders as antibiotics, robotic surgery, miniaturized electronics, laptop computers, and the Internet.

The United States leads the world in research and development spending.

Political Environment

Use **Key Term** *Political Environment* here. Use **Chapter Objective** 4 here. Use **Application Question** 2 here.

Legislation Regulating Business

Governments develop ***public policy*** to guide commerce.

Increasing Legislation. Legislation affecting business around the world has increased steadily over the years.

Business legislation has been enacted for a number of reasons.

1. To *protect companies* from each other.
2. To *protect consumers* from unfair business practices.
3. To *protect the interests of society* against unrestrained business behavior.

Changing Government Agency Enforcement. Because government agencies have discretion in enforcing laws, they can have an impact on a company's marketing performance.

Use **Table** 3-1 here. Use **Focus on Ethics** here.

Increased Emphasis on Ethics and Socially Responsible Actions

Socially Responsible Behavior. Enlightened companies encourage their managers to "do the right thing."

The boom in Internet marketing has created a new set of social and ethical issues.

Cause-Related Marketing. Many companies are now linking themselves to worthwhile causes.

Cause-related marketing has stirred some controversy.

Cultural Environment

Use **Key Term** *Cultural Environment* here. Use **Application Question** 3 here.

The **cultural environment** is made up of institutions and other forces that affect a society's basic values, perceptions, preferences, and behaviors.

Persistence of Cultural Values

Core beliefs and values are passed on from parents to children and are reinforced by schools, churches, business, and government.

Secondary beliefs and values are more open to change.

Shifts in Secondary Cultural Values

Use **Discussing the Issues** 5 here.

Marketers want to predict cultural shifts in order to spot new opportunities or threats.

People's Views of Themselves. People vary in their emphasis on serving themselves versus serving others.

The Yankelovich Monitor identifies consumer segments whose purchases are motivated by self-views. Two examples:

- *Do-It-Yourselfers—Recent Movers.*
- *Adventurers.*

People's Views of Others. Shifts in people's attitudes toward others has been noted.

Trend trackers see a new wave of "cocooning."

People's Views of Organizations. People are willing to work for major organizations and expect them to carry out society's work.

Many people see work as a required chore to earn money to enjoy their nonwork hours.

People's Views of Society. People vary in their attitudes toward their society.

People's Views of Nature. Recently, people have recognized that nature is finite and fragile, that it can be destroyed by human activities.

This renewed love of things natural has created a 63-million-person "lifestyles of health and sustainability" (LOHAS) market.

The U.S. organic-food market generated $15.9 billion in sales last year, a 325 percent increase over since 1997.

People's Views of the Universe. Religious conviction and practice have been dropping off gradually through the years.

Use **Linking the Concepts** here.

Responding to the Marketing Environment

Many companies think the marketing environment is an uncontrollable element to which they have to adapt.

Other companies take an ***environmental management perspective*** to affect the publics and forces in their environment.

Marketing managers should take a ***proactive*** rather than ***reactive*** approach to the marketing environment.

Use **Chapter Objective** 5 here. Use **Marketing at Work** 3-2 here. Use **Discussing the Issues** 6 here.

Travel Log

Discussing the Issues

1. Name and describe the elements of a company's microenvironment and give an example showing why each is important. (AASCB: Communication)

   Answer:

   The **microenvironment** consists of the actors close to the company that affect its ability to serve its customers—the company, suppliers, marketing intermediaries, customer markets, competitors, and publics. In designing marketing plans, marketing management takes other company groups into account—groups such as top management, finance, research and development (R&D), purchasing, operations, and accounting. All these interrelated groups form the internal environment. Suppliers form an important link in the company's overall customer value delivery system as they provide the resources needed by the company to produce its goods and services. Marketing intermediaries help the company to promote, sell, and distribute its products to final buyers. They include resellers, physical distribution firms, marketing services agencies, and financial intermediaries. The company needs to study five types of customer markets closely: consumer markets, business markets, reseller markets, government markets, and international markets. The marketing concept states that to be successful, a company must provide greater customer value and satisfaction than its competitors do. Thus, marketers must do more than simply adapt to the needs of target consumers. They also must gain strategic advantage by positioning their offerings strongly against competitors' offerings in the minds of consumers. Finally, the company's marketing environment also includes various publics—any group that has an actual or potential interest in or impact on an organization's ability to achieve its objectives. Seven types are identified: financial, media, citizen-action, local, general, government, and internal publics.

2. What is *demography* and why are marketers interested in it? List some of the demographic trends of interest to marketers. (AACSB: Communication)

   Answer:

   Demography is the study of human populations in terms of size, density, location, age, gender, race, occupation, and other statistics. The demographic environment is of major interest to marketers because it involves people, and people make up markets. The major trends discussed in the chapter include the changing age structure of the population, the changing American family, geographic shifts in population, a better-educated, more white-collar, more professional population, and increasing diversity.

3. Discuss the trends in the natural environment that marketers must be aware of and provide examples of companies' responses to them. (AACSB: Communication)

   Answer:

   The **natural environment** involves the natural resources that are needed as inputs by marketers or that are affected by marketing activities. Marketers should be aware of several trends in the natural environment. The first involves growing **shortages of raw materials**. Marketers need to rely less on nonrenewable resources and use renewable resources more wisely. A second environmental trend is **increased pollution**. Industry will almost always damage the quality of the natural environment. A third trend is **increased government intervention** in natural resource management. The governments of different countries vary in their concern and efforts to promote a clean environment. The general hope is that companies around the world will accept more social responsibility, and that less expensive devices can be found to control and reduce pollution.

   Concern for the natural environment has spawned the so-called green movement. Today, enlightened companies go beyond what government regulations dictate. They are developing **environmentally sustainable** strategies and practices in an effort to create a world economy that the planet can support indefinitely. They are responding to consumer demands with more environmentally responsible products, such as recyclable or biodegradable packaging, recycled materials and components, better pollution controls, and more energy-efficient operations. More and more, they are recognizing the link between a healthy ecology and a healthy economy. They are learning that environmentally responsible actions can also be good business.

4. Discuss reasons why business legislation is enacted. What role do businesses and industry groups play in shaping such legislation? (AACSB: Communication; Reflective Thinking)

   Answer:

   Business legislation has been enacted for a number of reasons. The first is to **protect companies** from each other. Laws define and prevent unfair competition. In the United States, such laws are enforced by the Federal Trade Commission and the Antitrust Division of the Attorney General's office. The second purpose of government regulation is to **protect consumers** from unfair business practices. Some firms, if left alone, would make shoddy products, invade consumer privacy, tell lies in their advertising, and deceive consumers through their packaging and pricing. Unfair business practices have been defined and are enforced by various agencies. The third purpose of government regulation is to **protect the interests of society** against unrestrained business behavior. Profitable business activity does not always create a better quality of life. Regulation arises to ensure that firms take responsibility for the social costs of their production or products.

   New laws and their enforcement will continue to increase. Businesses and industry groups must watch these developments when planning their products and marketing programs. Marketers need to know about the major laws protecting competition, consumers, and society. They need to understand these laws at the local, state, national, and international levels.

5. Compare and contrast core beliefs/values and secondary beliefs/values. Provide an example of each and discuss the potential impact marketers have on each. (AACSB: Communication; Reflective Thinking)

   Answer:

   Core beliefs and values are passed on from parents to children and are reinforced by schools, churches, business, and government. **Secondary beliefs and values** are more open to change. Believing in marriage is a core belief; believing that people should get married early in life is a secondary belief. Marketers have some chance of changing secondary values but little chance of changing core values.

6. How should marketers respond to the changing environment? (AACSB: Communication)

   Answer:

   Many companies view the marketing environment as an uncontrollable element to which they must react and adapt. They passively accept the marketing environment and do not try to change it. They analyze the environmental forces and design strategies that will help the company avoid the threats and take advantage of the opportunities the environment provides. Other companies take a *proactive* stance toward the marketing environment. Rather than simply watching and reacting, these firms take aggressive actions to affect the publics and forces in their marketing environment. Such companies hire lobbyists to influence legislation affecting their industries and stage media events to gain favorable press coverage. They run advertorials (ads expressing editorial points of view) to shape public opinion. They press lawsuits and file complaints with regulators to keep competitors in line, and they form contractual agreements to better control their distribution channels. By taking action, companies can often overcome seemingly uncontrollable environmental events. Marketing management cannot always control environmental forces. In many cases, it must settle for simply watching and reacting to the environment. For example, a company would have little success trying to influence geographic population shifts, the economic environment, or major cultural values. But whenever possible, smart marketing managers will take a *proactive* rather than *reactive* approach to the marketing environment.

Application Questions

1. China and India are emerging markets that will have a significant impact on the world in coming years. The term "Chindia" has been used to describe the growing power of these two countries. Discuss two trends related to Chindia's power and its impact on marketers in the United States. (AACSB: Communication; Reflective Thinking)

   Answer:

   Students' responses will vary but they can find articles on the growth of China and India, and on the "Chindia" phenomenon. For example, the article, "'Chindia Is the Future' Says Asburton," (2006), *Emerging Markets Monitor*, vol. 12 (December 18), pp. 1, 7-8, provides some trends that are of interest to United States marketers. In 2006, the working population in Chindia was 1.6 billion, but it will rise to 1.86 billion by 2020; nominal GDP will increase from $2 trillion US to $26 trillion US; auto sales will increase from 7 million to 32 million; and percentage of world energy consumption will increase from 15% to 25%. These trends pose both opportunities and threats to marketers in the United States. Opportunities arise because consumer demand will increase. But limited resources will be spread among more people, possibly driving up costs of raw materials.

2. The Federal Trade Commission (FTC) has regulatory authority over marketing practices. Visit www.ftc.gov to learn about this agency and how it regulates business activities in general and marketing activities in particular. Describe the process the FTC uses if a complaint is made and discuss one FTC case related to marketing. (AACSB: Communication; Use of IT)

   Answer:

   Students will have to search around the FTC's Web site to learn how the FTC brings an action. You may want to point them to the URL: www.ftc.gov/ftc/action.shtm. The best way to learn about current cases is to click on the "News" tab at the top of the Web site.

3. Cause-related marketing has grown considerably over the past ten years. Visit www.causemarketingforum.com and learn about companies that have won Halo Awards for outstanding cause-related marketing programs. Present two award-winning case studies to your class. (AACSB: Communication; Use of IT)

   Answer:

   Students' responses will vary. Students can click on "Winner Archives" on the left side of this Web site to learn about past winners of this award. Past recipients are highlighted with short explanations of their campaigns.

Under the Hood: Focus on Technology

First there was the television, then the computer, and now there's the "third screen"—mobile phones. The first and second screens—TV and the computer—are heavily commercialized, and so to will be the third screen. Mobile marketing involves any type of marketing message—voice, text, image, or video—delivered to a hand-held portable device such as a cellphone, iPhone, or BlackBerry. Though still in its infancy in the United States, mobile has grown rapidly in other countries. It has spawned an industry group—the Mobile Marketing Association (MMA)—and an academic journal entitled the *International Journal of Mobile Marketing*. Marketers in the United States are treading carefully but some are having success, such as Coca-Cola's Sprite campaign targeted to teens and Meijer's (a mid-West discount retail chain) "gas alerts" informing consumers of price changes three hours before they take effect.

1. Learn more about mobile marketing and discuss its applications. Develop a mobile marketing campaign for a brand of your choice. (AACSB: Communication; Reflective Thinking)

   Answer:

   Students' responses will vary but they should be able to find ample articles illustrating examples. Students can learn about campaigns through trade publications such as *Advertising Age* and at the Mobile Marketing Association's Web site: www.mmaglobal.com.

2. Which demographic group or groups will more likely accept mobile marketing? Explain your answer. (AACSB: Communication; Reflective Thinking)

   Answer:

   The text highlights some attributes of the Millennials. Most notably, they grew up on technology and have a high level of comfort with it. They can more easily overcome the learning curve for this technology than can older generations. In addition, they are an impatient, now-oriented generation. They also may feel aliened if they are not part of mobile marketing efforts.

Focus on Ethics

You've probably heard of a monopoly, in which one powerful seller controls a market of many buyers. But have you ever heard of a *monopsony*? A monopsony involves one powerful buyer and many sellers. The buyer is so powerful that it can drive prices down. And example is Wal-Mart, the world's largest retailer. Wal-Mart's power allows it to get the lowest possible prices from its suppliers. Similarly, wine-making giant Ernest & Gallo has so much power buying grapes that growers have to concede to the wine maker's demands for lower prices.

1. Is it fair that a buyer can exert so much power over a supplier? Are there any benefits to consumers? (AACSB: Communication; Ethical Reasoning)

   Answer:

   Some students will argue that it is the free market working and is inherently fair. However, whereas larger suppliers can meet the demands of the powerful buyer, smaller suppliers will not be able to compete. This may not be in the best interests of consumers if it reduces competition or if product quality suffers. However, the lower prices will be passed on to consumers, so some will argue that it is good for consumers. For example, Wal-Mart leverages its buying power to obtain lower prices, which it in turn passes on to consumers in the form of lower prices.

2. Do you think the government should step in and set minimum price levels? Discuss the consequences of your answer. (AACSB: Communication; Reflective Thinking)

   Answer:

   Students' responses will vary. Some students will argue that government intervention is necessary to protect the small suppliers. With minimum price levels set by the government, the smaller firms may be able to compete with the larger suppliers.

However, consumers may be hurt if suppliers must sell at a minimum price, resulting in higher prices for consumers.

Great Ideas

Barriers to Effective Learning

1. This is an intense chapter, and it presents a whole lot of information that might make some students' heads swim. If it hasn't happened before, this is where students really begin to get the picture that marketing managers need to be very analytical. Presenting the in-depth discussion of current macro trends as something that needs to be understood but not memorized helps.
2. Students will also be anxious about how a marketing manager successfully tracks these kinds of forces. Explaining the use of purchased marketing and economic reports, and what market researchers do for a living, helps relieve that anxiety.
3. As usual, examples of companies who successfully adapt to changing forces and factors will help students internalize the messages in this chapter.

Student Projects

1. Define the marketing environment for Starbucks (www.starbucks.com). Keep in mind that a company's marketing environment consists of the actors and forces outside marketing that affect marketing management's ability to build and maintain successful relationships with target customers.
2. What are the fundamental differences between consumer markets, business markets, and reseller markets?
3. Consider your college/university. What are the publics to which it must pay attention?
4. Over 14 percent of the U.S. population moves every year. How is this good for marketers?
5. Describe the differences in products which appeal to the middle class, working class, and upper class.

Small Group Assignment

Form students into groups of three to five. Each group should read the opening vignette to the chapter on McDonald's. Each group should answer the following questions:

1. What changes in the American lifestyle negatively impacted McDonald's, causing sales to slow markedly?
2. How has McDonald's attempted to cope with these slowing sales?
3. How effective have they been?

Each group should share its findings with the class.

Individual Assignment

Go online and compare the marketing strategies of McDonald's (www.mcdonalds.com), Wendy's (www.wendys.com), and Burger King (www.burgerking.com). What age group is each targeting? Do you agree with their strategy?

Think-Pair-Share

Consider the following questions, formulate and answers, pair with the student on your right, share your thoughts with one another, and respond to questions from the instructor.

1. What are the fundamental differences between Generation X and Generation Y?
2. How has the typical family changed just in your lifetime?
3. Overall, the U.S. population is becoming better educated. What implication does this hold for marketers?
4. By 2050, Hispanics will comprise an estimated 24 percent of the U.S. population. How will this impact the manner in which some products are marketed?
5. What is the one most significant trend in the natural environment, in your opinion, and how is it impacting marketing activities?

Classroom Exercise/Homework Assignment

Take a look at Wendy's (www.wendys.com). How is this company attempting to set themselves apart from their primary competitors? What publics do they appear to be concentrating on? Why do you believe this is the case?

Classroom Management Strategies

This will be the first time students will have thought about the marketing environment and what it means to companies in their marketing efforts. The concept of understanding consumer needs and wants will be totally foreign to them at worst, and at best a novel concept. Once the students begin to see the complexity of the marketing environment, however, there will be a tendency for their eyes to glaze over. As usual, working through several examples for each concept will help tremendously.

1. College is a place to break things down into their component parts to study them in isolation. The section on the company's microenvironment may well be the first time the students will have looked at marketing as needing to pay attention to anything other than marketing concepts. At least 15 minutes should be devoted to this topic in class. The difficult concepts will most likely be in the areas of marketing intermediaries and publics; spending sufficient time on these two topics will make the following chapters that much easier.
2. The majority of the class time, 30 to 40 minutes, should be spent on the macroenvironment. There is a tremendous amount of information in this section, particularly in the section describing the demographic environment. It's helpful here to link some of these concepts back to what they learned in sociology courses, or, if the students have not taken any of the social sciences,

you can point out how they interact with business. The next most intense part of this section is the political environment and the sheer number of laws passed that affect marketers. The cultural environment section is a good time to tie in principles of psychology.

CHAPTER 4
Managing Marketing Information to Gain Customer Insights

Previewing the Concepts: Chapter Objectives

1. Explain the importance of information in gaining insights about the marketplace and customers
2. Define the marketing information system and discuss its parts
3. Outline the steps in the marketing research process
4. Explain how companies analyze and use marketing information
5. Discuss the special issues some marketing researchers face, including public policy and ethics issues.

JUST THE BASICS

Chapter Overview

This chapter looks at how companies develop and manage information about important marketplace elements.

This chapter is an examination of marketing information systems designed to assess the firm's marketing information needs, develop the needed information, and help managers to use the information to gain actionable customer and market insights.

Annotated Chapter Notes/Outlines

Introduction

ZIBA is a new-product design consultancy.

It digs in and really gets to know consumers.

At the heart of ZIBA's success is its Consumer Insights and Trends Group.

ZIBA teaches its clients that successful new products don't begin in their R&D labs.

They begin with a deep understanding of customers and their emotional connections to the products they buy and use.

Marketers must *use* the information to gain powerful *customer and market insights.*

Marketing Information and Customer Insights

Companies use such customer insights to develop competitive advantage.

To gain good customer insights, marketers must effectively manage marketing information from a wide range of sources.

The real value of marketing research and marketing information lies in how it is used—in the **customer insights** that it provides.

Use **Key Term** *Customer Insights* here.

Customer insights group collect customer and market information from a wide variety of sources.

A **marketing information system (MIS)** consists of people and procedures for assessing information needs, developing the needed information, and helping decision makers to use the information to generate and validate actionable customer and market insights. (Figure 4.1)

Use **Key Term** *Marketing Information System* here. Use **Chapter Objectives** 1 and 2 here. Use **Figure** 4.1 here.

Assessing Marketing Information Needs

A good marketing information system balances the information users would *like* to have against what they really *need* and what is *feasible* to offer.

Sometimes the company cannot provide the needed information, either because it is not available or because of MIS limitations.

By itself, information has no worth; its value comes from its *use*.

Developing Marketing Information

Internal Data

Use **Key Term** *Internal Database* here.

Internal databases are electronic collections of consumer and market information obtained from data sources within the company network.

Information in the database can come from many sources.

Problems with internal data:

- It may be incomplete or in the wrong form for making marketing decisions.
- Keeping the database current requires a major effort, because data ages quickly.
- All the data must be well integrated and readily accessible.

Marketing Intelligence

Use **Key Term** *Marketing Intelligence* here.

Marketing intelligence is the systematic collection and analysis of publicly available information about consumers, competitors, and developments in the marketplace.

Marketing intelligence gathering has grown dramatically.

Firms use competitive intelligence to gain early warnings of competitor moves and strategies.

Much competitor intelligence can be collected from people inside the company.

Competitors often reveal intelligence information through their annual reports, business publications, trade show exhibits, press releases, advertisements, and Web pages.

Most companies are now taking steps to protect their own information.

Use **Application Question** 3 here.

The growing use of marketing intelligence raises a number of ethical issues.

Use **Key Term** *Marketing Research* here. Use **Chapter Objective** 3 here.

Marketing Research

Marketing research is the systematic design, collection, analysis, and reporting of data relevant to a specific marketing situation facing an organization.

Use **Figure** 4-2 here. Use **Discussing the Issues** 1 & 2 here.

The marketing research process has ***four steps*** (see Figure 4.2):

1. Defining the Problem and Research Objectives

Defining the problem and research objectives is often the hardest step in the research process.

A marketing research project might have one of three types of objectives.

Use **Key Terms** *Exploratory Research, Descriptive Research,* and *Causal Research* here. Use **Discussing the Issues** 3 here.

1. **Exploratory research:** to gather preliminary information that will help define the problem and suggest hypotheses.
2. **Descriptive research:** to describe things, such as the market potential for a product.
3. **Causal research:** to test hypotheses about cause-and-effect relationships.

Start with exploratory research and later follow with descriptive or causal research.

2. Developing the Research Plan

The research plan outlines sources of existing data and spells out the specific research approaches, contact methods, sampling plans, and instruments that researchers will use to gather new data.

Research objectives must be translated into specific information needs.

The research plan should be presented in a *written proposal.*

Secondary data consist of information that already exists somewhere, having been collected for another purpose.

Primary data consist of information collected for the specific purpose at hand.

Gathering Secondary Data

Researchers usually start by gathering secondary data.

Using **commercial online databases**, marketing researchers can conduct their own searches of secondary data sources.

Use **Key Term** *Commercial Online Database* here.

Can usually be obtained more quickly and at a lower cost than primary data.

Can provide data an individual company cannot collect on its own.

Use **Key Term** *Secondary Data* here. Use **Table** 4-1 here.

Secondary data can present problems.

- The needed information may not exist.
- The data might not be very usable.
    - *relevant* (fits research project needs), *accurate* (reliably collected and reported),
    - *current* (up-to-date enough for current decisions), and
    - *impartial* (objectively collected and reported).

Primary Data Collection

Use **Key Term** *Primary Data* here. Use **Table** 4-2 here.

Research Approaches

Observational Research involves gathering primary data by observing relevant people, actions, and situations.

Use **Key Term** *Observational Research* here.

Observational research can obtain information that people are unwilling or unable to provide.

Disadvantages:

- Some things cannot be observed.
- Long-term or infrequent behavior is also difficult to observe.
- Observations can be very difficult to interpret.

Ethnographic research involves sending trained observers to watch and interact with consumers in their "natural habitat."

Use **Key Term** *Ethnographic Research* here.

Ethnographic research often yields the kinds of details that just don't emerge from traditional research questionnaires or focus groups.

Survey Research, the most widely used method for primary data collection, is the approach best suited for gathering ***descriptive*** information.

Use **Key Terms** *Survey Research* here.

The major advantage of survey research is its flexibility.

Disadvantages:

- Sometimes people are unable to answer survey questions.
- People may be unwilling to respond to unknown interviewers or about things they consider private.
- Respondents may answer survey questions even when they do not know the answer.
- People may not take the time, or they might resent the intrusion into their privacy.

Experimental Research is best suited for gathering ***causal*** information.

Use **Key Term** *Experimental Research* here.

Contact Methods

Mail, Telephone, and Personal Interviewing

Mail questionnaires can be used to collect large amounts of information at a low cost per respondent.

Respondents give more honest answers to more personal questions.

No interviewer is involved to bias the respondent's answers.

Disadvantages:

- Not very flexible,
- Take longer to complete,
- The response rate is very low,
- The researcher often has little control over the mail questionnaire sample.

Telephone interviewing is the one of the best methods for gathering information quickly, and it provides greater flexibility than mail questionnaires.

Interviewers can explain difficult questions.

Response rates are higher than with mail questionnaires.
Disadvantages:

- Cost per respondent is higher than with mail questionnaires,
- People may not want to discuss personal questions with an interviewer,

- Introduces interviewer bias,
- Different interviewers may interpret and record responses differently,
- Increasingly high rates of hang-ups.

Personal interviewing takes two forms—individual and group interviewing.

- *Individual interviewing* involves talking with people one-on-one.
- *Group interviewing* (**focus group interviewing**) consists of inviting six to ten people to meet with a trained moderator to talk about a product, service, or organization.

Use **Key Term** *Focus Group Interviewing* here. Use **Table** 4-3 here. Use **Application Question** 2 here.

Online Marketing Research

Increasingly, researchers are collecting primary data through **online marketing research.**

Use **Key Term** *Online Marketing Research* here. Use **Under the Hood: Focus on Technology** here.

Online research spending by U.S. companies has soared to $1.35 billion, up from just $253 million in 2000.

Web-based research now accounts for 17 percent of all U.S. marketing research spending.

The Internet is well suited to ***quantitative*** research.

Online research usually costs much less than research conducted through mail, phone, or personal interviews.

Sample size has little impact on costs.

Use **Key Term** *Online Focus Group* here.

The primary qualitative Web-based research approach is **online focus groups.**

Disadvantages:

- Restricted Internet access can make it difficult to get a broad cross section of respondents. Controlling who's in the online sample is difficult.

- Online surveys can be dry and lacking in dynamics compared with other approaches.
- Consumer privacy is a major issue.

Sampling Plan

A **sample** is a segment of the population selected for marketing research to represent the population as a whole.

Use **Key Term** *Sample* here.

Designing the sample requires three decisions.

1. *Who* is to be surveyed (what *sampling unit*)?
2. *How many* people should be surveyed (what *sample size*)?
3. *How* should the people in the sample be *chosen* (what *sampling procedure*)?

Table 4.4 describes different kinds of samples.

Use **Table** 4-4 here.

The two types of samples are:

- ***Probability samples,***
- ***Nonprobability samples.***

Research Instruments

The ***questionnaire*** is the most common data collection instrument.

Closed-end questions include all the possible answers, and subjects make choices among them.

Open-end questions allow respondents to answer in their own words.

Care should be given to the ***wording*** and ***ordering*** of questions.

Use **Table** 4-5 here.

Researchers also use ***mechanical instruments*** to monitor consumer behavior. *People meters* and *checkout scanners* are examples.

Use **Discussing the Issues** 4 here.

3. Implementing the Research Plan

The data collection phase of the marketing research process is generally the most expensive and the most subject to error.

Researchers must process and analyze the collected data to isolate important information and findings.

4. Interpreting and Reporting the Findings

Researchers should present important findings and insights that are useful in the major decisions faced by management.

Analyzing and Using Marketing Information

Use **Chapter Objective** 4 here.

Customer Relationship Management (CRM)

Companies capture information at every possible customer ***touch point.***

Customer relationship management (CRM) is used to manage detailed information about individual customers and carefully manage customer touch points in order to maximize customer loyalty.

Use **Key Term** *Customer Relationship Management (CRM)* here.

CRM integrates everything that a company knows about individual customers to provide a 360-degree view of the customer relationship.

A ***data warehouse*** is a companywide electronic database of finely detailed customer information that needs to be sifted through for gems.

Data mining is the use of high-powered techniques to sift through the mounds of data and dig out interesting findings about customers.

CRM is just one part of an effective overall ***customer relationship management strategy.***

Use **Discussing the Issues** 5 here.

Distributing and Using Marketing Information

The marketing information system must make the information available to managers and others who make marketing decisions or deal with customers.

Many companies use an ***intranet*** to facilitate information distribution. The intranet provides ready access to data, stored reports, and so forth.

Companies are increasingly allowing key customers and value-network members to access account and product information, along with other information. The systems that do this are called ***extranets***.

Applying the Concept

Many auto companies have extranets with their suppliers; they also can include their dealerships, which are their product delivery channels. What kind of information might be shared among suppliers, the manufacturer, and the dealer? Why is it important that they share this information?

Other Marketing Information Considerations

Use **Chapter Objective** 5 here.

Marketing Research in Small Businesses and Nonprofit Organizations

Managers of small businesses and nonprofit organizations can obtain marketing insights by ***observing*** things around them.

Managers can conduct ***informal surveys*** using small convenience samples.

Managers can conduct their own simple ***experiments***.

Small organizations can obtain most of the secondary data available to large businesses.

Use **Application Question** 1 here.

International Marketing Research

International marketing researchers follow the same steps as domestic researchers.

The international researcher may have a difficult time finding good secondary data.

International researchers often must collect their own primary data.

Reaching respondents is often not easy in other parts of the world.

Cultural differences from country to country cause additional problems for international researchers.

Language is the most obvious obstacle.

Even when respondents are *willing* to respond, they may not be *able* to because of high functional illiteracy rates.

Use **Discussing the Issues** 6 here.

Public Policy and Ethics in Marketing Research

Intrusions on Consumer Privacy

Many consumers strongly resent or even mistrust marketing research.

Increasing consumer resentment has led to lower survey response rates in recent years.

The best approach is for researchers to ask only for the information they need, to use it responsibly to provide customer value, and to avoid sharing information without the customer's permission.

Use **Focus on Ethics** here.

Misuse of Research Findings

Many research studies appear to be little more than vehicles for pitching the sponsor's products.

Several associations have developed codes of research ethics and standards of conduct.

Travel Log

Discussing the Issues

1. Describe a marketing information system (MIS) and discuss the real value of marketing research and marketing information. (AACSB: Communication)

   Answer:

   A **marketing information system (MIS)** consists of people and procedures for assessing information needs, developing the needed information, and helping decision makers to use the information to generate and validate actionable customer and market insights. Figure 4.1 shows that the MIS begins and ends with information users—marketing managers, internal and external partners, and others who need marketing information. First, it interacts with these information users to assess information needs. Next, it interacts with the marketing environment to develop needed information through internal company databases, marketing intelligence activities, and marketing research. Finally, the MIS helps users to analyze and use the information to develop **customer insights**, making marketing decisions, and manage customer relationships. The real value of marketing research and marketing information lies in how it is used—in the customer insights that it provides. That is, an MIS provides marketing information that can be used to develop important customer insights from which the company can create more value for its customers. Thus, effective marketing information systems give managers the right information, in the right form, at the right time and help them to use this information to create customer value and stronger customer relationships.

2. Compare and contrast internal databases, marketing intelligence, and marketing research as means for developing marketing information. (AACSB: Communication)

   Answer:

   Marketers can obtain needed information from internal data, market intelligence, and marketing research. **Internal databases** are electronic collections of consumer and market information obtained from data sources within the company network. Information can come from many sources. For example, information on customer transactions, demographics, psychographics, and buying behavior can come from the marketing department. The customer service department can provide information on customer satisfaction or service problems. The accounting department can provide financial data. Operations reports on production schedules, shipments, and inventories. The sales force can provide information on resellers and competitors, and channel partners provide point-of-sale data.

   Marketing intelligence is the systematic collection and analysis of publicly available information about consumers, competitors, and developments in the marketplace. The goal is to better understand the environment to improve strategic decision making. A key difference between this source of information and internal databases is that other companies have access to the same marketing intelligence information.

   Marketing research is the systematic design, collection, analysis, and reporting of data relevant to a specific marketing situation facing an organization. That is, available information in an internal database or information gleaned through marketing intelligence activities may not provide the customer and/or market insights desired. The marketing research process has four steps: defining the problem and research objectives, developing the research plan, implementing the research plan, and interpreting and reporting the findings. Information from internal databases and marketing intelligence may be used to achieve the research objectives, but new data may need to be collected to achieve the research objectives.

3. Name and describe the three research approaches for gathering primary data. Explain when each approach is appropriate. (AACSB: Communication)

Answer:

Research approaches for gathering primary data include observation, surveys, and experiments. **Observational research** involves gathering primary data by observing people, actions, and situations. It is appropriate when researchers can't simply ask customers questions to glean customer insights. One type of observation research, ethnographic research, is appropriate when researchers want to observe and interact with consumers in their "natural habitat," yielding details that just don't emerge from traditional research questionnaires or focus groups. This research approach is best suited for exploratory research.

Survey research is the approach best suited for gathering descriptive information. Information about people's knowledge, attitudes, preferences, or buying behavior can often be obtained by asking them directly. Survey research is very flexible and can be used to obtain many different kinds of information in many different situations using many different contact methods (i.e., phone, mail, in person, or online).

Experimental research is best suited for gathering causal information. Experiments involve selecting matched groups of subjects, giving them different treatments, controlling unrelated factors, and checking for differences in group responses. This approach tries to explain cause-and-effect relationships.

4. Discuss the pros and cons of using questionnaires versus mechanical devices to collect primary data. (AACSB: Communication)

   Answer:

   Questionnaires are very flexible because there are many ways to ask questions. Closed-end questions, such as multiple-choice questions and scale questions, include all the possible answers respondents can choose. However, open-end questions allow respondents to answer in their own words, which is especially useful in exploratory research. On the negative side, though, questionnaires need to be prepared with caution as the order of the questions may produce bias or the wording may be difficult for respondents to understand.

   Unlike questionnaires, **mechanical devices** can measure actual behavior, even without respondents being aware that they are being observed. Whereas respondents know they are participating in research when completing a survey, mechanical devices can be used without respondents' knowledge. However, while these devices can monitor actions, they cannot provide insight as to why a respondent behaved that way. Questionnaires are useful in understanding why.

5. Explain customer relationship management (CRM) and how it helps companies develop customer insights. (AACSB: Communication)

Answer:

Customer relationship management (CRM) is used to manage detailed information about individual customers and carefully manage touch points to maximize customer loyalty. Smart companies capture information at every possible customer touch point, which can include customer purchases, sales force contacts, service and support calls, Web site visits, satisfaction surveys, credit and payment interactions, market research studies—basically every contact between the customer and the company. CRM consists of sophisticated software and analytical tools that integrate this information, analyze it, and apply the results to build stronger customer relationships. Customer insights can be gained using data mining techniques to dig out interesting findings about customers.

6. Discuss the challenges U.S. researchers might encounter when conducting research in other countries. (AACSB: Communication)

   Answer:

   There are several challenges U.S. researchers might encounter. Whereas domestic researchers deal with fairly homogeneous markets within a single country, international researchers deal with diverse markets in many different countries that often vary greatly in their levels of economic development, cultures and customs, and buying patterns. International researchers also may have a difficult time finding good secondary data as many countries have almost no research services at all. Even when secondary information is available, it usually must be obtained from many different sources on a country-by-country basis, making it difficult to combine or compare information. Thus, international researchers often must collect their own primary data, which also is fraught with problems (e.g., adequate samples, collecting data, cultural differences, translation problems, high illiteracy rates, etc.).

Application Questions

1. Describe the research process for a small business or nonprofit organization in your community. How does it differ compared to that for a larger business or organization? (AACSB: Communication; Reflective Thinking)

   Answer:

   Students' responses will vary depending on the organization chosen for this exercise, but the basic research process should be the same: defining the problem and research objectives, developing the research plan, implementing the research plan, and interpreting and reporting the findings (see Figure 4.2). Regardless of the type or business or nonprofit organization chosen, students should define a problem and state the objective of the research. Once this is done, then an appropriate research plan should be developed. The research plan should outline sources of existing data and spell out the specific research approach, contact method, sampling plan, and instrument used to gather data.

Students should indicate that the process should be the same regardless of the size or type of organization. However, smaller businesses and nonprofit organizations might use less expensive methods to collect data. For example, simply observing their customers can provide valuable information. Also, simple experiments, such as changing the themes in regular fund-raising mailings, can be conducted to determine which strategies work best. Finally, small and nonprofit organizations can obtain most of the secondary data available to large businesses, and many local organizations may provide useful information.

2. Assume you work for Outback Steakhouse, and your work group is tasked to assess customer satisfaction. Assign a different contact method used in marketing research to each member of your group to discuss the strengths and weaknesses of each. Write a brief report explaining which method your work group agreed would be appropriate for this task and support your recommendation. (AACSB: Communication; Reflective Thinking)

Answer:

Information can be collected by mail, telephone, personal interview, or online. Table 4.3 highlights the strengths and weaknesses of each in terms of flexibility, quantity of data that can be collected, control over interviewer effects, control of sample, speed of data collection, response rate, and cost.

Mail questionnaires can be used to collect large amounts of information at a low cost per respondent, and respondents may be more willing to give honest answers to personal questions than if using another contact method such as the telephone or personal interview. Also, no interviewer bias is involved. On the downside, though, mail questionnaires are not flexible as all respondents answer the same questions in a fixed order. Other weaknesses include a long time for the data collection to take place, poor response rates, and little control over who completes the survey. However, mail surveys are relatively inexpensive.

Telephone interviewing is a good method for gathering information quickly, and it provides greater flexibility than mail questionnaires. While researchers have better control over who responds and can collect a fair amount of data quickly, response rates are poor and cost tends to be relatively high.

Personal interviewing can be done at the individual or group level. This method offers excellent flexibility and the ability to collect a large amount of data. It is also a good method for controlling the sample, collecting data quickly, and providing good response rates. However, this method is expensive and there is poor control over interviewer effects.

Online collection methods appear to be one of the best methods in terms of all criteria listed in Table 4.3. The Internet is especially well suited to quantitative research, but it is also used for qualitative research approaches.

Students' responses regarding the appropriate method for this task will vary. However, many will probably indicate that online surveys would be best, as many retail stores and restaurants have started using this approach. For example, on the sales receipt, many restaurants offer customers a discount on their next visit if they go to their website to complete a survey.

3. One source of competitive marketing intelligence is a company's Web site. Visit Gateway's Web site (http://www.gateway.com) and identify information that might be useful to competitors. Write a brief report of what you found. (AACSB: Communication; Use of IT)

   Answer:

   Students' responses will vary on this activity as there is considerable information on this site that is useful to competitors. For example, all of Gateway's product offerings are described on this site. There is specific pricing information, product recall information, warrantee information, financial information, and information on careers at Gateway to name just a few. Visitors can search for job openings at different locations, which might indicate new product development activity if the competitor knows which plant produces certain products. Visitors can click on other countries (there are flags to click on) to see what Gateway offers in different markets. There is also target marketing information for the different customer segments (e.g., home, small business, government, education, etc.).

Under the Hood: Focus on Technology

Zoomerang is an online research tool used by many businesses and other organizations. It provides services such as online surveys, focus groups, sample selection from a national panel, and survey design. Conducting a survey can be as simple as adapting a current questionnaire to an online format and sampling current customers, or surveys can be developed by Zoomerang and a sample selected from the millions of respondents in their online panel. Zoomerang can even conduct a survey in several languages. Visit Zoomerang's Web site (http://info.zoomerang.com) and answer the following questions.

1. Discuss the benefits of using this service. (AACSB: Communication; Use of IT)

   Answer:

   This service offers all of the benefits of online marketing research discussed in the chapter. Users can adapt an existing questionnaire for online usage and use their own email list to send to respondents, or Zoomerang can assist in questionnaire development and provide the sample for users. This service also can host Web-based surveys as well as provide links on an organization's Web site to the research. Its online focus group service allows organizations to conduct focus groups online with experienced moderators in a fraction of the time and cost as traditional focus groups.

2. How might a university use this service to assess whether students are receiving a valuable education? (AACSB: Communication; Reflective Thinking)

Answer:

Students' responses will vary on this question, but they may indicate using this online tool to survey current students, alumni, or potential employers regarding the value of the education received. In this case, however, Zoomerang's online panel of over 2.5 million consumers would not be appropriate for drawing a sample because the research question deals specifically with the value of education received from this university. A survey could be used, or the online focus group could be used.

If the university currently has a questionnaire that they use, it can be easily adapted for this contact method. The university most likely already has email addresses of enrolled students and perhaps alumni and employers that can be used to distribute the survey. If email addresses are not available, then Zoomerang can provide a link on the university's Web site to the survey. If the university does not currently have a questionnaire, Zoomerang services can be used to develop one, or an online focus group can be conducted to assist in developing the appropriate questions.

While an online focus group could be used to assist in developing a questionnaire, it can also be used to answer the research question. However, users of this information need to be aware of the limitations regarding generalization of qualitative research.

Focus on Ethics

Marketing information is necessary for marketers to develop customer and market insights to better meet the needs of customers. Research respondents often are asked personal information that they might not want shared with others. Advances in technology enable the collection of large amounts of personal and behavioral information on consumers. However, gathering such information concerns individual consumers, consumer protection groups, and government agencies. Legitimate marketing researchers follow codes of ethics to use consumer information responsibly, and there are laws in place to protect consumers' privacy.

1. The Council of American Survey Research Organizations (CASRO) is a trade group representing survey researchers and provides a code of ethics for its members. Visit http://www.casro.org and write a brief summary of the code of ethics for survey researchers. (AACSB: Communication; Use of IT)

Answer:

Students should be able to find the code of ethics by clicking on "About CASRO." The code of ethics enumerates responsibilities to respondents, to clients, in reporting to clients and the public, and to outside contractors and interviewers. The set of responsibilities to respondents is most relevant to this exercise and guidelines for handling personally identifying information of respondents is provided.

2. Do consumers have a "right" to privacy? Discuss some federal laws in place to protect consumers' privacy. (AACSB: Communication)

   Answer:

   While many students may believe that, in the United States, we have a "right" to privacy, this is not the case. Surprisingly, there are relatively few federal laws in place regarding consumer privacy protection. For example, there is the Fair Credit Reporting Act and the Children's Online Privacy Protection Act. Students may discuss other laws, such as the Telephone Consumer Protection Act, but this does not involve the dissemination of information about consumers; rather, it involves restrictions on if and when marketers can call consumers. The federal Do Not Call list also restricts marketers from contacting consumers, but marketing research is exempt from this law.

   While the chapter does not directly address this issue, this is a good exercise to stress the two elements of privacy: the "right" to be left alone (i.e., the Do Not Call list), and the "right" to control dissemination of information about oneself (i.e., the Fair Credit Reporting Act). The latter is most relevant to this chapter because marketers are interested in information to glean relevant consumer insights.

Great Ideas

Barriers to Effective Learning

1. While today's students have grown up with computers, the idea of an "information system" may be very new to them. They typically will not have had to do any research, and any jobs they've held to this point in their lives will most likely have entailed very basic, entry-level type work. To get them past this, you could talk about the type of information the university will hold on each student—their major, the courses they've taken, the grades they've gotten, their current address, their home address, their parents' names, whether they are paying full tuition or are on any kind of scholarship, what high school they attended and their grade point average there, what sports they play or activities they participate in, and so forth. Then talk about how the university might use that information to understand their current student population to help them figure out how to target

future students while they are still in high school. This should help them grasp how data gets turned into information, and from that point to knowledge.

2. Virtually no one in class will be at all familiar with the market research process. They have not had to worry about collecting information in any large-scale process, although they might have been involved with collecting information from members of a student organization as to what activities the members would like to participate in. One effective way of discussing this issue is to talk about the course evaluations that are completed at the end of the semester. Explaining that this is not to rate the instructors but to provide valuable feedback to the university, the department and the instructor on course offerings, content within the courses, and only lastly to get an idea of the competence of instructors should help. Also, give examples of poorly designed surveys and show how they lead the respondent to answer in a given way. Especially helpful are questionnaires that use leading or loaded questions, or double-barreled questions that are difficult to answer.

3. A final barrier is the lack of understanding of commercial and/or online databases. Showing a database in class, such as the U.S. Census data or state information, both of which are available for free, will help them see the amount of data that is available. If possible, it would then be helpful to "find the story" in the data—that is, to apply the data to a small problem, such as where to locate a new Starbucks outlet. Using the data to show population clusters of mid- to upper-level income areas—the kind of consumer most likely to pay a premium for coffee—will help them internalize the power of using effective and relevant data in marketing decision making.

Student Projects

1. Imagine some situations where your school might make good use of exploratory research and/or descriptive research. Explain.
2. Secondary data consists of information that already exists, having been collected for another purpose. What are some secondary data sources you might take a look at if you were helping your school develop a recruitment strategy?
3. Observational research involves gathering primary data by observing people. Do you see any potential ethical conflicts with its use?
4. Why would you want to (or not want to) use a mail questionnaire to reach Generation Y individuals. Give both pros and cons.
5. Focus group interviewing can be a most effective interview technique. Under what situations does it make sense to use this technique?

Small Group Assignment

Form students into groups of three to five. Each group should read the opening vignette to the chapter on ZIBA. Each group should answer the following questions:

1. How is ZIBA's approach to marketing research different from the mainstream?
2. What disadvantages does ZIBA see in traditional forms of marketing research?

3. Do you believe their methods are a form of competitive advantage?

Each group should then share its findings with the class.

Individual Assignment

Construct two simple (5 question) survey that examines student's attitudes toward your school. One survey should contain open-ended questions only and the other only closed-ended questions. Be careful of your wording. Which of the two surveys do you believe would provide the greatest depth of information? Why?

Think-Pair-Share

Consider the following questions, formulate an answer, pair with the student on your right, share your thoughts with one another, and respond to questions from the instructor.

1. What are the four steps of the marketing research process?
2. What are the differences between causal, exploratory, and descriptive research methods?
3. Why does it make sense to use secondary data before you turn to primary data?
4. What are some of the more substantial drawbacks of observational research?
5. The internet is well suited for the collection of quantitative research. Why is not too good for qualitative research?

Classroom Exercise/Homework Assignment

Using observational research, gather data on your roommate's eating habits. What do your findings tell you? More importantly, what do you finding NOT tell you about his/her eating habits?

Classroom Management Strategies

This chapter will be a first introduction into managing any kind of information for most students. It is also a very brief introduction to marketing research. Figure 4-1 should figure prominently in the discussion about this chapter so that students don't lose track of all the varying sources of information marketers need.

1. Only 5 minutes should be spent on Assessing Marketing Information Needs. This is an introductory segment, and it also represents a topic that is necessarily company-driven rather than generic.
2. The majority of the class, probably 40 minutes, should be spent on Developing Marketing Information. This is the meat of the chapter, and it not only covers information sources such as internal data and marketing intelligence, but it also goes into some detail on performing marketing research. Most of the key terms from marketing research are defined and explained in this section.

3. The time remaining can be used to cover the last three sections of this chapter: Analyzing Marketing Information; Distributing and Using Marketing Information; and Other Marketing Information Considerations. Customer Relationship Management is covered in the first of these sections. Of the topics listed here, that will be the most important for students to comprehend.

CHAPTER 5
Understanding Consumer and Business Buyer Behavior

Previewing the Concepts: Chapter Objectives

1. Understand the consumer market and the major factors that influence consumer buyer behavior
2. Identify and discuss the stages in the buyer decision process
3. Describe the adoption and diffusion process for new products
4. Define the business market and identify the major factors that influence business buyer behavior
5. List and define the steps in the business buying decision process

JUST THE BASICS

Chapter Overview

In this chapter, we continue our marketing journey with a closer look at the most important element of the marketplace—customers.

The aim of marketing is to affect how customers think about and behave toward the organization and its market offerings.

But to affect the *whats, whens,* and *hows* of buying behavior, marketers must first understand the *whys.*

We look first at *final consumer* buying influences and processes and then at the buying behavior of *business customers.*

Annotated Chapter Notes/Outline

Introduction

Buyers of Harley-Davidson motorcycles are intensely loyal and devoted to the brand. Because of this, Harley-Davidson is at the top of the heavyweight motorcycle market.

Harley-Davidson's marketing managers spend a lot of time studying their buyers—they want to know who their customers are, what they think, how they feel, and why they buy a Harley rather than another brand.

Their research revealed seven core types: adventure-loving traditionalists, sensitive pragmatists, stylish status seekers, laid-back campers, classy capitalists, cool-headed loners, and cocky misfits.

Yet all Harley owners appreciated their bikes for the same basic reasons—independence, freedom, and power.

Consumer Markets and Consumer Buyer Behavior

Consumer buyer behavior refers to the buying behavior of final consumers—individuals and households who buy goods and services for personal consumption.

All of these consumers combine to make up the **consumer market**.:

The American consumer market consists of more than 300 million people.

The world consumer market consists of more than 6.6 *billion* people.

Use **Key Terms** *Consumer Market, Consumer Buyer Behavior* here. Use **Chapter Objective** 1 here.

Model of Consumer Behavior

The central question for marketers is: How do consumers respond to various marketing efforts the company might use?

The starting point is the stimulus-response model of buyer behavior shown in Figure 5.1.

Use **Figure** 5-1 here.

Marketing stimuli consist of the Four Ps.

Other stimuli include major forces and events in the buyer's environment: economic, technological, political, and cultural.

The marketer wants to understand how the stimuli are changed into responses inside the consumer's black box, which has two parts.

1. The buyer's characteristics influence how he or she perceives and reacts to the stimuli.
2. The buyer's decision process itself affects the buyer's behavior.

Characteristics Affecting Consumer Behavior

Cultural Factors

Culture is the most basic cause of a person's wants and behavior.

Marketers are always trying to spot *cultural shifts.*

Use **Key Term** *Culture* here.
Use **Figure** 5-2 here.

Subcultures are groups of people with shared value systems based on common life experiences and situations.

Use **Key Term** *Subculture* here.

The U.S. ***Hispanic market*** consists of 45 million consumers.

The ***African American*** market has an annual buying power of $799 million and is estimated to reach $981 billion by 2010.

Asian Americans are the most affluent U.S. demographic segment.

Mature consumers are becoming a very attractive market.

Now 68 million strong, the population of U.S. seniors will more than double in the next 25 years.

Social Classes are society's relatively permanent and ordered divisions whose members share similar values, interests, and behaviors. (See Figure 5.3)

Social class is not determined by a single factor, but is measured as a combination of occupation, income, education, wealth, and other variables.

Use **Key Term** *Social Class* here.
Use **Figure** 5-3 here.
Use **Discussing the Issues** 1 here.
Use **Focus on Ethics** here.

Social Factors

Groups and Social Networks. A person's behavior is influenced by many small **groups**.

Use **Key Terms** *Group and Opinion Leader* here.

Opinion leaders are people within a reference group who, because of special skills, knowledge, personality, or other characteristics, exert social influence on others.

These 10 percent of Americans are called the ***influentials*** or ***leading adopters***.

Marketers use ***buzz marketing*** to spread the word about their brands.

Online social networks are online spaces where people socialize or exchange information and opinions.

Use **Marketing at Work** 5-1 here.

Family is the most important consumer buying organization in society.

70 percent of women hold jobs outside the home.

Men now account for about 40 percent of all food-shopping dollars.

The nation's 36 million kids age 3 to 11 control an estimated $18 billion in disposable income.

Roles and Status. A role consists of the activities people are expected to perform. Each role carries a status reflecting the general esteem given to it by society.

Personal Factors

Age and Life-Cycle Stage. People change the goods and services they buy over their lifetimes.

Marketers are increasingly catering to a growing number of alternative, nontraditional stages such as unmarried couples, singles marrying later in life, childless couples, same-sex couples, single parents, extended parents (those with young adult children returning home), and others.

RBC Royal Bank has identified five life-stage segments.

1. The *youth* segment includes customers younger than 18.
2. *Getting Started* consists of customers aged 18 to 35 who are going through first experiences.
3. *Builders,* customers aged 35 to 50, are in their peak earning years.
4. *Accumulators*, aged 50 to 60, worry about saving for retirement and investing wisely.
5. *Preservers,* customers over 60, want to maximize their retirement income to maintain a desired lifestyle.

Occupation. A person's occupation affects the goods and services bought.

Economic Situation. A person's economic situation will affect product choice.

Lifestyle is a person's pattern of living as expressed in his or her psychographics.

Use **Key Term** *Lifestyle* here.

AIO dimensions are activities (work, hobbies, shopping, sports, social events), interests (food, fashion, family, recreation), and opinions (about themselves, social issues, business, products).

Personality and Self-Concept.

Personality refers to the unique psychological characteristics that lead to relatively consistent and lasting responses to one's own environment.

Use **Key Term** *Personality* here.

A ***brand personality*** is the specific mix of human traits that may be attributed to a particular brand. One researcher identified five brand personality traits:

1. Sincerity (down-to-earth, honest, wholesome, and cheerful)
2. Excitement (daring, spirited, imaginative, and up-to-date)
3. Competence (reliable, intelligent, and successful)
4. Sophistication (upper class and charming)
5. Ruggedness (outdoorsy and tough)

The basic ***self-concept*** premise is that people's possessions contribute to and reflect their identities; that is, "we are what we have."

Psychological Factors

Motivation.

A **motive** (or drive) is a need that is sufficiently pressing to direct the person to seek satisfaction.

Use **Key Term** *Motive (or Drive)* here.

Freud suggests that a person's buying decisions are affected by subconscious motives that even the buyer may not fully understand.

Motivation research refers to qualitative research designed to probe consumers' hidden, subconscious motivations.

Maslow sought to explain why people are driven by particular needs at particular times. (Figure 5.4)

Use **Figure** 5.4 here.

Perception is the process by which people select, organize, and interpret information to form a meaningful picture of the world.

Use **Key Term** *Perception* here.

Selective attention is the tendency for people to screen out most of the information to which they are exposed.

Selective distortion describes the tendency of people to interpret information in a way that will support what they already believe.

Selective retention is the retaining of information that supports their attitudes and beliefs.

Subliminal advertising refers to marketing messages received without consumers knowing it. Studies find no link between subliminal messages and consumer behavior.

Learning describes changes in an individual's behavior arising from experience.

Use **Key Term** *Learning* here.

A ***drive*** is a strong internal stimulus that calls for action.

A drive becomes a **motive** when it is directed toward a particular ***stimulus object.***

Cues are minor stimuli that determine when, where, and how the person responds.

Beliefs and Attitudes

A ***belief*** is a descriptive thought that a person has about something.

Attitude describes a person's relatively consistent evaluations, feelings, and tendencies toward an object or idea.

Use **Application Question** 1 here.

The Buyer Decision Process (Figure 5.5)

The buyer decision process consists of five stages:

1. *need recognition,*
2. *information search,*
3. *evaluation of alternatives,*
4. *purchase decision,* and
5. *postpurchase behavior.*

Use **Chapter Objective** 2 here. Use **Figure** 5.5 here.

Need Recognition

The buyer recognizes a problem or need.

The need can be triggered by either an:

- *internal stimuli* or
- *external stimuli.*

Information Search

Information search may or may not occur.

Consumers can obtain information from any of several sources.

- *Personal sources* (family, friends, neighbors, acquaintances),
- *Commercial sources* (advertising, salespeople, Web sites dealers, packaging, displays),
- *Public sources* (mass media, consumer-rating organizations, Internet searches), and
- *Experiential sources* (handling, examining, using the product).

Commercial sources ***inform*** the buyer.

Personal sources ***legitimize*** or ***evaluate*** products for the buyer.

Use **Discussing the Issues** 3 here.

Evaluation of Alternatives

Alternative evaluation: how the consumer processes information to arrive at brand choices.

How consumers go about evaluating purchase alternatives depends on the individual consumer and the specific buying situation.

In some cases, consumers use careful calculations and logical thinking.

At other times, the same consumers do little or no evaluating; instead they buy on impulse and rely on intuition.

Purchase Decision

Generally, the consumer's **purchase decision** will be to buy the most preferred brand.

Two factors can come between the purchase ***intention*** and the purchase ***decision***.

1. *Attitudes of others.*
2. *Unexpected situational factors.*

Postpurchase Behavior

The difference between the consumer's expectations and the perceived performance of the good purchased determines how satisfied the consumer is.

If the product falls short of expectations, the consumer is disappointed; if it meets expectations, the consumer is satisfied; if it exceeds expectations, the consumer is said to be delighted.

Cognitive dissonance, or discomfort caused by postpurchase conflict, occurs in most major purchases.

Use **Key Term** *Cognitive Dissonance* here.
Use **Marketing at Work** 5-1 here.
Use **Discussing the Issues** 2 here.

Let's Discuss This

Think of the last time you were unhappy with a purchase or with a company. How many people did you tell? Did you let the company know about it? Why or why not? Have you ever returned to that store or brand?

Use **Under the Hood/Focus on Technology** here.

The Buyer Decision Process for New Products

A **new product** is a good, service, or idea that is perceived by some potential customers as new.

The **adoption process** is the mental process through which an individual passes from first learning about an innovation to final adoption.

Use **Key Term** *New Product* here.
Use **Chapter Objective** 3 here.

Adoption is the decision by an individual to become a regular user of the product.

Use **Key Term** *Adoption Process* here.

Stages in the Adoption Process

Consumers go through five stages in the process of adopting a new product:

- *Awareness:* The consumer becomes aware of the new product, but lacks information about it.
- *Interest:* The consumer seeks information about the new product.
- *Evaluation:* The consumer considers whether trying the new product makes sense.
- *Trial:* The consumer tries the new product on a small scale to improve his or her estimate of its value.
- *Adoption:* The consumer decides to make full and regular use of the new product.

Individual Differences in Innovativeness

People differ greatly in their readiness to try new products.

People can be classified into the adopter categories shown in Figure 5.6.

Use **Figure** 5.6 here.

The five adopter groups have differing values.

1. *Innovators* are venturesome—they try new ideas at some risk.
2. *Early adopters* are guided by respect—they are opinion leaders in their communities and adopt new ideas early but carefully.
3. The *early majority* are deliberate—although they rarely are leaders, they adopt new ideas before the average person.
4. The *late majority* are skeptical—they adopt an innovation only after a majority of people have tried it.
5. *Laggards* are tradition bound—they are suspicious of changes and adopt the innovation only when it has become something of a tradition itself.

Use **Discussing the Issues** 4 here.

Influence of Product Characteristics on Rate of Adoption

Five characteristics are important in influencing an innovation's rate of adoption.

- *Relative advantage*: the degree to which the innovation appears superior to existing products.

- *Compatibility*: the degree to which the innovation fits the values and experiences of potential consumers.
- *Complexity*: the degree to which the innovation is difficult to understand or use.
- *Divisibility*: the degree to which the innovation may be tried on a limited basis.
- *Communicability*: the degree to which the results of using the innovation can be observed or described to others.

Use **Linking the Concepts** here.
Use **Application Question** 2 here.

Business Markets and Business Buyer Behavior

Business buyer behavior refers to the buying behavior of the organizations that buy goods and services for use in the production of other products and services that are sold, rented, or supplied to others.

Use **Key Term** *Business Buyer Behavior* here.
Use **Chapter Objective** 4 here.
Use **Figure** 5-7 here.
Use **Discussing the Issues** 5 here.

In the ***business buying process,*** business buyers determine which products and services their organizations need to purchase, and then find, evaluate, and choose among alternative suppliers and brands.

Business-to-business (B-to-B) marketers must do their best to understand business markets and business buyer behavior.

Business Markets

Business markets involve far more dollars and items than do consumer markets.

The main differences between business markets and consumer markets are in

- *market structure and demand,*
- *nature of the buying unit,*
- *types of decisions and the decision process involved.*

1. Market Structure and Demand

The business marketer normally deals with ***far fewer but far larger buyers*** than the consumer marketer does.

Business demand is **derived demand**—it ultimately derives from the demand for consumer goods.

Use **Key Term** *Derived Demand* here.

Many business markets have ***inelastic demand***; that is, total demand for many business products is not affected much by price changes.

Business markets have more ***fluctuating demand.***

2. Nature of the Buying Unit

Business purchases usually involve ***more decision participants*** and a ***more professional purchasing effort***.

3. Types of Decisions and the Decision Process

Business buyers usually face ***more complex*** buying decisions than do consumer buyers.

The business buying process tends to be ***more formalized***.

The buyer and seller are often much ***more dependent*** on each other.

Supplier development is systematically developing networks of supplier-partners to ensure an appropriate and dependable supply of products and materials that they will use in making their own products or resell to others.

Business Buyer Behavior

Figure 5.7 shows a model of business buyer behavior.

Within the organization, buying activity consists of two major parts:

1. The buying center and
2. The buying decision process.

Major Types of Buying Situations

Straight rebuy: the buyer reorders something without any modifications.

Modified rebuy: the buyer wants to modify product specifications, prices, terms, or suppliers.

New-task buy: the company is buying a product or service for the first time.

Use **Key Terms** *Straight Rebuy, Modified Rebuy, New Task* here.

Systems selling is often a key business marketing strategy because many business buyers prefer to buy a packaged solution to a problem from a single seller.

In this situation, a buyer may ask sellers to supply the components and assemble the package or system.

Use **Key Term** *Systems Selling* here.
Use **Application Question** 3 here.

Participants in the Business Buying Process

Buying center is all the individuals and units that play a role in the business purchase decision-making process.

The buying center is not a fixed and formally identified unit within the buying organization.

Use **Key Term** *Buying Center* here.

Major Influences on Business Buyers

Most B-to-B marketers recognize that emotion plays an important role in business buying decisions.

When suppliers' offers are very similar, buyers can allow personal factors to play a larger role in their decisions.

However, when competing products differ greatly, business buyers are more accountable for their choice and tend to pay more attention to economic factors.

Figure 5.8 lists various groups of influences on business buyers.

Use **Figure** 5.8 here.

Environmental factors include the current and expected economic environment, as well as shortages of key materials.

Technological, political, and competitive developments can also affect business buyers.

Culture and customs can also influence buyer reactions to the marketer's behavior and strategies.

Organizational factors are important because each buying organization has its own objectives, policies, procedures, structure, and systems.

Interpersonal factors influence the business buying process. These can be very difficult to ascertain.

Individual factors are involved as well. Each participant in the business buying process brings in personal motives, perceptions, and preferences.

These are, in turn, influenced by personal characteristics such as age, income, education, professional identification, personality, and attitudes toward risk.

Use **Chapter Objective** 5 here. Use **Figure** 5.9 here.

The Business Buying Process (Figure 5.9)

1. **Problem recognition**: The buying process begins when someone in the company recognizes a problem or need that can be met by acquiring a specific product or service.
2. A **general need description** is generated to describe the characteristics and quantity needed of an item.
3. The **product specification** includes the technical product specifications. ***Value analysis*** is an approach to cost reduction in which components are studied carefully to determine if they can be redesigned, standardized, or made by less costly methods of production.

Use **Key Term** *Value Analysis* here.

4. A **supplier search** is conducted to find the best vendors. The newer the buying task, and the more complex and costly the item, the greater the amount of time the buyer will spend searching for suppliers.
5. The **proposal solicitation** is the stage in which the buyer invites qualified suppliers to submit proposals.
6. **Supplier selection** occurs after the buying center reviews the proposals.
7. An **order-routine specification** includes the final order with the chosen supplier or suppliers.
8. Buyers conduct a **performance review**. This review may lead the buyer to continue, modify, or drop the arrangement with the seller.

E-Procurement: Buying on the Internet

Companies can do e-procurement in any of several ways.

- They can conduct *reverse auctions*, in which they put their purchasing requests online and invite suppliers to bid for the business.
- They can use online *trading exchanges,* through which companies work collectively to facilitate the trading process.
- Companies can set up their own *company buying sites.*
- They can create *extranet links* with key suppliers.

Use **Key Term** *e-Procurement* here. Use **Discussing the Issues** 6 here.

Business-to-business e-procurement yields many benefits.

1. It shaves transaction costs and results in more efficient purchasing for both buyers and suppliers.
2. It reduces the time between order and delivery.
3. It frees purchasing people to focus on more-strategic issues.

The use of e-purchasing presents some problems.

1. It can erode decades-old customer-supplier relationships.
2. It can create potential security disasters.

Travel Log

Discussing the Issues

1. Explain why marketers study buyer behavior and discuss characteristics affecting consumer behavior. Which characteristic(s) would have the greatest impact on your decision to purchase a computer and why? (AACSB: Communication; Reflective Thinking)

   Answer:

   Marketers study buyer behavior to understand *why* consumers behave as they do. Consumer purchases are influenced by cultural, social, personal, and psychological characteristics.

   Culture is the most basic cause of a person's wants and behavior as human behavior is largely learned. Every group or society has a culture, and cultural influences on buying behavior may vary greatly from country to country. **Subcultures** exist within cultures and are groups of people with shared value systems based on common life experiences and situations (i.e., nationalities, religions, racial groups, and geographic regions). **Social class** is another aspect of culture and represents a society's relatively permanent and ordered divisions whose members share similar values, interests, and behaviors.

Social influences include small groups, family, and social roles and status. **Groups** that influence consumers can include groups that have a direct influence as well as those with an indirect influence. Marketers of brands subjected to strong group influence must figure out how to reach **opinion leaders**—people within a reference group who exert social influence on others. **Family** can strongly influence buyer behavior and is the most important consumer buying organization in society. Finally, **roles and status** refer to a person's position in each group, and people usually choose products appropriate to their roles and status.

Personal factors affecting a buyer's decision include age and life-cycle stage, occupation, economic situation, lifestyle, and personality and self-concept. As people **age**, the products they buy over their lifetimes will differ. Also, the **stage of the family life cycle** they are experiencing will impact purchases. A person's **occupation** affects the products they buy as well, and **economic situation** will affect product choices. **Lifestyle** is a person's pattern of living as expressed in his or her psychographics—activities, interests, and opinions (AIOs). **Personality** refers to the unique psychological characteristics that lead to relatively consistent and lasting responses to one's own environment. Finally, **self-concept** relates to a person's identity, and possessions contribute to it and reflect it.

Psychological factors include motivation, perception, learning, and beliefs and attitudes. A **motive** (or drive) is a need that is sufficiently pressing to direct the person to seek satisfaction. Perception is the process by which people select, organize, and interpret information to form a meaningful picture of the world. **Learning** describes changes in behavior arising from experience. Finally, beliefs and attitudes influence behavior. A **belief** is a descriptive thought that a person has about something, and an **attitude** describes a person's relatively consistent evaluations, feelings, and tendencies toward an object or idea.

Students' responses regarding which characteristic(s) would have the greatest impact on their decision to purchase a computer will vary.

2. Discuss the stages of the consumer buyer decision process and describe how you or your family used this process to make a purchase. (AACSB: Communication; Reflective Thinking)

   Answer:

   Students' responses regarding how they used the buyer decision process will vary, but they should demonstrate an understanding of the five stages: need recognition, information search, evaluation of alternatives, purchase decision, and postpurchase behavior. The process starts with **need recognition**, where the buyer recognizes a problem or need. The consumer may then undertake an **information search**, and sources include personal sources, commercial sources, public sources, and experiential sources. Next, the consumer will **evaluate the alternatives** to arrive at a brand choice. Generally, the consumer's **purchase decision** will be to buy the most preferred brand, but the purchase decision can be influenced by the attitudes of others and unexpected situational factors. After purchasing the product, the consumer will be satisfied or dissatisfied and will engage in **postpurchase behavior**. Major purchases may result in cognitive dissonance, or discomfort caused by postpurchase conflict.

3. How might a marketer influence a consumer's information search through each of the four information sources discussed in the chapter? Which source do you think marketers should focus on to build long-term relationships with customers? (AACSB: Communication; Reflective Thinking)

   Answer:

   The four sources include **personal sources** (family, friends, neighbors, acquaintances), **commercial sources** (advertising, salespeople, Web sites, dealers, packaging, displays), **public sources** (mass media, consumer-rating organizations, Internet searches), and **experiential sources** (handling, examining, using the product). Examples of how a marketer might influence consumers are encouraging opinion leaders to share their thoughts about the product, targeting advertising to select groups of consumers, encouraging media stories about products and services, and giving consumers free samples or trial offers. It might be that personal sources offer the most influence and will help in building long-term relationships.

4. Explain why a new product doesn't necessarily have to be "new," and discuss the adoption process individuals go through when deciding whether to adopt a new product. (AACSB: Communication)

   Answer:

   A **new product** is a good, service, or idea that is *perceived* by some potential customers as new—it may have been around for a while. Marketers are interested in how consumers learn about products for the first time and make a decision on whether to adopt them. The **adoption process** is a mental process in which an individual learns about an innovation to finally adopting it. The stages in the adoption process are:

   - **Awareness:** The consumer becomes aware of the new product, but lacks information about it.
   - **Interest:** The consumer seeks information about the new product.

- **Evaluation:** The consumer considers whether trying the new product makes sense.
- **Trial:** The consumer tries the new product on a small scale to improve his or her estimate of its value.
- **Adoption:** The consumer decides to make full and regular use of the new product.

5. Discuss how business markets are similar to and different from consumer markets. What does this mean for a company attempting to sell goods to other organizations? (AACSB: Communication)

   Answer:

   In some ways, business markets are similar to consumer markets. Both involve people who assume buying roles and make purchase decisions to satisfy needs. However, business markets differ in many ways from consumer markets. The main differences are in market structure and demand, the nature of the buying unit, and the types of decisions and the decision process involved.

   Market Structure and Demand: The business marketer normally deals with **far fewer but far larger buyers** than the consumer marketer does. Further, business demand is **derived demand**—it ultimately derives from the demand for consumer goods. Many business markets have **inelastic demand**; that is, total demand for many business products is not affected much by price changes, especially in the short run. Finally, business markets have more **fluctuating demand**. The demand for many business goods and services tends to change more—and more quickly—than the demand for consumer goods and services does.

   Nature of the Buying Unit: Compared with consumer purchases, a business purchase usually **involves more decision participants** and a **more professional purchasing** effort.

   Types of Decisions and the Decision Process: Business buyers usually face more **complex buying** decisions than do consumer buyers. The business buying process also tends to be **more formalized** than the consumer buying process. Finally, the buyer and seller are often much **more dependent** on each other.

   Companies attempting to sell products or services to other organizations need to be particularly aware of the buying unit dynamics and the decision process for each organization as these can vary considerably among organizations.

6. Name and describe the major types of buying situations for business buyers. (AACSB: Communication)

Answer:

There are three major types of buying situations. At one extreme is the straight rebuy, which is a fairly routine decision. At the other extreme is the new task, which may call for thorough research. In the middle is the modified rebuy, which requires some research. In a **straight rebuy**, the buyer reorders something without any modification. In a **modified rebuy**, the buyer wants to modify product specifications, prices, terms, or suppliers. A company buying a product or service for the first time faces a **new-task** situation. The buyer makes the fewest decisions in the straight rebuy and the most in the new-task decision. In the new-task situation, the buyer must decide on product specifications, suppliers, price limits, payment terms, order quantities, delivery times, and service terms.

Application Questions

1. Interview a college student and an older adult (middle-aged or older) regarding the purchase of their automobiles. Based on what you learned in this chapter, ask them which, if any, cultural, social, personal, and psychological factors influenced their decision process and choice. Ask them to describe the process they went through in making their decision and explain it in terms of the consumer buying process discussed in the chapter. Ask them if they are satisfied or dissatisfied with their purchase and if they took any action based on that. Write a report about your interviews. (AACSB: Communication)

   Answer:

   Students' responses will vary, but they should exhibit an understanding of the factors influencing consumer behavior and the buyer decision process (see questions 1-3 in Discussing the Issues above).

2. Talk to five people about purchasing a high definition television (regardless of whether they have purchased one or not). Try to talk to individuals of different ages, genders, income levels, and occupations. Based on your understanding of the adopter categories discussed in the chapter, categorize each individual and explain why you have identified him or her in that category. (AACSB: Communication; Reflective Thinking)

   Answer:

   Students' answers will vary, but they should demonstrate an understanding of the adopter categories. People can be classified into the adopter categories shown in Figure 5.6. Innovators are defined as the first 2.5 percent of the buyers to adopt a new idea (those beyond two standard deviations from mean adoption time); the early adopters are the next 13.5 percent (between one and two standard deviations); and so forth. The five adopter groups have differing values. **Innovators** are venturesome—they try new ideas at some risk. **Early adopters** are guided by respect—they are opinion leaders in their communities and adopt new ideas early but carefully. The **early majority** are deliberate—although they rarely are leaders, they adopt new ideas before the average person. The **late majority** are skeptical—they adopt an innovation only after a majority of people have tried it. Finally, **laggards** are tradition bound—they are suspicious of changes and adopt the innovation only when it has become something of a tradition itself.

3. Interview a business person to learn how purchases are made in his or her organization. Ask this person to describe a straight rebuy, a modified rebuy, and a new-task buying situation that took place recently or that he or she is aware of (define them if necessary). Did the buying process differ based on the type of product or purchase situation? Ask the business person to explain the role he or she played in a recent purchase and to discuss the factors that influenced the decision. Write a brief report of your interview by applying the concepts you learned in this chapter regarding business buyer behavior. (AACSB: Communication; Reflective Thinking)

   Answer:

   Students' answers will vary, but students should demonstrate an understanding of business markets, the three types of buying situations, factors influencing business buyer behavior, and the stages in the business buying process. The business person interviewed will probably discuss the nature of business markets with respect to the nature of the buying unit (i.e., several decision participants and a professional purchasing effort) and the types of decisions and the decision process (i.e., complex, formalized, buyers and sellers dependent on each other). The three types of business buying situations are straight rebuy, modified rebuy, and new-task (see question 6 in Discussing the Issues for a description). The factors that may influence the purchase decision are environmental factors, organizational factors, interpersonal factors, and individual factors (see Figure 5.8). Finally, the stages of the business buying process are problem recognition, general need description, product specification, supplier search, proposal solicitation, supplier selection, order-routine specification, and performance review.

Under the Hood: Focus on Technology

There are several sources for buyers to research when making complex decisions such as purchasing an automobile. Kelly Blue Book is one such source (http://www.kbb.com). This Web site helps consumers find a car based on criteria such as price range, manufacturer, type of automobile, gas mileage, number of passengers, and others. Once the consumer selects what he or she desires, this site provides alternatives for consideration. Consumers can then compare different alternatives that they might be considering. This source also provides reviews and ratings from other sources (such as J.D. Powers Quality Ratings, Safety Ratings).

1. Describe the types of information sources from which consumers can obtain information and explain the type of information source Kelly Blue Book represents.

Click on the "About Us" link at the bottom of the home page to learn more about Kelly Blue Book. Do you think this source is very effective in influencing consumers? Explain why or why not. (AACSB: Communication; Use of IT; Reflective Thinking)

Answer:

Consumers can obtain information from any of several sources. These include *personal sources* (family, friends, neighbors, acquaintances), *commercial sources* (advertising, salespeople, Web sites, dealers, packaging, displays), *public sources* (mass media, consumer-rating organizations, Internet searches), and *experiential sources* (handling, examining, using the product). Kelly Blue Book represents a public source as it is not sponsored by any auto manufacturer.

The relative influence of these information sources varies with the product and the buyer. Generally, the consumer receives the most information about a product from commercial sources—those controlled by the marketer. Kelly Blue Book is a very popular and well-respected source of information about automobiles and is likely to have a considerable influence on consumers. The most effective sources, however, tend to be personal. Commercial sources normally *inform* the buyer, but personal sources *legitimize* or *evaluate* products for the buyer.

2. Click on the "Perfect Car Finder" under the "Compare and Explore" link on the left side of the home page and select the features you would like in your next automobile. Once you have a set of alternatives, compare at least two of them using the "Compare Cars" link under the "Compare and Explore" link. Do you think this resource would help you when making an actual purchase decision? Explain the stage(s) of the consumer buyer decision process to which this exercise represents. (AACSB: Communication; Use of IT; Reflective Thinking)

   Answer:

   Students' opinions will vary regarding whether this resource would be helpful when making an actual automobile purchase decision. This exercise applies to the information search and the evaluation of alternatives stages of the consumer buyer decision process.

Focus on Ethics

One factor that influences consumers' purchase decisions is culture, and one important element of a society's culture is social class. In the United States, the lines between social classes are not fixed and rigid as people can move to a higher or lower class. However, in other countries, such as India, this is not the case. India has a complex caste system in which members are born into one caste and expected to remain at that level, which influences their lifestyles and consumption behavior. India's complex caste system is rooted in Hinduism and includes thousands of castes and sub-castes that are traditionally related to occupations. With India's high-tech boom, though, American companies are increasingly coming into India and hiring workers regardless of social caste. While some higher-caste citizens and the government are supportive of advancing lower-caste workers, others are criticizing these companies for disregarding the long-standing social caste system.

1. Learn more about India's caste system and describe how economic growth is changing the culture in that country. What impact does this have on consumer behavior? (AACSB: Communication; Reflective Thinking)

   Answer:

   An article in *The Wall Street Journal* (see Beckett, Paul (2007), "Caste Away," *The Wall Street Journal*, (June 23), A1, A12) discusses the changes that are occurring in India due to foreign investment. You might want to assign this article along with the exercise. The castes and sub-castes can be categorized into the following basic categories: Brahmins (priests, scholars, and teachers); Kshatriyas (warriors and rulers); Vaishyas (traders); Sudras (manual workers and servants); and Dalits (perform unpleasant jobs and were known as "untouchables"). However, American companies don't really care about that, they just want talent. As a result, workers from the lowest caste are becoming middle class consumers. However, the social class system still has a strong influence on behavior.

2. Is it ethical for U.S. companies operating in India to ignore the country's caste system? Alternatively, is it ethical by U.S. standards to reinforce such a system when operating in India? (AACSB: Communication; Multicultural and Diversity; Ethical Reasoning)

   Answer:

   Students' opinions will vary. There are no "correct" answers to these questions. Businesses face many difficult ethical situations. In this case, businesses disregarding the social caste system in India are choosing immediate sales-producing actions, but their actions might be described as immoral or even amoral. However, individuals from the U.S. might view India's culture as immoral because it is so different and restrictive from our own. Chapter 16 further elaborates on guiding principles on issues of ethics and social responsibility. One philosophy is that such issues are decided by the free market and legal system. Under this principle, companies and their managers are not responsible for making moral judgments. Companies can, in good conscience, do whatever the market and legal systems allow. India has changed from a Socialist-modeled economy to a market-driven one, and the government has an affirmative-action program to promote the advancement of lower-caste workers. Thus, some could argue that foreign companies are not doing anything wrong by encouraging a change in the social system. However, the same argument can be made for reinforcing the social caste system when operating in India. Because the caste system continues to exist, that is what the market and legal systems also allow, and foreign businesses can justify perpetuating the system.

GREAT IDEAS

Barriers to Effective Learning

1. By and large, students have not been exposed to the consumer behavior concepts in this chapter before. If they have taken a sociology or human behavior course, chances are very high that the concepts were not presented in a way that allowed the students to understand them as they apply to business in general and marketing in particular. After presenting the concepts of consumer behavior, have the students discuss the concepts in terms of their own buying habits, their backgrounds, and how they differ from others in the class.
2. There is a lot of material in this chapter; although it hits only the high points of consumer behavior, the authors have done a good job of summarizing the constructs in a way that allows students to comprehend, albeit in a basic way, why these concepts are important to marketing managers. Explaining that consumer behavior is usually offered as a course unto itself can actually relieve some of their anxiety. Also helpful is continually reminding them of how they can apply this material to more fully appreciating their own motivations for their purchases. This can then lead them to understand how a marketer could approach understanding consumers' motives in general.
3. Understanding business buyer behavior and the business buying process can be especially difficult for students. Very few have ever had any experience with business purchasing decisions. This requires thorough explanation; the strategic use of personal experience in this regard is particularly helpful. If the instructor has no personal experience in business buying situations, it could be very helpful to bring in a guest speaker for this topic.
4. Business buying centers can be a very nebulous topic for students, particularly their dynamic nature. Discussing the importance and uses of inter-departmental teamwork in this section can be highly enlightening. This can then lead to a discussion of the different types of influencers, users, and so forth that could be found in a business buying center, and what their functions could be in the buying decision–making process.

Student Projects

1. Every culture contains smaller subcultures. In the U.S., the rapidly increasing Hispanic market holds opportunities for many businesses. Look around your community and make a list of those businesses that may well prosper from this increasing subculture. Why do you think this is so?
2. Within the U.S. Hispanic market there exist many distinct subsegments. Research these subsegments and detail the characteristics unique to each.

3. What social class do you belong to? Why? What would it take for you to move up a class?
4. How does social class in the U.S. differ from social class in India?
5. Think about the online social networks (such as Facebook or MySpace). How are marketers trying to use these networks to promote their products?

Small Group Assignment

Form students into groups of three to five. Each group should read the opening vignette to the chapter on Harley-Davidson. Each group should then answer the following questions:

1. Who rides a Harley?
2. How has Harley-Davidson gained such a devoted following?
3. How has Harley used advertising to evoke strong emotions and motivations?

Share your findings with the class.

Individual Assignment

Take a look at the websites for Harley-Davidson (www.harley-davidson.com), Yamaha (www.yamaha-motor.com), and Indian (www.indianmotorcycle.com). How are each of these companies appealing to their potential customer? Are they using emotion, facts, comparisons, etc. How effective do you believe each of them to be?

Think-Pair-Share

Consider the following questions, formulate an answer, pair with the student on your right, share your thoughts with one another, and respond to the questions from the instructor.

1. Describe the "black box."
2. Describe a cultural shift that has had an impact on marketers.
3. Highlight some of the more significant differences in purchase habits between African-Americans and the U.S. Hispanic market.
4. What factors determine social class in the U.S.?
5. How are online social networks changing the face of marketing?

Classroom Exercise/Homework Assignment

Age and lifecycle changes have a dramatic impact on the many and type of products we purchase and consume. Go to Toyota's website (www.toyota.com) and examine their complete product offering. How has Toyota tried to reach consumers of all ages and stages of the lifecycle?

Classroom Management Strategies

This chapter has a tremendous amount of material. Consumer buying behavior, in particular, presents an incredible amount of information, and all of this information is key to understanding marketing. As in Chapter 3, it is helpful to tie in both sociological and psychological principles in discussing this chapter.

1. More than half the class should be spent on Consumer Markets and Consumer Buyer Behavior. A thorough understanding of this section will make the business part of this chapter that much easier to comprehend. It is divided up into the "why" of buying and the "how" of buying. The former is guaranteed to never have crossed the students' mind prior to this, so lots of examples will help drive home the importance of understanding why people buy what they do. Using their own buying history helps, particularly when really drilling down into why they really choose the school they are attending, the clothes they are wearing, etc. The actual buying process can be illustrated through examples of buying something very complex, such as a computer or a car, and then something very simple, such as salt. The new product buying decision process is also covered, and several minutes should be spent on this topic.
2. The remaining third or so of this class will then be spent on Business Markets and Business Buyer Behavior. Again, the section is divided into the "why" of buying, and then the "how." There is also a discussion of the different market structure and demand characteristics of business markets. The terminology of business buying is different, and you should be certain the students understand the differences between straight rebuy, modified rebuy and new tasks. Also, the buying process is more complex and more likely to be followed in practice, particularly for very expensive or very large purchases. Students will need to be aware of the eight steps in the business buying process as well as all of the participants in this process and the roles they play.

CHAPTER 6
Customer-Driven Marketing Strategy: Creating Value for Target Customers

Previewing the Concepts: Chapter Objectives

1. Define the four major steps in designing a customer-driven marketing strategy: market segmentation, market targeting, differentiation, and positioning
2. List and discuss the major bases for segmenting consumer and business markets
3. Explain how companies identify attractive market segments and choose a market targeting strategy
4. Discuss how companies differentiate and position their products for maximum competitive advantage

JUST THE BASICS

Chapter Overview

This chapter looks further into key customer-driven marketing strategy decisions—how to divide up markets into meaningful customer groups (***segmentation***), choose which customer groups to serve (***targeting***), create market offerings that best serve targeted customers (***differentiation***), and positioning the offerings in the minds of consumers (***positioning***).

Then, the chapters that follow explore the tactical marketing tools—**the Four Ps**—by which marketers bring these strategies to life.

Annotated Chapter Notes/Outline

Introduction

William Rosenberg opened the first Dunkin' Donuts in Quincy, Massachusetts, in 1950.

In the mid-1990s, Dunkin' shifted its focus from doughnuts to coffee in the hope that promoting a more frequently consumed item would drive store traffic. The coffee push worked. Coffee now makes up 62 percent of sales—doughnuts make up 15 percent of sales.

Dunkin' and Starbucks target very different customers, who want very different things from their favorite coffee shops.

Starbucks is strongly positioned as a sort of high-brow "third place"—outside the home and office.

Dunkin' has a decidedly more low-brow, "everyman" kind of positioning.

Dunkin's research showed that although loyal Dunkin' customers want nicer stores, they were bewildered and turned off by the atmosphere at Starbucks.
Dunkin' knows that it'll take some time to refresh its image. And whatever else happens, it plans to stay true to the needs and preferences of the Dunkin' tribe.

Dunkin's "not going after the Starbucks coffee snob," says one analyst, it's "going after the average Joe."

Most companies have moved away from mass marketing and toward ***target marketing***—identifying market segments, selecting one or more of them, and developing products and marketing programs tailored to each.

Figure 6.1 shows the four major steps in designing a customer-driven marketing strategy.

Use **Chapter Objective** 1 here. Use **Figure** 6.1 here.

Market segmentation involves dividing a market into smaller groups of buyers with distinct needs, characteristics, or behaviors that might require separate marketing strategies or mixes.

Market targeting (or **targeting**) consists of evaluating each market segment's attractiveness and selecting one or more market segments to enter.

Use **Key Term** *Market Targeting (Targeting)* here.

Differentiation involves actually differentiating the firm's market offering to create superior customer value.

Positioning consists of arranging for a market offering to occupy a clear, distinctive, and desirable place relative to competing products in the minds of target consumers.

Use **Discussing the Issues** 1 here.

Market Segmentation

Through market segmentation, companies divide large, heterogeneous markets into smaller segments that can be reached more efficiently and effectively with products and services that match their unique needs.

Use **Key Term** *Market Segmentation* here. Use **Chapter Objective** 2 here.

Segmenting Consumer Markets

Table 6.1 outlines the major variables that might be used in segmenting consumer markets.

Use **Key Term** *Geographic Segmentation* here. Use **Table** 6.1 here. Use **Discussing the Issues** 2 here.

Geographic Segmentation

Geographic segmentation calls for dividing the market into different geographical units such as nations, regions, states, counties, cities, or even neighborhoods.

Demographic Segmentation

Demographic segmentation divides the market into groups based on variables such as age, gender, family size, family life cycle, income, occupation, education, religion, race, generation, and nationality.

Demographic factors are the most popular bases for segmenting customer groups.

Use **Key Term** *Demographic Segmentation* here.

Age and Life-Cycle Stage is offering different products or using different marketing approaches for different age and life-cycle groups.

Gender segmentation has long been used in clothing, cosmetics, toiletries, and magazines.

Income segmentation has long been used by the marketers of products and services such as automobiles, clothing, cosmetics, financial services, and travel.

Psychographic Segmentation

Psychographic segmentation divides buyers into different groups based on social class, lifestyle, or personality characteristics.

Marketers use ***personality*** variables to segment markets.

Use **Key Terms** *Age and Life-Cycle Segmentation, Gender Segmentation, Income Segmentation, Psychographic Segmentation* here.

Applying the Concept

How might Ford utilize psychographic segmentation for its various automobile brands, such as Mustang, Explorer, and the luxury car Jaguar?

Behavioral Segmentation

Use **Key Term** *Behavioral Segmentation* here.

Behavioral segmentation divides buyers into groups based on their knowledge, attitudes, uses, or responses to a product.

Occasion segmentation is grouping buyers according to occasions when they get the idea to buy, actually make their purchase, or use the purchased item.

Benefit segmentation is grouping buyers according to the different *benefits* that they seek from the product.

Use **Key Terms** *Benefit Segmentation, Occasion Segmentation* here.

User Status is segmenting markets into nonusers, ex-users, potential users, first-time users, and regular users of a product.

Usage Rate is grouping markets into light, medium, and heavy product users.

Loyalty Status is dividing buyers into groups according to their degree of loyalty.

Use **Application Question** 1 here.

Using Multiple Segmentation Bases

Marketers rarely limit their segmentation analysis to only one or a few variables.

PRIZM NE (one of the leading segmentation systems) classifies every American household based on a host of demographic factors.

Segmenting Business Markets

Consumer and business marketers use many of the same variables to segment their markets.

Business marketers also use some additional variables, such as customer *operating characteristics*, *purchasing approaches*, *situational factors*, and *personal characteristics*.

Many marketers believe that *buying behavior* and *benefits* provide the best basis for segmenting business markets.

Use **Discussing the Issues** 3 here.
Use **Video Case** here.

Segmenting International Markets

Companies can segment international markets using one or a combination of several variables.

- ***Geographic factors:*** Nations close to one another will have many common traits and behaviors.
- ***Economic factors:*** Countries may be grouped by population income levels or by their overall level of economic development.
- ***Political and legal factors:*** Type and stability of government, receptivity to foreign firms, monetary regulations, and the amount of bureaucracy.
- ***Cultural factors:*** Grouping markets according to common languages, religions, values and attitudes, customs, and behavioral patterns.

Intermarket segmentation is segmenting of consumers who have similar needs and buying behavior even though they are located in different countries.

Use **Key Term** *Intermarket Segmentation* here.

Requirements for Effective Segmentation

To be useful, market segments must be:

- *Measurable:* The size, purchasing power, and profiles of the segments can be measured.
- *Accessible:* The market segments can be effectively reached and served.
- *Substantial:* The market segments are large or profitable enough to serve.
- *Differentiable:* The segments are conceptually distinguishable and respond differently to different marketing mix elements and programs.
- *Actionable:* Effective programs can be designed for attracting and serving the segments.

Use **Linking the Concepts** here.

Market Targeting

Evaluating Market Segments

In evaluating different market segments, a firm must look at three factors:

1. Segment size and growth,
2. Segment structural attractiveness, and
3. Company objectives and resources.

The largest, fastest-growing segments are not always the most attractive ones for every company.

The company also needs to examine major structural factors that affect long-run segment attractiveness.

- A segment is less attractive if it already contains many strong and aggressive ***competitors***.
- The existence of many actual or potential ***substitute products*** may limit prices and the profits.
- The relative ***power of buyers*** also affects segment attractiveness.
- A segment may be less attractive if it contains ***powerful suppliers*** who can control prices.

Selecting Target Market Segments

A **target market** consists of a set of buyers who share common needs or characteristics that the company decides to serve. (Figure 6.2)

Use **Key Term** *Target Market* here.

Undifferentiated Marketing

Using an **undifferentiated marketing** (or **mass-marketing**) strategy, a firm might decide to ignore market segment differences and target the whole market with one offer.

This mass-marketing strategy focuses on what is ***common*** in the needs of consumers rather than on what is ***different***.

Differentiated Marketing

Using a **differentiated marketing** (or **segmented marketing**) strategy, a firm decides to target several market segments and designs separate offers for each.

Concentrated Marketing

Using a **concentrated marketing** (or **niche marketing**) strategy, instead of going after a small share of a large market, the firm goes after a large share of one or a few smaller segments or niches.

Use **Marketing at Work** 6.1 here.

It can market more ***effectively*** by fine-tuning its products, prices, and programs to the needs of carefully defined segments.

It can market more ***efficiently***, targeting its products or services, channels, and communications programs toward only consumers that it can serve best and most profitably.

Use **Key Terms** *Undifferentiated (or Mass) Marketing, Differentiated (or Segmented) Marketing, Concentrated (or Niche) Marketing* here.
Use **Figure** 6.2 here.
Use **Discussing the Issues** 4 here.

Micromarketing

Micromarketing is the practice of tailoring products and marketing programs to suit the tastes of specific individuals and locations.

Micromarketing includes ***local marketing*** and ***individual marketing***.

Local marketing involves tailoring brands and promotions to the needs and wants of local customer groups—cities, neighborhoods, and even specific stores.

Local marketing has drawbacks.

- It can drive up manufacturing and marketing costs by reducing economies of scale.
- It can create logistics problems.
- The brand's overall image might be diluted if the product and message vary too much in different localities.

Individual marketing is the tailoring of products and marketing programs to the needs and preferences of individual customers.

Individual marketing has also been labeled ***one-to-one marketing, mass customization,*** and ***markets-of-one marketing***.

Use **Key Terms** *Micromarketing, Local Marketing, Individual Marketing* here.

Use **Under the Hood/Focus on Technology** here.

Choosing a Targeting Strategy

Which strategy is best depends on:

- ***Company resources.***
- ***Product variability.***
- ***Product's life-cycle stage.***
- ***Market variability.***
- ***Competitors' marketing strategies.***

Use **Chapter Objective** 3 here.

Socially Responsible Target Marketing

Target marketing sometimes generates controversy and concern. Issues usually involve the targeting of vulnerable or disadvantaged consumers with controversial or potentially harmful products.

Problems arise when marketing adult products to kids, whether intentionally or unintentionally.

The growth of the Internet and other carefully targeted direct media has raised concerns about potential targeting abuses.

The issue is not so much who is targeted, but how and for what. Controversies arise when marketers attempt to profit when they unfairly target vulnerable segments or target them with questionable products or tactics.

Socially responsible marketing calls for segmentation and targeting that serve not just the interests of the company, but also the interests of those targeted.

Use **Focus on Ethics** here.

Differentiating and Positioning

Value proposition: How a company will create differentiated value for targeted segments and what positions it wants to occupy in those segments.

A **product's position** is the way the product is ***defined by consumers*** on important attributes.

Use **Key Terms** *Competitive Advantage, Product Position* here. Use **Chapter Objective** 4 here.

Positioning Maps

Perceptual positioning map show consumer perceptions of their brands versus competing products on important buying dimensions.

Choosing a Differentiation and Positioning Strategy

The differentiation and positioning task consists of three steps:

1. Identifying a set of differentiating competitive advantages upon which to build a position,
2. Choosing the right competitive advantages, and
3. Selecting an overall positioning strategy.

Use **Discussing the Issues** 5 here.

1. Identifying Possible Value Differences and Competitive Advantages

To the extent that a company can differentiate and position itself as providing superior customer value, it gains **competitive advantage.**

It can differentiate along the lines of *product*, *services*, *channels*, *people*, or *image*.

Use **Marketing at Work** 6.2 here.

Choosing the Right Competitive Advantages

How Many Differences to Promote

Ad man Rosser Reeves believes a company should develop a *unique selling proposition* (USP) for each brand and stick to it.

Other marketers think that companies should position themselves on more than one differentiator.

Which Differences to Promote

A difference is worth establishing to the extent that it satisfies the following criteria:

- *Important*: The difference delivers a highly valued benefit to target buyers.
- *Distinctive*: Competitors do not offer the difference, or the company can offer it in a more distinctive way.
- *Superior*: The difference is superior to other ways that customers might obtain the same benefit.
- *Communicable*: The difference is communicable and visible to buyers.
- *Preemptive*: Competitors cannot easily copy the difference.

- *Affordable*: Buyers can afford to pay for the difference.
- *Profitable*: The company can introduce the difference profitably.

Selecting an Overall Positioning Strategy

The full positioning of a brand is called the brand's **value proposition. (See Figure 6.4)**

Use **Key Term** *Value Proposition* here. Use **Application Questions** 2 and 3 here.

More for More positioning involves providing the most upscale product or service and charging a higher price to cover the higher costs.

More for the Same positioning involves introducing a brand offering comparable quality but at a lower price.

The Same for Less positioning can be a powerful value proposition—everyone likes a good deal.

Less for Much Less positioning is offering products that offer less and therefore cost less.

"Less-for-much-less" positioning involves meeting consumers' lower performance or quality requirements at a much lower price.

More for Less positioning is the winning value proposition.

In the long run, companies will find it very difficult to sustain such best-of-both positioning.

Use **Discussing the Issues** 6 here.

Developing a Positioning Statement

Company and brand positioning should be summed up in a **positioning statement.**

Use **Key Term** *Positioning Statement* here.

The statement should follow the form: *To (target segment and need) our (brand) is (concept) that (point of difference).*

Communicating and Delivering the Chosen Position

Once it has chosen a position, the company must take strong steps to deliver and communicate the desired position to target consumers. All the company's marketing mix efforts must support the positioning strategy.

Travel Log

Discussing the Issues

1. List and briefly describe the four major steps in designing customer-driven marketing strategy. (AACSB: Communication)

   Answer:

   Figure 6.1 shows the four major steps in designing a customer-driven marketing strategy. In the first two steps, the company selects the customers that it will serve. **Market segmentation** involves dividing a market into smaller groups of buyers with distinct needs, characteristics, or behaviors that might require separate marketing strategies or mixes. The company identifies different ways to segment the market and develops profiles of the resulting market segments. **Market targeting** (or **targeting**) consists of evaluating each market segment's attractiveness and selecting one or more market segments to enter. In the final two steps, the company decides on a value proposition—on how it will create value for target customers. **Differentiation** involves actually differentiating the firm's market offering to create superior customer value. **Positioning** consists of arranging for a market offering to occupy a clear, distinctive, and desirable place relative to competing products in the minds of target consumers.

2. Name and describe the four major variables that might be used in segmenting consumer markets. For each, give an example of a brand using that segmenting variable. (AACSB: Communication; Reflective Thinking)

   Answer:

   Consumer markets are typically segmented using four major variables: *geographic*, *demographic*, *psychographic*, and *behavioral* variables.

   Geographic segmentation calls for dividing the market into different geographical units such as nations, regions, states, counties, cities, or even neighborhoods. Some examples include Kraft Monterrey Jack cheese with jalapeno peppers in the southern United States, Coca-Cola soft drink formulated slightly differently in different regions of the world (stronger in South America), and magazines catering to different regions of the country (such as *Midwest Living*, *Southern Living*, and *Coastal Living*).

   Demographic segmentation divides the market into groups based on variables such as age, gender, family size, family life cycle, income, occupation, education, religion, race, generation, and nationality. Some examples include Centrum Silver vitamin supplement for older individuals, Disney Cruise Line for families with young children, or Waterford crystal for higher income individuals.

Psychographic segmentation divides buyers into different groups based on social class, lifestyle, or personality characteristics. People in the same demographic group can have very different psychographic makeups. Some examples include magazines targeted to groups of people with specific political orientations (such as the *Weekly Standard* for conservatives), vacations targeted to activity-oriented adults (such as Discovery Cove from Disney), or Starbuck's Coffee for more culture-oriented consumers.

Behavioral segmentation divides buyers into groups based on their knowledge, attitudes, uses, or responses to a product. Buyers can be grouped according to (1) *occasions* when they get the idea to buy, actually make their purchase, or use the purchased item, (2) the *benefits* people look for in the product class, (3) *user status* (nonusers, ex-users, potential users, first-time users, and regular users of a product), (4) *usage rate* (light, medium, and heavy product users), and (5) loyalty *status*. An example of occasion segmentation is FTD Florists targeting consumers to purchase floral arrangements for specific holidays. Benefit segmentation is exemplified when Heavenly Ham exclaims in advertisements, "When taste matters." Airline frequent flyer programs and hotel frequent guest programs are examples of behavioral segmentation based on both usage rate and loyalty status.

3. Explain how segmenting business markets is similar to, yet different from, segmenting consumer markets. (AACSB: Communication; Reflective Thinking)

   Answer:

   Consumer and business marketers use many of the same variables to segment their markets. Business buyers can be segmented geographically, demographically (industry, company size), or by benefits sought, user status, usage rate, and loyalty status. Yet, business marketers also use some additional variables, such as customer *operating characteristics*, *purchasing approaches*, *situational factors*, and *personal characteristics*.

4. After evaluating different segments, marketers must decide which segment(s) to target. Name and describe the options available and discuss the pros and cons of each. (AACSB: Communication)

   Answer:

   Market targeting can be carried out at several different levels. Companies can target very broadly (undifferentiated marketing), very narrowly (micromarketing), or somewhere in between (differentiated or concentrated marketing).

Using an **undifferentiated marketing** (or **mass-marketing**) strategy, a firm might decide to ignore market segment differences and target the whole market with one offer focusing on what is *common* in the needs of consumers rather than on what is *different*. The company designs a product and a marketing program that will appeal to the largest number of buyers. Difficulties arise in developing a product or brand that will satisfy all consumers. Moreover, mass marketers often have trouble competing with more-focused firms that do a better job of satisfying the needs of specific segments and niches.

Using a **differentiated marketing** (or **segmented marketing**) strategy, a firm decides to target several market segments and designs separate offers for each. By offering product and marketing variations to segments, companies hope for higher sales and a stronger position within each market segment. Developing a stronger position within several segments creates more total sales than undifferentiated marketing across all segments. But differentiated marketing also increases the costs of doing business—extra marketing research, forecasting, sales analysis, promotion planning, and channel management.

Using a **concentrated marketing** (or **niche marketing**) strategy, instead of going after a small share of a large market, the firm goes after a large share of one or a few smaller segments or niches. Through concentrated marketing, the firm achieves a strong market position because of its greater knowledge of consumer needs in the niches it serves and the special reputation it acquires. It can market more *effectively* by fine-tuning its products, prices, and programs to the needs of carefully defined segments. It can also market more *efficiently*, targeting its products or services, channels, and communications programs toward only consumers that it can serve best and most profitably. Concentrated marketing can be highly profitable, but it involves higher-than-normal risks, especially if the segment turns sour. Another problem is the potential for larger competitors entering the same segment with greater resources.

Micromarketing is the practice of tailoring products and marketing programs to suit the tastes of specific individuals and locations. Rather than seeing a customer in every individual, micromarketers see the individual in every customer. Micromarketing includes *local marketing* and *individual marketing*.

5. In the context of marketing, what is a product's "position"? How do marketers know what it is? (AACSB: Communication)

Answer:

A **product's position** is the way the product is *defined by consumers* on important attributes—the place the product occupies in consumers' minds relative to competing products. Marketers often prepare *perceptual positioning maps* to show consumer perceptions of their brands versus competing products on important buying dimensions. Figure 6.3 is an illustration, and the position of each circle on the map indicates the brand's perceived positioning on two dimensions and the size of each circle indicates the brand's relative market share.

Students should understand that marketers actively try to influence a product's position through their selection of a differentiation and positioning strategy.

6. Name and define the five winning value propositions described in the chapter. Which value proposition describes Starbuck's Coffee? Explain your answer. (AACSB: Communication; Reflective Thinking)

   Answer:

   Figure 6.4 shows possible value propositions upon which a company might position its products. The five winning value propositions are: more for more; more for the same; the same for less; les for much less; and more for less.

   More for more positioning involves providing the most upscale product or service and charging a higher price to cover the higher costs. In **more for the same** positioning, companies can attack a competitor's more-for-more positioning by introducing a brand offering comparable quality but at a lower price. Offering the **same for less** can be a powerful value proposition—everyone likes a good deal. The **less for much less** value proposition seeks consumers who do not need, want, or can afford "the very best" in everything they buy. Finally, the **more for less** value proposition is possible in the short run but is difficult to sustain in the long run as offering more usually costs more, making it difficult to deliver on the "for-less" promise.

   Students will probably indicate that the *more for more* value proposition best describes Starbuck's Coffee. Prices are higher but Starbuck's offers more than just coffee drinks and food. It offers the "Starbuck's experience," and consumers are willing to pay more for that brand.

Application Questions

1. The chapter described psychographics as one major variable used by marketers when segmenting consumer markets. SRI Consulting has developed a typology of consumers based on values and lifestyles. Go to SRI Consulting's Web site (http://www.sric-bi.com), click on the VALS survey on the right side of the Web site, and complete the VALS survey. How accurately do your primary and secondary VALS types describe you? How can marketers use this information? Write a brief report of your findings. (AACSB: Communication; Use of IT; Reflective Thinking)

   Answer:

Students' responses will vary, but they should report that their primary and secondary VALS types are one of the following: innovators, thinkers, achievers, experiencers, believers, strivers, makers, and survivors. Marketers can use this type of information to develop market offerings to consumers based on their lifestyles.

2. Suppose you are a brand manager for Van's footwear. You have identified two market segments: young men/boys who are into "pop" culture and skateboarding, and older men wanting shoes that do not need to be tied. You are now deciding which target marketing strategy to pursue. What criteria should you consider to ensure that the identified segments are effective? (AACSB: Communication; Reflective Thinking)

   Answer:

   To be useful, market segments must be:

   - *Measurable:* The size, purchasing power, and profiles of the segments can be measured.
   - *Accessible:* The market segments can be effectively reached and served.
   - *Substantial:* The market segments are large or profitable enough to serve. A segment should be the largest possible homogenous group worth pursuing with a tailored marketing program.
   - *Differentiable:* The segments are conceptually distinguishable and respond differently to different marketing mix elements and programs.
   - *Actionable:* Effective programs can be designed for attracting and serving the segments.

3. In a small group, develop the positioning strategies for an energy drink targeted to three separate target markets segmented by one or more of the four consumer segmenting variables described in the chapter. Describe each market segment and what your brand will offer that target market. For each target market, choose a differentiation and positioning strategy by identifying possible value differences and competitive advantages for your brand, choose the best competitive advantages, select an overall positioning strategy for each target market, and develop a positioning statement for each brand targeted to a specific market. (AACSB: Communication; Reflective Thinking)

   Answer:

   Students' responses will vary, but they should identify three market segments that they want to target and follow the steps for choosing a differentiation and positioning strategy for each target market chosen. Recall that consumer markets typically are segmented using four major variables: geographic, demographic, psychographic, and behavioral variables. Once three target markets are identified, students can then develop an offering for each target market. Once value differences and competitive advantages are identified, they should then select an overall positioning strategy (more for more, more for the same, same for less, less for much less, or more for less). Finally, the positioning statement should follow the form: *To (target segment and need) our (brand) is (concept) that (point of difference).*

Under the Hood: Focus on Technology

Today's micromarketing technology enables marketers to mass customize products ranging from clothing, skin care products, and vitamin supplements to furniture, automobiles, and even postage stamps. And through behavioral targeting technologies, marketing communications also can be customized based on Web surfing behavior and television viewership, often without consumers being aware that their behavior is tracked. Explore micromarketing at the following sites and report on what you find.

1. Consumers can design their own shoes at Nike's Web site. Visit this site at http://NikeID.com and design your own shoe. Print out your shoe design and bring it to class. Do you think the price is appropriate for the value you received from being able to customize your shoe? Find two other Web sites that allow buyers to customize products and write a brief report on what you learned. (AACSB: Communication; Use of IT)

   Answer:

   Students' responses will vary. However, some other Web sites where consumers can customize products are Only Yourx custom skin care products (http://www.onlyyourx.com), Zazzle for a variety of custom products such as shirts and mugs (http://www.zazzle.com), stamps at http://stamps.com, and furniture through Norwalk furniture's "variations" program (http://www.norwalkfurniture.com).

2. Tacoda Inc. is a behavior ad network that allows marketers to deliver Internet ads to individuals based on their Internet behavior. Visit http://www.tacoda.com to learn more about this company. Explore this Web site to learn how marketers are able to send Internet ads to targeted consumers and write a brief report explaining behavioral targeting and how marketers are using it. (AACSB: Communication; Use of IT)

   Answer:

   TACODA is the largest behavioral targeting advertising network that delivers Internet ads to individuals based on their Internet behavior. For example, if a consumer is interested in health-related issues, marketers of health-related products can have their ads appear on specific sites when that individual visits that site. While not specifically described on this Web site, cookies (electronic files that track Internet behavior) are used to track individual Internet behavior, usually without the knowledge of the consumer. Several success stories are highlighted on this Web site: Snapple Green Tea, FAO Schwarz, Panasonic, LATimes.com and Macy's, and Weather.com and Scott's lawn products (accessed July 2, 2007).

Focus on Ethics

As more companies go global, segmentation is becoming more common. However, manufactured goods marketed in one country sometimes end up in another country for which that product was not intended. Or products sometimes end up in intended markets, but through unauthorized channels. This is called gray marketing or parallel importing. It involves genuinely branded products—not counterfeit or "knock-off" products. One factor that encourages such activities is that a given product may be priced differently for different international markets, depending on the economic conditions of those markets. Gray marketers purchase these products at the lower price, import them into another country, and sell them for more than they paid but lower than the price authorized distributors charge in that country.

1. Research gray marketing. Write a report explaining (1) how it occurs, (2) the impact it has on manufacturers and distributors, (3) any positive outcomes of this practice, and (4) what manufacturers can do about it. (AACSB: Communication; Reflective Thinking)

   Answer:

   Students should be able to find several articles on gray markets. Some suggested articles you might want to assign with this exercise are Antia, Kersi D., Mark Bergen, and Shantanu Dutta (2004), "Competing With Gray Markets," *Sloan Management Review*, (Fall), 63-69 and Myers, Mattthew B. and David A. Griffith (1999), "Strategies for Combating Gray Market Activity," *Business Horizons*, (November-December), 2-8.

   Gray markets occur when a company's products are sold through unauthorized dealers. The products are genuinely branded products that were intended for other geographic markets, typically international markets. If prices are lower in the other markets, there is incentive for gray marketers to purchase the products and import them to other countries. Gray market sales are often at much lower prices than authorized sales, and authorized dealers suffer loss of sales. Manufacturers have been known to be their own gray marketers in order to increase overall sales by reaching price sensitive consumers that would otherwise not be able to purchase their products. Antia et al. (2004) discuss several reasons for the condemnation of gray markets: (1) dilution of exclusivity for distributors, (2) authorized distributors cutting corners on service to reduce costs, (3) damaged channel relationships, (4) undermining segmented pricing strategies, and (5) damaged manufacturer reputation and greater legal liability. However, some argue that consumers benefit from the lower-priced genuine brands. In many cases, though, warranties may not apply and the product information may be written in a foreign language.

Bergen et al. (2004) point out several instances when gray markets can help a manufacturer: (1) incremental sales because previously untapped markets can be reached, (2) they may enable suppliers to overcome supply constraints, (3) competitive necessity—if companies do not follow competitors, they risk losing market strength, (4) allows companies to segment markets outside of existing distribution structures, (5) can adapt more quickly to changing market conditions, and (6) can gather market intelligence.

These authors suggest that sensing, speed, and severity are keys to controlling gray markets. That is, companies should have mechanisms for sensing that the activity is occurring, act quickly to deter the activity, and take severe actions against violations. Myers and Griffin (1999) suggest several strategies for combating this activity: (1) horizontal coordination of the distribution channel to encourage information sharing across distributors, (2) keeping current on regulations, (3) pay close attention to differentiated products across markets, (4) minimize the autonomy of distributors and sales people to set prices, and (5) maintain close communication with distributors.

2. As a consumer, do you see any benefits of gray markets? Is it ethical for consumers to purchase products through gray markets? (AACSB: Communication; Reflective Thinking; Ethical Reasoning)

   Answer:

   Students' responses will vary, but most will probably discuss the reduced cost to consumers as the greatest benefit. However, warranties may not be honored and service cannot be obtained as they would when purchasing through an authorized dealer. However, many consumers will not know the difference between an authorized and an unauthorized dealer and will likely end up dissatisfied with the manufacturer if problems arise. Some students might argue that it is a smart shopper that purchases a branded product at a lower price, so it's the "right" thing to do. Others may claim that when something is "too good to be true," then they probably shouldn't do it—perhaps not because it is wrong, though. It might end up to be a poor economic decision if they have problems with the product.

GREAT IDEAS

Barriers to Effective Learning

1. Understanding the concept of a market segment can be very difficult for students. Working through breaking down a market, such as their own university, into separate groups can help tremendously, as can drawing a big box on the board, and then breaking the box down into separate sections to represent pieces of a larger market.

2. Also difficult to understand is the concept that there is no one, single way to segment a market. Students will often point out that companies segment on a single variable frequently, not understanding that the concept is much broader than that. Using a simple pen as an example, you can point out the various segmentation variables, such as income, occasion (such as graduations), and lifestyle that a pen manufacturer could study to determine effective segments. While Mont Blanc might segment based on income and occasion factors, Bic could very well look at lifestyle or even age.
3. Segmenting business markets could also pose some problems, particularly in the discussion of operating characteristics and purchasing styles. Contrasting large corporations with small, local enterprises could help here, as can asking the students about their parents' business lives and any responsibility they might have in purchasing goods and services for the firms they work for.
4. If anyone knows anything about target marketing before coming to class, they will think of it as simply selling to one type of customer. But most students will never have heard of this concept, either. Use the "box" principle in #1, showing how a company could choose one or more of the sections to address will help in students' understanding. This can also be expanded to show how companies might move from focusing on one target segment to moving along to another when penetration of the first has been accomplished, even though this goes beyond the scope of this textbook.
5. Development of a positioning statement is also a difficult concept. It requires students to boil down a company's strategy into one sentence, which can be quite tricky. Going through the examples in the book, and then applying them to something within the students' sphere of knowledge (books, soft drinks, breakfast foods, coffee, etc.) can enrich the explanations in the text.

Student Projects

1. Go to iTunes (www.apple.com) or Rhapsody (www.rhapsody.com). What unique market segments appear to be the target of specific genres of music? How did you determine the segments?
2. You've agreed to help a friend with a home furnishings business segment her market. Suggest a way to segment the market for her. Select a target market to go after, keeping in mind segment size and growth, structural attractiveness, and probable company resources. What target marketing strategy would you use (using Figure 6.2)? Explain your answers.
3. There are many ways to segment a market. Using the four segmentation variables discussed in the chapter, discuss which variables would be ***most important*** for segmenting (a) candidates for cataract surgery and (b) possible enrollees in a culinary school. Explain your choices.

4. Collect advertisements that demonstrate the positioning of different watch brands. Sort the various brands into categories of brands with similar positions.
5. Find ads for several different types of watches. For instance, select one diver's watch, one prestige watch, one economy watch, and one *avant garde* watch. What market is each trying to reach? What type of segmentation is the advertiser using?

Small Group Assignment

Form students into groups of three to five. Each group should read the opening vignette to the chapter on Dunkin' Donuts. Each group should then answer the following questions:

1. What is Dunkin' Donuts' strategy?
2. What is unique about their market segmentation strategy?
3. Is their strategy really product differentiation (as opposed to market segmentation)?
4. Are there weaknesses in the Dunkin' Donut strategy? If so, what are they?
5. Do you see any uncovered market segments? If so, what are they? How would you exploit this?

Each group should share its findings with the class.

Individual Assignment

You have been asked by your college/university to help develop a market segmentation strategy for them. What market segments would you encourage them to pursue and why?

Think-Pair-Share

Consider the following questions, formulate an answer, pair with the student on your right, share your thoughts with one another, and respond to questions from the instructor.

1. How would you define market segmentation?
2. How does geographic segmentation differ from demographic segmentation?
3. Which one segmentation form do you consider the most valuable? Why?
4. What is benefit segmentation? Give a good example.
5. List the requirements for effective segmentation.

Classroom Exercise/Homework Assignment

Review the requirements for effective market segmentation. Now, log on to Rhapsody (www.rhapsody.com). How are they attempting to segment their markets? Rate Rhapsody on each of the five requirements for effective segmentation. Do you believe they are doing a good job on each? What suggestions for improvement would you recommend?

Classroom Management Strategies

Most students will still be thinking, even at this point in the semester, that marketing is all about getting everyone to buy your product. This chapter will set them straight. It uses three sections to discuss the three important topics of segmentation, targeting, and positioning.

1. Divide this chapter up equally. Spend about 20 minutes on market segmentation, with the majority of that time spent on segmenting consumer markets. Students will understand geographic and demographic segmentation fairly quickly, but benefit and occasion segmentation will take a little more time. Business and international markets can be covered fairly quickly.
2. Target marketing should also take about 20 minutes. It is important for the students to grasp that once they've divided the market, they then need to decide which of those segments to address. Evaluating and selecting segments to target should be the primary topics in this section.
3. Finally, positioning should take the remainder of the class. Discussing a brand you are especially loyal to, so you can speak about it emotionally, often helps the students realize the importance of positioning, and also how dependent positioning is on the responses of the consumer to the product itself as well as the messaging about the product.

CHAPTER 7
Products, Services, and Brands: Building Customer Value

Previewing the Concepts: Chapter Objectives

1. Define *product* and the major classifications of products and services
2. Describe the decisions companies make regarding their individual products and services, product lines, and product mixes
3. Discuss branding strategy—the decisions companies make in building and managing their brands
4. Identify the four characteristics that affect the marketing of a service and the additional marketing considerations that services require

JUST THE BASICS

Chapter Overview

In this and the next chapter, we'll study how companies develop and manage products and brands. The product is usually the first and most basic marketing consideration.

This chapter begins with a deceptively simple question: *What is a product*? After addressing this question, we look at ways to classify products in consumer and business markets.

Then we discuss the important decisions that marketers make regarding individual products, product lines, and product mixes.

Next, we look into the critically important issue of how marketers build and manage brands.

Finally, we examine the characteristics and marketing requirements of a special form of product—services.

Annotated Chapter Notes/Outline

Introduction

Many old-timers still think of Las Vegas as "Sin City." The new Vegas has reinvented itself as a luxury destination.

To visitors, Vegas is an emotional connection, a total brand experience.

The research showed that the when people come to Las Vegas, they're a little naughtier. "We found that [the Las Vegas experience] centered on adult freedom," says Ralenkotter. "People could stay up all night and do things they wouldn't normally do in their own towns."

Based on these consumer insights, the LVCVA coined a now-familiar catchphrase—"Only Vegas: What happens here, stays here."

"It's all about branding," says CEO Ralenkotter. "The slogan captures the city's experiences rather than amenities, the image that Las Vegas represents freedom."

What is a Product?

A **product** is anything that can be offered to a market for attention, acquisition, use, or consumption that might satisfy a want or need.

Use **Key Term** *Product* here. Use **Chapter Objective** 1 here.

Broadly defined, "products" also include services, events, persons, places, organizations, ideas, or mixes of these.

Services are a form of product that consists of activities, benefits, or satisfactions offered for sale that are essentially intangible and do not result in the ownership of anything.

Use **Key Term** *Service* here.

Products, Services, and Experiences

A company's market offering often includes both tangible goods and services.

At one extreme, the offer may consist of a ***pure tangible good***, such as soap or toothpaste.

At the other extreme are ***pure services***, for which the offer consists primarily of a service.

To differentiate their offers, marketers are creating and managing customer ***experiences*** with their brands or company.

Levels of Product and Services (Figure 7.1)

Use **Figure** 7.1 here.

Product planners need to think about products and services on three levels.

1. *Core customer value*, which addresses the question, *What is the buyer really buying?*
2. *Actual product*.
3. *Augmented product,* which is created around the core benefit and actual product by offering additional consumer services and benefits.

Use **Under the Hood/Focus on Technology** here.

When developing products, marketers first must identify the ***core customer value*** that consumers seeks from the product. They must then design the ***actual*** product and find ways to ***augment*** it in order to create this customer value and the most satisfying customer experience.

Use **Discussing the Issues** 1 here.

Product and Service Classifications

Consumer Products

Consumer products are products and services bought by final consumers for personal consumption.

Consumer products include (see Table 7.1):

- **Convenience products** are consumer products and services that customers usually buy frequently, immediately, and with a minimum of comparison and buying effort.
- **Shopping products** are less frequently purchased consumer products and services that customers compare carefully on suitability, quality, price, and style.
- **Specialty products** are consumer products and services with unique characteristics or brand identification for which a significant group of buyers is willing to make a special purchase effort.
- **Unsought products** are consumer products that the consumer either does not know about or knows about but does not normally think of buying.

Use **Key Terms** *Consumer Product, Convenience Product, Shopping Product, Specialty Product,* and *Unsought Product* here. Use **Table** 7.1 here. Use **Discussing the Issues** 2 here.

Industrial Products

Industrial products are those purchased for further processing or for use in conducting a business.

Use **Key Term** *Industrial Product* here.

The distinction between a consumer product and an industrial product is based on the ***purpose*** for which the product is bought.

The three groups of industrial products and services are:

- ***Materials and parts*** include raw materials and manufactured materials and parts.
- ***Capital items*** are industrial products that aid in the buyer's production or operations, including installations and accessory equipment.
- ***Supplies and services*** include operating supplies and maintenance and repair services.

Use **Discussing the Issues** 3 here.

Organizations, Persons, Places, and Ideas

Organization marketing consists of activities undertaken to create, maintain, or change the attitudes and behavior of target consumers toward an organization.

Person marketing consists of activities undertaken to create, maintain, or change attitudes or behavior toward particular people.

Place marketing involves activities undertaken to create, maintain, or change attitudes or behavior toward particular places.

Social marketing is the use of commercial marketing concepts and tools in programs designed to influence individuals' behavior to improve their well-being and that of society.

Use **Key Term** *Social Marketing* here.

Product and Service Decisions

Individual Product and Service Decisions (Figure 7.2)

Use **Figure** 7.2 here.

Product and Service Attributes

Developing a product or service involves defining the benefits that it will offer. These benefits are communicated and delivered by product attributes such as ***quality, features***, and ***style and design.***

Product Quality is creating customer value and satisfaction.

Total quality management (TQM) is an approach in which all the company's people are involved in constantly improving the quality of products, services, and business processes.

Product quality has two dimensions: **level** and **consistency**.

Use **Key Term** *Product Quality* here.

The quality level means performance quality or the ability of a product to perform its functions. Quality conformance means quality consistency, freedom from defects, and consistency in delivering a targeted level of performance.

Product Features are a competitive tool for differentiating the company's product from competitors' products.

The company should periodically survey buyers who have used the product and ask these questions: How do you like the product? Which specific features of the product do you like most? Which features could we add to improve the product?

Product Style and Design is another way to add customer value.

Style describes the appearance of a product. ***Design*** contributes to a product's usefulness as well as to its looks.

Applying the Concept
Over the last several years, cell phones have evolved from being quite large and clunky to being extremely small. Discuss how these style and design changes have benefited consumers. Do you think the penetration of this kind of technology was accelerated because of these changes?

Branding

A **brand** is a name, term, sign, symbol, or design, or a combination of these, that identifies the maker or seller of a product or service.

Use **Key Term** *Brand* here.

Branding helps buyers in many ways.

- Brand names help consumers identify products that might benefit them.
- Brands say something about product quality and consistency.

Branding gives the seller several advantages.

- The brand name becomes the basis on which a whole story can be built about a product.
- The brand name and trademark provide legal protection for unique product features.
- The brand name helps the seller to segment markets.

Packaging

Packaging involves designing and producing the container or wrapper for a product.

Use **Key Term** *Packaging* here.

Labeling

Labels perform several functions.

- The label ***identifies*** the product or brand.
- The label ***describes*** several things about the product.
- The label ***promotes*** the brand.

Labeling also raises concerns. As a result, several federal and state laws regulate labeling.

The most prominent is the Fair Packaging and Labeling Act of 1966.

Labeling has been affected in recent times by:

- ***unit pricing*** (stating the price per unit of standard measure),
- ***open dating*** (stating the expected shelf life of the product), and
- ***nutritional labeling*** (stating the nutritional values in the product).

Product Support Services

The first step is to survey customers periodically to assess the value of current services and to obtain ideas for new ones.

Next, the company can take steps to fix problems and add new services that will both delight customers and yield profits to the company.

Product Line Decisions

Use **Chapter Objective** 2 here.

A **product line** is a group of products that are closely related because they function in a similar manner, are sold to the same customer groups, are marketed through the same types of outlets, or fall within given price ranges.

Use **Key Term** *Product Line* here.

Product line length is the number of items in the product line.

Product line filling involves adding more items within the present range of the line.

Product line stretching occurs when a company lengthens its product line beyond its current range.

Companies located at the upper end of the market can stretch their lines ***downward***.

Companies located at the lower end of the market can stretch their product lines ***upward***.

Companies located in the middle range of the market can stretch their lines in ***both directions***.

Product Mix Decisions

Product mix (or **product portfolio**) consists of all the product lines and items that a particular seller offers for sale.

Use **Key Term** *Product Mix (*or *Product Portfolio)* here.

A company's product mix has four dimensions: **width, length, depth,** and **consistency**.

- Product mix ***width*** refers to the number of different product lines the company carries.
- Product mix ***length*** refers to the total number of items the company carries within its product lines.
- Product mix ***depth*** refers to the number of versions offered of each product in the line.
- Product mix ***consistency*** refers to how closely related the various product lines are in end use, production requirements, distribution channels, or some other way.

Use **Application Question** 1 here.

The company can increase its business in four ways.

1. It can add new product lines, widening its product mix.
2. It can lengthen its existing product lines.
3. It can add more versions of each product, deepening its product mix.
4. It can pursue more product line consistency.

Use **Linking the Concepts** here.

Branding Strategy: Building Strong Brands

Some analysts see brands as *the* major enduring asset of a company.

Use **Marketing at Work** 7.1 here.
Use **Chapter Objective** 3 here.

Brand Equity is the positive differential effect that knowing the brand name has on customer response to the product or service.

Use **Key Term** *Brand Equity* here.
Use **Discussing the Issues** 4 here.

Young & Rubicam's Brand Asset Evaluator measures brand strength along four consumer perception dimensions:

1. ***differentiation*** (what makes the brand stand out),
2. ***relevance*** (how consumers feel it meets their needs),
3. ***knowledge*** (how much consumers know about the brand), and
4. ***esteem*** (how highly consumers regard and respect the brand).

Brand valuation is the process of estimating the total financial value of a brand.

High brand equity provides a company with many competitive advantages.

- High level of consumer brand awareness and loyalty.
- More leverage in bargaining with resellers.
- More easily launch line and brand extensions.
- Defense against fierce price competition.
- Forms the basis for building strong and profitable customer relationships.

The fundamental asset underlying brand equity is ***customer equity***—the value of the customer relationships that the brand creates.

Building Strong Brands (Figure 7.3)

Use **Figure** 7.3 here.

Brand Positioning

Marketers can position brands at any of three levels.

1. They can position the brand on ***product attributes.***
2. They can position the brand with a desirable ***benefit.***
3. They can position the brand on ***beliefs and values.***

Brand Name Selection

Desirable qualities for a brand name include the following:

(1) It should suggest something about the product's benefits and qualities.
(2) It should be easy to pronounce, recognize, and remember.
(3) The brand name should be distinctive.
(4) It should be extendable.
(5) The name should translate easily into foreign languages.
(6) It should be capable of registration and legal protection.

Use **Application Question** 2 here.

Brand Sponsorship

A manufacturer has four sponsorship options.

(1) The product may be launched as a ***manufacturer's brand*** (or national brand).
(2) The manufacturer may sell to resellers who give it a ***private brand*** (also called a *store brand* or *distributor brand*).
(3) The manufacturer can market ***licensed brands.***
(4) Two companies can join forces and ***cobrand*** a product

National Brands versus Store Brands

National brands (or manufacturers' brands) have long dominated the retail scene. In recent times, an increasing number of retailers and wholesalers have created their own **store brands** (or *private brands*).

Use **Key Term** *Store Brand (Private Brand)* here.

Private brands now capture more than 20 percent of all North American consumer package goods sales and will capture an estimated 27 percent by 2010

41 percent of U.S. consumers now identify themselves as frequent buyers of store brands, up from just 12 percent in the early 1990s.

82 percent of consumers now believe that stores brands generally match the quality of national brands.

In the ***battle of the brands*** between national and private brands, retailers have many advantages.

- Retailers often price their store brands lower than comparable national brands.
- Store brands yield higher profit margins for the reseller.
- Store brands give resellers exclusive products that cannot be bought from competitors.

Licensing

Name and character licensing has grown rapidly in recent years. Annual retail sales of licensed products in the United States and Canada have grown from only $4 billion in 1977 to $55 billion in 1987 and more than $175 billion today.

Cobranding

Use **Key Term** *Cobranding* here.

Cobranding occurs when two established brand names of different companies are used on the same product.

Cobranding offers many advantages.

- The combined brands create broader consumer appeal and greater brand equity.
- Cobranding also allows a company to expand its existing brand into a category it might otherwise have difficulty entering alone.

Cobranding also has limitations.

- Such relationships involve complex legal contracts and licenses.
- Cobranding partners must carefully coordinate their advertising, sales promotion, and other marketing efforts.
- Each partner must trust the other will take good care of its brand.

Brand Development

Use **Figure** 7.4 here.

A company has four choices when it comes to developing brands (see Figure 7.4).

(1) **Line Extensions** occur when a company extends existing brand names to new forms, colors, sizes, ingredients, or flavors of an existing product category.
(2) **Brand Extensions** extend a current brand name to new or modified products in a new category.

Use **Key Terms** *Line Extension, Brand Extension* here.

(3) **Multibranding** introduces additional brands in the same category.
(4) **New Brands**.

Use **Video Case** here.

Megabrand strategy—weeding out weaker brands and focusing their marketing dollars only on brands that can achieve the number-one or number-two market share positions in their categories.

Managing Brands

The ***brand experience*** is customers coming to know a brand through a wide range of contacts and touchpoints.

Use **Focus on Ethics** here.

Companies need to periodically audit their brands' strengths and weaknesses.

Services Marketing

Services account for close to 79 percent of U.S. gross domestic product.

Services make up 64 percent of gross world product.

Nature and Characteristics of a Service

A company must consider four service characteristics when designing marketing programs: ***intangibility***, ***inseparability***, ***variability***, and ***perishability*** (see Figure 7.5).

Use **Figure** 7.5 here.
Use **Key Terms** *Service Inseparability, Service Intangibility, Service Perishability* and *Service Variability* here.
Use **Chapter Objective** 4 here.
Use **Discussing the Issues** 6 here.

(1) **Service intangibility** means that services cannot be seen, tasted, felt, heard, or smelled before they are bought.
(2) **Service inseparability** means that services cannot be separated from their providers, whether the providers are people or machines. Because the customer is also present as the service is produced, ***provider-customer interaction*** is a special feature of services marketing.
(3) **Service variability** means that the quality of services depends on who provides them as well as when, where, and how they are provided.
(4) **Service perishability** means that services cannot be stored for later sale or use.

Marketing Strategies for Service Firms

The Service-Profit Chain

In a service business, the customer and front-line service employee *interact* to create the service.

Use **Key Term** *Service-Profit Chain* here.
Use **Marketing at Work** 7.2 here.

The **service-profit chain** consists of five links:

- *Internal service quality:* superior employee selection and training, a quality work environment, and strong support for those dealing with customers, which results in...
- *Satisfied and productive service employees:* more satisfied, loyal, and hardworking employees, which results in...
- *Greater service value:* more effective and efficient customer value creation and service delivery, which results in...
- *Satisfied and loyal customers:* satisfied customers who remain loyal, repeat purchase, and refer other customers, which results in...
- *Healthy service profits and growth:* superior service firm performance.

Service marketing requires ***internal marketing*** and ***interactive marketing.*** (Figure 7.6)

Internal marketing means that the service firm must orient and motivate its customer-contact employees and supporting service people to work as a *team* to provide customer satisfaction.

Interactive marketing means that service quality depends heavily on the quality of the buyer-seller interaction during the service encounter.

Use **Key Terms** *Interactive Marketing, Internal Marketing* here. Use **Figure** 7.6 here.

Service companies face three major marketing tasks: They want to increase their ***service differentiation***, ***service quality***, and ***service productivity.***

Managing Service Differentiation

Service companies can differentiate their service *delivery* by having more able and reliable customer-contact people, by developing a superior physical environment in which the service product is delivered, or by designing a superior delivery process.

Service companies can work on differentiating their *images* through symbols and branding.

Managing Service Quality

Service quality is harder to define and judge than product quality.

Service quality will always vary, depending on the interactions between employees and customers.

Good ***service recovery*** can turn angry customers into loyal ones.

Managing Service Productivity

Service firms are under great pressure to increase service productivity.

- They can train current employees better or hire new ones who will work harder or more skillfully.
- They can increase the quantity of their service by giving up some quality.
- They can harness the power of technology.

Use **Application Questions** 3 here.

Travel Log

Discussing the Issues

1. What is a product and how can product planners build customer value? (AACSB: Communication)

   Answer:

   A **product** is anything that can be offered to a market for attention, acquisition, use, or consumption that might satisfy a want or need Products include more than just tangible objects Broadly defined, "products" also include services, events, persons, places, organizations, ideas, or mixes of these A product can be thought about on three levels (see Figure 8.1) Each level adds more customer value The most basic level is the **core customer value**, which addresses the question *What is the buyer really buying?* When designing products, marketers must first define the core, problem-solving benefits or services that consumers seek At the second level, product planners must turn the core benefit into an **actual product** They need to develop product and service features, design, a quality level, a brand name, and packaging Finally, product planners must build an **augmented product** around the core benefit and actual product by offering additional consumer services and benefits

2. Name and describe the four types of consumer products Provide an example of each (AACSB: Communication; Reflective Thinking)

   Answer:

   Consumer products include *convenience products*, *shopping products*, *specialty products*, and *unsought products* These products differ in the ways consumers buy them and therefore in how they are marketed (see Table 8.1) **Convenience products** are products and services that customers usually buy frequently, immediately, and with a minimum of comparison and buying effort Examples include soft drinks, bath soap, and candy Convenience products are usually low priced, and marketers place them in many locations to make them readily available when customers need them **Shopping products** are less frequently purchased products and services that customers compare carefully on suitability, quality, price, and style When buying shopping products and services, consumers spend much time and effort in gathering information and making comparisons Examples include furniture, clothing, appliances, and hotel and airline services Shopping products marketers usually distribute their products through fewer outlets but provide deeper sales support to help customers in their comparison efforts **Specialty products** are products and services with unique characteristics or brand identification for which a significant group of buyers is willing to make a special purchase effort Examples include specific brands of cars, high-priced photographic equipment, designer clothes, and the services of medical or legal specialists Buyers normally do not compare specialty products They invest only the time needed to reach dealers carrying the wanted products **Unsought products** are products that the consumer either does not know about or knows about but does not normally think of buying Classic examples of known but unsought products and services are life insurance, preplanned funeral services, and blood donations By their very nature, unsought products require a lot of advertising, personal selling, and other marketing efforts.

3. Discuss the individual product and service decisions facing marketers (AACSB: Communication)

   Answer:

   Figure 7.2 shows the important decisions in the development and marketing of individual products and services: *product attributes*, *branding*, *packaging*, *labeling*, and *product support services* Developing a product or service involves defining the benefits that it will offer These benefits are communicated and delivered by product **attributes** such as *quality*, *features*, and *style and design* A **brand** is a name, term, sign, symbol, or design, or a combination of these, that identifies the maker or seller of a product or service **Packaging** involves designing and producing the container or wrapper for a product Traditionally, the primary function of the package was to hold and protect the product In recent times, however, numerous factors have made packaging an important marketing tool as well **Labels** range from simple tags attached to products to complex graphics that are part of the package They perform the functions of (1) identifying the product or brand, (2) describing several things about the product—who made it, where it was made, when it was made, its contents, how it is to be used, and how to use it safely, and (3) promoting the brand, supporting its positioning, and connecting with customers. Customer **service** is another element of product strategy A company's offer usually includes some support services, which can be a minor or a major part of the total offering.

4. Define brand equity. What competitive advantages does high brand equity provide a company? (AACSB: Communication)

   Answer:

   Brand equity is the positive differential effect that knowing the brand name has on customer response to the product or service It's a measure of the brand's ability to capture consumer preference and loyalty High brand equity provides a company with many competitive advantages: (1) high level of consumer brand awareness and loyalty, (2) more leverage in bargaining with resellers because consumers expect stores to carry the brand, (3) ease of launching line and brand extensions due to the brand name's high credibility, (4) defense against fierce price competition, and (5) a basis for building strong and profitable customer relationships The fundamental asset underlying brand equity is *customer equity*—the value of the customer relationships that the brand creates A powerful brand is important, but what it really represents is a profitable set of loyal customers The proper focus of marketing is building customer equity, with brand management serving as a major marketing tool

5. Compare and contrast the four choices a company has regarding developing brands Provide an example of each (AACSB: Communication)

   Answer:

   A company has four choices when it comes to developing brands (see Figure 8.4) It can introduce *line extensions*, *brand extensions*, *multibrands*, or *new brands* **Line extensions** occur when a company extends existing brand names to new forms, colors, sizes, ingredients, or flavors of an existing product category Examples include microwave Quaker oatmeal, Skippy low fat peanut butter, and Kleenex facial tissue with lotion A **brand extension** extends a current brand name to new or modified products in a new category Examples include Apple's iPhone, Quaker oatmeal breakfast squares, and Arm & Hammer carpet deodorizer With **multibranding**, companies introduce additional brands in the same category For example, Procter & Gamble markets many different brands in each of its product categories Finally, a company might believe that the power of its existing brand name is waning and a **new brand** name is needed Or it may create a new brand name when it enters a new product category for which none of the company's current brand names are appropriate.

6. Name and describe the four special characteristics of services. How do the services offered by a hair salon differ from those offered by an auto-parts store regarding these characteristics? (AACSB: Communication, Reflective Thinking)

   Answer:

   The four special characteristics of services are: *intangibility*, *inseparability*, *variability*, and *perishability* **Service intangibility** means that services cannot be seen, tasted, felt, heard, or smelled before they are bought **Service inseparability** means that services cannot be separated from their providers, whether the providers are people or machines **Service variability** means that the quality of services depends on who provides them as well as when, where, and how they are provided **Service perishability** means that services cannot be stored for later sale or use Services offered by a hair salon are much more intangible, inseparable, variable, and perishable than those offered by an auto-parts store because the hair salon offers more of a pure service than does a store that sells merchandise Compared to the services offered by an auto-parts store, it is more difficult to evaluate the quality of the service provided by a hair salon prior to purchase, the consumer must be present and is actively involved in the creation of the service, no two haircuts are alike—even if performed by the same stylist, and the time spent creating the service cannot be stored for later purchase if the customer misses an appointment

Application Questions

1. Visit the Kraft Foods Web site (www.kraft.com/brands/index.html) and examine its list of different brands Name and define the four dimensions of a company's product mix and describe Kraft's product mix on these dimensions (AACSB: Communication; Reflective Thinking; Use of IT)

   Answer:

   A company's product mix has four important dimensions: width, length, depth, and consistency Product mix **width** refers to the number of different product lines the company carries Kraft has identified five broad product lines: beverages, convenient meals, cheese & dairy, grocery, and snacks Product mix **length** refers to the total number of items the company carries within its product lines The length of Kraft's product mix varies from four in the beverage category to twenty in the grocery category Product mix **depth** refers to the number of versions offered of each product in the line As with product mix length, Kraft's product mix depth varies by category For example, the company offers 25 different cereal brands but only one brand of hot dogs Finally, the **consistency** of the product mix refers to how closely the various product lines are related in end use, production requirements, distribution channels, or some other way Within each major product category, Kraft's product lines are fairly consistent in that they are all convenience products (food) and go through the same distribution channels (grocery stores).

2. In a small group, develop a brand name for a line of clothing targeted to college students Your brand is positioned as affordable yet stylish for the student on the go Use the desirable qualities for a brand name described in the chapter when selecting your brand name (AACSB: Communication; Reflective Thinking)

   Answer:

   Students' responses will vary Desirable qualities for a brand name include the following: (1) It should suggest something about the product's benefits and qualities; (2) It should be easy to pronounce, recognize, and remember; (3) The brand name should be distinctive; (4) It should be extendable; (5) The name should translate easily into foreign languages; and (6) It should be capable of registration and legal protection.

3. Find five examples of service-provider attempts to reduce service intangibility (AACSB: Communication; Reflective Thinking)

   Answer:

   Students' responses will vary, but several examples can be found in just the insurance industry alone—All State (You're in Good Hands), Hartford (The Rock), and State Farm (Like a Good Neighbor) Other examples include Merrill Lynch's tagline

"Bullish on America" (a bull represents a strong market), banks and law firms often have large, prestigious-looking buildings, and using spokespersons to lend credibility.

Under the Hood: Focus on Technology

After years of rumors and anticipation, Apple launched the iPhone in June 2007 It's more than just a phone—it's also a music player, a video player, a camera, and an Internet device with Web surfing and e-mail capabilities Like its predecessor, the iPod, the design is sleek The touch screen and keyboard enable a world of information at the user's fingertips This product doesn't come without high costs, however When it was launched, the 4GB version retailed for $499 and the 8GB version for $599 And because AT&T was the sole service provider, purchasers had to sign up for a two-year service contract with AT&T Moreover, some businesses were concerned because the iPhone was not compatible with current wireless e-mail systems used by companies At the time of the launch, most companies were using BlackBerry software and there was fear that iPhone users would circumvent security systems and jeopardize company networks.

1. Visit Apple's Web site to learn more about the iPhone (www.apple.com) Discuss the three levels of this product (AACSB: Communication; Reflective Thinking; Use of IT)

   Answer:

   The three levels of product include the core benefit, the actual product, and the augmented product The most basic level is the **core customer value**, which addresses the question *What is the buyer really buying?* With the iPhone, the core customer value is mobility Users can communicate with others, access information, and be entertained virtually anywhere At the second level, the core benefit is turned into an **actual product** This includes product and service features, design, a quality level, a brand name, and packaging In this case, the iPhone is an actual product Its name, parts, styling, features, packaging, and other attributes have all been combined carefully to deliver the core customer value of staying connected The third level is the **augmented product**, which is built around the core benefit and actual product by offering additional consumer services and benefits Apple provides product warranties, offers accessories such as Bluetooth headsets, provides purchasers with usage information from the Web site, and offers free hour-long workshops at select Apple retail stores so users can learn more and interact with other iPhone customers.

2. Chapter 5 described the product characteristics influencing the rate of new product adoption Review these factors and discuss how each factor will influence the rate of adoption of the iPhone (AACSB: Communication; Reflective Thinking)

   Answer:

   Five characteristics are especially important in influencing an innovation's rate of adoption:

- ***Relative advantage:*** *the degree to which the innovation appears superior to existing products The greater the perceived relative advantage of using the iPhone over current offerings, such as the BlackBerry or the Trio, will increase the rate of adoption.*
- ***Compatibility:*** *the degree to which the innovation fits the values and experiences of potential consumers This also means how compatible the new innovation is with how the user's needs are currently being met In the case of the iPhone, it is not compatible with current corporate software or with many users' current wireless providers Thus, the rate at which this product is adopted will be slower than if there was complete compatibility.*
- ***Complexity:*** *the degree to which the innovation is difficult to understand or use For some users, the iPhone will be simple but for others it will be more difficult to use One indication of how complex this product might be is the fact that Apple is offering free workshops on usage.*
- ***Divisibility:*** *the degree to which the innovation may be tried on a limited basis Adopters can only try the iPhone on a very limited basis—basically in an Apple or AT&T store However, as more users adopt the product, friends, relatives, and co-workers will show others its benefits.*
- ***Communicability:*** *the degree to which the results of using the innovation can be observed or described to others. Because the iPhone lends itself to demonstration and description, its use will spread faster among consumers.*

Other characteristics influence the rate of adoption, such as initial and ongoing costs, risk and uncertainty, and social approval The initial price and service agreement requirements will deter many consumers, but as prices drop and other contracts expire, the rate of adoption will increase.

Focus on Ethics

Arm & Hammer Baking Soda has been around for more than 150 years Sodium bicarbonate is a baking ingredient, but this brand has found hundreds of other uses around the house Use it to eliminate odors in your refrigerator, to brush your teeth, to sooth a stomach ache, to clean battery acid corrosion off your car, or to freshen up your carpet, laundry, or cat's litter box Arm & Hammer now offers separate products that meet several of these needs, such as laundry detergent, carpet freshener, toothpaste, and kitty litter deodorizer While a box of Arm & Hammer Baking Soda costs about 50¢, the other products cost $2.00 to $4.00, raising issues about the ethics of Arm & Hammer pricing.

1. Visit Arm & Hammer's Web site (www.armhammer.com) to learn more about this product Identify four ways this brand can be used other than for baking For each use, identify a product Arm & Hammer has developed for that use What brand development strategy is Arm & Hammer using? (AACSB: Communication; Reflective Thinking; Use of IT)

Answer:

This Web site provides a wealth of other uses for Arm & Hammer Baking Soda Students can "Tour Our House" for solutions for their home, family, and body Several of the uses have links to the other products Arm & Hammer offers to meet that need, such as oral care products, laundry detergent, carpet and room deodorizer, cat litter deodorizer, and deodorant The overall brand development strategy Arm & Hammer is using is **brand extension**—extending a current brand name to new or modified products in a new category Arm & Hammer Baking Soda was the original product for this brand, but it has extended the Arm & Hammer brand name to other product categories.

2. Visit a store where the Arm & Hammer products you identified in question #1 can be purchased and find the price of each product Compare the price per ounce for each of these products to the price per ounce for Arm & Hammer Baking Soda Is it ethical for Arm & Hammer to sell different products at considerably higher costs to consumers that meet basically the same needs as the other uses identified for the baking soda product? Develop an argument justifying the higher cost for these products (AACSB: Communication; Ethical Reasoning)

Answer:

Prices will vary depending on the products students identify as well as the location and type of store visited. Some example prices for Arm & Hammer brands found at WalMart are:

16 ounce package of baking soda for $0.54 = 3.4¢ per ounce

42.6 ounce package of carpet deodorizer for $1.94 = 4.5¢ per ounce

50 ounce liquid laundry detergent for $3.37 = 6.74¢ per ounce

20 ounce package of cat litter deodorizer for $2.17 = 10.8¢ per ounce

6 ounce tube of toothpaste for $2.43 = 40.5¢ per ounce
2.8 ounce deodorant for $1.98 = 70.7¢ per ounce

Students' responses will vary regarding the ethicality of developing higher-priced products to meet the same needs that the lower-priced baking soda product can meet However, the argument justifying the higher-cost should be based on the premise that these products create **greater customer value** than the original baking soda product For example, the refrigerator package has vents to allow the odor absorbing capabilities of the baking soda without the potential for a messy spill The carpet deodorizer is priced very closely to the price of plain baking soda, but it comes with different fragrances The laundry detergent is offered in a liquid version and performs more than a deodorizing function Brushing teeth with baking soda and peroxide can be dangerous because peroxide is poisonous, but consumers can get the same benefits from the convenient and safer toothpaste These products create greater value by offering greater convenience

GREAT IDEAS

Barriers to Effective Learning

1. Students will most likely have difficulty understanding the levels of products exhibited in Figure 7.1; no one in class is likely to have thought of a product in that level of detail before. This is a critical piece of information the students will need, however, so it is worthwhile going through several products and services to get at the core benefit, actual product, and augmented product in each so that they can see how to apply this concept.
2. Students' eyes can glaze over at the concepts of brand equity and brand sponsorship. Asking questions such as the students' perceptions of well-known brands such as Starbucks, Coke, Nike, and the like will help them understand what brand equity is all about. You can also tie in the discussion of the three levels of product with this idea of brand equity. Finally, by using different products with different brand sponsorships—several examples from Sears, auto companies, department store private labels, and various licensed properties from Disney or Warner Brothers will do—you can bring students to an understanding of this important concept.
3. The service characteristics of intangibility, inseparability, variability, and perishability are usually picked up fairly easily, but again, various examples from day-to-day life may help. For instance, everyone has had to cancel at least one doctor's appointment in his or her life—that beautifully illustrates the problem of perishability. Girls will understand inseparability by talking about the beauty salons they use. Ask: If the hairdresser you used left, would you easily switch to another person at the salon? Many students today travel heavily, so talking about airline personnel can illustrate service variability. Intangibility is the easiest characteristic to appreciate, as most students will have suffered through having to choose between several universities from whom they had received acceptances.

Student Projects

1. What is your all-time favorite brand? What do you most like about the product and/or brand name? What (if anything) do you dislike? What image does the brand have in your mind? How loyal are you toward the brand? Why?
2. Go to the supermarket and take a look at the brand extensions that exist for Coke. Do you think this makes sense or not? When is brand extension a good strategy? When is it a poor one?
3. Consider Starbucks Coffee. Consumers sometimes bond very closely with their preferred brands. What type of brand equity do you believe they have established over the years? How did this happen?

4. What do you like about your bank? How would you compare the services you receive from your bank to other competing banks and to your "ideal" bank? What is good about the service you currently receive? Review the service using the material from the chapter. What specifics about the service make it very good from a marketing standpoint?

Small Group Assignment

Read the chapter opening vignette on Las Vegas. Form students into groups of three to five. Each group should then answer the following questions:

1. What is Las Vegas selling? And what are visitors really buying?
2. As Vegas continues to grow in popularity, how important are the two dimensions of product quality?
3. Discuss the brand equity of Las Vegas versus that of another Top 3 gaming destination-Biloxi, Mississippi.

Each group should share its findings with the class.

Individual Assignment

Review the gaming industry in Mississippi. How has that industry positioned itself in the overall gaming market? How have they attempted to build customer value? How successful do you believe they have been in this effort?

Think-Pair-Share

Consider the following questions, formulate an answer, pair with the student on your right, share your thoughts with one another, and respond to questions from the instructor:

1. Define "product."
2. How do products and services really differ?
3. Your text states that "The product is the key element in the overall market offering." What does this mean?
4. When a buyer purchases a product, what are they *really* buying?
5. What is the difference between shopping goods and specialty goods?

Classroom Exercise/Homework Assignment

In many parts of the world, birth control is an unsought product. Assume you have been given the task of promoting birth control in a region of the world where it has traditionally been unused. How would you attempt to make inroads?

Classroom Management Strategies

This chapter will challenge the students to think more deeply about the concepts of products, services, and branding strategy.

1. The first major section of this chapter "What Is a Product?" should take 10 minutes. The primary focus should be on the classification of products and services, which will aid in the comprehension of the next section.
2. Product and Service Decisions should be covered in 20 minutes. The individual product decisions have the most material, and by and large students will never have focused on how important issues such as packaging and labeling are. Bringing in several products to discuss these attributes is helpful. Students will generally be confused about the product line and product mix decisions, and so a careful discussion of these topics is beneficial.
3. Branding Strategy should also take 20 minutes. Branding decisions are closely tied in with positioning discussed in the last chapter, but now would also be a good time to cover such areas as naming and sponsorship. Again, confusion can enter the student's mind regarding line extensions, brand extensions, multibrands, and new brands, so examples of each are very helpful.
4. Services marketing can be covered in 10 minutes. The special characteristics of services, outlined in Figure 7.5, are very important to understanding the differences between products and services. The service-profit chain seems a difficult concept to students until they work through the fact that each link in the chain leads to the next.

CHAPTER 8
New-Product Development and Life-Cycle Strategies

Previewing the Concepts: Chapter Objectives

1. Explain how companies find and develop new-product ideas
2. List and define the steps in the new-product development process and the major considerations in managing this process
3. Describe the stages of the product life cycle
4. Describe how marketing strategies change during the product's life cycle
5. Discuss two additional product and services issues: socially responsible product decisions and international product and services marketing

JUST THE BASICS

Chapter Overview

In this chapter, we'll look into two product topics:

1. Developing new products
2. Managing products through their life cycles.

New-product development is risky, and many new products fail.

The first part of this chapter lays out a process for finding and growing successful new products.

In the second part of the chapter, we see that every product passes through several life-cycle stages and that each stage poses new challenges requiring different marketing strategies and tactics.

Finally, we look at two additional considerations, social responsibility in product decisions and international product and services marketing.

Annotated Chapter Notes/Outline

Introduction

Then things took an ugly turn for Apple. In 1985, after tumultuous struggles with the new president he'd hired only a year earlier, Steve Jobs left Apple.

With Jobs gone, Apple's creative fires cooled. By the mid- to late-1990s, Apple's sales had plunged to $5 billion, 50 percent off previous highs.

Yet Apple has engineered a remarkable turnaround. Last years sales soared to a record $19 billion, more than triple sales just three years earlier.

After returning, Jobs next unleashed Mac OS X.

The iMac and Mac OS X put Apple back on the map in personal computing.

The iPod ranks as one of the greatest consumer electronics hits of all time. By March of 2007, Apple had sold more than 88 million iPods, and more than two billion songs, 50 million TV shows, and 1.3 million movies had been downloaded from the iTunes Store.

Thus, almost overnight, it seems, Steve Jobs has transformed Apple from a failing niche computer maker to a major force in consumer electronics, digital music and video, and who knows what else in the future. And he's done it through innovation.

Every product seems to go through a life cycle.

This product life cycle presents two major challenges:

1. Because all products eventually decline, a firm must be good at developing new products to replace aging ones (the challenge of *new-product development*).
2. The firm must be good at adapting its marketing strategies in the face of changing tastes, technologies, and competition as products pass through life-cycle stages (the challenge of *product life-cycle strategies*).

New-Product Development Strategy

Use **Key Term** *New Product Development* here. Use **Chapter Objective** 1 here.

A firm can obtain new products in two ways.

1. *Acquisition*—by buying a whole company, a patent, or a license to produce someone else's product.
2. **New-product development** efforts.

The New-Product Development Process

Figure 8.1 shows the eight major steps in the ***new-product development process.***

Use **Figure** 8-1 here. Use **Chapter Objective** 2 here. Use **Discussing the Issues** 1 and 2 here.

1. Idea Generation

Use **Key Term** *Idea Generation* here. Use **Application Questions** 2 here.

Idea generation is the systematic search for new-product ideas.

Internal Idea Sources

Using ***internal sources***, the company can find new ideas through formal research and development. Or it can pick the brains of employees—from executives to scientists, engineers, and manufacturing staff to salespeople.

Use **Under the Hood/Focus on Technology** here.

External Idea Sources

Companies can also obtain good new-product ideas from any of a number of external sources, such as ***distributors and suppliers*** or even **competitors.**

Perhaps the most important source of new-product ideas is ***customers*** themselves.

2. Idea Screening

Use **Key Term** *Idea Screening* here.

The first idea-reducing stage is **idea screening**, which helps spot good ideas and drop poor ones as soon as possible.

3. Concept Development and Testing

Use **Key Terms** *Product Concept, Concept Testing* here. Use **Table** 8.1 here. Use **Application Question** 1 here.

A ***product idea*** is an idea for a possible product that the company can see itself offering to the market.

A ***product concept*** is a detailed version of the idea stated in meaningful consumer terms.

A ***product image*** is the way consumers perceive an actual or potential product.

Concept Development

In **concept development**, several descriptions of the product are generated to find out how attractive each concept is to customers. From these concepts, the best one is chosen.

Concept Testing

Concept testing calls for testing new-product concepts with groups of target consumers.

4. **Marketing strategy development** is designing an initial marketing strategy for introducing this car to the market.

Use **Key Term** *Marketing Strategy Development* here.

The ***marketing strategy statement*** consists of three parts.

1. A description of the target market; the planned value proposition; and the sales, market share, and profit goals for the first few years.
2. Outline of the product's planned price, distribution, and marketing budget for the first year.
3. Description of the planned long-run sales, profit goals, and marketing mix strategy:

5. **Business Analysis**

Use **Key Term** *Business Analysis* here.

Business analysis involves a review of the sales, costs, and profit projections for a new product to find out whether they satisfy the company's objectives.

Use **Applications Questions** 3 here.

6. **Product Development**

Use **Key Term** *Product Development* here.

Let's Discuss This
What kind of safety testing might a new baby stroller need to go through? How about a new flashlight? A new telephone?

In **product development**, R&D or engineering develops the product concept into a physical product.

The product development step calls for a large jump in investment.

7. Test Marketing

Use **Key Term** *Test Marketing* here.

Test marketing is the stage at which the product and marketing program are introduced into realistic market settings.

8. Commercialization

Use **Key Term** *Commercialization* here.

Commercialization is introducing the new product into the market.

Decisions must be made concerning:

- *Timing,*
- *Where* to launch the new product
- *Market rollout.*

Use **Video Case** here.

Managing New-Product Development

Customer-Centered New-Product Development

Use **Key Term** *Customer-Centered New-Product Development* here.

New-product development ***must*** be customer centered.

Customer-centered new-product development focuses on finding new ways to solve customer problems and create more customer-satisfying experiences.

Use **Discussing the Issues** 3 here.

Team-Based New-Product Development

Under the ***sequential product development*** approach, one company department works individually to complete its stage of the process before passing the new product along to the next department and stage.

This orderly, step-by-step process can help bring control to complex and risky projects. But it also can be dangerously slow.

In order to get their new products to market more quickly, many companies use a **team-based new-product development** approach.

Use **Key Term** *Team-Based New-Product Development* here. Use **Marketing at Work** 8-1 here. Use **Linking the Concepts** here.

Under this approach, company departments work closely together in cross-functional teams, overlapping the steps in the product development process to save time and increase effectiveness.

Instead of passing the new product from department to department, the company assembles a team of people from various departments that stay with the new product from start to finish.

Systematic New-Product Development

An ***innovation management system*** can be used to collect, review, evaluate, and manage new-product ideas.

The innovation management system approach yields two favorable outcomes.

1. It helps create an innovation-oriented company culture.
2. It will yield a larger number of new-product ideas, among which will be found some especially good ones.

Product Life-Cycle Strategies

Figure 8.2 shows a typical **product life cycle** (PLC), the course that a product's sales and profits take over its lifetime.

Use **Key Term** *Product Life Cycle (PLC)* here. Use **Figure** 8.2 here. Use **Chapter Objective** 3 here.

The product life cycle has five distinct stages:

Product development begins when the company finds and develops a new-product idea. During product development, sales are zero and the company's investment costs mount.

Introduction is a period of slow sales growth as the product is introduced in the market. Profits are nonexistent in this stage because of the heavy expenses of product introduction.

Growth is a period of rapid market acceptance and increasing profits.

Maturity is a period of slowdown in sales growth because the product has achieved acceptance by most potential buyers. Profits level off or decline because of increased marketing outlays to defend the product against competition.

Decline is the period when sales fall off and profits drop.

Use **Discussing the Issues** 4 here.

The PLC concept can describe a ***product class*** (gasoline-powered automobiles), a ***product form*** (SUVs), or a ***brand*** (the Ford Escape).

Product classes have the longest life cycles.

Product forms have the standard PLC shape.

Product brand PLC can change quickly because of changing competitive attacks and responses.

The PLC can be applied to styles, fashions, and fads (Figure 8.3).

- A **style** is a basic and distinctive mode of expression.
- A **fashion** is a currently accepted or popular style in a given field.
- **Fads** are temporary periods of unusually high sales driven by consumer enthusiasm and immediate product or brand popularity.

Use **Key Terms** *Style, Fashion,* and *Fad* here. Use **Figure** 8.3 here.

Strategies for each of the other life-cycle stages:

Introduction Stage

Use **Key Term** *Introduction Stage* here.

The **introduction stage** starts when the new product is first launched.

In this stage, profits are negative or low, promotion spending is relatively high, only basic versions of the product are produced.

Growth Stage

Use **Key Term** *Growth Stage* here.

The **growth stage** is where sales begin to climb quickly.

New competitors will enter the market. They will introduce new product features, and the market will expand.

The increase in competitors leads to an increase in the number of distribution outlets.

Prices remain stable.

Profits increase during the growth stage.

Maturity Stage

Use **Key Term** *Maturity Stage* here. Use **Linking the Concepts** here.

The **maturity stage** is characterized by slowing product growth.

The slowdown in sales growth results in many producers with many products to sell.

Competitors begin marking down prices, increasing their advertising and sales promotions, and upping their product-development budgets to find better versions of the product.

These steps lead to a drop in profit.

Product managers should consider modifying the market, product, and marketing mix.

In ***modifying the market***, the company tries to increase the consumption of the current product.

In ***modifying the product***, the company tries changing characteristics such as quality, features, style, or packaging to attract new users and to inspire more usage.

In ***modifying the marketing mix***, the company tries changing one or more marketing mix elements.

Decline Stage

Use **Key Term** *Decline Stage* here. Use **Table** 8.2 here. Use **Chapter Objective** 4 here.

Applying the Concept
Discuss several soft drinks that are on the market today. Define which stage of the PLC you think each is in and why.

The sales of most product forms and brands eventually dip. This is the **decline stage.**

Management may decide to ***maintain*** its brand without change in the hope that competitors will leave the industry.

Management may decide to ***harvest*** the product, which means reducing various costs (plant and equipment, maintenance, R&D, advertising, sales force) and hoping that sales hold up

Management may decide to ***drop*** the product from the line.

Use **Discussing the Issues** 5 here.

Additional Product and Service Considerations

Product Decisions and Social Responsibility

Marketers should consider public policy issues and regulations regarding acquiring or dropping products, patent protection, product quality and safety, and product warranties.

Regarding new products, the government may prevent companies from adding products through acquisitions if the effect threatens to lessen competition.

Manufacturers must comply with specific laws regarding product quality and safety.

Congress passed the Magnuson-Moss Warranty Act in 1975. The act requires that full warranties meet certain minimum standards, including repair "within a reasonable time and without charge" or a replacement or full refund if the product does not work "after a reasonable number of attempts" at repair.

Use **Focus on Ethics** here.

International Product and Services Marketing

Use **Chapter Objective 5** here.

International product and service marketers face special challenges.

- They must figure out what products and services to introduce and in which countries.
- They must decide how much to standardize or adapt their products and services for world markets.
- Packaging presents new challenges for international marketers.

The trend toward growth of global service companies will continue, especially in banking, airlines, telecommunications, and professional services.

Use **Discussing the Issues** 6 here.

Travel Log

Discussing the Issues

1. Think of a product that failed. Discuss the reasons why new products fail and indicate which reasons you think caused the failure of the product you chose. (AACSB: Communication; Reflective Thinking)

   Answer:

   Students' responses will vary regarding an example of a product failure. Several examples include the Ford Edsel, McDonald's Arch Deluxe, New Coke, Crystal Pepsi, Sony Betamax, and the Segway Scooter. There are several reasons why new products fail. Although an idea may be good, the company may overestimate market size. The actual product may be poorly designed. Or it might be incorrectly positioned, launched at the wrong time, priced too high, or poorly advertised. A high-level executive might push a favorite idea despite poor marketing research findings. Sometimes the costs of product development are higher than expected and sometimes competitors fight back harder than expected.

2. Name and describe the major steps in the new-product development process. (AACSB: Communication)

   Answer:

   Figure 8.1 shows the eight major steps in this process:

   - **Idea generation**—the systematic search for new-product ideas. Major sources of new-product ideas include internal sources and external sources. The purpose of idea generation is to create a large number of ideas. The purpose of the succeeding stages is to *reduce* that number.
   - **Idea screening**—helps spot good ideas and drop poor ones as soon as possible.
   - **Product concept**—a detailed version of the idea stated in meaningful consumer terms.
   - **Concept testing**—testing with groups of target consumers. The concepts may be presented to consumers symbolically or physically.
   - **Marketing strategy development**—designing an initial marketing strategy for introducing the product to the market. The marketing strategy

statement describes the target market, the planned value proposition, and the sales, market share, and profit goals for the first few years.

- **Business analysis**—a review of the sales, costs, and profit projections for a new product to find out whether they satisfy the company's objectives. If they do, the product can move to the product development stage.
- **Product development**—R&D or engineering develops the product concept into a physical product
- **Test marketing**—the stage at which the product and marketing program are introduced into realistic market settings.
- **Commercialization**—introducing the new product into the market.

3. Successful new-product development requires a customer-centered, team-based, and systematic effort. Explain what this means. (AACSB: Communication)

Answer:

Successful new-product development begins with a thorough understanding of what consumers need and value. **Customer-centered new-product development** focuses on finding new ways to solve customer problems and create more customer-satisfying experiences. Good new-product development also requires a total-company, cross-functional effort. In order to get their new products to market more quickly, many companies use a **team-based new-product development** approach in which company departments work closely together in cross-functional teams, overlapping the steps in the product development process to save time and increase effectiveness. Instead of passing the new product from department to department, the company assembles a team of people from various departments that stay with the new product from start to finish. Finally, the new-product development process should be **holistic and systematic** rather than compartmentalized and haphazard. Otherwise, few new ideas will surface, and many good ideas will sputter and die. To avoid these problems, a company can install an *innovation management system* to collect, review, evaluate, and manage new-product ideas. The innovation management system approach yields two favorable outcomes. First, it helps create an innovation-oriented company culture. It shows that top management supports, encourages, and rewards innovation. Second, it will yield a larger number of new-product ideas, among which will be found some especially good ones. The good new ideas will be more systematically developed, producing more new-product successes.

4. Briefly describe the five stages of the product life cycle. Identify a product class, form, or brand that is in each stage. (AACSB: Communication; Reflective Thinking)

Answer:

Figure 8.2 shows a typical product life cycle (PLC), the course that a product's sales and profits take over its lifetime. The product life cycle has five distinct stages:

1. **Product development** begins when the company finds and develops a new-product idea. During product development, sales are zero and the company's investment costs mount. Examples for this stage may be difficult for students to think of because the products are not yet introduced into the market. Solar-powered automobiles might be in the product development stage.
2. **Introduction** is a period of slow sales growth as the product is introduced in the market. Profits are nonexistent in this stage because of the heavy expenses of product introduction. An example of a product form in this stage might be hybrid automobiles.
3. **Growth** is a period of rapid market acceptance and increasing profits. Examples of brands in this stage are wireless Internet devices such as BlackBerry, Trio, and iPhone.
4. **Maturity** is a period of slowdown in sales growth because the product has achieved acceptance by most potential buyers. Profits level off or decline because of increased marketing outlays to defend the product against competition. Most products are in this stage, such as laundry detergent, toothpaste, and soft drinks.
5. **Decline** is the period when sales fall off and profits drop. An example of a product form in this stage is videotape players and recordings.

5. Explain the difference between maintaining, harvesting, and dropping a brand in the decline stage. (AACSB: Communication)

   Answer:

   Management may decide to **maintain** its brand without change in the hope that competitors will leave the industry. Or management may decide to reposition or reinvigorate the brand in hopes of moving it back into the growth stage of the product life cycle. Management may decide to **harvest** the product, which means reducing various costs (plant and equipment, maintenance, R&D, advertising, sales force) and hoping that sales hold up. If successful, harvesting will increase the company's profits in the short run. Or management may decide to **drop** the product from the line. It can sell it to another firm or simply liquidate it at salvage value.

6. Discuss the special challenges facing international product and services marketers. (AACSB: Communication)

   Answer:

   International product and service marketers face special challenges. First, they must figure out what products and services to introduce and in which countries. Then, they must decide how much to standardize or adapt their products and services for world markets. Standardization helps a company to develop a consistent worldwide image and lowers the product design, manufacturing, and marketing costs of offering a large variety of products. However, markets and consumers around the world differ widely. Companies must usually respond to these differences by adapting their product offerings. Packaging also presents new challenges for international marketers. For example, names, labels, and colors may not translate easily from one country to another. Packaging may also need to be tailored to meet the physical characteristics of consumers in various parts of the world. Thus, although product and package standardization can produce benefits, companies must usually adapt their offerings to the unique needs of specific international markets. Service marketers also face special challenges when going global. The global growth of professional and business services industries such as accounting, management consulting, and advertising have followed the globalization of the client companies they serve.

Application Questions

1. Visit the Product Development and Management Association's Web site (http://www.pdma.org) to learn about this organization. Click on "OCI Award" on the left side of the page. Briefly describe the criteria used when granting this award and write a brief report about a company receiving this award. (AACSB: Communication; Use of IT)

   Answer:

   This organization advocates best practices in product development and provides several resources for members. The OCI Award stands for Outstanding Corporate Innovator and there are four basic requirements for receiving this award:

   1. A sustained record of successful new product launches over a five-year period.
   2. New product success that leads to significant company growth.
   3. The company has a defined new product development process.
   4. An innovative culture within the organization.

   Companies receiving this award each year are highlighted on the site. Recent recipients include Xerox Corporation, Bank of America, Nextel, Air Force Laboratory, and Harley-Davidson. Students can click on each organization to learn why they were granted this distinction.

2. If your campus is like most college campuses, you probably experience parking frustrations. Wouldn't you like to know where parking spots are available so you don't have to drive around looking for a spot? In a small group, brainstorm ideas for a new product or service that satisfies this need. (AACSB: Communication; Reflective Thinking)

Answer:

Students' responses will vary and are limited only by their imaginations. Some examples include a special radio station that reports on parking conditions and availability, posting radio-equipped traffic directors on campus to send cars to available spots, and using technology (such as infrared-sensing devices or radar) to indicate an available spot.

3. Select the product concept from the previous question that you believe is the most viable. Develop a marketing-strategy statement and describe how you would conduct a business analysis for the new product based on that concept. (AACSB: Communication; Analytic Skills; Reflective Thinking)

   Answer:

   Students' responses will vary, but the marketing-strategy statement and the business analysis should include elements described in the chapter. For example, the first part of the **strategy statement** describes the target market; the planned value proposition; and the sales, market share, and profit goals for the first few years. The second part of the marketing strategy statement outlines the product's planned price, distribution, and marketing budget for the first year. The third part of the marketing strategy statement describes the planned long-run sales, profit goals, and marketing mix strategy. **Business analysis** involves a review of the sales, costs, and profit projections for a new product to find out whether they satisfy the company's objectives. Students should discuss how they would estimate sales and expected costs to analyze the new product's financial attractiveness.

Under the Hood: Focus on Technology

Could you and a fellow student develop a business that would employ more that 10,000 people and be valued at over $120 billion in just over a decade? That's exactly what two Stanford University graduate students, Larry Page and Sergey Brin, did. They founded Google, the world's largest Internet search engine. Google is used in more than 100 countries and generates revenues from its online search services and highly targeted advertising. At Google's headquarters in Mountain View, CA, known as "Googleplex," employees ("Googlers") are encouraged to be innovative. As a result, in addition to its original search engine capabilities, Google has launched a host of new products.

1. Identify five products Google has introduced in addition to its search engine service. Are they successful? How many of these were you aware of before this exercise? Visit Goggle Labs (labs.google.com) to learn about new products that are still in the testing stage—"a few of our favorite ideas that still aren't quite ready for primetime." Briefly discuss what you found. (AACSB: Communication; Use of IT)

Answer:

Google has launched several new products, such as Google Talk, Google Finance, GMail, Orkut, Google News, Google Apps, and Google Checkout to name a few. Google's primary revenue sources are targeted advertising and online search services, and some observers state that all the other services offered are mediocre, at best.

A visit to Google Labs will be interesting to students. The content changes, so students' experiences will vary. For example, when accessed in August 2007, visitors could test timelines and maps. One application allowed users to view a timeline and map of PGA events. There were several more applications to test.

2. Read the article about Google's new-product development process at http://www.businessweek.com/technology/content/jun2006/tc20060629_411177.htm. What is Google's philosophy regarding new products? Do you think it is appropriate? (AACSB: Communication; Reflective Thinking; Use of IT)

   Answer:

   This article is from June 30, 2006 *BusinessWeek.com*. It describes Google's philosophy regarding new product introductions and provides several links to other articles about Google's new products and the company's new-product development process. Google's philosophy is to "launch early and often" and that a "high failure rate is baked into their strategy." They expect that up to 60% to 80% of their new products may fail. Employees are encouraged to generate ideas. The company relies on word-of-mouth to promote new products, so it seems that very little is invested in new products. However, no products other than Google's Internet search engine are market leaders.

   Students' opinions regarding whether this approach is appropriate will vary. However, some may indicate that this strategy is appropriate as there really is little financial risk for failure regarding the types of new products launched. Others may point out, though, that a large number of failures will hurt Google's brand equity.

Focus on Ethics

"Green marketing" has been around for a long time and has experienced renewed growth in the last decade. In response, several companies are developing eco-friendly products and touting their environmental conscientiousness. Greenpeace, an environmental activist group, is pushing legislation that would ban the production of incandescent light bulbs. It called Philips Electronics a "climate criminal" because it produces these types of light bulbs. However, not all of the new products developed in response to consumers' desires for more environmentally-friendly products live up to their promises.

1. Find examples of new products developed in response to growing environmental concern. Have marketers been successful with these new products? (AACSB: Communication; Reflective Thinking)

   Answer:

   Although students' responses will vary, most will probably discuss hybrid automobiles. The Toyota Prius is the market leader in this product class, but sales still pale in comparison to gas-powered counterparts. Ford and Honda have announced that they will discontinue some of their offerings in this category. The higher purchase prices and the negative press associated with some of these products are hindering growth. Hybrids cost $5,000 to $15,000 more and the delivered gas mileage is not as good as promised.

2. Not all "green" products live up to their claims. Is it ethical for marketers to continue to offer these products? (AACSB: Communication; Ethical Reasoning)

   Answer:

   Students' responses will vary. Some students may point out that hybrid automobiles do not deliver the gas mileage promised and fluorescent light bulbs contain mercury that is harmful to the environment if not disposed of properly. Some have argued that the true cost to plan, build, deliver, sell, operate, and dispose of eco-friendly products far exceeds that of conventional products. Some consumers purchase organic products thinking that they are less harmful to the environment, but those products must still be transported, which causes environmental damage.

GREAT IDEAS

Barriers to Effective Learning

1. Understanding the systematic nature of the new product development process will cause problems for some students. They will have some difficulty understanding why a process is needed at all, and they will also not realize how development costs rise at each and every stage. Finally, the amount of analysis that goes into the screening phases might be a surprise to them. To overcome these barriers, come up with a new product idea in class and review how you might develop it into a viable product.
2. The commercialization phase of the new product development process could also be somewhat difficult for the students to comprehend. They may not be aware that not all products are launched nationally or globally when first introduced. Some examples of products that are available only regionally—food and drink products frequently are regional—may help them to understand the logistics of launching a new product.

3. The phases of the product life cycle, and the fact that it can apply to product classes, forms, and brands, can cause some difficulty. Discussing brands that are in each stage helps tremendously, as does discussing products that have successfully moved back from decline into maturity or growth (e.g., Arm & Hammer baking soda).
4. The differences among fads, fashions, and styles can be explained through asking the students to discuss clothing in those terms. Because these items are routinely discussed in terms of fashions and styles, students can easily internalize the differences in meaning of these terms.

Student Projects

1. Go to Research in Motion's (the makers of the Blackberry phone) website (www.rim.com) and read about one of their newest offerings, the 8300 Curve. Imagine if you had been assigned the job of developing questions for the concept test of this product. Develop a series of five questions that you would have included.
2. Why is test marketing so important for marketers? Why is not more often used?
3. Find two products that you believe are in the Introduction stage of the Product Life Cycle. Justify your beliefs.
4. What is the difference between Fads, Styles, and Fashions?
5. In what ways do the Growth and Maturity stages of the Product Life Cycle differ?

Small Group Assignment

Form students into groups of three to five. Each group should read the opening vignette to the chapter about Apple. Each group should then answer the following questions:

1. How did Apple, an early industry leader which almost faced extinction, manage to make such a stunning comeback?
2. How did Apple use creativity in the development of the iPod?
3. How has Apple built customer-driven innovation into its organization?
4. Trace the iPod through the product life cycle stages.

Each group should share its findings with the class.

Individual Assignment

Read the opening vignette to the chapter. Think about the answers to the following questions:

1. How did Apple, an early industry leader which almost faced extinction, use creativity?
2. Why would Apple feel the need to launch so many new products in such a few years?

3. How has Apple built customer-driven innovation into its organization?
4. Are iPods styles, fashions, or fads?

Share your findings with the class.

Think-Pair-Share

Consider the following questions, formulate an answer, pair with the student on your right, share your thoughts with one another, and respond to questions from the instructor.

1. How do companies find new products?
2. Define the stages of the New Product Development Process.
3. What stage of the PLC do you believe currently holds Apple's iPhone? Why?
4. How are *competitors* a source of new product ideas?
5. What are the advantages of team-based new product development?

Classroom Exercise/Homework Assignment

Research the bottled water market. Check out the websites for Evian (www.evian.com/us), Aqua Pacific (www.aquapacific.com), Mountain Valley Spring Water (www.mountainvalleyspring.com), and Perrier (www.usa.perrier.com). What stage of the PLC would you say bottled water occupies? How is each of these companies attempting to maintain or grow sales of their products?

Classroom Management Strategies

This is a relatively short chapter, and so you have the luxury of really being able to focus on each section. Still, there is a lot of material to discuss, so effective use of time is important. The majority of class time should be spent on the New Product Development section, with slightly less than half being devoted to Product Life-Cycle Strategies.

1. An introductory 5 minutes should be spent on the discussion of Apple's development as an example of why companies need to continually offer new products and services.
2. Another 5 minutes should be spent discussing the reasons why a systematic new product development process is important, rather than developing products in a haphazard manner. Tie this discussion back to earlier in the term when you talked about marketing strategies, mission statements, and goals and objectives for the company as a whole.
3. Spend about 35 minutes going through the eight stages of the new product development process. At each phase, using examples from your own and the students' experience will help tremendously. Having a guest speaker from a company that has developed and launched several products is a unique way of driving home the importance of a systematic process.
4. Finally, spend 15 minutes discussing the PLC and the marketing strategies that can accompany each stage. Going online and looking at Web sites for various

kinds of products at each of the different stages could make this more interesting for the students, while also providing a more detailed introduction to the meaning of a product life cycle.

CHAPTER 9
Pricing: Understanding and Capturing Customer Value

Previewing the Concepts: Chapter Objectives

1. Discuss the importance of understanding customer value perceptions and company costs when setting prices.

2. Identify and define the other important internal and external factors affecting a firm's pricing decisions.

3. Describe the major strategies for pricing imitative and new products.

4. Explain how companies find a set of prices that maximize the profits from the total product mix.

5. Discuss how companies adjust their prices to take into account different types of customers and situations.

6. Discuss the key issues related to initiating and responding to price changes.

JUST THE BASICS

Chapter Overview

Firms successful at creating customer value with the other marketing mix activities must capture this value in the prices they earn.

Despite its importance, many firms do not handle pricing well.

In this chapter, we begin with the question, What is a price? Next, we look at customer-value perceptions, costs, and other factors that marketers must consider when setting prices.

Price can be defined as the sum of all the values that customers give up in order to gain the benefits of having or using a product or service. Pricing decisions are subject to an incredibly complex array of company, environmental, and competitive forces.

Finally, we examine pricing strategies for new-product pricing, product mix pricing, price adjustments, and dealing with price changes.

Annotated Chapter Notes/Outline

Introduction

One airline appears to have found a radical new pricing solution, one that customers are sure to love: Make flying *free*!

Even without free flights, Ryanair has become one of Europe's most popular carriers.

Although its average fare is just $53 compared with U.S. low-cost leader Southwest's $92, Ryanair's net margins are 18 percent, more than double Southwest's 7 percent.

The secret? Ryanair's austere cost structure makes even cost-conscious Southwest look like a reckless spender. In addition, the Irish airline puts a price on virtually everything except tickets, from baggage check-in to seat-back advertising space.

Add it all up—relentless cost cutting on the operations side, combined with innovative efforts to extract more revenue from each traveler—and Ryanair's plan to give away half of its seats by 2010 starts to look quite sane.

What is a Price?

In the narrowest sense, **price** is the amount of money charged for a product or service.

Use **Key Term** *Price* here.

More broadly, **price** is the sum of all the values that customers give up in order to gain the benefits of having or using a product or service.

Price is the only element in the marketing mix that produces revenue.

Price is one of the most flexible marketing mix elements.

Factors to Consider When Setting Prices

Figure 9.1 summarizes the major considerations in setting price.

Use **Chapter Objective** 1 here. Use **Figure** 9.1 here. Use **Discussing the Issues** 1 here.

Customer Perceptions of Value

In the end, the customer will decide whether a product's price is right.

Value-Based Pricing

Use **Key Term** *Value-Based Pricing* here. Use **Figure** 9.2 here.

Value-based pricing uses buyers' perceptions of value, not the seller's cost, as the key to pricing.

Price is considered along with the other marketing mix variables *before* the marketing program is set.

Use **Application Question** 1 here.

Figure 9.2 compares value-based pricing with cost-based pricing.

Cost-based pricing is product driven.

"Good value" is not the same as "low price."

Two types of value-based pricing are *good-value pricing* and *value-added pricing.*

Use **Key Term** *Good-Value Pricing* here.

1. **Good-Value Pricing. Good-value pricing** is offering just the right combination of quality and good service at a fair price.

Everyday low pricing (EDLP) involves charging a constant, everyday low price with few or no temporary price discounts.

High-low pricing involves charging higher prices on an everyday basis but running frequent promotions to lower prices temporarily on selected items.

2. **Value-Added Pricing. Value-added pricing** is the strategy of attaching value-added features and services to differentiate their offers and thus support higher prices.

Use **Key Term** *Value-Added Pricing* here. Use **Under the Hood/Focus on Technology** here.

Company and Product Costs

Cost-based pricing involved setting prices based on the costs for producing, distributing, and selling the product plus a fair rate of return for its effort and risk.

Types of Costs

Fixed costs (also known as overhead) are costs that do not vary with production or sales level.

Variable costs vary directly with the level of production. They are called variable because their total varies with the number of units produced.

Use **Key Terms** *Fixed Costs, Variable Costs* here. Use **Application Question** 2 here.

Total costs are the sum of the fixed and variable costs for any given level of production.

Use **Key Term** *Total Costs* here.

Cost-Based Pricing

Use **Key Term** *Cost-Based Pricing* here.

The simplest pricing method is **cost-plus pricing**—adding a standard markup to the cost of the product.

Does using standard markups to set prices make sense? Generally, no.

Markup pricing remains popular for many reasons.

1. Sellers are more certain about costs than about demand.
2. When all firms in the industry use this pricing method, prices tend to be similar and price competition is thus minimized.
3. Many people feel that cost-plus pricing is fairer to both buyers and sellers.

Another cost-oriented pricing approach is **break-even pricing**, or a variation called **target profit pricing**. The firm tries to determine the price at which it will break even or make the target profit it is seeking.

The major problem with this analysis is that it fails to consider customer value and the relationship between price and demand.

As the *price* increases, *demand* decreases.

Use **Chapter Objective** 2 here. Use **Key Terms** *Cost-Plus Pricing, Breakeven Pricing (Target Profit Pricing)* here. Use **Figure** 9.3 here. Use **Linking the Concepts** here. Use **Discussing the Issues** 2 here.

Other Internal and External Considerations Affecting Price Decisions

Overall Marketing Strategy, Objectives, and Mix

General pricing objectives might include survival, current profit maximization, market share leadership, or customer retention and relationship building.

Price is only one of the marketing mix tools that a company uses to achieve its marketing objectives.

Price decisions must be coordinated with product design, distribution, and promotion decisions to form a consistent and effective integrated marketing program.

Use **Video Case** here.

Companies often position their products on price and then tailor other marketing mix decisions to the prices they want to charge.

Target costing starts with an ideal selling price based on customer-value considerations, and then targets costs that will ensure that the price is met.

Use **Key Term** *Target Costing* here.

Companies may deemphasize price and use other marketing mix tools to create ***nonprice*** positions.

Organizational Considerations

In small companies, prices are often set by top management rather than by the marketing or sales departments.

In large companies, pricing is typically handled by divisional or product line managers.

In industrial markets, salespeople may be allowed to negotiate with customers within certain price ranges.

In industries in which pricing is a key factor, companies often have pricing departments to set the best prices or to help others in setting them.

The Market and Demand

Pricing in Different Types of Markets

Pure competition: The market consists of many buyers and sellers trading in a uniform commodity. No single buyer or seller has much effect on the going market price.

In a purely competitive market, marketing research, product development, pricing, advertising, and sales promotion play little or no role. Thus, sellers in these markets do not spend much time on marketing strategy.

Monopolistic competition: The market consists of many buyers and sellers who trade over a range of prices rather than a single market price. A range of prices occurs because sellers can differentiate their offers to buyers.

Oligopolistic competition: The market consists of a few sellers who are highly sensitive to each other's pricing and marketing strategies.

There are few sellers because it is difficult for new sellers to enter the market.

Pure monopoly: The market consists of one seller. The seller may be a government monopoly, a private regulated monopoly, or a private nonregulated monopoly.

Use **Marketing at Work** 9-1 here.

Applying the Concept

Name one company in each of the following categories: a purely competitive market, a monopolistic competition, an oligopolistic market, and a pure monopoly. How do they differ in terms of products or services offered and how responsive they are to customers? How about in how they price their products and services?

Analyzing the Price-Demand Relationship

The relationship between the price charged and the resulting demand level is shown in the **demand curve** (Figure 9.4).

Use **Key Term** *Demand Curve* here.
Use **Figure** 9.4 here.

In the case of prestige goods, the demand curve sometimes slopes upward. Consumers think that higher prices mean more quality.

In a monopoly, the demand curve shows the total market demand resulting from different prices.

If the company faces competition, its demand at different prices will depend on whether competitors' prices stay constant or change with the company's own prices.

Price Elasticity of Demand

Price elasticity: How responsive demand will be to a change in price.

If demand hardly changes with a small change in price, we say demand is ***inelastic***.

If demand changes greatly with a small change in price, we say the demand is ***elastic***.

Use **Key Term** *Price Elasticity* here.

Competitors' Strategies and Prices

In assessing competitors' pricing strategies, the company should ask several questions.

1. How does the company's market offering compare with competitors' offerings in terms of customer value?
2. How strong are current competitors and what are their current pricing strategies?
3. How does the competitive landscape influence customer price sensitivity?

Other External Factors

Economic conditions can have a strong impact on the firm's pricing strategies.

The company must also consider what impact its prices will have on other parties in its environment, such as resellers and the government.

Social concerns may have to be taken into account.

New-Product Pricing Strategies

Market-Skimming Pricing

Market-skimming pricing (or **price skimming**) is setting high initial prices to "skim" revenues layer by layer from the market.

Market skimming makes sense under certain conditions.

1. The product's quality and image must support its higher price and enough buyers must want the product at that price.
2. The costs of producing a smaller volume cannot be so high that they cancel the advantage of charging more.

3. Competitors should not be able to enter the market easily and undercut the high price.

Use **Key Term** *Market-Skimming Pricing* here. Use **Chapter Objective** 3 here. Use **Discussing the Issues** 3 here.

Market-Penetration Pricing

Market-penetration pricing is setting a low initial price in order to ***penetrate*** the market quickly and deeply—to attract a large number of buyers quickly and win a large market share.

Several conditions must be met for this strategy to work.

1. The market must be highly price sensitive so that a low price produces more market growth.
2. Production and distribution costs must fall as sales volume increases.
3. The low price must help keep out the competition, and the penetration pricer must maintain its low-price position.

Use **Key Term** *Market-Penetration Pricing* here.

Product Mix Pricing Strategies (Table 9.1)

In **product line pricing**, management must decide on the price steps to set between the various products in a line.

Use Table **9.1** here.

The price steps should take into account cost differences between the products in the line.

Use **Key Term** *Product Line Pricing* here. Use **Chapter Objective** 4 here. Use **Application Question** 3 here.

Optional-product pricing is offering to sell optional or accessory products along with their main product.

Use **Key Term** *Optional-Product Pricing* here.

In **captive-product pricing,** companies make products that must be used along with a main product.

Use **Key Term** *Captive-Product Pricing* here.

In the case of services, captive-product pricing is called ***two-part pricing***. The price of the service is broken into a ***fixed fee*** plus a ***variable usage rate.***

Using **by-product pricing**, the company seeks a market for the by-products produced in the generation of some products and services.

Use **Key Term** *By-Product Pricing* here.

Using **product bundle pricing**, sellers often combine several of their products and offer the bundle at a reduced price.

Use **Key Term** *Product Bundle Pricing* here. Use **Discussing the Issues** 4 here.

Price Adjustment Strategies (Table 9.2)

Use **Chapter Objective** 5 here. Use Table **9.2** here.

Discounts include:

- ***Cash discount***, a price reduction to buyers who pay their bills promptly.
- ***Quantity discount*** is a price reduction to buyers who buy large volumes.
- ***Functional discount*** (also called a ***trade discount***) is offered by the seller to trade-channel members who perform certain functions.
- ***Seasonal discount*** is a price reduction to buyers who buy merchandise or services out of season.

Allowances are a reduction from the list price.

- ***Trade-in allowances*** are price reductions given for turning in an old item when buying a new one.
- ***Promotional allowances*** are payments or price reductions to reward dealers for participating in advertising and sales support programs.

Use **Key Terms** *Discount, Allowance* here.

Segmented pricing occurs when the company sells a product or service at two or more prices, even though the difference in prices is not based on differences in costs.

- ***Customer-segment pricing:*** different customers pay different prices for the same product or service.
- ***Product-form pricing:*** Different versions of the product are priced differently but not according to differences in their costs.
- ***Location pricing:*** A company charges different prices for different locations, even though the cost of offering each location is the same.
- ***Time pricing:*** A firm varies its price by the season, the month, the day, and even the hour.

Use **Key Term** *Segmented Pricing* here.

Applying the Concept
Why would a movie theater use segmented pricing? How is it applied? What kinds of companies use product-form pricing? Give some examples.

Other names for segmented pricing include: *revenue management* and *yield management.*

Psychological pricing occurs when sellers consider the psychology of prices and not simply the economics.

One aspect of psychological pricing is **reference prices**—prices that buyers carry in their minds and refer to when looking at a given product.

Use **Key Terms** *Psychological Pricing, Reference Prices* here.
Use **Discussing the Issues** 5 here.

With **Promotional pricing**, companies will temporarily price their products below list price and sometimes even below cost to create buying excitement and urgency.

- ***Loss leaders:*** Selling a product at less than cost.
- ***Special-event pricing:*** Pricing differently in certain seasons to draw more customers.
- ***Cash rebates:*** Consumers who buy the product from dealers within a specified time; the manufacturer sends the rebate directly to the customer.

Promotional pricing can have adverse effects.

1. Price promotions can create "deal-prone" customers who wait until brands go on sale before buying them.
2. Constantly reduced prices can erode a brand's value in the eyes of customers.
3. Promotional pricing can lead to industry price wars.

Use **Key Term** *Promotional Pricing* here.
Use **Linking the Concepts** here.

Geographical Pricing involves deciding how to price its products for customers located in different parts of the country or world.

Use **Key Term** *Geographical Pricing* here.

- **FOB-origin pricing:** The goods are placed ***free on board*** (hence, *FOB*) a carrier. At that point the title and responsibility pass to the customer, who pays the freight from the factory to the destination.
- **Uniform-delivered pricing** is the opposite of FOB pricing. Here, the company

charges the same price plus freight to all customers, regardless of their location.

- **Zone pricing** falls between FOB-origin pricing and uniform-delivered pricing. All customers within a given zone pay a single total price; the more distant the zone, the higher the price.
- **Basing-point pricing**: The seller selects a given city as a "basing point" and charges all customers the freight cost from that city to the customer location, regardless of the city from which the goods are actually shipped.
- **Freight-absorption pricing**. Using this strategy, the seller absorbs all or part of the actual freight charges in order to get the desired business.

Use **Focus on Ethics** here.

Dynamic Pricing is adjusting prices continually to meet the characteristics and needs of individual customers and situations.

Dynamic pricing offers many advantages:

- Internet sellers can mine their databases to gauge a specific shopper's desires, measure his or her means, and instantaneously tailor products to fit that shopper's behavior, and price products accordingly.

- Internet buyers benefit from the Web and dynamic pricing. A wealth of ***shopping bots***—such as Bizrate.com—offer instant product and price comparisons from thousands of vendors.

- Buyers can also negotiate prices at online auction sites and exchanges.

International Pricing

The price that a company should charge in a specific country depends on many factors, including economic conditions, competitive situations, laws and regulations, and development of the wholesaling and retailing system.

Costs play an important role in setting international prices.

Price Changes

Initiating Price Cuts

Several situations may lead a firm to consider cutting its price.

- Excess capacity.
- Falling demand in the face of strong price competition.
- Desire to dominate market.

Initiating Price Increases

Use **Discussing the Issues** 6 here.

A major factor in price increases is cost inflation.

When raising prices, the company must avoid being perceived as a price gouger.

Techniques for avoiding this problem:

- Maintain a sense of fairness surrounding any price increase.
- Making low-visibility price moves first:

Buyer Reactions to Price Changes

They may view price *cuts* or price *increases* in several ways.

Competitor Reactions to Price Changes

Competitors are most likely to react when the number of firms involved is small, when the product is uniform, and when the buyers are well informed about products and prices.

Responding to Price Changes (Figure 9.5)

The firm needs to consider several issues: Why did the competitor change the price? Is the price change temporary or permanent? What will happen to the company's market share and profits if it does not respond? Are other competitors going to respond?

Figure 9.5 shows the ways a company might assess and respond to a competitor's price cut.

Use **Figure** 9.5 here.

1. The company could ***reduce its price*** to match the competitor's price.
2. The company could maintain its price but ***raise the perceived value*** of its offer.
3. The company could *improve quality and increase price*, moving its brand into a higher price-value position.
4. The company could ***launch a low-price "fighting brand"***—adding a lower-price item to the line or creating a separate lower-price brand.

Use **Chapter Objective** 6 here.

Public Policy and Pricing

Figure 9.6 shows the major public policy issues in pricing.

Use **Figure** 9.6 here.

Pricing Within Channel Levels

Federal legislation on ***price-fixing*** states that sellers must set prices without talking to competitors. Otherwise, price collusion is suspected.

Sellers are prohibited from using ***predatory pricing***—selling below cost with the intention of punishing a competitor or gaining higher long-run profits by putting competitors out of business.

Pricing Across Channel Levels

The Robinson-Patman Act seeks to prevent unfair ***price discrimination*** by ensuring that sellers offer the same price terms to customers at a given level of trade.

Laws prohibit ***retail (or resale) price maintenance***—a manufacturer cannot require dealers to charge a specified retail price for its product.

Although the seller can propose a manufacturer's ***suggested*** retail price to dealers, it cannot refuse to sell to a dealer who takes independent pricing action, nor can it punish the dealer by shipping late or denying advertising allowances.

Deceptive pricing occurs when a seller states prices or price savings that mislead consumers or are not actually available to consumers.

Other deceptive pricing issues include ***scanner fraud*** and ***price confusion***.

<u>Travel Log</u>

Discussing the Issues

1. What is price? List five other words that mean the same thing as price (for example, tuition). (AACSB: Communication; Reflective Thinking)

   Answer:

   In the narrowest sense, **price** is the amount of money charged for a product or service. More broadly, price is the sum of all the values that customers give up in order to gain the benefits of having or using a product or service. Examples of other terms used for price are rent, fee, rate, tax, toll, commission, and assessment.

2. Explain the differences between value-based pricing and cost-based pricing and describe the methods of implementing each. (AACSB: Communication)

Answer:

Cost-based pricing is product driven. The company designs what it considers to be a good product, totals the costs of making the product, and sets a price that covers costs plus a target profit. The simplest pricing method is **cost-plus pricing**—adding a standard markup to the cost of the product. Another cost-oriented pricing approach is **break-even pricing**, or a variation called **target profit pricing**. The firm tries to determine the price at which it will break even or make the target profit it is seeking. Target pricing uses the concept of a *break-even chart*, which shows the total cost and total revenue expected at different sales volume levels.

Value-based pricing uses buyers' perceptions of value, not the seller's cost, as the key to pricing. Value-based pricing means that the marketer cannot design a product and marketing program and then set the price. The company sets its target price based on customer perceptions of the product value. The targeted value and price then drive decisions about product design and what costs can be incurred. **Good-value pricing** strategies offer just the right combination of quality and good service at a fair price. In many cases, this has involved introducing less-expensive versions of established, brand name products. In other cases, good-value pricing has involved redesigning existing brands to offer more quality for a given price or the same quality for less. An important type of good-value pricing at the retail level is *everyday low pricing (EDLP)*. EDLP involves charging a constant, everyday low price with few or no temporary price discounts. To increase their pricing power, many companies adopt **value-added pricing** strategies. Rather than cutting prices to match competitors, they attach value-added features and services to differentiate their offers and thus support higher prices.

3. Why would a marketer of high-tech innovative products choose market-skimming pricing rather than market-penetration pricing when launching a new product? (AACSB: Communication)

   Answer:

   Many companies that invent new products set high initial prices to "skim" revenues layer by layer from the market, a strategy called **market-skimming pricing** (or **price skimming**). Market skimming makes sense only under certain conditions. First, the product's quality and image must support its higher price and enough buyers must want the product at that price. Second, the costs of producing a smaller volume cannot be so high that they cancel the advantage of charging more. Finally, competitors should not be able to enter the market easily and undercut the high price.

4. Name and briefly describe the five product mix pricing decisions. (AACSB: Communication)

Answer:

The product mix pricing situations are: (1) product line pricing, (2) optional-product pricing, (3) captive-product pricing, (4) by-product pricing, and (5) product bundle pricing.

In **product line pricing**, management must decide on the price steps to set between the various products in a line. The price steps should take into account cost differences between the products in the line. More importantly, they should account for differences in customer perceptions of the value of different features.

Many companies use **optional-product pricing**—offering to sell optional or accessory products along with their main product. Pricing these options is a sticky problem, though, as automobiles marketers found when advertising the most basic, stripped down version of their cars.

Companies that make products that must be used along with a main product are using **captive-product pricing**. Examples of captive products are razor blade cartridges, video games, and printer cartridges. Producers of the main products (razors, video game consoles, and printers) often price them low and set high markups on the supplies. Companies using captive-product pricing must be careful—consumers trapped into buying expensive supplies may come to resent the brand that ensnared them. In the case of services, captive-product pricing is called *two-part pricing*. The price of the service is broken into a *fixed fee* plus a *variable usage rate*.

Producing products and services often generates by-products. If the by-products have no value and if getting rid of them is costly, this will affect the pricing of the main product. Using **by-product pricing**, the company seeks a market for these by-products to help offset the costs of disposing of them and to help make the price of the main product more competitive. The by-products themselves can even turn out to be profitable.

Using **product bundle pricing**, sellers often combine several of their products and offer the bundle at a reduced price. For example, fast-food restaurants bundle a burger, fries, and a soft drink at a "meal" price.

5. Psychological pricing is a price-adjustment strategy often used by retailers. Explain this pricing strategy. How do reference prices affect psychological pricing decisions? (AACSB: Communication; Reflective Thinking)

Answer:

In using **psychological pricing**, sellers consider the psychology of prices and not simply the economics. For example, consumers usually perceive higher-priced products as having higher quality. When they can judge the quality of a product by examining it or by calling on past experience with it, they use price less to judge quality. But when they cannot judge quality because they lack the information or skill, price becomes an important quality signal. **Reference prices** are prices that buyers carry in their minds and refer to when looking at a given product. The reference price might be formed by noting current prices, remembering past prices, or assessing the buying situation.

6. Under what conditions will a marketer consider a price increase and what factors must be considered before raising price? (AACSB: Communication)

   Answer:

   A successful price increase can greatly improve profits. For example, if the company's profit margin is 3 percent of sales, a 1 percent price increase will boost profits by 33 percent if sales volume is unaffected. A major factor in price increases is cost inflation. Rising costs squeeze profit margins and lead companies to pass cost increases along to customers. Another factor leading to price increases is overdemand—when a company cannot supply all that its customers need, it may raise its prices, ration products to customers, or both. When raising prices, the company must avoid being perceived as a price gouger. There are some techniques for avoiding this problem. One is to maintain a sense of fairness surrounding any price increase. Price increases should be supported by company communications telling customers why prices are being raised. Making low-visibility price moves first is also a good technique: Some examples include dropping discounts, increasing minimum order sizes, and curtailing production of low-margin products. The company sales force should help business customers find ways to economize.

Application Questions

1. Visit U.S. *News & World Report* at http://www.usnews.com/usnews/edu/college/rankings/bvrankindex_brief.php for a list of schools that offer the best value. Click on the "Best Colleges Home" tab and then on the "About the Rankings" tab. Under "Methodology" click on "Best Values Methodology" to learn how value is defined. Is this a valid definition of value? (AACSB: Communication; Use of IT; Reflective Thinking)

   Answer:

   U.S. News & World Report calculates value based on the academic ranking of the school in relation to the average cost to a student once financial aid is considered. It can be argued that this formula does not truly take into account the *customer's* perception of value because it does not survey customers as to the benefits they perceive they receive from the university.

2. In a small group, brainstorm ideas about a service targeted toward college students (such as laundry pick up and delivery). Have each member of your group talk to five other students about their perceptions of value regarding this service, what they desire

is this type of service, and the price they are be willing to pay for it. Write a brief report on what your group learned and discuss the basis on which price is determined. (AACSB: Communication; Reflective Thinking)

Answer:

Students' responses will vary, but they should indicate that this is a form of value-based pricing. **Value-based pricing** uses buyers' perceptions of value, not the seller's cost, as the key to pricing. Value-based pricing means that the marketer cannot design a product and marketing program and then set the price. Price is considered along with the other marketing mix variables *before* the marketing program is set.

3. You are an owner of a small independent chain of coffee houses competing head-to-head with Starbuck's. The retail price your customers pay for coffee is exactly the same as at Starbuck's. The wholesale price you pay for roasted coffee beans has increased by 25 percent. You know that you cannot absorb this increase and that you must pass it on to your customers. However, you are concerned about the consequences of an open price increase. Discuss three alternative price-increase strategies that address these concerns. (AACSB: Communication; Reflective Thinking)

   Answer:

   Students' responses will vary, but some suggestions are provided here. One alternative is to communicate to the customers the real reason for the price increase—no rain or too much rain in Antigua, increase in transportation costs, tariff increases, and so on. Another alternative is to implement a low-visibility price increase. Some examples include eliminating discounts, increasing minimum order sizes, and curtailing production of low-margin products. A third alternative is to increase price with an announced change to a higher quality coffee, or to consider the introduction of a lower-quality product at the old prices.

Under the Hood: Focus on Technology

Consumers have always been price conscious, and price comparison shopping is now easier than ever. Comparing prices used to require that shoppers visit stores or call to get price information. But now, with the click of a mouse, buyers can compare the prices of several retailers instantaneously. At one time, some experts even predicted that Internet "shopping bots" would make price comparisons so simple that prices would be driven down as retailers were forced to match each others' prices to stay in business.

1. Identify three comparison price shopping Web sites and shop for an MP3 player of your choice. Compare the price ranges given at these three Web sites. Has price compression occurred as predicted? (AACSB: Communication; Use of IT)

Answer:

There are several online comparison price shopping sites, such as www.BizRate.com, www.PriceGrabber.com, www.Shopzilla.com, www.Pricescanner.com, www.mysimon.com, and www.DealTime.com.

Students' responses will vary depending on the product chosen, but just a quick search of a 30GB iPod came back with prices ranging from under $200 to more than $300. Searches for other MP3 players and brands will most likely result in wide variations in price as well.

2. Although price is important, other factors influence consumers' purchase decisions. What information, in addition to price, is available from the comparison shopping Web sites you accessed? (AACSB: Communication; Use of IT)

   Answer:

   Many of the shopping comparison Web sites include reviews of retailers to help consumers decide whether or not to trust an unfamiliar retailer. Some of the comparison shopping Web sites even highlight the "best price from a trusted retailer."

Focus on Ethics

Marketers often use pricing to influence consumer behavior. For example, movie theaters smooth out demand by charging less for an afternoon matinee to draw more patrons at this slower time. Similarly, airlines charge lower prices for flyers staying over a Saturday night, causing many buyers to stay an extra night rather than flying home before the weekend. Such pricing shifts demand from one time period to another. A relatively new form of this pricing strategy is called *congestion pricing*. Used in London since 2003, such pricing encourages commuters to use public transportation to relieve congestion—to shift modes of transportation rather than times. However, rather than rewarding individuals for performing the desired behavior, it punishes them for undesirable behavior. Londoners must pay £8 per day to travel across 8.5 square miles of central London. Singapore and Stockholm are using a tolling scheme as well. In the United States, if lawmaker's approve Mayor Bloomberg's plan, New York City's proposed congestion pricing plan will receive more than $350 million in Federal funding. Although several U.S. cities are congested, New York is ideal for congestion pricing. Manhattan, the most congested area of New York City, is surrounded by water, making it relatively easy to charge drivers both coming and going.

1. Research congestion pricing and discuss three pros and three cons of this pricing strategy. (AACSB: Communication; Reflective Thinking)

Answer:

Students will find considerable information on congestion pricing. Examples of pros and cons are provided below.

Pros:

- Reduces gridlock
- Increases air quality
- Proceeds can be used to enhance public transit
- Increases residential values in congested areas

Cons:

- Reduces property values as businesses move out of congested areas
- Reduces parking lot values
- Increases congestion at entry points (toll booths)
- Reduces retail sales as shoppers stay home
- Hurts businesses that must travel within congested areas (such as delivery trucks)

2. Some critics argue that this type of pricing potentially harms small businesses that operate within congested areas (florists, for example) or employees who must travel to such areas for their jobs. Is it ethical for governments to charge drivers in this way? Suggest some compromise solutions. (AACSB: Communication; Ethical Reasoning)
Answer:

Students' responses will vary. Some may discuss the radio tags that are in use at several toll locations that allow drivers to move through more quickly. Discounts could be given to various drivers or types of businesses based on their need for traveling into the congested area.

GREAT IDEAS

Barriers to Effective Learning

1. Even if a few students have worked in a family business, it is a very safe bet that none of them have ever set prices on anything. Even if they are a devotee of eBay and have been buying and selling items for years, they still won't have set prices because of the auction environment of that and other sites that have sprung up in the years since the explosion of the World Wide Web. So, although the "What Is a Price?" section is very short, it is well worth spending some time talking about the difference between fixed-price policies and dynamic pricing. A discussion of what it's like to buy a meal at a restaurant, where you cannot typically haggle on price, and buying a car, where you are expected to haggle on price, can drive

home the difference between the two. A discussion of what has happened with auctions and exchanges online will also help.

2. There are so many factors to consider in setting prices that the students might begin to feel overwhelmed very early in the chapter. It might be easier to discuss this in the context of a new business the class will launch—say, a laundry service on campus. Most students hate doing laundry, so they are willing to pay for someone to do it for them, especially with pickup and delivery service. You can easily run through the internal and external factors that would affect such a service, and even discuss pricing strategy if a competitor were to develop a similar service.
3. Students may also need further explanation regarding why cost-based pricing isn't the right way to price everything. It's simple, it's easy to apply a formula, and there is no guesswork involved. You need to drive home the point that it ignores the customer completely—cost-based pricing is internally focused, without a thought to the demand parameters or competitors' prices. You can talk about this from the perspective of a high-cost manufacturer—how much would they be able to sell if their product cost 50% more than the competition simply because the company hadn't figured out how to manufacture it effectively?
4. Value-based pricing could engender a considerable amount of conversation, particularly if someone thinks it is unethical to charge a price for something that yields the company a very large margin. Why wouldn't you treat customers "right" by charging them less? A discussion of the meaning of customer focus and of benefits to the customer will help the class to understand that if the customer thinks he is getting value, he will happily pay the price.
5. After this discussion, the students might then be quite confused that value pricing and everyday low pricing are subsets of value-based pricing. It might be helpful here to differentiate between value-based pricing in a business market and value or EDLP in the consumer market. Many businesses will buy based on a value they assign to a product or service, often in terms of ROI for themselves. Consumers will rarely do that explicitly and, at least for basic necessities, will often buy based on price. It is still value-based pricing.
6. Product line pricing can easily be illustrated with the example of gasoline. Virtually every gas station in this country sets the prices of each of its grades of gas between 8 and 10 cents apart (e.g., regular for $2.93, the next grade for $3.03, and the premium grade for $3.13). This is an everyday example of price steps with which everyone will have experience. Captive-product pricing will also be a fairly easy concept to understand with the example of razors and razor blades. Optional-product pricing could cause some problems, however. Discussing the example of buying a computer with or without a service agreement could help explain how this is done.
7. Segmented pricing can easily be explained by using the examples of senior citizen discounts or the discount you get at the movies for going during the day (matinee prices). Most students today have traveled, so it is also useful to talk about the airlines' use of yield management.
8. Geographical pricing can cause some problems. Although the students might have heard of FOB pricing, it will not be a common term for them. Explaining that this

is basically a decision between the customer paying the freight and the company paying the freight will help, especially because the majority of the students will have purchased at least something online, so they will have experience with freight or delivery charges.

Student Projects

1. Take a drive around town and look at the pricing of gasoline at a variety of different stations. Use Product Line Pricing to explain what you are seeing.
2. How does Wal-Mart make use of Good-Value Pricing?
3. Explain how companies such as Dell use Cost-Plus Pricing. What are the competitive disadvantages of such pricing strategies?
4. Take a look at Rolex watches (www.rolex.com/en). What pricing strategy is being employed here? What message is this pricing strategy sending to potential consumers?
5. Walk though your favorite supermarket or discount store. Make a list of 10 products that employ Captive-Product Pricing.

Small Group Assignment

Form students into groups of three to five. Each group should read the opening vignette to the chapter on Ryanair. Each group should then answer the following questions:

1. Is Ryanair utilizing an effective pricing strategy?
2. How has Ryanair been able to maintain their current pricing strategy in the wake of the turbulent air travel market?
3. What is Ryanair's position in the mind of the customer?

Each group should share its findings with the class.

Individual Assignment

Product Bundle Pricing has become a very popular pricing strategy. Review and compare the current pricing strategies being used by your local cable provider and that offered by DirectTV (www.directtv.com). Are they making the most of product bundle pricing? What suggestions could you offer to improve their competitive positions against one another?

Think-Pair-Share

Consider the following questions, format an answer, pair with the student on your right, share your thoughts with one another, and respond to questions from the instructor.

1. Under what conditions should market-penetration pricing be used?
2. Provide examples of when promotional pricing may be considered unethical.
3. What is predatory pricing and why is its use questionable?

4. When raising prices, care must be taken so that the company does not appear to be a price gouger. What techniques can be employed to assist in this?
5. Give examples of unfair price discrimination.

Classroom Exercise/Homework Assignment

For the ultimate in Dynamic Pricing, one need only look to the air travel industry. Go online to Expedia (www.expedia.com), one popular booking engine, and "book" yourself a flight to Cancun for the Christmas break. Examine the vast differences in prices offered and explain why this is occurring. Now, "book" this same trip to Cancun, put add in a hotel stay for six night. Again, examine and explain the vast differences in prices offered.

Classroom Management Strategies

This is a very long chapter, and it might be best to break it into two class periods. It is noted below where a reasonable break would be if you are able to do so.

1. Discussing the history of pricing, and the differences between fixed prices and dynamic prices is worthy of at least 5 minutes. You can also tie dynamic pricing back into the individual markets that were discussed in a previous chapter to drive home the value of dynamic pricing.
2. If you are breaking the chapter into two class sessions, spend 20 minutes on Factors to Consider when Setting Prices. If you do not have that luxury, 10 minutes will suffice. In this case, you will want to hit the major factors of marketing objectives and marketing mix strategy for internal factors, and the market and demand for the external factors.
3. Another 20 minutes should be spent on General Pricing Approaches in a two-session approach to this chapter. If covering the material in one session, spend 10 minutes on this. In this approach, focus on the differences among the three pricing approaches.
4. New Product Pricing Strategies should be covered in 15 minutes. In one class session, spend about 5 minutes covering the differences between market skimming and market penetration. This would also be where you should break for the session if you are going to continue with the chapter in the next class.
5. Product Mix Pricing Strategies covers a lot of information. In the second class session, spend 20 minutes on this topic, being sure to cover each of the five subsections. In one class period, you can cover this in 10 minutes by focusing on the three pricing strategies, briefly explaining the last two.
6. Price-Adjustment Strategies also covers a lot of material. In a second class section, 20 minutes should also be spent on this topic. In one, again you can cover this in 10 minutes by focusing on the first three subsections.
7. Regardless of whether you are presenting this material in one class or two, spend 15 minutes on Price Changes. This is an important element to understanding pricing, and this is the area where many marketing managers make their money when it comes to pricing.

CHAPTER 10
Marketing Channels: Delivering Customer Value

Previewing the Concepts: Chapter Objectives

1. Explain why companies use marketing channels and discuss the functions these channels perform
2. Discuss how channel members interact and how they organize to perform the work of the channel
3. Identify the major channel alternatives open to a company
4. Explain how companies select, motivate, and evaluate channel members
5. Discuss the nature and importance of marketing logistics and integrated supply chain management

JUST THE BASICS

Chapter Overview

This chapter deals with distribution.

An individual firm's success depends not only on how well *it* performs but also on how well its *entire marketing channel* competes with competitors' channels.

To be good at customer relationship management, a company must also be good at partner relationship management.

The first part of this chapter explores the nature of marketing channels and the marketer's channel design and management decisions.

We then examine physical distribution—or logistics—an area that is growing dramatically in importance and sophistication.

Annotated Chapter Notes/Outline

Introduction

Caterpillar sells more than 300 products in nearly 200 countries, with sales of more than $41 billion annually. Over the past five years, sales have more than doubled and profits have shot up more than four-fold.

"Buy the Iron, Get the Company"—that's a powerful value proposition. It means that when you buy Cat equipment, you become a member of the Caterpillar family.

Caterpillar and its dealers work in close harmony to find better ways to bring value to customers.

The partnership between Caterpillar and its dealers rests on a handful of basic principles and practices:

- *Dealer profitability:* Caterpillar's rule: "Share the gain as well as the pain."
- *Extraordinary dealer support:* The Company ships 80 percent of parts orders immediately and 99 percent on the same day the order is received.
- *Communications:* Caterpillar communicates with its dealers—fully, frequently, and honestly.
- *Dealer performance:* Caterpillar does all it can to ensure that its dealerships are run well.
- *Personal relationships:* Cat forms close personal ties with its dealers in a kind of family relationship.

Most firms cannot bring value to customers by themselves. Instead, they must work closely with other firms in a larger value-delivery network.

Use **Chapter Objective** 1 here.

Supply Chains and the Value Delivery Network

The ***supply chain*** consists of "upstream" and "downstream" partners.

Upstream from the company is the set of firms that supply the raw materials, components, parts, information, finances, and expertise needed to create a product or service.

Use **Key Term** *Marketing Channel (Distribution Channel)* here.

Marketers have traditionally focused on the "downstream" side of the supply chain—on the ***marketing channels*** (**or** ***distribution channels***) that look forward toward the customer.

A better term would be ***demand chain*** because it suggests a ***sense-and-respond*** view of the market.

Under this view, planning starts with the needs of target customers, to which the company responds by organizing a chain of resources and activities with the goal of creating customer value.

Use **Key Term** *Value Delivery Network* here.

As defined in Chapter 2, a **value delivery network** is made up of the company, suppliers, distributors, and ultimately customers who "partner" with each other to improve the performance of the entire system.

The Nature and Importance of Marketing Channels

Producers try to forge a **marketing channel** (or **distribution channel**)—a set of interdependent organizations that help make a product or service available for use or consumption by the consumer or business user.

Use **Figure** 10-1 here.
Use **Applications Questions** 1 here.

How Channel Members Add Value

Figure 10.1 shows how using intermediaries can provide economies.

The role of marketing intermediaries is to transform the assortments of products made by producers into the assortments wanted by consumers.

Members of the marketing channel perform many key functions. Some help to complete transactions:

- *Information:* Gathering and distributing marketing research and intelligence information about actors and forces in the marketing environment needed for planning and aiding exchange.
- *Promotion*: Developing and spreading persuasive communications about an offer.
- *Contact*: Finding and communicating with prospective buyers.
- *Matching*: Shaping and fitting the offer to the buyer's needs, including activities such as manufacturing, grading, assembling, and packaging.
- *Negotiation*: Reaching an agreement on price and other terms of the offer so that ownership or possession can be transferred.

Others help to fulfill the completed transactions:

- *Physical distribution*: Transporting and storing goods.
- *Financing*: Acquiring and using funds to cover the costs of the channel work.
- *Risk taking*: Assuming the risks of carrying out the channel work.

Let's Discuss This

Mobile phone manufacturers largely distribute their products through service providers such as Verizon, AT&T Wireless, and T-Mobile. Why have they chosen this method of distribution?

Number of Channel Levels

A **channel level** is each layer of marketing intermediaries that performs some work in bringing the product and its ownership closer to the final buyer.

Use **Key Term** *Channel Level* here.

The *number of intermediary levels* indicates the *length* of a channel. (Figure 10.2)

A **direct marketing channel** has no intermediary levels; the company sells directly to consumers.

An **indirect marketing channel** contains one or more intermediaries.

Use **Key Terms** *Direct Marketing Channel, Indirect Marketing Channel* here. Use **Figure** 10-2 here.

From the producer's point of view, a greater number of levels means less control and greater channel complexity.

Use **Chapter Objective** 2 here.

Channel Behavior and Organization

Channel Behavior

A marketing channel consists of firms that have partnered for their common good. Each channel member depends on the others.

Each channel member plays a specialized role in the channel. The channel will be most effective when each member assumes the tasks it can do best.

Use **Key Term** *Channel Conflict* here.

Disagreements over goals, roles, and rewards generate **channel conflict.**

Horizontal conflict occurs among firms at the same level of the channel.

Vertical conflict occurs between different levels of the same channel.
Vertical Marketing Systems

Use **Key Term** *Conventional Distribution Channel* here.

A **conventional distribution channel** consists of one or more independent producers, wholesalers, and retailers. Each is a separate business seeking to maximize its own profits, perhaps even at the expense of the system as a whole.

A **vertical marketing system (VMS)** consists of producers, wholesalers, and retailers acting as a unified system. One channel member owns the others, has contracts with them, or wields so much power that they must all cooperate. (Figure 10.3)

A ***Corporate VMS*** integrates successive stages of production and distribution under single ownership.

A ***Contractual VMS*** consists of independent firms at different levels of production and distribution who join together through contracts to obtain more economies or sales impact than each could achieve alone.

The **franchise organization** is the most common type of contractual relationship—a channel member called a ***franchisor*** links several stages in the production-distribution process.

There are three types of franchises.

1. The *manufacturer-sponsored retailer franchise system*—for example, Ford and its network of independent franchised dealers.
2. The *manufacturer-sponsored wholesaler franchise system*—Coca-Cola licenses bottlers (wholesalers) in various markets who buy Coca-Cola syrup concentrate and then bottle and sell the finished product to retailers in local markets.
3. The *service-firm-sponsored retailer franchise system*—examples are found in the auto-rental business (Avis), the fast-food service business (McDonald's), and the motel business (Ramada Inn).

In an ***Administered VMS,*** leadership is assumed not through common ownership or contractual ties but through the size and power of one or a few dominant channel members.

Use **Key Terms** *Vertical Marketing System (VMS), Corporate VMS, Contractual VMS, Franchise Organization,* and *Administered VMS* here.
Use **Figure** 10-3 here.
Use **Discussing the Issues** 1 here.
Use **Application Question** 2 here.

Horizontal Marketing Systems: Two or more companies at one level join together to follow a new marketing opportunity.

> Use **Key Term** *Horizontal Marketing System* here.
> Use **Discussing the Issues** 2 here.

> **Applying the Concept**
> Why are there bank branches in many grocery stores today? Discuss why this application of a horizontal marketing system makes sense for both the grocery store and the bank.

Multichannel Distribution Systems (often called ***hybrid marketing channels***)**:** Occurs when a single firm sets up two or more marketing channels to reach one or more customer segments. (Figure 10.4)

> Use **Key Term** *Multichannel Distribution System* here.
> Use **Figure** 10-4 here.

Changing Channel Organization

Disintermediation occurs when product or service producers cut out intermediaries and go directly to final buyers, or when radically new types of channel intermediaries displace traditional ones.

> Use **Key Term** *Disintermediation* here.
> Use **Linking the Concepts** here.
> Use **Discussing the Issues** 3 here.

Channel Design Decisions

Marketing channel design calls for analyzing consumer needs, setting channel objectives, identifying major channel alternatives, and evaluating them.

> Use **Key Term** *Marketing Channel Design* here.

Analyzing Consumer Needs

The company must balance consumer needs not only against the feasibility and costs of meeting these needs but also against customer price preferences.

Setting Channel Objectives

Companies should state their marketing channel objectives in terms of targeted levels of customer service.

The company should decide which segments to serve and the best channels to use in each case.

The company's channel objectives are influenced by the nature of the company, its products, its marketing intermediaries, its competitors, and the environment.

Environmental factors such as economic conditions and legal constraints may affect channel objectives and design.

Identifying Major Alternatives

Types of Intermediaries

A firm should identify the types of channel members available to carry out its channel work.

Number of Marketing Intermediaries

Companies must also determine the number of channel members to use at each level.

Three strategies are available:

1. **Intensive distribution:** Ideal for producers of convenience products and common raw materials. It is a strategy in which they stock their products in as many outlets as possible.
2. **Exclusive distribution:** Purposely limit the number of intermediaries handling their products. The producer gives only a limited number of dealers the exclusive right to distribute its products in their territories.
3. **Selective distribution:** This is the use of more than one, but fewer than all, of the intermediaries who are willing to carry a company's products.

Use **Key Terms** *Intensive Distribution, Exclusive Distribution,* and *Selective Distribution* here. Use **Discussing the Issues** 4 here. Use **Video Case** here. Use **Application Question** 3 here.

Responsibilities of Channel Members

The producer and intermediaries need to agree on the terms and responsibilities of each channel member.

They should agree on price policies, conditions of sale, territorial rights, and specific services to be performed by each party.

Evaluating the Major Alternatives

Using ***economic criteria***, a company compares the likely sales, costs, and profitability of different channel alternatives.

Using ***control issues*** means giving them some control over the marketing of the product, and some intermediaries take more control than others.

Using ***adaptive criteria*** means the company wants to keep the channel flexible so that it can adapt to environmental changes.

Designing International Distribution Channels

In some markets, the distribution system is complex and hard to penetrate, consisting of many layers and large numbers of intermediaries.

At the other extreme, distribution systems in developing countries may be scattered, inefficient, or altogether lacking.

Sometimes customs or government regulation can greatly restrict how a company distributes products in global markets.

Use **Chapter Objective** 3 here.

Channel Management Decisions

Marketing channel management calls for selecting, managing, and motivating individual channel members and evaluating their performance over time.

Use **Key Term** *Marketing Channel Management* here.

Selecting Channel Members

When selecting intermediaries, the company should determine what characteristics distinguish the better ones.

Managing and Motivating Channel Members

The company must sell not only *through* the intermediaries but *to* and *with* them.

Most companies practice strong ***partner relationship management (PRM)*** to forge long-term partnerships with channel members.

Evaluating Channel Members

The company should recognize and reward intermediaries who are performing well and adding good value for consumers.

A company may periodically "requalify" its intermediaries and prune the weaker ones.

Use **Linking the Concepts** here. Use **Chapter Objective** 4 here. Use **Discussing the Issues** 5 here.

Public Policy and Distribution Decisions

Use **Focus on Ethics** here.

Exclusive distribution occurs when the seller allows only certain outlets to carry its products.

Exclusive dealing occurs when the seller requires that these dealers not handle competitors' products.

Exclusive arrangements exclude other producers from selling to these dealers. This brings exclusive dealing contracts under the scope of the Clayton Act of 1914.

Exclusive territorial agreements occur when the producer agrees not to sell to other dealers in a given area, or the buyer may agree to sell only in its own territory.

Full-line pricing occurs when producers of a strong brand sell it to dealers only if the dealers will take some or all of the rest of the line. This is also known as a ***tying agreement.***

In general, sellers can drop dealers "for cause."

Marketing Logistics and Supply Chain Management

Use **Key Term** *Marketing Logistics (Physical Distribution)* here.

Nature and Importance of Marketing Logistics

Marketing logistics—also called **physical distribution**—involves planning, implementing, and controlling the physical flow of goods, services, and related information from points of origin to points of consumption to meet customer requirements at a profit.

Marketing logistics involves ***outbound distribution*** (moving products from the factory to resellers and ultimately to customers), ***inbound distribution*** (moving products and materials from suppliers to the factory) and ***reverse distribution*** (moving broken, unwanted, or excess products returned by consumers or resellers).

Use **Key Term** *Supply Chain Management* here. Use **Figure** 10-5 here.

It involves entire **supply chain management**—managing upstream and downstream value-added flows of materials, final goods, and related information among suppliers, the company, resellers, and final consumers (Figure 10.5).

Companies today are placing greater emphasis on logistics for several reasons.

1. Companies can gain a powerful competitive advantage by using improved logistics to give customers better service or lower prices.
2. Improved logistics can yield tremendous cost savings to both the company and its customers.
3. The explosion in product variety has created a need for improved logistics management.
4. Improvements in information technology have created opportunities for major gains in distribution efficiency.

Goals of the Logistics System

The goal of marketing logistics should be to provide a ***targeted*** level of customer service at the least cost.

Major Logistics Functions

Warehousing

A company must decide on ***how many*** and ***what types*** of warehouses it needs and ***where*** they will be located.

Storage warehouses store goods for moderate to long periods.

Use **Key Term** *Distribution Center* here.

Distribution centers are designed to move goods rather than just store them.

Inventory Management

Just-in-time logistics systems: Producers and retailers carry only small inventories of parts or merchandise, often only enough for a few days of operations.

Transportation

Trucks have increased their share of transportation steadily and now account for nearly 35 percent of total cargo ton-miles (more than 60 percent of actual tonnage).

Trucks are highly flexible in their routing and time schedules, and they can usually offer faster service than railroads.

They are efficient for short hauls of high-value merchandise.

Railroads account for 31 percent of total cargo ton-miles moved.

They are one of the most cost-effective modes for shipping large amounts of bulk products—coal, sand, minerals, and farm and forest products—over long distances.

Water carriers account for 11 percent of cargo ton-miles, transport large amounts of goods by ships and barges on U.S. coastal and inland waterways.

Although the cost of water transportation is very low for shipping bulky, low-value, nonperishable products, it is the slowest mode and may be affected by the weather.

Pipelines account for 16 percent of cargo ton-miles, are a specialized means of shipping petroleum, natural gas, and chemicals from sources to markets.

Air carriers transport less than 5 percent of the nation's goods. Airfreight rates are much higher than rail or truck rates.

The ***Internet*** carries digital products from producer to customer via satellite, cable, or phone wire.

Use **Key Term** *Intermodal Transportation* here. Use **Discussing the Issues** 6 here.

Intermodal transportation: Combining two or more modes of transportation.

- ***Piggyback:*** Rail and trucks;
- ***Fishyback:*** Water and trucks;
- ***Trainship**:* Water and rail;
- ***Airtruck:*** Air and trucks.

Logistics Information Management

Electronic data interchange (EDI) is the computerized exchange of data between organizations.

Vendor-managed inventory **(VMI)** systems or ***continuous inventory replenishment*** systems, is the customer sharing real-time data on sales and current inventory levels with the supplier. The supplier then takes full responsibility for managing inventories and deliveries.

Use **Key Term** *Integrated Logistics Management* here.

Integrated Logistics Management

Integrated logistics management is a concept which recognizes that providing better customer service and trimming distribution costs require ***teamwork***, both inside the company and among all the marketing channel organizations.

Cross-Functional Teamwork inside the Company

The goal of integrated supply chain management is to harmonize all of the company's logistics decisions.

Close working relationships among departments can be achieved in several ways.

- Permanent logistics committees, made up of managers responsible for different physical distribution activities.
- Supply chain manager positions that link the logistics activities of functional areas.
- System-wide supply chain management software.

Building Logistics Partnerships

***Cross-functional, cross-company teams*:** For example, P&Gers work jointly with their counterparts at Wal-Mart to find ways to squeeze costs out of their distribution system.

***Shared projects*:** For example, Home Depot allows key suppliers to use its stores as a testing ground for new merchandising programs.

Third-Party Logistics

Third-party logistics (3PL) providers help clients tighten up overstuffed supply chains, slash inventories, and get products to customers more quickly and reliably. (Also called ***outsourced logistics*** or ***contract logistics.***)

Companies use third-party logistics providers for several reasons.

1. These providers can often do it more efficiently and at lower cost.
2. Outsourcing logistics frees a company to focus more intensely on its core business.

3. Integrated logistics companies understand increasingly complex logistics environments.

Use **Key Term** *Third-Party Logistics (3PL) Provider* here. Use **Chapter Objective** 5 here.

Travel Log

Discussing the Issues

1. Explain how channel members add value for manufacturers and consumers. (AACSB: Communication)

   Answer:

   Producers use intermediaries because they create greater efficiency in making goods available to target markets. Through their contacts, experience, specialization, and scale of operation, intermediaries usually offer the firm more than it can achieve on its own. From the economic system's point of view, the role of marketing intermediaries is to transform the assortments of products made by producers into the assortments wanted by consumers. Producers make narrow assortments of products in large quantities, but consumers want broad assortments of products in small quantities. Marketing channel members buy large quantities from many producers and break them down into the smaller quantities and broader assortments wanted by consumers. Thus, intermediaries play an important role in matching supply and demand.

   In making products and services available to consumers, channel members add value by bridging the major time, place, and possession gaps that separate goods and services from those who would use them. Members of the marketing channel perform many key functions: information, promotion, contact, matching, negotiation, physical distribution, financing, and risk taking.

   The question is not *whether* these functions need to be performed—they must be—but rather *who* will perform them. To the extent that the manufacturer performs these functions, its costs go up and its prices have to be higher. When some of these functions are shifted to intermediaries, the producer's costs and prices may be lower, but the intermediaries must charge more to cover the costs of their work. In dividing the work of the channel, the various functions should be assigned to the channel members who can add the most value for the cost.

2. Discuss the differences between a conventional distribution channel, a corporate VMS, a contractual VMS, and an administered VMS. Give one example of each. (AACSB: Communication; Reflective Thinking)

   Answer:

   A conventional distribution channel consists of one or more independent producers, wholesalers, and retailers. A **corporate VMS** integrates successive stages of production and distribution under single ownership. Coordination and conflict management are attained through regular organizational channels (Luxottica). A **contractual VMS** consists of independent firms at different levels of production and distribution who join together through contracts to obtain more economies or sales impact than each could achieve alone (Holiday Inn). In an **administered VMS,** leadership is assumed not through common ownership or contractual ties but through the size and power of one or a few dominant channel members (Home Depot).

3. Define *disintermediation.* List three industries for which changes in channel systems have resulted in disintermediation. (AACSB: Communication; Reflective Thinking)

   Answer:

   Disintermediation occurs when product or service producers cut out intermediaries and go directly to final buyers, or when radically new types of channel intermediaries displace traditional ones. Companies such as Dell and American Airlines sell directly to final buyers, cutting retailers from their marketing channels altogether. In addition, consumers can buy flowers from Calyx & Corolla (calyxandcorolla.com); clothes from llbean.com or gap.com; and books, videos, toys, jewelry, consumer electronics, and almost anything else from Amazon.com— all without ever stepping into a traditional retail store. Online music download services such as iTunes and Musicmatch are threatening the very existence of traditional music-store retailers.

4. Compare and contrast intensive, selective, and exclusive distribution. Give an example of a product or brand that is distributed at each level. (AACSB: Communication; Reflective Thinking)

   Answer:

   Producers of convenience products and common raw materials typically seek **intensive distribution**—a strategy in which they stock their products in as many outlets as possible. These products must be available where and when consumers want them. For example, toothpaste, candy, and other similar items are sold in millions of outlets to provide maximum brand exposure and consumer convenience. By contrast, some producers purposely limit the number of intermediaries handling their products. The extreme form of this practice is **exclusive distribution,** in which the producer gives only a limited number of dealers the exclusive right to distribute its products in their territories. Exclusive distribution is often found in the distribution of luxury automobiles and prestige women's clothing. For example, Bentley dealers are few and far between—even large cities may have only one dealer. By granting exclusive distribution, Bentley gains stronger distributor selling support and more control over dealer prices, promotion, credit, and services. Exclusive distribution also enhances the car's image and allows for higher markups. Between intensive and exclusive distribution lies **selective distribution**—the use of more than one, but fewer than all, of the intermediaries who are willing to carry a company's products. Most television, furniture, and home appliance brands are distributed in this manner. For example, Whirlpool and General Electric sell their major appliances through dealer networks and selected large retailers. By using selective distribution, they can develop good working relationships with selected channel members and expect a better-than-average selling effort. Selective distribution gives producers good market coverage with more control and less cost than does intensive distribution.

5. Suppose a company has identified several channel alternatives and wants to select the one that will best satisfy its long-run objectives. Discuss the criteria that should be evaluated in making this decision. (AACSB: Communication)

   Answer:

   Each alternative should be evaluated against economic, control, and adaptive criteria. Using **economic criteria**, a company compares the likely sales, costs, and profitability of different channel alternatives. What will be the investment required by each channel alternative, and what returns will result? The company must also consider **control issues**. Using intermediaries usually means giving them some control over the marketing of the product, and some intermediaries take more control than others. Other things being equal, the company prefers to keep as much control as possible. Finally, the company must apply **adaptive criteria**. Channels often involve long-term commitments, yet the company wants to keep the channel flexible so that it can adapt to environmental changes. Thus, to be considered, a channel involving long-term commitments should be greatly superior on economic and control grounds.

6. List and briefly describe the major logistics functions. Provide an example of a decision a logistics manager would make for each major function. (AACSB: Communication; Reflective Thinking)

   Answer:

   The major logistics functions include **warehousing** (storing their tangible goods while they wait to be sold), **inventory management** (maintaining the delicate balance between carrying too little inventory and carrying too much), **transportation** (choice of transportation carriers), and **logistics information management.** A manager might decide on how many and what types of warehouses are needed and where they will be located, how much inventory to carry, and which of the five main transportation modes to employ (truck, rail, water, pipeline, and air), along with an alternative mode for digital products (the Internet, or how to share information).

Application Questions

1. Category management is used by channel members to better meet the needs of consumers. Visit www.acnielsen.com/pubs/2004_q3_ci_consumer.shtml to learn about category management and write a brief report on how marketers and distributors implement it as well as a company such as ACNielsen's role. (AACSB: Communication; Use of IT; Reflective Thinking)

   Answer:

   Category management involves analyzing store-level data on a category basis (such as salty snacks or laundry products). Each category is analyzed at the individual store level to develop the optimum assortment and replenishment for that store. ACNielsen is one of the largest suppliers of point-of-sale data that enables either retailers or manufacturers to perform this analysis.

2. In a small group, interview three franchise owners in your community. Ask them why they chose to become a franchisee and the benefits associated with it. Write a brief report describing what you learned about franchising. (AACSB: Communication; Reflective Thinking)

   Answer:

   Students' responses will vary. Instructors may suggest students learn more about franchising before interviewing franchisees. One useful source is www.franchising.com.

3. Direct selling is a legitimate means for selling products to consumers. However, some people equate direct selling with pyramid selling schemes, which are illegal. Go to www.dsa.org to learn more about direct selling. Explain what it is, the impact it has on distribution, and how it differs from pyramid selling schemes. (AACSB: Communication; Use of IT; Reflective Thinking)

   Answer:

   Direct selling is a way to sell products to consumers person-to-person outside of a retail context, and some students may be employed in this activity. For example, Cutco Knives are sold through direct selling using college students as the salespeople. Most products are sold through in-home parties or demonstrations. Each salesperson is independent and the focus is on selling the product. Pyramid schemes, however, do not focus on selling products to consumers, but rather focus on recruiting more sales people. Each new recruit pays money to get into the scheme and the people at the top reap the benefits. Soon the pyramid collapses and those at the bottom lose their money.

Under the Hood: Focus on Technology

RFID, radio frequency identification, is one of the most exciting recent technical innovations relating to logistics operations. Applications involve placing small tags containing tiny electronic RFID chips on containers, pallets, cartons, or even individual products. The tags transmit a radio signal to readers, which translate and store the product-identification data. In the past, RFID tags have been prohibitively expensive. However, thanks to improved semiconductor technology, chips can now be produced at reasonable prices. Improvements in software, telecommunications, and data sharing have all worked to move RFID to center stage for logistics managers. In fact, Wal-Mart, a pioneer in RFID application, has issued mandates to its suppliers, forcing them to begin using RFID tags on pallet shipments. As additional retailers adopt this technology and spread it through their value networks, analysts expect that RFID will become the standard for product identification.

1. What impact will RFID applications have on each of the major logistical functions? (AACSB: Communication; Reflective Thinking)

   Answer:

   Warehousing – Products could be more easily identified when coming into the warehouse and their location within the warehouse could be easily ascertained.

   Inventory – RFID could help reduce stockouts, theft, error, and vendor fraud.

   Transportation – Better tracking from ocean liner, rail, and trucking will help ensure on-time delivery.

   Information management – Supply chain members could easily share data and locate freight within minutes.

2. With advancing technology and decreasing costs, it may soon be feasible for potentially every product you purchase to contain an RFID tag. One company has even developed washable RFID tags that can be sown into clothing. Tags can also be embedded in banknotes. With this technology, there is the potential to know how consumers use products, from purchase all the way to disposal. Discuss the benefits and risks of placing these tags on individual products. (AACSB: Communication; Reflective Thinking)

   Answer:

   The benefits to manufacturers are that consumption behavior can be tracked from the point of purchase to the time of disposal. This will allow a better understanding of consumption behavior because it is actually tracking behavior. However, students will likely discuss the privacy issue of having their product usage tracked by marketers. Encourage students to learn more about this issue. For example, tags are now useless outside of the store. However, as readers become more prevalent, that will change.

Focus on Ethics

Firearms-related violence is a major societal issue in the United States. More than 300,000 violent crimes involving firearms are committed each year, killing nearly 30,000 people and injuring another 80,000, costing more than $100 billion for medical, security, and legal services. Although gun sales are legal, most crimes are committed using weapons obtained through diverted sales. The distribution channel for this product is multi-tiered, with manufacturers selling to wholesale distributors that sell to dealers who sell to the public. Several federal, state, and local laws regulate the sale of firearms. The federal enforcement agency is the Bureau of Alcohol, Tobacco, Firearms, and Explosives (known as the ATF or BATF). Firearms are sold to the public by BATF licensed dealers, known as federal firearms licensees (FFLs). The FFLs must follow laws and safeguards, selling firearms only to individuals who are considered legal purchasers (for example, over 18 years of age; not a convicted criminal; not mentally defective). However, the major channels for firearms diversion include gun shows, straw man purchases (that is, a legal purchaser buys a gun on behalf of someone who cannot legally buy one), theft, nonstore FFLs (also known as "basement bandits" or "car trunk" dealers"), unlicensed sellers, and corrupt FFLs. Gun control advocates, public safety groups, and several municipal governments have launched lawsuits against manufacturers, distributors, and dealers, claiming that industry members are not doing enough to stop diverted sales.

1. One solution to firearms diversion is to completely ban the production and sale of firearms in the United States. What are your thoughts about this solution? Is it right to ban the production and sale of firearms? (AACSB: Communication; Ethical Reasoning)

   Answer:

   Students' response will vary and the debate will likely be heated. One point is that citizens of the United States are given the right to bear arms by our Constitution, which would make a ban a constitutional violation. Another point that will probably be brought up is that banning the production and sale of this product will not solve the violent crime problem because there will still be an illegal market for this product. Individuals that intend to do harm with firearms will still be able to obtain them.

2. For a discussion on the issue of firearms marketing, see Kevin D. Bradford, Gregory T. Gundlach, and William L. Wilkie, "Countermarketing in the Courts: The Case of Marketing Channels and Firearms Diversion," *Journal of Public Policy & Marketing*, Fall 2005, pp. 284-298. Suggest ways to minimize firearms diversion. (AACSB: Communication; Reflective Thinking)

Answer:

This is a very good article on this issue. It highlights the concepts of countermarketing and demarketing and suggests ways in which they can be used in this situation. This article also applies several concepts from this chapter (such as corporate VMS, contractual VMS, and administered VMS; exclusive and selective distribution) as potential solutions to this problem.

Although not discussed in this article, RFID technology discussed above may be useful in the distribution of this product. For example, tracing of firearms used in crimes is one mechanism for identifying firearms diversion. However, this information is obtained *after* the crime has been committed. If each firearm had an RFID tag, perhaps diverted sales could be detected *before* the gun is used to commit a crime. Of course, this raises privacy concerns. However, that might be a small price legitimate guns owners are willing to pay to deter illegal use of this product.

GREAT IDEAS

Barriers to Effective Learning

1. Students will probably not have previously considered the complicated nature of getting products to consumers before, and the concepts of "supply chain" and "value delivery network" will most likely be foreign. Figure 10.1 is excellent in showing how complex delivery networks could become without intermediaries, and an early focus should be placed on this figure.
2. Vertical marketing systems can be difficult to understand. It might actually be easier to begin discussion of the contractual VMS with the illustration of franchises. Most students understand that McDonald's is a franchise organization, and so the concept will be understood quickly and easily. A corporate VMS then becomes easy to understand, because those consumer outlets are all owned by the company whose logo is on the door. Administered VMSs can be illustrated by the example of Wal-Mart, whose marketplace power has been making news.
3. Students will recognize horizontal VMSs if they have been in a grocery store recently. The addition of bank branches, and in some grocery stores, Starbucks outlets, easily explains this concept.
4. Multichannel distribution systems can be illustrated through the example of many PC manufacturers. HP, for instance, sells through many retail outlets, but they also have their own sales force for businesses. IBM will sell to consumers via its Web site, to large companies through its own sales force, and to small businesses through many certified resellers.
5. In marketing logistics, the concepts of inbound and reverse logistics should be fully explained. Most students, at this point in the chapter, will have no problems with outbound logistics.

Student Projects

1. Why do some manufacturers establish contractual relationship with their dealers instead of owning them?
2. Draw the diagram of the channel of distribution for Green Giant canned corn and Rolex watches. (You may have to do a little internet research, if you're not familiar with the brands.) How does distribution differ between these two products?
3. How do channel members add value? Give specific examples.
4. One of the major trends is *disintermediation*. Why are companies turning to this? What are the primary advantages and disadvantages associated with disintermediation? Under what conditions does it make the most sense?

Small Group Assignment

Form students into groups of three to five. Each group should read the opening vignette to the chapter on Caterpillar. Each group should then answer the following questions:

1. How is Caterpillar's strategy different from other competitors' strategies?
2. Why are dealers so important to Caterpillar?
3. How has Caterpillar attempted to build strong dealer relationships?
4. Most firms cannot bring value to customers by themselves. How does Caterpillar bring value to its customers?
5. What is the source of Caterpillar's competitive advantage? Can competitors easily duplicate this? Explain.

Each group should share its findings with the class.

Individual Assignment

Mobile phone manufacturers largely distribute their products through service providers like T-Mobile and AT&T. Why do you believe this is so? Do you think this is the most efficient method?

Think-Pair-Share

Consider the following questions, formulate an answer, pair with the student on your right, share your thoughts with one another, and respond to questions from the instructor.

1. What are the major channel alternatives open to a company?
2. What are some of the ways that companies have to evaluate channel members?
3. What is the difference between an "upstream" channel member and a "downstream" member?
4. The term "supply chain" seems pretty limiting. What phrase would you use to replace it? Why?

5. What are some of the key functions that members of the marketing channel typically perform?

Classroom Exercise/Homework Assignment

Read about Starbuck's commitment to helping out indigenous farmers in underdeveloped countries. (www.starbucks.com) After reading, write up your interpretation of the full distribution channel – from beans in the field to the finished cup of coffee you enjoy at your local Starbucks.

Classroom Management Strategies

We have a chapter with a lot of very important material, but planned carefully, this chapter can easily be covered in one class period.

1. The first two sections of this chapter, Supply Chains and the Value Delivery Network and The Nature and Importance of Marketing Channels, can be covered in 5 minutes each. Both sections are important for establishing a vocabulary and baseline for the remainder of the chapter and, as such, are relatively short and to the point. Utilizing Figures 10.1 and 10.2 will be extremely helpful.
2. The next section, Channel Behavior and Organization, should be covered in 15 minutes. The concept of vertical marketing systems will most likely take the majority of that time, because it can be a difficult concept to comprehend. Utilizing lots of examples will help
3. Channel Design Decisions should also take 15 minutes to discuss. In this section, an equal amount of time should be spent on virtually all the subheadings, although Identifying Major Alternatives may take several minutes longer than the remaining sections.
4. The next two major sections, Channel Management Decisions and Public Policy and Distribution Decisions, can be covered in 5 minutes each. Again, these sections are short, with the information presented in a concise manner.
5. Finally, Marketing Logistics and Supply Chain Management can be covered in 10 minutes. Half of this time should be spent on the subsection Major Logistics Functions. If the students are required to take an Operations Management course, they will cover these topics in more detail, but if not, this could be the only time they are exposed to these concepts while in college.

CHAPTER 11
Retailing and Wholesaling

Previewing The Concepts: Chapter Objectives

1. Explain the roles of retailers and wholesalers in the distribution channel
2. Describe the major types of retailers and give examples of each
3. Describe the major types of wholesalers and give examples of each
4. Explain the marketing decisions facing retailers and wholesalers

JUST THE BASICS

Chapter Overview

This chapter is a continuation of the prior chapter on marketing channels; it provides more detail on retailing and wholesaling, two very important concepts in the value delivery network.

Retailers can be classified according to several characteristics, including the amount of service they offer, the breadth and depth of their product lines, the relative prices they charge, and how they are organized.

The major decisions retailers make are centered around their target market and positioning, their product assortment and services, their price, their promotion strategies, and where they are located.

The wheel of retailing concept says that many new retailing forms begin as low-margin, low-price, low-status operations. They challenge established retailers, and then the new retailers' success leads them to upgrade their facilities and offer more services. In turn, their costs increase, and eventually they become like the conventional retailers they replaced. The cycle begins again.

There are many types of wholesalers, including merchant wholesalers, agents and brokers, and manufacturers' sales branches and offices.

The distinction between large retailers and large wholesalers continues to blur.

Annotated Chapter Notes/Outline

Introduction

Costco is trouncing Wal-Mart at its own low-price game.
With about the same number of members but 50 fewer stores, Costco outsells Sam's Club

by 50 percent. Its $60 billion in sales makes Costco the nation's third-largest retailer, behind only Wal-Mart and Home Depot.

How is Costco beating Sam's Club at its own low-price game? The two retailers are very similar in many ways. But inside the store, Costco adds a certain merchandising magic that Sam's Club just can't match.

Both Costco and Sam's Club excel at low-cost operations and low prices.

As one industry analyst puts it, "While Wal-Mart stands for low prices, Costco is a retail treasure hunt, where one's shopping cart could contain a $50,000 diamond ring resting on top of a vat of mayonnaise."

Costco brings flair to an otherwise dreary setting.

Mixed in with its regular stock of staples, Costco features a glittering, constantly-shifting array of one-time specials such as discounted Prada bags, Calloway gold clubs, or Kenneth Cole Bags—deals you just won't find at Sam's Club.

Use **Key Terms** *Retailing, Retailer* here. Use **Chapter Objective** 1 here. Use **Discussing the Issues** 1 here.

Retailing

Retailing includes all the activities involved in selling products or services directly to final consumers for their personal, nonbusiness use.

Retailers: Businesses whose sales come ***primarily*** from retailing.

In recent years ***nonstore retailing*** has been growing much faster than has store retailing.

Types of Retailers (Table 11.1)

Use **Table** 11.1 here.

Amount of Service

Self-service retailers serve customers who are willing to perform their own "locate-compare-select" process to save time or money.

Limited-service retailers provide more sales assistance because they carry more shopping goods about which customers need information.

Full-service retailers include high-end specialty stores and first-class department stores.

Salespeople assist customers in every phase of the shopping process.

Let's Discuss This
What type of service strategy is implemented at a 7-Eleven? At J.C. Penney? At Neiman Marcus?

Product Line

Specialty stores carry narrow product lines with deep assortments within those lines.

Department stores carry a wide variety of product lines.

In recent years, department stores have been squeezed between more focused and flexible specialty stores on the one hand, and more efficient, lower-priced discounters on the other.

Supermarkets are the most frequently shopped type of retail store.

Supermarkets also have been hit hard by the rapid growth of out-of-home eating.

Supermarkets' share of the groceries and consumables market plunged from 73 percent in 1998 to 51 percent in 2005.

Convenience stores are small stores that carry a limited line of high-turnover convenience goods.

Superstores are much larger than regular supermarkets and offer a large assortment of routinely purchased food products, nonfood items, and services.

Supercenters (called **hypermarkets** in some countries) are very large combination food and discount stores.

Category killers are superstores that are actually giant specialty stores. (Best Buy and Circuit City are examples.)

Service retailers include hotels and motels, banks, airlines, colleges, hospitals, movie theaters, tennis clubs, bowling alleys, restaurants, repair services, hair salons, and dry cleaners.

Service retailers in the United States are growing faster than product retailers.

Use **Key Terms** *Specialty Store, Department Store, Supermarket, Convenience Store, Superstore,* and *Category Killer* here. Use **Discussing the Issues** 2 here. Use **Focus on Ethics** here.

Relative Prices

Discount stores sells standard merchandise at lower prices by accepting lower margins and selling higher volume.

Off-price retailers offer products to fill the ultra low-price, high-volume gap by pricing lower than discount stores.

The three main types of off-price retailers are:

1. **Independent off-price retailers** either are independently owned and run or are divisions of larger retail corporations.
2. **Factory outlets**—manufacturer-owned and operated stores—sometimes group together in ***factory outlet malls*** and ***value-retail centers***.
3. **Warehouse clubs** (or ***wholesale clubs*** or ***membership warehouses***), operate in huge, drafty, warehouse-like facilities and offer few frills.

Use **Key Terms** *Discount Store, Off-Price Retailer, Independent Off-Price Retailers, Factory Outlet,* and *Warehouse Club* here. Use **Chapter Objective** 2 here.

Organizational Approach (Table 11.2)

Use **Discussing the Issues** 3 here.

Chain stores are two or more outlets that are commonly owned and controlled.

They have many advantages over independents.

- Their size allows them to buy in large quantities at lower prices and gain promotional economies.
- They can hire specialists to deal with areas such as pricing, promotion, merchandising, inventory control, and sales forecasting.

There are three forms of contractual associations:

1. ***Voluntary chain***—a wholesaler-sponsored group of independent retailers that engages in group buying and common merchandising.
2. ***Retailer cooperative***—a group of independent retailers that bands together to set up a jointly owned, central wholesale operation and conducts joint merchandising and promotion efforts.
3. ***Franchise***— The main difference between franchise organizations and other contractual systems is that franchise systems are normally based on some unique product or service; on a method of doing business. Franchises command 40 percent of all retail sales in the United States.

Merchandising conglomerates are corporations that combine several different retailing forms under central ownership. An example is Limited Brands, which operates The Limited, Express, Victoria's Secret, and others.

Use **Key Terms** *Chain Store, Franchise* here. Use **Table** 11-2 here. Use **Application Questions** 1 here.

Retailer Marketing Decisions (Figure 11.1)

Use **Figure** 11.1 here.

Segmentation, Targeting, Differentiation, and Positioning Decisions

Too many retailers fail to define their target markets and positions clearly. They try to have "something for everyone" and end up satisfying no market well.

In contrast, successful retailers define their target markets well and position themselves strongly.

Product Assortment and Services Decision

Retailers must decide on three major product variables:

1. ***Product assortment*** should differentiate the retailer while matching target shoppers' expectations.
2. ***Services mix*** can help set one retailer apart from another.
3. ***Store atmosphere*** is another important element in the reseller's product arsenal.

Price Decision

Most retailers seek ***either:***

- High markups on lower volume (most specialty stores)
- Low markups on higher volume (mass merchandisers and discount stores).

Other pricing decisions:

- ***"High-low" pricing***—charging higher prices on an everyday basis, coupled with frequent sales and other price promotions to increase store traffic, clear out unsold merchandise, create a low-price image, or attract customers who will buy other goods at full prices.
- ***Everyday low pricing (EDLP)***, charging constant, everyday low prices with few sales or discounts.

Promotion Decision

Retailers use any or all of the promotion tools—advertising, personal selling, sales promotion, public relations, and direct marketing—to reach consumers.

Place Decision

Retailers often point to three critical factors in retailing success: ***location, location,*** and ***location***!

It's very important that retailers select locations that are accessible to the target market in areas that are consistent with the retailer's positioning.

Location options include:

- ***Central business districts*** which were the main form of retail cluster until the 1950s.
- ***Shopping centers*** which are a group of retail businesses planned, developed, owned, and managed as a unit.
    - ***Regional shopping centers***, or ***regional shopping malls***, are the largest and most dramatic shopping center, contains from 40 to over 200 stores, including two or more full-line department stores.
    - ***Community shopping centers*** contain between 15 and 40 retail stores. It normally contains a branch of a department store or variety store, a supermarket, specialty stores, professional offices, and sometimes a bank.
    - ***Neighborhood shopping centers*** or ***strip malls*** that generally contain between 5 and 15 stores. They are close and convenient for consumers.

      The average American makes three trips to the mall a month, shopping for an average of 81.5 minutes per trip and spending about $90.

- ***Power centers*** are huge unenclosed shopping centers consisting of a long strip of retail stores, including large, freestanding anchors. This is the current trend.
- ***Lifestyle centers*** are smaller malls with upscale stores, convenient locations, and non-retail activities such as dining and a movie theater.

Use **Key Term** *Shopping Center* here. Use **Application Questions** 2 here.

The Future of Retailing

New Retail Forms and Shortening Retail Life Cycles

New retail forms continue to emerge to meet new situations and consumer needs, but the life cycle of new retail forms is getting shorter.

The **wheel-of-retailing concept** states that many new types of retailing forms begin as low-margin, low-price, low-status operations.

Use **Key Term** *Wheel of Retailing Concept* here. Use **Discussing the Issues** 4 here. Use **Application Questions** 3 here. Use **Under the Hood/Focus on Technology** here.

The new retailers' success leads them to upgrade their facilities and offer more services, forcing them to increase their prices.

Eventually, the new retailers become like the conventional retailers they replaced.

The cycle begins again.

Growth of Nonstore Retailing

Americans are increasingly avoiding the hassles and crowds at malls by doing more of their shopping by phone or computer.

Much of the anticipated growth in online sales will go to multichannel retailers—the click-and-brick marketers who can successfully merge the virtual and physical worlds.

Retail Convergence

The merging of consumers, products, prices, and retailers is called ***retail convergence***.

Such convergence means greater competition for retailers and greater difficulty in differentiating offerings.

The Rise of Megaretailers

The megaretailers are shifting the balance of power between retailers and producers. A relative handful of retailers now control access to enormous numbers of consumers, giving them the upper hand in their dealings with manufacturers.

Growing Importance of Retail Technology

Many retailers now routinely use technologies such as touch-screen kiosks, customer-loyalty cards, electronic shelf labels and signs, handheld shopping assistants, smart cards, and self-scanning checkout systems.

Global Expansion of Major Retailers

Retailers with unique formats and strong brand positioning are increasingly moving into other countries.

Many are expanding internationally to escape mature and saturated home markets.

Most U.S retailers are still significantly behind Europe and Asia when it comes to global expansion.

Retail Stores as "Communities" or "Hangouts"

With the rise in the number of people living alone, working at home, or living in isolated and sprawling suburbs, there has been a resurgence of establishments that, regardless of the product or service they offer, also provide a place for people to get together.

Use **Discussing the Issues** 5 here.

Wholesaling

Wholesaling includes all activities involved in selling goods and services to those buying for resale or business use.

Wholesalers are those firms engaged *primarily* in wholesaling activities.

Use **Key Terms** *Wholesaling, Wholesaler* here. Use **Chapter Objective** 3 here.

Wholesalers buy mostly from producers and sell mostly to retailers, industrial consumers, and other wholesalers.

Wholesalers add value by performing one or more of the following channel functions:

- *Selling and promoting:* Wholesalers' sales forces help manufacturers reach many small customers at a low cost.
- *Buying and assortment building:* Wholesalers can select items and build assortments needed by their customers, thereby saving the consumers much work.
- *Bulk-breaking:* Wholesalers save their customers money by buying in carload lots and breaking bulk (breaking large lots into small quantities).
- *Warehousing:* Wholesalers hold inventories, thereby reducing the inventory costs and risks of suppliers and customers.
- *Transportation:* Wholesalers can provide quicker delivery to buyers because they are closer than the producers.
- *Financing:* Wholesalers finance their customers by giving credit, and they finance their suppliers by ordering early and paying bills on time.
- *Risk bearing:* Wholesalers absorb risk by taking title and bearing the cost of

theft, damage, spoilage, and obsolescence.

- *Market information:* Wholesalers give information to suppliers and customers about competitors, new products, and price developments.
- *Management services and advice:* Wholesalers often help retailers train their salesclerks, improve store layouts and displays, and set up accounting and inventory control systems.

Use **Discussing the Issues** 6 here.

Types of Wholesalers

Wholesalers fall into three major groups (see Table 11.3):

Use **Table** 11.3 here.

1. **Merchant wholesalers** are the largest single group of wholesalers, accounting for roughly 50 percent of all wholesaling. Merchant wholesalers include two broad types:
   a. ***Full-service wholesalers*** provide a full set of services.
   b. ***Limited-service wholesalers*** offer fewer services to their suppliers and customers.

The different types of ***limited-service wholesalers*** perform varied specialized functions:

2. ***Brokers*** and ***agents*** differ from merchant wholesalers in two ways:
   a. They do not take title to goods.
   b. They perform only a few functions.

   A **broker** brings buyers and sellers together and assists in negotiation.
   Agents represent buyers or sellers on a more permanent basis. ***Manufacturers' agents*** (also called manufacturers' representatives) are the most common type of agent wholesaler.

3. **Manufacturers' sales branches and offices** are wholesaling by sellers or buyers themselves rather than through independent wholesalers.

Use **Key Terms** *Merchant Wholesaler, Broker, Agent, Manufacturers' Sales Branches* and *Office* here.

Wholesaler Marketing Decisions (Figure 11.2)

Segmentation, Targeting, Differentiation, and Positioning Decisions

Like retailers, wholesalers must segment and define their target markets and differentiate and position themselves effectively—they cannot serve everyone.

Marketing Mix Decisions

Wholesalers add customer value though the ***products and services*** they offer.

They are often under great pressure to carry a full line and to stock enough for immediate delivery. But this practice can damage profits.

Price is an important wholesaler decision.

Most wholesalers are not ***promotion*** minded.

Their use of trade advertising, sales promotion, personal selling, and public relations are largely scattered and unplanned.

Distribution (***location***) is important—wholesalers must choose their locations, facilities, and Web locations carefully.

Use **Chapter Objective** 4 here. Use **Figure** 11-2 here.

Trends in Wholesaling

The industry remains vulnerable to one of the most enduring trends of the last decade—fierce resistance to price increases and the winnowing out of suppliers who are not adding value based on cost and quality.

The distinction between large retailers and large wholesalers continues to blur.

Wholesalers will continue to increase the services they provide to retailers—retail pricing, cooperative advertising, marketing and management information reports, accounting services, online transactions, and others.
Many large wholesalers are now going global.

<u>Travel Log</u>

Discussing the Issues

1. Define *retailing* and *wholesaling* and discuss how each adds value to the marketing system. (AACSB: Communication; Reflective Thinking)

   Answer:

   Retailing includes all the activities involved in selling products or services directly to final consumers for their personal, nonbusiness use. Retailing plays a very important role in most marketing channels—they connect brands to consumers. **Wholesaling**

includes all activities involved in selling goods and services to those buying for resale or business use. Wholesalers buy mostly from producers and sell mostly to retailers, industrial consumers, and other wholesalers. Wholesalers add value by performing one or more of the following channel functions: selling and promoting, buying and assortment building, bulk-breaking, warehousing, transportation, financing, risk bearing, market information, and management services and advice.

2. Distinguish between specialty stores, department stores, supermarkets, convenience stores, superstores, and category killers. Give one example of each. (AASCB: Communication; Reflective Thinking)

   Answer:

   Specialty stores carry narrow product lines with deep assortments within those lines. Hallmark and f.y.e. are examples of specialty stores. In contrast, **department stores** carry a wide variety of product lines. Examples of department stores include Sear's, Macy's, Dillard's, and Neiman-Marcus. **Supermarkets** sell food and other items and are the most frequently shopped type of retail store. Examples include Kroger, Albertson's, Safeway, and Winn-Dixie. **Convenience stores** are small stores that carry a limited line of high-turnover convenience goods, and examples include 7-11 and Circle K. **Superstores** are much larger than regular supermarkets and offer a large assortment of routinely purchased food products, nonfood items, and services. Wal-Mart, Target, and Meijer are examples. Recent years have also seen the explosive growth of superstores that are actually giant specialty stores, the so-called **category killers**. They are large stores and carry a very deep assortment of a particular line with a knowledgeable staff. Examples include Best-Buy, Bed Bath and Beyond, Sports Academy, PetSmart, and Toys-R-Us.

3. Discuss the different organizational approaches for retailers and provide an example of each. (AACSB: Communication; Reflective Thinking)

   Answer:

   The major types of retail organizations—*corporate chains*, *voluntary chains* and *retailer cooperatives*, *franchise organizations* and *merchandising conglomerates*—are described in Table 11.2. **Chain stores** are two or more outlets that are commonly owned and controlled. They have many advantages over independents. Their size allows them to buy in large quantities at lower prices and gain promotional economies. They can hire specialists to deal with areas such as pricing, promotion, merchandising, inventory control, and sales forecasting. The great success of corporate chains caused many independents to band together in one of two forms of contractual associations. One is the **voluntary chain**—a wholesaler-sponsored group of independent retailers that engages in group buying and common merchandising. Examples include Independent Grocers Alliance (IGA), Western Auto, and Do-It Best hardware. The other type of contractual association is the **retailer cooperative**—a group of independent retailers that bands together to set up a jointly owned, central wholesale operation and conducts joint merchandising and promotion efforts. Examples are Associated Grocers and Ace Hardware. These organizations give independents the buying and promotion economies they need to meet the prices of corporate chains.

Another form of contractual retail organization is a **franchise**. The main difference between franchise organizations and other contractual systems (voluntary chains and retail cooperatives) is that franchise systems are normally based on some unique product or service; on a method of doing business; or on the trade name, goodwill, or patent that the franchiser has developed. Franchising has been prominent in fast food and restaurants, motels, health and fitness centers, auto sales and service, and real estate.

Merchandising conglomerates are corporations that combine several different retailing forms under central ownership. An example is Limited Brands, which operates The Limited (fashion-forward women's clothing), Express (trendy private-label women's and men's apparel), Victoria's Secret (glamorous lingerie and beauty products), Bath & Body Works (natural but luxurious beauty and body-care products), and The White Barn Candle Company (home fragrance and décor items).

4. What is the wheel-of-retailing concept? Does it apply to online retailing? (AACSB: Communication; Reflective Thinking)

   Answer:

   Many retailing innovations are partially explained by the **wheel-of-retailing concept**. According to this concept, many new types of retailing forms begin as low-margin, low-price, low-status operations. They challenge established retailers that have become "fat" by letting their costs and margins increase. The new retailers' success leads them to upgrade their facilities and offer more services. In turn, their costs increase, forcing them to increase their prices. Eventually, the new retailers become like the conventional retailers they replaced. The cycle begins again when still newer types of retailers evolve with lower costs and prices. The wheel-of-retailing concept seems to explain the initial success and later troubles of department stores, supermarkets, and discount stores, and the recent success of off-price retailers.

   Online retailers certainly began as low-margin operations—in fact, so low-margin that many of them went out of business. To succeed, they had to increase prices and offer new services. Now we see online prices that are comparable to those of offline stores, thus moving online sellers through the wheel.

5. List and briefly discuss the trends impacting the future of retailing. (AACSB: Communication)

Answer:

- New retail forms and shortening retail life cycles
- Growth of nonstore retailing
- Retail convergence
- The rise of megaretailers
- Growing importance of retail technology
- Global expansion of major retailers
- Retail stores as "communities" or "hangouts"

6. Name and describe the different types of wholesalers. (AACSB: Communication)

   Answer:

   Wholesalers fall into three major groups (see Table 11.3): *merchant wholesalers, agents and broker,* and *manufacturers' sales branches and offices*. **Merchant wholesalers** are the largest single group of wholesalers and include two broad types: full-service wholesalers and limited-service wholesalers. *Full-service wholesalers* provide a full set of services, whereas the various *limited-service wholesalers* offer fewer services to their suppliers and customers. The several different types of limited-service wholesalers perform varied specialized functions in the distribution channel.

   Brokers and *agents* differ from merchant wholesalers in two ways: They do not take title to goods, and they perform only a few functions. Like merchant wholesalers, they generally specialize by product line or customer type. A **broker** brings buyers and sellers together and assists in negotiation. **Agents** represent buyers or sellers on a more permanent basis. *Manufacturers' agents* (also called manufacturers' representatives) are the most common type of agent wholesaler. The third major type of wholesaling is that done in **manufacturers' sales branches and offices** by sellers or buyers themselves rather than through independent wholesalers.

Application Questions

1. Store brands (or private labels) have existed for years but have only recently seen increasing popularity in the United States. These are brands that can only be purchased at a specific store, such as Wal-Mart's Great Value or Equate brands. Store brands now account for 15 percent of all retail sales (19 percent of food sales) and are priced about 30 percent below national brands. Visit a grocery store, a drug store, a discount store, and a department store and identify the private label store brands for each. Compare store brand prices with national brand prices and write a brief report of what you found. (AACSB: Communication; Reflective Thinking)

   Answer:

   Students' response will vary depending on the stores visited, but some examples include A&P's America's Choice, Dillard's department store's Roundtree & Yorke, and Walgreen's brand by the same name. Prices will vary, but they will be much lower for the store brands.

2. Deciding on a target market and positioning for a retail store are very important marketing decisions. In a small group, visit a local mall and evaluate five stores. What is the target market for each store? How is each store positioned? Do the retail atmospherics of each store enhance this positioning effectively to attract and satisfy the target market? (AACSB: Communication; Reflective Thinking)

   Answer:

   Students' responses will vary. However, they should describe the target market for each store in terms of demographic and lifestyle variables. Some stores, such as Abercrombie and Fitch, target young teens and adults and design their stores to appeal to this segment. Vivid graphics, loud music, "pushing the envelope," and dark stores appeal to this group. It might be interesting to discuss how this retailer repositioned itself to appeal to this segment. The store was originally positioned to appeal to older men and women. Similarly, Banana Republic used to sell safari type adventure clothing and play big band music!

3. The Mall of America, located in Bloomington, Minnesota, is the largest mall in the world. Visit www.mallofamerica.com to learn more about this shopping center. Write a brief report describing the center and classify what type of shopping center it is. (AACSB: Communication; Reflective Thinking)

   Answer:

   This mall is truly phenomenal with more than 500 stores, 30 restaurants, an amusement park, an aquarium, and several other entertainment diversions. Families take vacations to visit this mall. It is so unique that it doesn't really fit in the classifications of shopping centers given in the chapter: regional shopping mall, community shopping centers, neighborhood shopping centers, etc. Technically, it is classified as a regional shopping mall, but it is in a league of its own.

Under the Hood: Focus on Technology

Gift card giving has grown dramatically over the past few years, but some consumers feel such cards constitute a thoughtless or impersonal gift. Not anymore! Macy's is testing customized gift card kiosks in some of its stores. The kiosks allow customers to customize gift cards with their photo, message, and color. Each kiosk is equipped with a digital camera for those wanting an impromptu photo, but customers also can upload pictures from a disc or from their own digital camera. Cardways is the company providing this technology, and at its Web site consumers can now customize gift cards for other retailers (such as Circuit City, Linens 'N Things, Lowe's, and Travelocity).

1. This is an example of which retailer marketing decision? Explain your answer. (AACSB: Communication; Reflective Thinking)

   Answer:

   This is an illustration of the product assortment and service decision. By offering kiosks throughout the store or the ability to customize offerings on a Web site, customers are provided an additional service of personalizing gift cards.

2. Go to www.cardways.com and create your own gift card. Was it easy to use? How much does it cost to customize a card and do you think the benefit you receive is worth the cost? (AACSB: Communication; Reflective)

   Answer:

   Students will probably have some fun customizing either a greeting card or a greeting card/gift card combination. The price for a single greeting card is $3.25 and $4.50 if a gift card is added (plus the value of the gift card). Shipping costs range from.41 cents for standard mail to more that $16.00 for faster delivery. Students' responses will vary concerning the value received, and this is a good illustration to remind students that value is based on consumers' perceptions.

Focus on Ethics

You would think that city officials would want to encourage retail growth but that isn't the always the case. For example, the Chicago City Council passed an ordinance that has been labeled "living wage legislation." It required retailers with more that $1 billion in profits and more than 90,000 square feet of floor space to pay a "living wage" to employees, defined as $10 per hour in pay plus an additional $3 per hour in benefits. As a result, large retailers such as Wal-Mart, Target, and Lowe's threatened to curtail their expansion plans in that city. The mayor of Chicago vetoed the law. But this type of legislation is in effect in other cities, such as Santa Fe, New Mexico and San Francisco, California. Other cities are considering different kinds of restrictive legislation. For example, Fresno, California banned altogether stores larger than 100,000 square feet that devote at least 5 percent of that space to groceries (such as Wal-Mart Superstores). And Austin, Texas requires retail developments greater than 100,000 square feet to obtain conditional use permits and notifies local residents of the development.

1. Why would city officials enact these types of ordinances? (AACSB: Communication; Reflective Thinking)

   Answer:

   The Chicago "living wage legislation" was targeted primarily at Wal-Mart, which has a reputation for paying low wages. However, this law may have had the opposite effect if retailers cancelled plans to expand in the city—citizens would have lost jobs.

"Ban ordinances" against giant retailers have to do with maintaining a level competitive playing field for local merchants and limiting the sprawl that such large stores create.

2. Is it right to single out a few retailers and limit their growth this way? (AACSB: Communication; Ethical Reasoning)

Answer:

Students' responses will vary. Arguments can be made in support of bans on superstores, such as protecting small merchants and maintaining the character of the community. However, students can argue that it is discriminatory against these retailers, and that consumers end up losing because they will not have the benefit of lower prices and employment opportunities that such retailers provide.

GREAT IDEAS

Barriers to Effective Learning

1. Retailing is generally not a difficult concept for students. However, the different types of retailers should be thoroughly explained to the students to ensure their understanding. Table 11.1 is an excellent resource in this regard. The differing types of retail organizations are also critical to understand; Table 11.2 helps here.
2. The decisions retailers need to make will be easily understood with a review of Figure 11.1. It is very clear in this figure that the marketing mix elements studied earlier in the text are being applied in a retail environment. Explain carefully how the type of retail organization chosen affects the marketing mix, and vice versa.
3. Nonstore retailing should be familiar to students, but perhaps not by this name. Many students may not realize that they are visiting a retailer when they buy books or CDs from Amazon.com, or select an item from a catalog and order it over the phone.
4. Wholesaling, by contrast, could be a difficult subject for many students. Although the concept was introduced in an earlier chapter, there is more detail here, and there are many more terms for the students to learn.
5. The description of the types of wholesalers is brief but important. Examples will help tremendously, even though most wholesalers, by their nature and as discussed in the text, are virtually unknown to consumers. Some students, however, might be familiar with distributors who service grocery stores and other retail outlets from summer jobs or those held by family members. Table 11.3 will be helpful in this discussion.

Student Projects

1. Go to a local power center. Make a list of all the stores located there. Which of these stores serve as the anchor and which stores are dependant on the anchor?

2. Visit a local discount store (Wal-Mart, Target, etc.) and a local off-price store (T.J. Maxx, Stein Mart, etc.). Examine the product mix and pricing strategies of both stores. Who would you say is the target market of each? Why?
3. Describe the major types of wholesalers located in your community and give an example of each.
4. In your town, locate a merchant at each stage of the Wheel of Retailing.

Small Group Assignment

Form students into groups of three to five. Each group should read the opening vignette to the chapter on Costco and then answer the following questions:

1. What is Costco's basic strategy?
2. Describe Costco based on the types of retailers described in the text—via service, product line, prices, and organizational approach.
3. Describe the decisions that Costco has made for each variable of the marketing mix.
4. If you were a wholesaler, how would you approach Costco to carry your products?

Each group should share its findings with the class.

Individual Assignment

Become an internet detective and do some research on the history of Wal-Mart. Trace the evolution of the company from its humble beginnings to the global powerhouse it is today. Give a time-line of the company as it passes through the stages of Wheel-of-Retailing. At what stage do you believe Wal-Mart finds itself today? Justify your answer.

Think-Pair-Share

Consider the following questions, formulate an answer, pair with the student on your right, share your thoughts with one another, and respond to questions from the instructor.

1. How would you define retailing? How does it fundamentally differ from wholesaling?
2. What is a category killer? Why do you believe they have become so popular in recent years?
3. What are the stages of the Wheel of Retailing? What stage do you believe Costco is in? Why?
4. What are the basic functions that wholesalers perform? Why don't retailers perform these functions instead?
5. What does it mean that the Retail Life Cycle is becoming shorter?

Classroom Exercise/Homework Assignment

Consider both Wal-Mart (www.walmart.com) and Amazon (www.amazon.com). In what ways do these two companies compete? Compare them using the variables of the marketing mix. Specifically, take a look at how both companies market their music offerings. Which do you believe has the upper hand? Why?

Classroom Management Strategies

This chapter can easily be covered in one standard class period. Although the terminology will be new to students, particularly the types of retailers and wholesalers, the material itself is easily understood as a general rule, and students will tend to be pretty familiar with retailing in particular.

1. The majority of the class, perhaps 40 minutes in a 60-minute class, should be spent on retailing. This can be broken down further, with 15 minutes on the Types of Retailers, 15 minutes on Retailer Marketing Decisions, and 10 minutes on the Future of Retailing. You can liberally use examples and the various questions from the chapter in going through this material.
2. The remaining 20 minutes of the class will be spent on the Wholesaling section. Here, it is very important that time be spent on discussing the various types of wholesalers and what kinds of functions they perform. Students will be less familiar with this type of business, so several examples should be gathered to discuss in class. The Classroom Exercise/Homework Assignment provided previously can be very useful.

CHAPTER 12
Communicating Customer Value: Advertising and Public Relations

Previewing the Concepts: Chapter Objectives

1. Discuss the process and advantages of integrated marketing communications in communicating customer value
2. Define the five promotion tools and discuss the factors that must be considered in shaping the overall promotion mix
3. Describe and discuss the major decisions involved in developing an advertising program
4. Explain how companies use public relations to communicate with their publics.

JUST THE BASICS

Chapter Overview

This chapter concentrates on the final element of the marketing mix—promotion.

Companies use promotion to clearly and persuasively communicate that value.

Promotion is not a single tool but rather a mix of several tools.

Ideally, under the concept of ***integrated marketing communications***, the company will carefully coordinate these promotion elements to deliver a clear, consistent, and compelling message about the organization and its products.

The chapter begins by introducing the various promotion mix tools.

Next, it examines the rapidly changing communications environment and the need for integrated marketing communications.

Finally, the chapter looks closely at two of the promotion tools—advertising and public relations.

Annotated Chapter Notes/Outline

Introduction

Until about ten years ago, GEICO was a little-known player in the auto insurance industry.

But now, thanks in large part to an industry-changing advertising campaign featuring a likable spokes-lizard, an indignant clan of cavemen, and an enduring tagline, GEICO has grown to become a major industry player.

Like all good advertising, the GEICO campaign began with a simple but enduring theme. Every single one of the more than 150 commercials produced in the campaign drives home the now-familiar tagline: "15 minutes could save you 15 percent or more on car insurance."

In 1999, GEICO ran a 15-second spot in which the now-famous, British-accented gecko calls a press conference and pleads: "I am a gecko, not to be confused with a GEICO, which could save you hundreds on car insurance. So stop calling me."

Then came the cavemen. The company's new advertising slogan is "It's so easy to use GEICO.com, even a caveman could do it."

The indignant cavemen have taken on a cult status all their own.

Not only have the gecko and cavemen helped GEICO grow, they've changed the face of the auto insurance industry.

The Promotion Mix

Use **Key Term** *Promotion Mix (Marketing Communications Mix)* here. Use **Chapter Objective** 1 here.

The **promotion mix** is also called the **marketing communications mix.**

It consists of five tools:

Advertising: Any paid form of nonpersonal presentation and promotion of ideas, goods, or services by an identified sponsor.

Sales promotion: Short-term incentives to encourage the purchase or sale of a product or service.

Personal selling: Personal presentation by the firm's sales force for the purpose of making sales and building customer relationships.

Public relations: Building good relations with the company's various publics by obtaining favorable publicity, building up a good corporate image, and handling or heading off unfavorable rumors, stories, and events.

Direct marketing: Direct connections with carefully targeted individual consumers to both obtain an immediate response and cultivate lasting customer relationships.

Use **Key Terms** *Advertising, Sales Promotion, Public Relations, Personal Selling,* and *Direct Marketing* here. Use **Chapter Objective** 2 here.

Integrated Marketing Communications

The New Marketing Communications Landscape

Factors which are changing the face of marketing communications:

1. Consumers are changing. They are better informed and more communications-empowered.
2. Marketing strategies are changing. As mass markets have fragmented, marketers are shifting away from mass marketing.
3. Changes in communications technology are causing changes in the ways in which companies and customers communicate with each other.

Use **Discussing the Issues** 2 here.

The Shifting Marketing Communications Model

Although television, magazines, and other mass media remain very important, their dominance is declining.

Companies are doing less *broadcasting* and more *narrowcasting*.

Consumers, especially younger ones, appear to be turning away from the major television networks in favor of cable TV or altogether different media.

Many large advertisers are shifting their advertising budgets away from network television in favor of more targeted, cost-effective, interactive, and engaging media.

The Need for *Integrated* Marketing Communications

Integrated marketing communications (IMC) requires the company to carefully integrate its many communications channels to deliver a clear, consistent, and compelling message about the organization and its brands. (Figure 12.1)

Use **Key Term** *Integrated Marketing Communications* here. Use **Figure** 12.1 here.

IMC calls for recognizing all contact points where the customer may encounter the company and its brands.

Each ***brand contact*** will deliver a message, whether good, bad, or indifferent.

IMC ties together all of the company's messages and images.

Shaping the Overall Promotion Mix

The Nature of Each Promotion Tool

Use **Discussing the Issues** 1 here.

Each promotion tool has unique characteristics and costs.

Advertising

Advantages:

1. Advertising can reach masses of geographically dispersed buyers at a low cost per exposure, and it enables the seller to repeat a message many times.
2. Large-scale advertising says something positive about the seller's size, popularity, and success.
3. Consumers tend to view advertised products as more legitimate.

Shortcomings:

1. Advertising is impersonal and cannot be as directly persuasive as can company salespeople.
2. Advertising can carry on only a one-way communication with the audience.
3. Advertising can be very costly.

Personal Selling

Advantages:

1. Personal selling is the most effective tool at certain stages of the buying process, particularly in building up buyers' preferences, convictions, and actions.
2. It involves personal interaction between two or more people.
3. With personal selling, the buyer usually feels a greater need to listen and respond.

Shortcomings:

1. A sales force requires a longer-term commitment than does advertising.
2. Personal selling is the company's most expensive promotion tool.

Sales Promotion

Sales promotion includes a wide assortment of tools—coupons, contests, cents-off deals, premiums, and others.

Advantages:

1. They attract consumer attention.
2. They offer strong incentives to purchase.
3. They can be used to dramatize product offers and to boost sagging sales.
4. Sales promotions invite and reward quick response

Shortcomings:

1. Sales promotion effects are often short-lived.
2. They are often are not as effective as advertising or personal selling in building long-run brand preference and customer relationships.

Public Relations

- Public relations is very believable—news stories, features, sponsorships, and events seem more real and believable to readers than ads do.
- Public relations can reach many prospects who avoid salespeople and advertisements.
- Public relations can dramatize a company or product.

Direct Marketing

Although there are many forms of direct marketing, they all share four distinctive characteristics:

1. Direct marketing is ***nonpublic***:
2. Direct marketing is ***immediate.***
3. Direct marketing is ***customized.***
4. Direct marketing is ***interactive.***

Promotion Mix Strategies (Figure 12.2)

Marketers can choose from two basic promotion mix strategies—***push*** promotion or ***pull*** promotion.

- A **push strategy** involves "pushing" the product through marketing channels to final consumers.
- A **pull strategy** involves the producer directing its marketing activities toward final consumers to induce them to buy the product.

Most large companies use some combination of both strategies.

Use **Discussing the Issues** 3 here.

Factors to consider when designing promotion mix strategies include ***type of product/market*** and the ***product life-cycle stage.***

Use **Key Terms** *Push Strategy, Pull Strategy* here. Use **Figure** 12.2 here. Use **Application Questions** 2 here.

Advertising

U.S. advertisers now spend in excess of $285 billion yearly on advertising.

Use **Figure** 12.3 here. Use **Chapter Objective** 3 here.

The four decisions to make when developing an advertising program are (see Figure 12.3):

1. **Setting Advertising Objectives**

Advertising objectives should be based on past decisions about the target market, positioning, and the marketing mix, which define the job that advertising must do in the total marketing program.

Use **Key Term** *Advertising Objective* here.

An **advertising objective** is a specific communication ***task*** to be accomplished with a specific *target* audience during a specific period of ***time***.

Advertising objectives can be classified by primary purpose (Table 12.1):

Use **Table** 12.1 here.

- ***Informative advertising*** is used heavily when introducing a new product category.
- ***Persuasive advertising*** becomes important as competition increases. Here, the company's objective is to build selective demand.
    - ***Comparative advertising*** is directly or indirectly comparing one brand with another.
- ***Reminder advertising*** is important for mature products—it helps to maintain customer relationships and keep consumers thinking about the product.

2. Setting the Advertising Budget

Here are the four common methods used to set the total budget for advertising:

Affordable Method

The **affordable method** is setting the promotion budget at the level believed to be what the company can afford.

Small businesses often use this method.

Shortcomings:

- It ignores the effects of promotion on sales.
- It tends to place promotion last among spending priorities, even in situations in which advertising is critical to the firm's success.
- It leads to an uncertain annual promotion budget.
- It more often results in underspending.

Percentage-of-Sales Method

The **percentage-of-sales method** is setting the promotion budget at a certain percentage of current or forecasted sales.

It is simple to use and helps management think about the relationships between promotion spending, selling price, and profit per unit.

Shortcomings:

- It wrongly views sales as the ***cause*** of promotion rather than as the ***result***.
- It is based on availability of funds rather than on opportunities.
- It may prevent the increased spending sometimes needed to turn around falling sales.
- Because the budget varies with year-to-year sales, long-range planning is difficult.
- The method does not provide any basis for choosing a ***specific*** percentage.

Competitive-Parity Method

The **competitive-parity method** is setting the promotion budgets to match competitors' outlays.

Two arguments support this method.

- Competitors' budgets represent the collective wisdom of the industry.
- Spending what competitors spend helps prevent promotion wars.

Neither argument is valid.

Objective-and-Task Method

The most logical budget-setting method is the **objective-and-task method**, whereby the company sets its promotion budget based on what it wants to accomplish with promotion.

This budgeting method entails:

(1) defining specific promotion objectives,
(2) determining the tasks needed to achieve these objectives, and
(3) estimating the costs of performing these tasks.

The advantage of the objective-and-task method is that it forces management to spell out its assumptions about the relationship between dollars spent and promotion results.

It is the most difficult method to use.

Use **Key Terms** *Affordable Method, Competitive-Parity Method, Percentage-of-Sales Method,* and *Objective-and-Task Method* here. Use **Discussing the Issues** 4 here.

Let's Discuss This
Compare and contrast what happens to an advertising budget when sales are slipping using each budget setting method described.

3. **Developing Advertising Strategy**

Advertising strategy consists of two major elements:

- Creating advertising ***messages***
- Selecting advertising ***media***.

Creating the Advertising Message

Consumers are exposed to as many as 3,000 to 5,000 commercial messages every day.

Breaking through the Clutter

Ads are sandwiched in with a clutter of other commercials, announcements, and network promotions, totaling more than 20 minutes of nonprogram material per prime-time hour with commercial breaks coming every six minutes on average.

Use **Under the Hood/Focus on Technology** here.

Such clutter in television and other ad media has created an increasingly hostile advertising environment.

Just to gain and hold attention, today's advertising messages must be better planned, more imaginative, more entertaining, and more rewarding to consumers.

Message Strategy

The first step in creating effective advertising messages is to plan a ***message strategy***—to decide what general message will be communicated to consumers.

Developing an effective message strategy begins with identifying customer ***benefits*** that can be used as advertising appeals.

The advertiser must next develop a compelling ***creative concept***—or *"big idea"*—that will bring the message strategy to life in a distinctive and memorable way.

Advertising appeals should have three characteristics:

- They should be *meaningful.*
- Appeals must be *believable.*
- Appeals should be *distinctive.*

Message Execution

The advertiser has to turn the big idea into an actual ad execution that will capture the target market's attention and interest.

Execution styles include the following:

- *Slice of life*: This style shows one or more "typical" people using the product in a normal setting.
- *Lifestyle:* This style shows how a product fits in with a particular lifestyle.
- *Fantasy:* This style creates a fantasy around the product or its use. For instance, many ads are built around dream themes.

- *Mood or image:* This style builds a mood or image around the product or service, such as beauty, love, or serenity.
- *Musical:* This style shows people or cartoon characters singing about the product.
- *Personality symbol:* This style creates a character that represents the product.
- *Technical expertise:* This style shows the company's expertise in making the product.
- *Scientific evidence:* This style presents survey or scientific evidence that the brand is better or better liked than one or more other brands.
- *Testimonial evidence or endorsement:* This style features a highly believable or likable source endorsing the product.

Use **Application Questions** 1 here. Use **Focus on Ethics** here.

The advertiser must choose a ***tone, words,*** and ***format*** for the ad.

Consumer-Generated Messages

Taking advantage of today's interactive technologies, many companies are now tapping consumers for message ideas or actual ads.

If used carefully, consumer-generated advertising efforts can produce big benefits.

- For little expense, companies can collect new creative ideas.
- These campaigns can boost consumer involvement and get consumers talking and thinking about a brand and its value to them.

Selecting Advertising Media

The major steps in **advertising media** selection are (1) deciding on *reach, frequency*, and *impact*; (2) choosing among major *media types*; (3) selecting specific *media vehicles*; and (4) deciding on *media timing.*

Deciding on Reach, Frequency, and Impact

Reach is a measure of the ***percentage*** of people in the target market who are exposed to the ad campaign during a given period of time. ***Frequency*** is a measure of how many ***times*** the average person in the target market is exposed to the message.

The advertiser must decide on the desired ***media impact***—the ***qualitative value*** of a message exposure through a given medium.

Typically, the advertiser wants to choose media that will ***engage*** consumers rather than simply reach them.

Choosing Among Major Media Types (Table 12.2)

The media planner has to know the reach, frequency, and impact of each of the major media types.

Use **Table** 12.2 here. Use **Discussing the Issues** 5 here.

The major media types are:

- Television,
- Newspapers,
- Direct mail,
- Magazines,
- Radio,
- Outdoor,
- Internet.

Selecting Specific Media Vehicles

The media planner now must choose the best ***media vehicles***—specific media within each general media type.

Media planners must compute the cost per thousand persons reached by a vehicle.

The media planner must also consider the costs of producing ads for different media.

The media planner must balance media costs against several media effectiveness factors.

- *Audience quality.*
- *Audience engagement.*
- *Editorial quality.*

Deciding on Media Timing

The advertiser must decide how to schedule the advertising over the course of a year.

Some marketers do *only* seasonal advertising: For instance, Hallmark advertises its greeting cards only before major holidays.

The advertiser has to choose the pattern of the ads.

- ***Continuity*** means scheduling ads evenly within a given period.
- ***Pulsing*** means scheduling ads unevenly over a given time period.

4. Evaluating Advertising Effectiveness and Return on Advertising Investment

Advertising accountability and **return on advertising investment** have become hot issues for most companies.

Advertising effectiveness has fallen 40 percent over the past decade and 37.3 percent of advertising budgets are wasted.

Advertisers should regularly evaluate two types of advertising results:

- Measuring the ***communication effects*** of an ad or ad campaign tells whether the ads and media are communicating the ad message well.
- ***Sales and profits*** effects of advertising are often harder to measure. Sales and profits are affected by many factors besides advertising—such as product features, price, and availability.

One way to measure the sales and profit effects of advertising is to compare past sales and profits with past advertising expenditures.

Use **Application Questions** 3 here.

Other Advertising Considerations

Organizing for Advertising

Different companies organize in different ways to handle advertising.

In small companies, advertising might be handled by some-one in the sales department.

Large companies set up advertising departments whose job it is to set the advertising budget, work with the ad agency, and handle advertising not done by the agency.

Use **Key Term** *Advertising Agency* here. Use **Video Case** here.

Advertising agencies employ specialists who can often perform advertising tasks better than the company's own staff.

Most large advertising agencies have the staff and resources to handle all phases of an advertising campaign for its clients, from creating a marketing plan to developing ad campaigns and preparing, placing, and evaluating ads.

International Advertising Decisions

International advertisers face many complexities not encountered by domestic advertisers.
The most basic issue concerns the degree to which global advertising should be adapted to the unique characteristics of markets in various countries.

Standardization produces many benefits—lower advertising costs, greater global advertising coordination, and a more consistent worldwide image.

There are also drawbacks. It ignores the fact that country markets differ greatly in their cultures, demographics, and economic conditions.

Global advertisers face several special problems.

- Advertising media costs and availability differ vastly from country to country.
- Countries also differ in the extent to which they regulate advertising practices.
- Although advertisers may develop global strategies to guide their overall advertising efforts, specific advertising programs must usually be adapted to meet local cultures and customers, media characteristics, and advertising regulations.

Public Relations

Public relations departments may perform any or all of the following functions:

- *Press relations or press agency:* Creating and placing newsworthy information in the news media to attract attention to a person, product, or service.
- *Product publicity:* Publicizing specific products.
- *Public affairs:* Building and maintaining national or local community relations.
- *Lobbying:* Building and maintaining relations with legislators and government officials to influence legislation and regulation.
- *Investor relations:* Maintaining relationships with shareholders and others in the financial community.
- *Development:* Public relations with donors or members of nonprofit organizations to gain financial or volunteer support.

Public relations is used to promote products, people, places, ideas, activities, organizations, and even nations.

Use **Chapter Objective** 4 here.

The Role and Impact of Public Relations

Public relations can have a strong impact on public awareness at a much lower cost than advertising can.

The company does not pay for the space or time in the media.

If the company develops an interesting story or event, it could be picked up by several different media, having the same effect as advertising that would cost millions of dollars.

It has more credibility than advertising.

Public relations is sometimes described as a marketing stepchild because of its often limited and scattered use.

Major Public Relations Tools

Public relations uses several tools:

- *News.*
- ***Speeches.***
- ***Special events.***
- ***Written materials.***
- ***Audiovisual materials.***
- ***Corporate identity materials.***
- ***Public service activities.***

Use **Discussing the Issues** 6 here.

Management should set PR objectives, choose the PR messages and vehicles, implement the PR plan, and evaluate the results.

Use **Application Questions** 3 here.

<u>Travel Log</u>

Discussing the Issues

1. List and briefly describe the five major promotion mix tools. (AASCB: Communication)

Answer:

Advertising: Any paid form of nonpersonal presentation and promotion of ideas, goods, or services by an identified sponsor.

Sales promotion: Short-term incentives to encourage the purchase or sale of a product or service.

Personal selling: Personal presentation by the firm's sales force for the purpose of making sales and building customer relationships.

Public relations: Building good relations with the company's various publics by obtaining favorable publicity, building up a good corporate image, and handling or heading off unfavorable rumors, stories, and events.

Direct marketing: Direct connections with carefully targeted individual consumers to both obtain an immediate response and cultivate lasting customer relationships—the use of direct mail, the telephone, direct-response television, e-mail, the Internet, and other tools to communicate directly with specific consumers.

2. Discuss the three major factors changing the face of today's marketing communications. (AACSB: Communication)

Answer:

First, **consumers are changing**. In this digital, wireless age, they are better informed and more communications empowered. Rather than relying on marketer-supplied information, they can use the Internet and other technologies to seek out information on their own. More than that, they can more easily connect with other consumers to exchange brand-related information or even to create their own marketing messages.

Second, **marketing strategies are changing**. As mass markets have fragmented, marketers are shifting away from mass marketing. More and more, they are developing focused marketing programs designed to build closer relationships with customers in more narrowly defined micromarkets. Vast improvements in information technology are speeding the movement toward segmented marketing. Today's marketers can amass detailed customer information, keep closer track of customer needs, and tailor their offerings to narrowly target groups.

Finally, **sweeping changes in communications technology** are causing remarkable changes in the ways in which companies and customers communicate with each other. The digital age has spawned a host of new information and communication tools—from cellphones, and iPods to the Internet and satellite and cable television systems. The new communications technologies give companies exciting new media for interacting with targeted consumers. At the same time, they give consumers more control over the nature and timing of messages they choose to send and receive.

3. Compare and contrast pull and push promotion strategies. Which promotion tools are most effective in each? (AACSB: Communication)

   Answer:

   Marketers can choose from two basic promotion mix strategies—*push* promotion or *pull* promotion. Figure 12.2 contrasts the two strategies. The relative emphasis on the specific promotion tools differs for each. A **push strategy** involves "pushing" the product through marketing channels to final consumers. The producer directs its marketing activities (primarily personal selling and trade promotion) toward channel members to induce them to carry the product and to promote it to final consumers. Using a **pull strategy**, the producer directs its marketing activities (primarily advertising and consumer promotion) toward final consumers to induce them to buy the product. If the pull strategy is effective, consumers will then demand the product from channel members, who will in turn demand it from producers. Thus, under a pull strategy, consumer demand "pulls" the product through the channels.

4. Name and describe the common methods for setting total advertising budgets. (AACSB: Communication)

   Answer:

   Affordable method – The brand manager looks at revenues from last year and the expected revenues for the coming year and deducts all costs. The manager would then choose a portion of the remaining funds for advertising.

   Percentage-of-sales method – After forecasting sales, the brand manager would apply a percentage to these sales to determine the budget.

   Competitive-Parity method – The manager would use market research to determine what the competitor is spending for promotions. He or she could use industry sources, retailer contacts, and salespeople to determine this spending. The manager would then set the budget at roughly the same relative dollar value as the competitor.

   Objective-and-Task method – The marketing manager determines the marketing objectives. These may be based on measurable outcomes, including awareness, trial, sales, or market share. The manager then determines the marketing tactics to achieve these objectives – advertising, consumer promotion, trade promotion, internet, or direct mail. The costs for these tactics are then estimated and used to determine the budget.

5. Define the terms *reach, frequency*, and *impact*. (AACSB: Communication)

Answer:

Reach is a measure of the *percentage* of people in the target market who are exposed to the ad campaign during a given period of time. For example, the advertiser might try to reach 70 percent of the target market during the first three months of the campaign. **Frequency** is a measure of how many *times* the average person in the target market is exposed to the message. For example, the advertiser might want an average exposure frequency of three. But advertisers want to do more than just reach a given number of consumers a specific number of times. The advertiser also must decide on the desired **media impact**—the *qualitative value* of a message exposure through a given medium. For example, the same message in one magazine (say, *Newsweek*) may be more believable than in another (say, the *National Enquirer*).

6. Discuss the tools used by public relations professionals. (AACSB: Communication)

Answer:

Public relations uses several tools. One of the major tools is **news.** PR professionals find or create favorable news about the company and its products or people. Sometimes news stories occur naturally, and sometimes the PR person can suggest events or activities that would create news. **Speeches** can also create product and company publicity. Increasingly, company executives must field questions from the media or give talks at trade associations or sales meetings, and these events can either build or hurt the company's image. Another common PR tool is **special events,** ranging from news conferences, press tours, grand openings, and fireworks displays to laser shows, hot air balloon releases, multimedia presentations, or educational programs designed to reach and interest target publics. Public relations people also prepare **written materials** to reach and influence their target markets. These materials include annual reports, brochures, articles, and company newsletters and magazines. **Audiovisual materials**, such as slide-and-sound programs, DVDs, and online videos are being used increasingly as communication tools. **Corporate identity materials** can also help create a corporate identity that the public immediately recognizes. Logos, stationery, brochures, signs, business forms, business cards, buildings, uniforms, and company cars and trucks—all become marketing tools when they are attractive, distinctive, and memorable. Finally, companies can improve public goodwill by contributing money and time to **public service activities**. Many marketers are now also designing **buzz marketing** campaigns to generate excitement and favorable word-of-mouth for their brands.

Application Questions

1. Any message can be presented using different message styles. Find two good print advertisements (such as magazine ads) and identify the execution style used. For each advertisement, design an alternative execution style delivering the same message to the target audience but in a different way. (AACSB: Communication; Reflective Thinking)

Answer:

Students' responses will vary, but they should indicate knowledge of the different execution styles discussed in the chapter:

- *Slice of life*: This style shows one or more "typical" people using the product in a normal setting.
- *Lifestyle:* This style shows how a product fits in with a particular lifestyle.
- *Fantasy:* This style creates a fantasy around the product or its use.
- *Mood or image:* This style builds a mood or image around the product or service, such as beauty, love, or serenity. Few claims are made about the product except through suggestion.
- *Musical* (probably not applicable in this exercise): This style shows people or cartoon characters singing about the product.
- *Personality symbol:* This style creates an animated or real character that represents the product.
- *Technical expertise:* This style shows the company's expertise in making the product.
- *Scientific evidence:* This style presents survey or scientific evidence that the brand is better or better liked than one or more other brands.
- *Testimonial evidence or endorsement:* This style features a highly believable or likable source endorsing the product. It could be ordinary people saying how much they like a given product, or it might be a celebrity presenting the product.

2. Gather advertising rate information for a magazine, a newspaper, a local radio station, and a television program (national or local). Which medium has the lowest cost per exposure? Which has the lowest total cost? Which would be most effective for an advertiser like Nike? How about for a local retail store? (AACSB: Communication; Reflective Thinking)

Answer:

Students' responses will vary, and instructors might want to assign individual students different media to research. Rate information can be found on the Internet. For example, searching "media rate cards" using Google brings up several examples, such as *Newsweek*. A four-color full page ad in this magazine costs $231,525. This magazine boasts of 3.1 million readers, so the cost per thousand readers is about $75. Students can visit local radio stations or newspapers or check their Web sites. While television advertising rates vary with the program, students can obtain this information from a local sales representative or search publications such as *Advertising Age* to learn rates on network and cable programming. Nike is a national brand, so the most effective and efficient media will be magazines and national television, whereas a local retailer would use local media such as local television, newspapers, and radio.

3. In a small group, discuss the major public relations tools and develop three public relations items for the Humane Society in your community. (AACSB: Communication; Reflective Thinking)

   Answer:

   Students' responses will vary, but they should use the major public relations tools discussed in the chapter (explained in question #6): news stories, speeches, special events, written materials, audio visual materials, corporate identity materials, buzz marketing, and Web sites.

Under the Hood: Focus on Technology

Second Life is a virtual world launched in 2003 by Linden Labs in San Francisco, California. It boasts more than nine million inhabitants who connect for fun and to escape. Registered members create online digital alter egos called avatars, and now users can actually speak to each other. The currency is called Linden dollars, with $1 equal to about 270 Linden dollars. Users can purchase land in Second Life to start a business or build a home. The world started with 64 acres but now has more than 65,000 acres as it expanded to meet users' demand. Second Life is not the only virtual world. Approximately $200 million of real money moves through virtual worlds overall. Second Life is more adult-oriented but there are other worlds, such as Habbo and Nictropolis, targeted to children. Marketers see opportunities for research and promotion in virtual worlds. Useful insights into consumer preferences and behavior can be gleaned from observing virtual behavior, but some skeptics claim this might not be valid due to consumers not being themselves in these worlds. However, marketers such as IBM, Sony, Adidas, Pontiac, Kraft, and Coca-Cola have a strong presence, much like product placement in other forms of media. Kraft launched 70 new products in a virtual supermarket and found that consumers do go grocery shopping in their fantasy world and that they do read product information.

1. Visit Second Life at www.secondlife.com to learn more about this virtual world. What are some advantages and disadvantages for marketers using a virtual world to promote products? (AACSB: Communication; Use of IT; Reflective Thinking)

   Answer:

   Students' responses will vary. Instructors may want to assign the following article that highlights the pros and cons of promoting in virtual worlds: "Virtual Worlds," *Bullet Point*, July/August 2007, p. 20. This article briefly discusses advantages and disadvantages. Advantages discussed are:

- extended brand presence
- improved internal and external communications—people tend to be more outspoken online
- research consumer behavior
- build online communities
- advertise and make sales

Disadvantages include:

- small world
- deceptive audience because people disguise themselves
- no mass marketing—Second Life venues cannot handle more than 50 visitors at one time
- risk of backlash—Reebok's Second Life shop was raided, but it did boost visits
- dubious associations—sometimes the content is not what marketers want to be association with
- new worlds—virtual worlds like Second Life may not remain dominant as more are created

2. What other online venues feature brands as part of their content? (AACSB: Communication; Reflective Thinking)

   Answer:

   Students' responses will vary, but they will probably mention similar platforms such as MySpace and YouTube. Brands are placed in online video games as well.

Focus on Ethics

Splenda (sucralose) was introduced to the consumer market in 1999. It is now a common sweetener found in more than 3,500 food products. Splenda's advertising slogan is "made from sugar, so it tastes like sugar." Manufactured and marketed by packaged goods giant Johnson & Johnson, Splenda now captures a substantial percentage of the artificial sweetener market and is beginning to cut into sugar's market share. But Splenda's campaign has attracted much attention from competitors, social advocacy groups, and nutritional experts. According to these groups, Splenda has clearly violated "truth in advertising" codes with its "made from sugar" slogan. Although currently produced from a sugar molecule, they claim, Splenda is an artificial sweetener that can be produced without sugar. In addition, the chemical name assigned to Splenda—sucralose—is misleading because it closely resembles the chemical name of sugar, sucrose.

The strongest opponent to the Splenda "made from sugar" campaign is The Sugar Association, which has launched a large and expensive campaign of its own to educate the public and to expose Splenda's unethical behavior. The association's Web site (www.truthaboutsplenda.com) urges consumers to take action by contacting friends, sending letters to the FTC and the FDA, and sending letters of complaint directly to

Johnson & Johnson. Another area of the Web site, labeled Fact vs. Fiction, highlights serious consumer misunderstandings that might result from Splenda's advertising. It describes in detail how Splenda is not natural sugar and notes that there exist no conclusive tests regarding long-term safety of consuming Splenda.

1. What is the objective of Splenda's "made from sugar, so it tastes like sugar" message and campaign? Is this slogan effective? (AACSB: Communication; Reflective Thinking)

   Answer:

   One of the objectives is to inform consumers about the product, its origin, and its taste. In addition, for those familiar with this sweetener, the objective is to persuade them that Splenda tastes more like sugar than other artificial sweeteners.

2. Check the "truth in advertising" guidelines at the FTC Web site (www.ftc.gov/bcp/conline/pubs/buspubs/ad-faqs.htm). Has Splenda followed these guidelines? (AACSB: Communication; Ethical Reasoning)

   Answer:

   According to the FTC commission advertising must:
   - be Truthful and non-deceptive
   - have evidence to back up claims
   - be fair

   Students will probably argue that since it is currently produced from the sugar molecule and there is no strong evidence that the product is harmful, that it is not violating truth in advertising guidelines. In the discussion, be certain that students both sides of the issue—Johnson & Johnson's and the Sugar Association's.

<u>GREAT IDEAS</u>

Barriers to Effective Learning

1. Some students will need to have explained in detail the differences among the various communication methods outlined in the chapter. Figure 12.1 will help in this regard. Asking students for examples from each channel of communication will also help. Many students will be able to give examples from their parents' work.
2. There is a tremendous amount of information delivered in only a few pages in the advertising section. The differences among informative, persuasive, and reminder advertising may seem simple to students at first, but these concepts should be studied in some detail to ensure understanding. Again, examples are a tremendous help here.

3. Message execution is also a key concept. Many students will have trouble with the various execution styles and will particularly have difficulty with *slice of life* versus *lifestyle*. There may also be difficulty in understanding the difference between *fantasy* and *mood* or *image*. Again, use examples of your own and from the class, as well as those shown in the text.
4. Sales promotions, particularly consumer promotions, will be familiar to students. It is important that they understand the terminology, however. Trade promotion is also fairly simple, although the difference between a discount and an allowance is crucial to understand. Business promotions, as well, will go quickly. You can tie this section back into the push strategy to show how a strategy gets turned into tactics.
5. Public relations is a mystery to almost everyone. There will be some questions regarding the product publicity done by public relations versus that done by a marketing manager, but these questions can be answered by the notion of *free*, because the vast majority of what PR does is to get the company in the press. One of the examples of masterful public relations the book points out is Johnson & Johnson during the Tylenol product-tampering scare. This example alone is often enough to explain the importance of this communication channel.

Student Projects

1. Many supermarkets will give you coupons based on what you purchase. What type of promotion is this and do you believe it to be effective?
2. Pick up a Sunday newspaper (they always have the most advertisement in them). Remember the conversation on advertising objectives. Now find two examples of advertisements that inform, persuade, and remind.
3. Review the five components of the promotion mix. Find a merchant that is utilizing all five components and describe how they are using each.
4. Why are companies doing less *broadcasting* and more *narrowcasting?* What is a company that uses both and gives examples of how they are accomplishing this?
5. Describe the five promotion tools and discuss the factors that must be considered in shaping the overall promotion mix.

Small Group Assignments

Form students into groups of three to five. Each group should read the opening vignette to the chapter on GIECO. Each group should then answer the following questions:

1. How does GIECO approach setting advertising objectives? How does this differ from its competitors?
2. How do their ads break through the clutter?
3. Would GIECO's method of marketing communication work in an international environment? Why or why not?
4. What's next for GIECO? What new advertising direction would you suggest for them now?

Each group should share its findings with the class.

Individual Assignments

Marketers can choose from two basic promotion mix strategies—*push* or *pull* promotion. First, describe each. Larger companies typically use a combination of both strategies. Find two examples of companies that are making successful use of BOTH promotion mix strategies. Describe what they are doing and why you believe it to be successful.

Think-Pair-Share

Consider the following questions, formulate an answer, pair with the student on your right, share your thoughts with one another, and respond to questions from the instructor.

1. What is an advertising objective?
2. What is the main difference between reach and frequency? Write a definition of each.
3. How is public relations different from advertising and sales promotion?
4. What are the advantages and disadvantages of the various types of media?
5. What form of media do you believe would be best for reaching a 70-year-old retired school teacher? For reaching a 12-year-old girl?

Classroom Exercise/Homework Assignment

Examine the advertising for cigarettes over time. Spend some time researching how advertising for cigarettes has changed over the past 50 years. Look at old ads from the 1950s and 60s and compare them with modern ads. How has the message changed? During which time frame do you believe the advertising to be the most effective? Why?

Classroom Management Strategies

This chapter is full of good information. Make sure to keep the focus on integrating all communication channels as you go through the material. As discussed previously in Barriers to Effective Learning, use examples liberally through your discussion to drive home the importance of cohesive marketing messaging.

1. The introductory sections are short and can be covered in 10 minutes. These sections set the stage for the chapter and provide valuable background information so that the remaining material is put into the proper context. Figure 12.1 illustrates the tools in the communication process.
2. Setting the Overall Communication Mix goes through the different communications channels, and 10 minutes should be spent here. Attention should be paid to the push and pull strategies. Figure 12.2 illustrates these two strategies in a very clear format.

3. The section on Advertising is dense and should take 15 minutes. There are several subsections here, with the heart of the section in Developing Advertising Strategy. Table 12.1 discusses advertising objectives.
4. Sales Promotion should also be given 15 minutes.
5. Public relations can be covered in 10 minutes. Be sure to talk in some detail about the different tools PR managers have at their disposal so that the students understand this is not just about getting mentions in the newspapers, even though that is extremely important and one of the key focus points for PR departments.

CHAPTER 13
Communicating Customer Value: Personal Selling and Sales Promotion

Previewing the Concepts: Chapter Objectives

1. Discuss the role of a company's salespeople in creating value for customers and building customer relationships
2. Identify and explain the six major sales force management steps
3. Discuss the personal selling process, distinguishing between transaction-oriented marketing and relationship marketing
4. Explain how sales promotion campaigns are developed and implemented

JUST THE BASICS

Chapter Overview

This chapter concentrates on two more IMC elements—**personal selling** and **sales promotion**.

Personal selling is the interpersonal arm of marketing communications, in which the sales force interacts with customers and prospects to build relationships and make sales.

Sales promotion consists of short-term incentives to encourage purchase or sale of a product or service.

Although this chapter examines personal selling and sales promotion as separate tools, they must be carefully integrated with other elements of the promotion mix.

Annotated Chapter Notes/Outline

Introduction

CDW Corporation, the nation's largest reseller of technology products and services, is thriving.

The company owes its success to its highly effective "clicks and people" direct marketing strategy.

CDW has traditionally targeted small and midsize businesses (SMBs).

When someone says "salesperson", you may still think of the stereotypical "traveling salesman"—the fast-talking, ever-smiling peddler who travels his territory foisting his wares on reluctant customers.

Such stereotypes, however, are out of date.

Today, like CDW's account managers, most professional salespeople are well-educated, well-trained men and women who work to build valued customer relationships.

Personal Selling

Robert Louis Stevenson once noted that "everyone lives by selling something."

The Nature of Personal Selling

Personal selling is one of the oldest professions in the world.

The people who do the selling go by many names: salespeople, sales representatives, district managers, account executives, sales consultants, sales engineers, agents, and account development reps to name just a few.

Use **Key Terms** *Personal Selling* and *Salesperson* here.

The term **salesperson** covers a wide range of positions.

At one extreme, a salesperson might be an ***order taker***, such as the department store salesperson standing behind the counter.

At the other extreme are ***order getters***, whose positions demand ***creative selling*** and ***relationship building*** for products and services ranging from appliances to industrial equipment.

The Role of the Sales Force

Personal selling is the interpersonal arm of the promotion mix.

The role of personal selling varies from company to company.

Some firms have no salespeople at all—for example, companies that sell only online or through catalogs, or companies that sell through manufacturer's reps, sales agents, or brokers. In most firms, however, the sales force plays a major role.

Linking the Company with Its Customers

The sales force serves as a critical link between a company and its customers.

- They *represent the company to customers.*
- They *represent customers to the company.*

Coordinating Marketing and Sales

A company can take several actions to help bring its marketing and sales functions closer together.

- It can *increase communications* between the two groups by arranging joint meetings and by spelling out when and with whom each group should communicate.
- The company can create *joint assignments*.
- The company can create *joint objectives and reward systems* for sales and marketing.
- They can appoint *marketing-sales liaisons*—people from marketing who "live with the sales force" and help to coordinate marketing and sales force programs and efforts.
- The firm can appoint a *chief revenue officer* (or *chief customer officer*)—a high-level marketing executive who oversees both marketing and sales.

Use **Chapter Objective** 1 here. Use **Discussing the Issues** 1 here.

Managing the Sales Force

Sales force management is defined as the analysis, planning, implementation, and control of sales force activities. (Figure 13.1)

Use **Key Term** *Sales Force Management* here. Use **Chapter Objective** 2 here. Use **Figure** 13.1 here.

Designing Sales Force Strategy and Structure

Sales Force Structure

A company can divide sales responsibilities along any of several lines.

Territorial Sales Force Structure: Each salesperson is assigned to an exclusive geographic area and sells the company's full line of products or services to all customers in that territory.

Characteristics:

- The organization defines each salesperson's job and fixes accountability.
- The organization increases the salesperson's desire to build local customer relationships.

- Because each salesperson travels within a limited geographic area, travel expenses are relatively small.

Product Sales Force Structure: The sales force sells along product lines.

This structure can lead to problems if a single large customer buys many different company products.

Customer Sales Force Structure: The sales force is organized along customer or industry lines.

Separate sales forces may be set up for different industries, for serving current customers versus finding new ones, and for major accounts versus regular accounts.

Complex Sales Force Structures: A company often combines several types of sales force structures when it sells a wide variety of products to many types of customers over a broad geographic area.

Use **Key Terms** *Territorial Sales Force Structure, Product Sales Force Structure,* and *Customer Sales Force Structure* here.
Use **Discussing the Issues** 2 here.

Sales Force Size

Sales force size may range in size from only a few salespeople to tens of thousands.

Workload approach: A company first groups accounts into different classes according to size, account status, or other factors related to the amount of effort required to maintain them. It then determines the number of salespeople needed to call on each class of accounts the desired number of times.

Other Sales Force Strategy and Structure Issues

Outside (*Field Sales force*) and Inside Sales Forces

Outside salespeople travel to call on customers in the field.

Inside salespeople conduct business from their offices via telephone, the Internet, or visits from buyers.

- ***Technical sales support people*** provide technical information and answers to customers' questions.
- ***Sales assistants*** provide administrative backup for outside salespeople.
- ***Telemarketers*** and ***Web sellers*** use the phone and Internet to find new leads and qualify prospects or to sell and service accounts directly.

Use **Key Terms** *Outside Sales Force (Field Sales Force), Inside Sales Force* here.
Use **Discussing the Issues** 3 here.
Use **Focus on Technology** here.

Most companies now use **team selling** to service large, complex accounts. Sales teams can unearth problems, solutions, and sales opportunities that no individual salesperson could.

Such teams might include experts from any area or level of the selling firm—sales, marketing, technical and support services, R&D, engineering, operations, finance, and others.

In team selling situations, the salesperson shifts from "soloist" to "orchestrator."

Shortcomings of team selling:

1. Salespeople who are used to having customers all to themselves may have trouble learning to work with and trust others on a team.
2. Selling teams can confuse or overwhelm customers who are used to working with only one salesperson.
3. Difficulties in evaluating individual contributions to the team selling effort can create some sticky compensation issues.

Use **Key Term** *Team Selling* here.

Recruiting and Selecting Salespeople

In a typical sales force, the top 30 percent of the salespeople might bring in 60 percent of the sales.

The best salespeople possess four key talents:

1. Intrinsic motivation.
2. Disciplined work style.
3. The ability to close a sale.
4. The ability to build relationships with customers.

When recruiting, companies should analyze the sales job itself and the characteristics of its most successful salespeople to identify the traits needed by a successful salesperson in their industry.

Sources of new potential hires:

- The human resources department gets names from current salespeople, using employment agencies, placing classified ads, searching the Web, and working

through college placement services.
- Another source is to attract top salespeople from other companies.

Use **Application Questions** 1 here.

Training Salespeople

Training programs have several goals.

1. The training program must teach them about different types of customers and their needs, buying motives, and buying habits.
2. It must teach them how to sell effectively and train them in the basics of the selling process.
3. The training program teaches them about the company's objectives, organization, and chief products and markets, and about the strategies of major competitors.

Many companies are adding **e-learning** to their sales training programs.

Most e-learning is Web-based but many companies now offer on-demand training for PDAs, cell phones, and even video iPods.

Compensating Salespeople

Management must decide what ***mix*** of compensation elements makes the most sense for each sales job.

Different combinations of fixed and variable compensation give rise to four basic types of compensation plans:

1. Straight salary,
2. Straight commission,
3. Salary plus bonus,
4. Salary plus commission.

The average salesperson's pay consists of about 67 percent salary and 33 percent incentive pay.

Compensation should direct salespeople force toward activities that are consistent with overall sales force and marketing objectives.

Supervising and Motivating Salespeople

The goal of ***supervision*** is to help salespeople "work smart" by doing the right things in the right ways.

The goal of ***motivation*** is to encourage salespeople to "work hard" and energetically toward sales force goals.

Companies vary in how closely they supervise their salespeople.

- The annual ***call plan*** shows which customers and prospects to call on and which activities to carry out.
- The ***time-and-duty analysis*** shows the time the salesperson spends selling, traveling, waiting, taking breaks, and doing administrative chores. (Figure 13.2)

Use **Figure** 13.2 here.

On average, active selling time accounts for only 10 percent of total working time!

Sales force automation systems: Computerized, digitized sales force operations that let salespeople work more effectively anytime, anywhere.

Perhaps the fastest-growing technology tool is the Internet.

Organizational climate describes the feeling that salespeople have about their opportunities, value, and rewards for a good performance.

Use **Key Term** *Sales Quotas* here.

Sales quotas: Standards stating the amount they should sell and how sales should be divided among the company's products.

Compensation is often related to how well salespeople meet their quotas.

Companies use various ***positive incentives*** to increase sales force effort:

- ***Sales meetings*** provide social occasions, breaks from routine, chances to meet and talk with "company brass," and opportunities to air feelings and to identify with a larger group.

- Companies also sponsor ***sales contests*** to spur the sales force to make a selling effort above what would normally be expected.

- Other incentives include ***honors, merchandise and cash awards, trips,*** and ***profit-sharing plans***.

Evaluating Salespeople and Sales-Force Performance

Management sources of salesperson information:

- *Sales reports,*
- *Call reports,*
- *Expense reports.*

Formal evaluation forces management to develop and communicate clear standards for judging performance and provides salespeople with constructive feedback and motivates them to perform well.

Use **Linking the Concepts** here. Use **Application Questions** 2 here.

The Personal Selling Process

Steps in the Selling Process (Figure 13.3)

Use **Key Term** *Selling Process* here. Use **Figure** 13.3 here. Use **Application Question** 2 here.

The selling process consists of seven steps:

1. Prospecting and qualifying,
2. Preapproach,
3. Approach,
4. Presentation and demonstration,
5. Handling objections,
6. Closing,
7. Follow-up.

1. Prospecting and Qualifying

Prospecting is identifying qualified potential customers.

The best source of prospects is referrals.

Sources of referrals:

- Current customers.
- Suppliers, dealers, noncompeting salespeople, and bankers.
- Directories or on the Web.

- Dropping in unannounced on various offices (a practice known as **"cold calling"**).

Qualifying a lead is knowing how to identify the good ones and screen out the poor ones.

Prospects can be qualified by:

- Their financial ability.
- Volume of business.
- Special needs.
- Location.
- Possibilities for growth.

2. **Preapproach**

The **preapproach** is the stage in which the salesperson learns as much as possible about the organization (what it needs, who is involved in the buying) and its buyers (their characteristics and buying styles).

Call objectives: The task of qualifying the prospect, gathering information, or making an immediate sale.

Other ***call objectives*** include: deciding on the best approach, the best timing, and a determination of the overall sales strategy for the account.

3. **Approach**

During the **approach** step, the salesperson should know how to meet and greet the buyer and get the relationship off to a good start.

4. **Presentation and Demonstration**

During the **presentation** step of the selling process, the salesperson tells the "value story" to the buyer, showing how the company's offer solves the customer's problems.

The ***customer-solution approach*** fits better with a relationship marketing focus.

But before salespeople can ***present*** customer solutions, they must ***develop*** solutions to present.

The qualities that buyers ***dislike most*** in salespeople include:

- Being pushy,
- Late,
- Deceitful,
- Unprepared or disorganized.

The qualities that buyers ***value most*** in salespeople include:

- Good listening,
- Empathy,
- Honesty,
- Dependability,
- Thoroughness,
- Follow-through.

5. Handling Objections

In **handling objections**, the salesperson should:

- Use a *positive* approach,
- *Seek* out hidden objections,
- *Ask* the buyer to clarify any objections,
- Take objections as *opportunities*,
- *Turn* the objections into reasons for buying.

Every salesperson needs training in the skills of handling objections.

6. Closing

Salespeople can use one of several **closing** techniques:

- Ask for the order,
- Review points of agreement,
- Offer to help write up the order,
- Ask whether the buyer wants this model or that one,
- Note that the buyer will lose out if the order is not placed now.

7. Follow-Up

Follow-up is necessary if the salesperson wants to ensure customer satisfaction and repeat business.

Use **Key Terms** *Prospecting, Preapproach, Approach, Presentation, Handling Objections, Closing,* and *Follow-Up* here.

Personal Selling and Managing Customer Relationships

Transaction orientation: Purpose is to help salespeople close a specific sale with a customer.

Relationship orientation: Purpose is to serve the customer over the long haul in a mutually profitable relationship.

Today's large customers favor suppliers who can sell and deliver a coordinated set of products and services to many locations, and who can work closely with customer teams to improve products and processes.

Use **Chapter Objective** 3 here.

Sales Promotion

Sales promotion consists of short-term incentives to encourage purchase or sales of a product or service.

Use **Key Term** *Sales Promotion* here.

Rapid Growth of Sales Promotion

Use **Discussing the Issues** 4 here.

Sales promotion tools are targeted toward final buyers (*consumer promotions*), retailers and wholesalers (*trade promotions*), business customers (*business promotions*), and members of the sales force *(sales force promotions*).

Today, in the average consumer packaged-goods company, sales promotion accounts for 74 percent of all marketing expenditures.

Several factors have contributed to the rapid growth of sales promotion:

1. Product managers face greater pressures to increase their current sales.
2. The company faces more competition and competing brands are less differentiated.
3. Advertising efficiency has declined.
4. Consumers have become more deal oriented.

The growing use of sales promotion has resulted in ***promotion clutter***. Consumers are increasingly tuning out promotions, weakening their ability to trigger immediate purchase.

Sales Promotion Objectives

Sales promotion objectives vary widely.

- ***Consumer promotions***: Urge short-term customer buying or to enhance customer brand involvement.
- ***Trade promotions***: Get retailers to carry new items and more inventory, buy ahead, or promote the company's products and give them more shelf space.
- ***Sales force***: Get more sales force support for current or new products or getting salespeople to sign up new accounts.

Sales promotions should help to reinforce the product's position and build long-term *customer relationships.*

Major Sales Promotion Tools

Many tools can be used to accomplish sales promotion objectives. Descriptions of the main consumer, trade, and business promotion tools follow.

Consumer Promotions

Use **Key Term** *Customer Promotions* here. Use **Application Question** 3 here.

The **consumer promotions** include a wide range of tools.

Samples are offers of a trial amount of a product.

Sampling is the most effective—but most expensive—way to introduce a new product or to create new excitement for an existing one.

Coupons are certificates that give buyers a saving when they purchase specified products.

Most major consumer goods companies are issuing fewer coupons and targeting them more carefully.

***Cash refunds* (or *rebates*)** are like coupons except that the price reduction occurs after the purchase rather than at the retail outlet.

Price packs (also called ***cents-off deals***) offer consumers savings off the regular price of a product.

Premiums are goods offered either free or at low cost as an incentive to buy a product.

Advertising specialties, also called ***promotional products***, are useful articles imprinted with an advertiser's name, logo, or message that are given as gifts to consumers.

Point-of-purchase (POP) promotions include displays and demonstrations that take place at the point of sale.

Contests, sweepstakes, and ***games*** give consumers the chance to win something.

- A ***contest*** calls for consumers to submit an entry to be judged.
- A ***sweepstakes*** calls for consumers to submit their names for a drawing.
- A ***game*** presents consumers with something every time they buy.

Event marketing (or ***event sponsorships***) allows companies to create their own brand marketing events or serve as sole or participating sponsors of events created by others.

Trade Promotions

Trade promotions persuade resellers to carry a brand, give it shelf space, promote it in advertising, and push it to consumers.

Use **Key Terms** *Event Marketing* and *Trade Promotions* here.
Use **Discussing the Issues** 5 here.
Use **Focus on Ethics** here.

Manufacturers direct more sales promotion dollars toward retailers and wholesalers (78 percent) than to final consumers (22 percent).

Manufacturers use several trade promotion tools:

- Offer a straight ***discount*** (also called a ***price-off***, ***off-invoice***, or ***off-list***).
- Offer an ***allowance*** (usually so much off per case).
- Offer ***free goods***.
- Offer ***push money***.
- Offer free ***specialty advertising items.***

Business Promotions

Business promotions are used to generate business leads, stimulate purchases, reward customers, and motivate salespeople.

Use **Key Term** *Business Promotions* here.

Conventions and trade shows: Firms selling to the industry show their products at the trade show.

Vendors receive many benefits:

- Opportunities to find new sales leads,
- Contact customers,
- Introduce new products,
- Meet new customers,
- Sell more to present customers,
- Educate customers with publications and audiovisual materials.
- Reach many prospects not reached through their sales forces.

Sales contests: Contests for salespeople or dealers to motivate them to increase their sales performance over a given period.

Sales contests work best when they are tied to measurable and achievable sales objectives (such as finding new accounts, reviving old accounts, or increasing account profitability).

Developing the Sales Promotion Program

Marketers must decide:

1. ***Size of the incentive.***
2. ***Conditions for participation.***
3. ***Promotion and distribution.***
4. ***Length of the promotion.***
5. ***Evaluation.***

Use **Chapter Objective** 4 here. Use **Discussing the Issues** 6 here. Use **Video Case** here.

Travel Log

Discussing the Issues

1. According to the chapter, salespeople serve "two masters." What does this mean? Is it a good or bad thing? (AASCB: Communication)

   Answer:

   The sales force serves as a critical link between a company and its customers. In many cases, salespeople serve both masters—the seller and the buyer. First, they represent the company to customers. They find and develop new customers and communicate information about the company's products and services. They sell products by approaching customers, presenting their products, answering objections, negotiating prices and terms, and closing sales. In addition, salespeople provide customer service and carry out market research and intelligence work. At the same time, salespeople represent customers to the company, acting inside the firm as "champions" of customers' interests and managing the buyer-seller relationship. Salespeople relay customer concerns about company products and actions back inside to those who can handle them. They learn about customer needs and work with other marketing and nonmarketing people in the company to develop greater customer value. This is a very good thing because customer value is created in this interaction. The company gains first-hand knowledge of the customer's need and demands and this knowledge may allow it to provide a much better product or service to the customer.

2. Explain how a company can enable marketing and sales to work better together. (AACSB: Communication)

   Answer:

   A company can take several actions to help bring its marketing and sales functions closer together. At the most basic level, it can **increase communications** between the two groups by arranging joint meetings and by spelling out when and with whom each group should communicate. The company can create **joint assignments.**
   A company can also create **joint objectives and reward systems** for sales and marketing or appoint **marketing-sales liaisons**—people from marketing who "live with the sales force" and help to coordinate marketing and sales force programs and efforts. Finally, the firm can appoint a **chief revenue officer** (or *chief customer officer*)—a high-level marketing executive who oversees both marketing and sales. Such a person can help infuse marketing and sales with the common goal of creating value for customers in order to capture value in return.

3. List and briefly describe the three sales force structures outlined in the chapter. What sales force structure does CDW employ? (AACSB: Communication)

Answer:

In the **territorial sales force structure**, each salesperson is assigned to an exclusive geographic area and sells the company's full line of products or services to all customers in that territory. With a **product sales force structure**, the sales force sells along product lines. More and more companies are now using a **customer sales force structure**, in which they organize the sales force along customer or industry lines. Separate sales forces may be set up for different industries, for serving current customers versus finding new ones, and for major accounts versus regular accounts. CDW uses the customer sales force structure.

4. Define *sales promotion* and discuss the factors contributing to its rapid growth. (AACSB: Communication)

   Answer:

   Sales promotion consists of short-term incentives to encourage purchase or sales of a product or service and includes tools such as coupons, sweepstakes, premiums, and trade allowances. Whereas advertising offers reasons to buy a product or service, sales promotion offers reasons to buy *now*. Several factors have contributed to the rapid growth of sales promotion, particularly in consumer markets. First, inside the company, product managers face greater pressures to increase their current sales, and promotion is viewed as an effective short-run sales tool. Second, externally, the company faces more competition and competing brands are less differentiated. Increasingly, competitors are using sales promotion to help differentiate their offers. Third, advertising efficiency has declined because of rising costs, media clutter, and legal restraints. Finally, consumers have become more deal oriented, and ever-larger retailers are demanding more deals from manufacturers.

5. Name and describe the types of trade sales promotions. (AACSB: Communication)

   Answer:

   Manufacturers use several trade promotion tools. Many of the tools used for consumer promotions—contests, premiums, displays—can also be used as trade promotions. Or the manufacturer may offer a straight **discount** off the list price on each case purchased during a stated period of time (also called a *price-off*, *off-invoice*, or *off-list*). Manufacturers also may offer an **allowance** (usually so much off per case) in return for the retailer's agreement to feature the manufacturer's products in some way. An advertising allowance compensates retailers for advertising the product. A display allowance compensates them for using special displays. Manufacturers may offer **free goods**, which are extra cases of merchandise, to resellers who buy a certain quantity or who feature a certain flavor or size. They may offer **push money**—cash or gifts to dealers or their sales forces to "push" the manufacturer's goods. Manufacturers may give retailers free **specialty advertising items** that carry the company's name, such as pens, pencils, calendars, paperweights, matchbooks, memo pads, and yardsticks.

6. Explain the decisions involved in designing a sales promotion program. (AACSB: Communication)

   Answer:

   Beyond selecting the types of promotions to use, marketers must make several other decisions in designing the full sales promotion program. First, they must decide on the **size of the incentive**. A certain minimum incentive is necessary if the promotion is to succeed; a larger incentive will produce more sales response. The marketer also must set **conditions for participation**. Incentives might be offered to everyone or only to select groups. Marketers must decide how to **promote and distribute the promotion** program itself. A $2-off coupon could be given out in a package, at the store, via the Internet, or in an advertisement. Each distribution method involves a different level of reach and cost. Increasingly, marketers are blending several media into a total campaign concept. The **length of the promotion** is also important. If the sales promotion period is too short, many prospects (who may not be buying during that time) will miss it. If the promotion runs too long, the deal will lose some of its "act now" force. **Evaluation** is also very important. The most common evaluation method is to compare sales before, during, and after a promotion. Marketers should ask, Did the promotion attract new customers or more purchasing from current customers? Can we hold onto these new customers and purchases? Will the long-run customer relationship and sales gains from the promotion justify its costs?

Application Questions

1. Explain how a company uses the workload method to determine sales force size. If a company has 4,300 customer accounts, each requiring four calls per year, and if an average salesperson makes 1,000 calls per year, how many salespeople will be needed? (AACSB: Communication; Reflective Thinking)

   Answer:

   Many companies use some form of **workload approach** to set sales force size. Using this approach, a company first groups accounts into different classes according to size, account status, or other factors related to the amount of effort required to maintain them. It then determines the number of salespeople needed to call on each class of accounts the desired number of times. In this application, there is just one class of account, and there are 4,300 accounts. Each account requires four calls per year, so that means the company will make 17,200 total sales calls (4,300 × 4 = 17,200). If

   Each salesperson makes 1,000 calls per year, then the company needs 17.2 or 18 salespeople (17,200 ÷ 1000 = 17.2).

2. Name and describe the steps in the selling process. In a small group, develop a plan for the selling process that an office equipment firm could use to sell to small businesses in your community. (AACSB: Communication; Reflective Thinking)

   Answer:

   Students' responses will vary, but they should demonstrate an understanding of the selling process. As shown in Figure 13.3, the selling process consists of seven steps: prospecting and qualifying, preapproach, approach, presentation and demonstration, handling objections, closing, and follow-up.

   The first step in the selling process is **prospecting**—identifying qualified potential customers. While referrals are the best approach to prospecting, students will likely search for prospects in directories, such as the Yellow Pages, or on the Web. Or they can drop in unannounced on various offices (a practice known as "cold calling"). Salespeople also need to know how to *qualify* leads—that is, how to identify the good ones and screen out the poor ones. Prospects can be qualified by looking at their financial ability, volume of business, special needs, location, and possibilities for growth.

   This second step is the **preapproach**, which involves learning as much as possible about a prospect. The salesperson can consult standard industry and online sources, acquaintances, and others to learn about the company.

   During the **approach** step, the salesperson should know how to meet and greet the buyer and get the relationship off to a good start. This step involves the salesperson's appearance, opening lines, and the follow-up remarks. Students should outline how they plan to approach prospects.

   During the **presentation** step of the selling process, the salesperson tells the "value story" to the buyer, showing how the company's offer solves the customer's problems. Students should provide an outline of the presentation they will use.

   In **handling objections**, the salesperson should use a positive approach, seek out hidden objections, ask the buyer to clarify any objections, take objections as opportunities to provide more information, and turn the objections into reasons for buying. Students should think about possible objections and how they will handle them.

   Students should plan how the firm will **close the sale**—that is, ask for the sale. Finally, the last step in the selling process—**follow-up**—is necessary if the salesperson wants to ensure customer satisfaction and repeat business. Right after closing, the salesperson should complete any details on delivery time, purchase terms, and other matters. The salesperson then should schedule a follow-up call when the initial order is received, to make sure there is proper installation, instruction, and servicing. Students should demonstrate an understanding of the follow-up activities that are relevant in this scenario.

3. Name and briefly describe the types of consumer promotions. Find examples of four of them and present them to your class. (AACSB: Communication; Reflective Thinking)

   Answer:

   Consumer promotions include a wide range of tools—from samples, coupons, refunds, and premiums, and point-of-purchase displays to contests, sweepstakes, and event sponsorships. **Samples** are offers of a trial amount of a product. **Coupons** are certificates that give buyers a saving when they purchase specified products. **Cash refunds** (or *rebates*) are like coupons except that the price reduction occurs after the purchase rather than at the retail outlet. The consumer sends a "proof of purchase" to the manufacturer, who then refunds part of the purchase price by mail. **Price packs** (also called *cents-off deals*) offer consumers savings off the regular price of a product. The producer marks the reduced prices directly on the label or package. Price packs can be single packages sold at a reduced price (such as two for the price of one), or two related products banded together (such as a toothbrush and toothpaste). **Premiums** are goods offered either free or at low cost as an incentive to buy a product. A premium may come inside the package (in-pack), outside the package (on-pack), or through the mail. **Advertising specialties**, also called *promotional products,* are useful articles imprinted with an advertiser's name, logo, or message that are given as gifts to consumers. Typical items include T-shirts and other apparel, pens, coffee mugs, calendars, key rings, mouse pads, matches, tote bags, coolers, golf balls, and caps. **Point-of-purchase (POP) promotions** include displays and demonstrations that take place at the point of sale. Contests, sweepstakes, and games give consumers the chance to win something, such as cash, trips, or goods, by luck or through extra effort. A **contest** calls for consumers to submit an entry to be judged by a panel that will select the best entries. A **sweepstakes** calls for consumers to submit their names for a drawing. A **game** presents consumers with something every time they buy, which may or may not help them win a prize. Finally, marketers can promote their brands through **event marketing** (or *event sponsorships*). They can create their own brand marketing events or serve as sole or participating sponsors of events created by others. The events might include anything from mobile brand tours to festivals, reunions, marathons, concerts, or other sponsored gatherings.

   Students will easily find examples of at least four of these types of promotions. They can be found in the Free Standing Inserts in newspapers, which are pre-printed inserts usually included in the Sunday newspaper. They can also find sales promotion examples in stores and on the Internet.

Under the Hood: Focus on Technology

Sales force automation (or SFA) allows salespeople to spend less time in their office and more time with customers. Web-based sales automation systems provide information at the touch of a button to salespeople out in the field. Such systems became more feasible with the advent of laptop computers. Now, wireless technology allows even more information to be accessed using small mobile devices such as smart phones, pocket PCs, and PDAs. Although not as available as computer-based systems, mobile data applications are expected to grow fastest and to generate more than $100 billion in revenue worldwide by 2012. Intuit Inc. offers mobile solutions through its Eclipse Mobile interface. Whereas most SFA platforms require salespeople to use laptop computers, the new generation of platforms allows the same or more applications to use handheld devices. One leader in sales force automation is Salesforce.com but there are many other companies in this field.

1. Visit www.salesforce.com to view a demonstration of how this service is used to automate the selling function. You will have to sign in to view the demonstration. Write a brief report on what you learned and discuss how the use of this type of technology helps a salesperson deliver greater customer value. (AACSB: Communication; Use of IT; Reflective Thinking)

   Answer:

   The introductory demonstration lasts about eight minutes and gives an overview of this company's sales force automation solution. This service provides real-time data dashboards that a company and/or salesperson can customize, such as lead conversion rates. It provides forecasts for sales representatives and allows sales managers to manage territories. The system allows the integration of existing or custom sales methodologies. The demonstration also includes a salesperson explaining the benefits, which provides a nice overview and reinforcement of the selling process described in the chapter for students.

   Though not enumerated in the demonstration students watch, they should be able to discuss how a system such as this can help the sales force deliver greater customer value. Salespeople can spend more time with customers than behind a desk because they have relevant information available to them in the field. Thus, they are able to deliver a higher quality of customer service.

2. Discuss drawbacks of using sales force automation in general and mobile SFA solutions in particular. (AACSB: Communication; Reflective Thinking)

   Answer:

   Students' responses will vary. However, a major concern is data security. What if the salesperson's laptop or mobile device is lost or stolen? Are company and customer data safe? Also, some salespeople may rely too much on automation and not develop the interpersonal relationships that are key to developing valuable customer relationships.

Focus on Ethics

Slotting fees, a type of allowance trade promotion, consist of a one-time fee paid by food manufacturers to retailers for allotting shelf space to a new product. The manufacturer buys the product's way into the marketing channel. An FTC survey shows that the average slotting fee per chain for a new product is about $10,000, and producers report total slotting fees in the $1,000,000 to $2,000,000 range. The many critics of this system claim that grocery retailers have too much power in this situation. They also assert that the slotting fee system is unfair to small manufacturers who cannot afford such large fees. Slotting fees have been called everything from a bribe to a retailer's addiction, a questionable source of income that many retailers now rely on to survive. Retailers claim that the fees are needed to offset the costs associated with new products. To stock a new product, they must shift other products on the shelf, move products in the warehouse, and update computer systems. In addition, retailers say they run the risk of costs associated with the potential failure of the product. In response to the cries of small manufacturers that these fees create unfair competition, retailers sometimes waive slotting fees for smaller companies.

1. Assess slotting fees from the viewpoints of both retailers and manufacturers. How does this type of allowance differ from the others described in the chapter? Is it fair for retailers to demand slotting fees from manufacturers? (AACSB: Communication; Ethical Reasoning)

   Answer:

   One key difference between this type of allowance and the others described in the chapter is that it is usually demanded by retailers, not offered to them by manufacturers. This issue often raises channel conflict. Students will take both sides. On the one hand, grocery margins are razor thin and this is an additional source of revenue that offsets the costs and risks associated with new products. On the other hand, slotting fees add costs for the producer and translate to higher consumer prices, which we all bear. In either situation, we definitely see that the retailer here has the upper hand.

2. Go to www.ftc.gov/opa/2003/11/slottingallowance.htm to read about the FTC report on slotting fees. What did you learn form this report? (AACSB: Communication; Reflective Thinking)

   Answer:

   Students will find the following:

   - There is variability in the fees depending on product category.

- Fees make up a substantial part of the revenues from new products in their first year.
- Slotting allowances are lower when the product does not have to travel through the retailer's warehouse.
- Slotting fees are only part of the negotiations involved between the channels for new product placements.

GREAT IDEAS

Barriers to Effective Learning

1. The issues surrounding managing the sales force can be difficult for some students. Individually, each of the decisions a sales manager needs to make seem reasonable enough, but bringing them all together to actually plan how to develop and manage the sales force appears complicated to most undergraduates. These issues can be made simpler by going through each of the concepts carefully and thoroughly. You may also want to have students design their own sales force for a product or service idea they have. This will really drive home the concepts of how you design the sales force, as well as all the management processes.
2. Sales to most students equates to retail sales, a field that many people dislike. Therefore, many students will not be planning on going into sales as a career, and this could cause them to "tune out" during this section. You can bring them back by talking about the nature of selling in various kinds of service firms (e.g., accounting firms) that many students may be heading toward after graduation. Also, a discussion of the sophistication and professionalism of the salespeople in companies such as IBM and other business-to-business companies can generate some enthusiasm for this important field.
3. The personal selling process will be a surprise to many students, again because they typically think of retail sales, if they've thought about sales at all. The importance of all of these steps in the sales process can be highlighted in the discussion of business-to-business sales.
4. Direct marketing is a hot topic these days because of the national Do-Not-Call list and the recently passed federal legislation on anti-spamming. The students should be able to maintain their interest in this topic, but they may well be surprised that direct marketing is not just for underfunded or shady enterprises.

Student Projects

1. Examine Dell (www.dell.com). How is Dell's sales force structured?
2. List and describe each step of the personal selling process. Analyze your own potential as a sales person at each step of the process. What steps of the process would be the easiest for you to handle and what steps the most difficult? Why?
3. Consider your college/university. How could they effectively use sales promotion as a recruiting tool?

4. What are the distinguishing features between transaction-oriented marketing and relationship marketing?
5. Discuss the pros and cons of the different sales force compensation methods.

Small Group Assignment

Form students into groups of three to five. Each group should read the opening vignette to the chapter on CDW. Each group should then answer the following questions:

1. What is the role of the sales force in CDW?
2. What sort of people would you recruit for the CDW sales force?
3. How would you motivate such highly-trained salespeople? Be specific.
4. In an Internet environment, how would you prospect for and qualify potential customers?

Each group should share its findings with the class.

Individual Assignment

The sales force serves as a critical link between a company and its customers. They represent the company to customers and they represent customers to the company. Explain how this would work for a company such as CDW.

Think-Pair-Share

Consider the following questions, formulate an answer, pair with the student on your right, share your thoughts with one another, and respond to questions from the instructor:

1. What are the major forms of saleforce compensation? Which do you believe to be superior? Why?
2. List and briefly describe the stages of the personal selling process.
3. What is direct marketing?
4. What do you believe to be the major advantages and disadvantages of team selling?
5. In the personal selling process, when would you consider the sell over? Why?

Classroom Exercise/Homework Assignment

Consider you are a sales person for the local Toyota dealership. A young, newly married couple enters the lot. Walk us through the personal selling process, using this couple as your target.

Classroom Management Strategies

This chapter describes the final two communications methods for integrated marketing communications. Most of the chapter is spent on the sales process, and then direct marketing is discussed.

1. The introduction and Personal Selling section can be covered in 5 minutes. These sections set the stage for the next two sections, and for that reason should not be rushed through.
2. Spend 20 minutes going over the section entitled Managing the Sales Force. This is critical information that the students will need to learn. Figure 13.1 provides an introduction to the steps in sales force management. Review Table 13.1 to show the connection between marketing strategy and sales force compensation.
3. The Personal Selling Process can be covered in 15 minutes. Be sure to work with the students to ensure their understanding of each step of the process. Having them team up to "sell" something to other teams is often helpful in this section, ensuring that they "prospect," develop their preapproach and approach, and then present, close, and follow-up. Figure 13.3 shows the complete selling process.
4. Direct Marketing is a packed section. Spend 20 minutes here, paying particular attention to the subsections on customer databases and the forms of direct marketing. Most students will come into this thinking only of telemarketing calls. Others will have trouble distinguishing between direct marketing and advertising.
5. Public policy as it relates to direct marketing is ever changing. Have the students investigate the current status of laws and proposals as they pertain to telemarketing and email marketing campaigns, and report back to the class. A discussion of the implication of these laws and proposals will drive home the complexity of the issues.

CHAPTER 14
Direct and Online Marketing: Building Direct Customer Relationships

Previewing the Concepts: Chapter Objectives

1. Define direct marketing and discuss its benefits to customers and companies
2. Identify and discuss the major forms of direct marketing
3. Explain how companies have responded to the Internet and other powerful new technologies with online marketing strategies
4. Discuss how companies go about conducting online marketing to profitably deliver more value to customers
5. Overview the public policy and ethical issues presented by direct marketing

JUST THE BASICS

Chapter Overview

This chapter looks at the final IMC element, direct marketing, and at its fastest-growing form, online marketing.

In many ways direct marketing constitutes an overall marketing approach—a blend of communication and distribution channels all rolled into one.

Annotated Chapter Notes/Outline

Introduction

In the United States, Dell is number one in desktop PC sales, number one in laptops, and number one in servers. It captures a 33.5 percent share of the U.S. PC market.

Dell owes its stunning success to it revolutionary business model—the *direct model.* Dell sells the lion's share of its product via the telephone and Internet.

The direct model results in more efficient selling and lower costs, which translate into lower prices for customers.

Selling direct has given Dell a tremendous competitive advantage. However, after decades of rocketing revenues and profits, Dell growth engine has stalled in the past few years.

Can Dell's direct-only model still deliver sales and profit growth for Dell in the fast-changing and highly competitive PC market? The answer depends on whom you ask.

Much of the recent growth in PC demand has come from consumers buying laptops at electronics retailers such as Best Buy and Circuit City.

Dell is reviewing its direct-only marketing strategy.

Dell now sells inexpensive PCs through Wal-Mart and is rumored to be talking with Best Buy, Circuit City, and CompUSA.

It appears poised to open its own chain of Dell-branded retail stores.

Does this mean that Dell will abandon its previously-sacred direct model? Michael Dell says no.

Direct marketing consists of direct connections with carefully targeted individual consumers to both obtain an immediate response and cultivate lasting customer relationships.

Direct marketers communicate directly with customers, often on a one-to-one, interactive basis.

Using detailed databases, they tailor their marketing offers and communications to the needs of narrowly defined segments or even individual buyers.

Use **Key Term** *Direct Marketing* here.

The New Direct Marketing Model

Most companies still use direct marketing as a supplementary channel or medium.

For a growing number of companies direct marketing constitutes a complete model for doing business.

Firms employing this new ***direct model*** use it as the ***only*** approach.

Growth and Benefits of Direct Marketing

Direct marketing has become the fastest-growing form of marketing.

The Internet now accounts for about 18 percent of direct marketing-driven sales.

The DMA predicts that over the next five years Internet marketing expenditures will grow at **17** percent a year, more than three times faster than expenditures in other direct marketing media.

Internet-driven sales will grow by almost **16** percent.

Benefits to Buyers

For buyers, direct marketing is convenient, easy, and private.

Advantages:

- Gives buyers ready access to a wealth of products.
- Gives buyers access to a wealth of comparative information about companies, products, and competitors.
- Is interactive and immediate.
- Gives consumers a greater measure of control.

Benefits to Sellers

- Can target small groups or individual consumers.
- Low-cost, efficient, speedy alternative for reaching their markets.
- Can offer greater flexibility.
- Gives sellers access to buyers that they could not reach through other channels.

Use **Chapter Objective** 1 here. Use **Discussing the Issues** 1 here.

Customer Databases and Direct Marketing

A **customer database** is an organized collection of comprehensive data about individual customers or prospects, including geographic, demographic, psychographic, and behavioral data.

Use **Key Term** *Customer Database* here. Use **Discussing the Issues** 2 here.

<u>In consumer marketing</u>, the customer database might contain a customer's demographics (age, income, family members, birthdays), psychographics (activities, interests, and opinions), and buying behavior (buying preferences and the recency, frequency, and monetary value—RFM—of past purchases).

<u>In business-to-business marketing</u>, the customer profile might contain the products and services the customer has bought; past volumes and prices; key contacts (and their ages, birthdays, hobbies, and favorite foods); competing suppliers; status of current contracts; estimated customer spending for the next few years; and assessments of competitive strengths and weaknesses in selling and servicing the account.

Companies use their databases in many ways.

- To locate good potential customers and to generate sales leads.
- To learn about customers in detail.

Forms of Direct Marketing

The major forms of direct marketing are:

Use **Figure** 14.1 here. Use **Chapter Objective** 2 here.

1. Personal selling,
2. Direct-mail marketing,
3. Catalog marketing,
4. Telephone marketing,
5. Direct-response television marketing,
6. Kiosk marketing,
7. New digital direct marketing technologies,
8. Online marketing. (Figure 14.1)

Personal selling was covered in detail in Chapter 13.

Direct-mail marketing involves sending an offer, announcement, reminder, or other item to a person at a particular address.

Use **Key Term** *Direct Mail Marketing* here. Use **Focus on Ethics** here.

Direct mail (including both catalog and non-catalog mail) accounts for more than a third of all U.S. direct marketing sales.

Characteristics:

- Well suited to direct, one-to-one communication.
- Permits high target-market selectivity,
- Can be personalized,
- Is flexible,
- Allows easy measurement of results.
- Costs more than mass media per thousand people reached, people reached are much better prospects.

New forms of delivery have become popular, such as *fax mail, voice mail,* and *e-mail.*

Fax mail and voice mail are subject to the same do-not-call restrictions as telemarketing.

E-mail is booming as a direct marketing tool.

Catalog Marketing

Use **Key Term** *Catalog Marketing* here.

Catalog used to be defined as printed, bound piece of at least eight pages, selling multiple products, and offering a direct ordering mechanism.

With Internet, more and more catalogs are going digital. A variety of Web-only catalogers have emerged, and most print catalogers have added Web-based catalogs.

Advantages of Web-based catalogs:

- Eliminate production, printing, and mailing costs.
- Allow real-time merchandising.

Printed catalogs are still thriving.

Advantages of printed catalogs:

- One of the best ways to convince consumers to use the online versions.
- Create emotional connections with customers.

Telephone Marketing

Use **Key Term** *Telephone Marketing* here. Use **Application Question** 2 here.

Telephone marketing involves using the telephone to sell directly to consumers and business customers.

Telephone marketing now accounts for **22** percent of all direct marketing-driven sales.

Outbound telephone marketing is used to sell directly to consumers and businesses.

Inbound toll-free 800 numbers are used to receive orders from television and print ads, direct mail, or catalogs.

Do-not-call legislation (National Do-Not-Call Registry) has hurt the telemarketing industry, but not all that much.

Do-not-call appears to be helping most direct marketers more than it's hurting them.

- Shifting call-center activity from making cold calls to managing existing customer relationships.
- Development of *"opt-in"* calling systems.

Direct-Response Television Marketing

Use **Key Term** *Direct-Response Television Marketing* here. Use **Discussing the Issues** 3 here.

Direct-response television marketing takes one of two major forms.

Direct-response television advertising **(DRTV)** is television spots which describe a product and give customers a toll-free number or Web site for ordering.

30-minute or longer advertising programs are called ***infomercials***.

Home shopping channels are television programs or entire channels dedicated to selling goods and services.

Kiosk Marketing

Kiosks are information and ordering machines.

New Digital Direct Marketing Technologies

Mobile Phone Marketing

A growing number of consumers—especially younger ones—are using their cell phones as a "third screen" for text messaging, surfing the Web, watching videos and shows, and e-mail.

Most people are initially skeptical about receiving cellphone ad messages. But they often change their minds if the ads deliver value.

A recent study found that 42 percent of cellphones users are open to mobile advertising if it's relevant.

Podcasts and Vodcasts

The name ***podcast*** derives from Apple's iPod.

With podcasting, consumers can download audio files (podcasts) or video files (vodcasts) via the Internet to an iPod or other handheld device, and then listen to or view them whenever they wish.

Interactive TV (ITV)

Interactive TV (ITV) lets viewers interact with television programming and advertising using their remote controls.

Online Marketing

Online marketing is the fastest-growing form of direct marketing.

Marketing and the Internet

Use **Key Term** *Online Marketing* and *Internet* here. Use **Focus on Technology** here.

The **Internet**, a vast public web of computer networks, connects users of all types all around the world to each other and to an amazingly large information repository.

Internet household penetration in the United States is approximately 69 percent, with more than 209 million people now using the Internet at home or at work.

The average U.S. Internet user spends some 33 hours a month surfing the Web at home, plus another 80 hours a month at work.

Worldwide, almost 500 million people now have Internet access.

Click-only companies operate only on the Internet.

Use **Key Terms** *Click-Only Companies* and *Click-and-Mortar Companies* here.

They include a wide array of firms:

- *E-tailers* such as Amazon.com and Expedia,
- *Search engines and portals* (such as Yahoo!, Google, and MSN),
- *Transaction sites* (eBay),
- *Content sites* (New York Times on the Web, and ESPN.com)

Click-and-mortar companies operate both as existing *brick-and-mortar* retailers and online.

Online Marketing Domains

Use **Discussing the Issues** 4 here.

The four major online marketing domains (Figure 14.2) are:

1. **Business to Consumer (B2C)**

Business-to-consumer (B2C) online marketing is selling goods and services online to final consumers.

Use **Key Term** *Business-to-Consumer (B2C) Online Marketing* here.
Use **Chapter Objective** 3 here.

65 percent of American online users use the Internet to shop.

The Internet now influences 27 percent of total retail sales.

2. **Business to Business (B2B)**

Business-to-business (B2B) online marketing is using online resources to reach new business customers, serve current customers more effectively, and obtain buying efficiencies and better prices.

Use **Key Term** *Business-to-Business (B2B) Online Marketing* here.

3. **Consumer to Consumer (C2C)**

Consumer-to-consumer (C2C) online marketing occurs on the Web between interested parties over a wide range of products and subjects.

EBay's C2C online trading community of more than 220 million registered users worldwide transacted some $52 billion in trades last year.

Use **Key Term** *Consumer-to-Consumer (C2C) Online Marketing* here.

Blogs are online journals where people post their thoughts, usually on a narrowly defined topic.

4. **Consumer to Business (C2B)**

Consumer-to-business (C2B) online marketing occurs when consumers communicate with companies.

Use **Key Term** *Consumer-to-Business (C2B) Online Marketing* here.

Consumers search out sellers on the Web, learn about their offers, initiate purchases, and give feedback.

Setting Up an Online Marketing Presence (Figure 14.4)

Creating a Web Site

For most companies, the first step in conducting online marketing is to create a Web site.

Types of Web Sites

Corporate (or Brand) Web site is the most basic.

Use **Key Terms** *Corporate Web Site* and *Marketing Web Site* here.

These sites are designed to build customer goodwill, collect customer feedback, and supplement other sales channels, rather than to sell the company's products directly.

Marketing Web site engages consumers in an interaction that will move them closer to a direct purchase or other marketing outcome.

Designing Effective Web Sites

Use **Chapter Objective** 4 here. Use **Application Question** 1 here.

A key challenge is designing a Web site that is attractive on first view and interesting enough to encourage repeat visits.

Online marketers should pay close attention to the seven *C*s of effective Web site design:

- *Context:* the site's layout and design
- *Content:* the text, pictures, sound, and video that the Web site contains
- *Community:* the ways that the site enables user-to-user communication
- *Customization:* the site's ability to tailor itself to different users or to allow users to personalize the site
- *Communication:* the ways the site enables site-to-user, user-to-site, or two-way communication
- *Connection:* the degree that the site is linked to other sites
- *Commerce:* the site's capabilities to enable commercial transactions

To keep customers coming back to the site, companies need to embrace yet another "C"—constant *change*.

Placing Ads and Promotions Online

Last year, U.S. companies spent nearly $17 billion on online advertising, up 35 percent over the previous year, and more than they spend on outdoor and radio advertising combined.

Use **Key Term** *Online Advertising* here.
Use **Discussing the Issues** 5 here.

Forms of Online Advertising

- *Banners* are banner-shaped ads found at the top, bottom, left, right, or center of a Web page.
- *Interstitials* are online display ads that appear between screen changes on a Web site, especially while a new screen is loading.
- *Pop-ups* are online ads that appear suddenly in a new window in front of the window being viewed.
- *Pop-unders* are online ads that appear in a new window that evades pop-up blockers by appearing behind the page you're viewing.
- *Rich media* display ads are online ads that incorporate animation, video, sound, and interactivity.
- *Search-related ads* (or *Contextual advertising*) are online advertising in which text-based ads and links appear alongside search engine results.

Other Forms of Online Promotion

Content sponsorships

Companies gain name exposure on the Internet by sponsoring special content on various Web sites.

Alliances** and **affiliate programs allow companies to promote each other.

Viral marketing is the Internet version of word-of-mouth marketing.

Viral marketing involves creating a Web site, video, e-mail message, or other marketing event that is so infectious that customers will want to pass it along to their friends.

Use **Key Terms** *Viral Marketing* and *Online Social Networks* here.
Use **Video Case** here.

Creating or Participating in Online Social Networks

Online social networks or **Web communities** are Web sites that give consumers online places to congregate, socialize, and exchange views and information. (Examples are MySpace and Facebook.)

Marketers can engage in online communities in two ways:

1. They can participate in existing Web communities
2. They can set up their own Web communities.

Participating successfully in existing online social networks presents challenges.

1. Online social networks are new and results are hard to measure.
2. Such Web communities are largely user controlled.

Using E-Mail

U.S. companies currently spend about $1.5 billion a year on e-mail marketing, up from just $164 million in 1999.

Spam: The unsolicited, unwanted commercial e-mail messages that clog up e-mailboxes.

Use **Key Term** *Spam* here.

Most legitimate marketers now practice ***permission-based e-mail marketing,*** which is sending e-mail pitches only to customers who "opt in."

The Promise and Challenges of Online Marketing

As it continues to grow, online marketing will prove to be a powerful direct marketing tool for improving sales, communicating company and product information, delivering products and services, and building customer relationships more efficiently and effectively.

Public Policy Issues in Direct Marketing

Irritation, Unfairness, Deception, and Fraud

Phishing is a type of identity theft that uses deceptive emails and fraudulent Web sites to fool users into divulging their personal data.

Online security issues continue to grow.

Consumers fear that unscrupulous snoopers will eavesdrop on their online transactions, picking up personal information or intercepting credit and debit card numbers.

Access by vulnerable or unauthorized groups is another area of concern.

For example, marketers of adult-oriented materials have found it difficult to restrict access by minors.

Invasion of Privacy

Invasion of privacy is perhaps the toughest public policy issue now confronting the direct-marketing industry.

Online privacy causes special concerns. Most online marketers have become skilled at collecting and analyzing detailed consumer information.

A Need for Action

All of this calls for strong actions by marketers to curb privacy abuses before legislators step in to do it for them.

TRUSTe, a nonprofit self-regulatory organization, works with many large corporate sponsors to audit companies' privacy and security measures and help consumers navigate the Web safely.

Use **Chapter Objective** 5 here. Use **Discussing the Issues** 6 here. Use **Application Question** 3 here.

<u>**Travel Log**</u>

Discussing the Issues

1. Discuss the benefits of direct marketing to both buyers and sellers. (AASCB: Communication)

   Answer:

   For buyers, direct marketing offers several benefits:
   - **convenient, easy, and private**—customers can shop and purchase from almost anywhere at any time.
   - **gives buyers ready access to a wealth of products**—for example, unrestrained by physical boundaries, direct marketers can offer an almost unlimited selection to consumers almost anywhere in the world.
   - **gives buyers access to a wealth of comparative information about companies, products, and competitors**—good catalogs or Web sites often provide more information in more useful forms than even the most helpful

retail salesperson can.

- **interactive and immediate**—buyers can interact with sellers by phone or on the seller's Web site to create exactly the configuration of information, products, or services they desire, and then order them on the spot.
- **greater measure of control**—consumers decide which catalogs they will browse and which Web sites they will visit.

Direct marketing also offers several benefits to sellers:

- **powerful tool for building customer relationships**—using database marketing, today's marketers can target small groups or individual consumers and promote their offers through personalized communications.
- **low-cost, efficient, speedy alternative for reaching markets**—compared to personal sales calls, lower-cost-per-contact media (such as telemarketing, direct mail, and company Web sites) often prove more cost effective. Similarly, online direct marketing results in lower costs, improved efficiencies, and speedier handling of channel and logistics functions, such as order processing, inventory handling, and delivery.
- **flexibility**—it allows marketers to make ongoing adjustments to its prices and programs, or to make immediate and timely announcements and offers.
- **access to buyers that they could not reach through other channels**—smaller firms can mail catalogs to customers outside their local markets and post 1-800 telephone numbers to handle orders and inquiries. Internet marketing is a truly global medium that allows buyers and sellers to click from one country to another in seconds.

2. Describe the qualities and features of an effective customer database. (AACSB: Communication)

Answer:

Like many other marketing tools, database marketing requires a special investment. Companies must invest in computer hardware, database software, analytical programs, communication links, and skilled personnel. The database system must be user-friendly and available to various marketing groups, including those in product and brand management, new-product development, advertising and promotion, direct mail, telemarketing, Web marketing, field sales, order fulfillment, and customer service. However, a well-managed database should lead to sales and customer-relationship gains that will more than cover its costs.

3. Name and describe the forms of direct-response television marketing and give an example of each. (AACSB: Communication)

Answer:

Direct-response television marketing takes one of two major forms. The first is **direct-response television advertising (DRTV)**. Direct marketers air television spots, often 60 or 120 seconds long, which persuasively describe a product and give customers a toll-free number or Web site for ordering. Basically, any commercial that includes a way for consumers to respond is considered direct-response television advertising. Television viewers also often encounter full 30-minute or longer advertising programs, or **infomercials**, for a single product.

Home shopping channels, another form of direct-response television marketing, are television programs or entire channels dedicated to selling goods and services. Some home shopping channels, such as the Quality Value Channel (QVC), Home Shopping Network (HSN), and ShopNBC, broadcast 24 hours a day.

4. Describe the four major e-marketing domains and provide an example of each. (AACSB: Communication)

   Answer:

   Business-to-consumer (B2C) e-commerce is the online selling of goods and services to final consumers. Amazon.com is a B2C marketer. **Business-to business (B2B)** e-marketers use trading networks, auction sites, spot exchanges, online product catalogs, barter sites, and other online resources to reach new customers, serve current customers more effectively, and obtain buying efficiencies and better prices. Trane is a B2B marketer. Much **consumer-to-consumer (C2C)** e-commerce and communication occurs on the Web between interested parties over a wide range of products and subjects. Ebay is a good example. The final e-commerce domain is **consumer-to-business (C2B)** e-commerce. Thanks to the Internet, today's consumers are finding it easier to communicate with companies. PlanetFeedback is a C2B site.

5. Compare and contrast the different forms of online advertising. What factors should a company consider in deciding among these different forms? (AACSB: Communication)

   Answer:

   The major forms of online advertising include display ads, search-related ads, and online classifieds. Online display ads might appear anywhere on an Internet user's screen. The most common form is **banners**, banner-shaped ads found at the top, bottom, left, right, or center of a Web page. Clicking on the ad takes consumers to the Web site. **Interstitials** are online display ads that appear between screen changes on a Web site, especially while a new screen is loading. **Pop-ups** are online ads that appear suddenly in a new window in front of the window being viewed. Such ads can multiply out of control, creating a major annoyance. As a result, Internet services and Web browser providers have developed applications that let users block most pop-ups. As a result, many advertisers have now developed **pop-unders**, new windows that evade pop-up blockers by appearing behind the page you're viewing. **Rich media** display ads incorporate animation, video, sound, and interactivity. Rich media ads attract and hold consumer attention better than traditional banner ads. They employ techniques such as float, fly, and snapback—animations that jump out and sail over the Web page before retreating to their original space.

Search-related ads (or *contextual advertising*) are text-based ads and links that appear alongside search engine results on sites such as Google and Yahoo! An advertiser buys search terms from the search site and pays only if consumers click through to it site.

Firms should consider the exposure rate for targeted consumers when selecting a form of advertising. In addition, firms should consider how well the form of advertising delivers the intended message.

6. Discuss the public policy issues in direct marketing. What are direct marketers doing to address these issues? (AACSB: Communication; Reflective Thinking)

   Answer:

   Policy issues related to direct marketing include irritating and offending consumers, deception and fraud, online security, and invasion of privacy. Direct-marketing excesses sometimes annoy or offend consumers. Television commercials can be irritating, mail boxes fill up with catalogs, and consumers get phone calls and emails they do not want. Beyond irritating consumers, some direct marketers have been accused of taking unfair advantage of impulsive or less-sophisticated buyers. Worse yet, so-called heat merchants design mailers and write copy intended to mislead buyers. Even well-known direct mailers have been accused of deceiving consumers. Fraudulent schemes, such as investment scams or phony collections for charity, have also multiplied in recent years.

   Internet fraud, including identity theft and financial scams, has become a serious problem. One common form of Internet fraud is *phishing,* a type of identity theft that uses deceptive emails and fraudulent Web sites to fool users into divulging their personal data. Many consumers also worry about online security. Internet shoppers are also concerned about contracting annoying or harmful viruses, spyware, and other "malware." Another Internet marketing concern is that of *access by vulnerable or unauthorized groups*, such as children being able to access adult content.

   Invasion of privacy is perhaps the toughest public policy issue now confronting the direct-marketing industry. Consumers often benefit from database marketing—they receive more offers that are closely matched to their interests. However, many critics worry that marketers may know *too* much about consumers' lives and that they may use this knowledge to take unfair advantage of consumers. At some point, they claim, the extensive use of databases intrudes on consumer privacy.

   Some of these issues have been addressed by the government, such as the FTC's Do Not Call Registry and the Children's Online Privacy Protection Act (COPPA).

However, the direct-marketing industry as a whole is also addressing public policy issues. For example, in an effort to build consumer confidence in shopping direct, the Direct Marketing Association (DMA) launched a "Privacy Promise to American Consumers." The Privacy Promise requires that all DMA members adhere to a carefully developed set of consumer privacy rules. Marketers themselves have also instituted policies to protect consumers' personal information and to allow them to opt-out of or opt-in to marketing programs.

Application Questions

1. In a small group, select a Web site of your choice and evaluate it according to the "7 C's" of effective Web site design. Present this to the rest of the class. (AACSB: Communication; Use of IT; Reflective Thinking)

   Answer:

   Students' responses will vary but they should demonstrate an application of the seven *C*s of effective Web site design:
   - *Context:* the site's layout and design
   - *Content:* the text, pictures, sound, and video that the Web site contains
   - *Community:* the ways that the site enables user-to-user communication
   - *Customization:* the site's ability to tailor itself to different users or to allow users to personalize the site
   - *Communication:* the ways the site enables site-to-user, user-to-site, or two-way communication
   - *Connection:* the degree that the site is linked to other sites
   - *Commerce:* the site's capabilities to enable commercial transactions

2. Visit www.donotcall.gov and click on "more Information" to learn more about the National Do Not Call registry. Write a brief report regarding who can register a number, who must comply with the registry, and consequences for non-compliance. (AACSB: Communication; Use of IT; Reflective Thinking)

   Answer:

   If students click on "More Information" they will find information for consumers, businesses, and media. They should be able to find considerable information regarding this registry from this source.

3. On-line marketing to children is of great concern to parents, consumer groups, businesses, and the government. Research the Children's Online Privacy Protection Act (COPPA) and the Children's Advertising Review Unit (CARU) of the National

Advertising Division. Discuss a recent case the CARU handled with respect to the COPPA. (AACSB: Communication; Reflective Thinking)

Answer:

Students can learn about COPPA by visiting www.ftc.gov or www.caru.org. By clicking on "News" at CARU's Web site, students will be able to find cases related to the Act. For example, a news release dated August 24, 2007 discussed how CARU recommended that Disney should change certain functions of it Web site, www.mdisney.com to ensure compliance with the Act.

Under the Hood: Focus on Technology

The future of Internet advertising is widgets. Widgets, also known as "gadgets," are tiny computer programs that allow anyone to incorporate professional-looking content into Web pages, such as news feeds, clocks, weather information, and so on. Widgets usually contain a brand name or promotional message. They can be simple or complex, such as those incorporating chat boxes, polls, video, and games. Whereas banner advertising is not very effective and video ads are annoying because they take over the screen, marketers see widgets as a promising route to reach consumers by integrating advertising onto the Web page. Moreover, widgets are a way to get on individuals' personal Web sites and may be the only way to get inside some Web spaces, such as My Space pages. As with banner ads, marketers can measure widget click-through-rates to assess the effectiveness of an ad. Yahoo! offers widgets, Google offers gadgets, and others, such as Microsoft and ThinkGeek, offer free programs for users to download. The only price to users is the promotional content that comes along with it.

1. Search "widgets" and "gadgets" on the Internet to learn more about this Web advertising tool. Search Web sites to see if you can find examples of this type of advertising. Write a brief report of what you learned. (AACSB: Communication; Use of IT; Reflective Thinking)

   Answer:

   Students' responses will vary but there is plentiful information available on this phenomenon.

2. Discuss the different forms of online advertising. Do you think this type of Internet advertising is more effective than the others? Explain why or why not. (AACSB: Communication; Reflective Thinking)

   Answer:

   Students' opinions regarding whether or not this is a more effective form of Web advertising will vary. However, they should discuss the different forms of online advertising: display ads, search-related ads, and online classifieds. These are explained in question #5 above.

Focus on Ethics

"Junk mail!" We all know what it is, but have you ever considered the environmental impact of all that unsolicited mail? The Department of the Environment estimates that Americans spend more than $320 million per year to dispose of junk mail. Approximately 42 billion pieces of unsolicited mail are delivered annually, representing 41 pounds of junk mail per adult each year. More than 100 million trees are cut down and 28 billion gallons of water are used each year to feed our junk mail addiction. Statistics such as these have lead some consumers and communities to fight back. For example, the San Francisco and Santa Barbara areas of California started a "Stop Junk Mail" campaign and provide useful tips for consumers at www.stopjunkmail.org. The United States is not the only concerned country. British Environment Minister David Miliband has declared a "war on junk mail" and has threatened legislation forcing direct marketers to go to an opt-in model of mailing. Charities responded that this was simply "hair-brained lunacy." The direct mail industry in the UK is already reeling from a government mandate that 30 percent of delivered direct mail in 2006 be recycled, amounting to proving that more than 600,000 pieces had been recycled by direct marketers by the end of that year.

1. Should the government enact laws to legislate the amount of mail a marketer can send? Is there any benefit to direct mailers of reducing unsolicited mailings? (AACSB: Communication; Ethical Reasoning)

   Answer:

   Students' positions will vary and will most likely be influenced by their personal environmental concerns. Some will argue that the government must step in because marketers will not regulate themselves. Others will argue the opposite, indicating that the industry provides services to consumers, such as the Direct Marketing Association's Mail Preference Service (MPS), to remove their names from mailing lists. Consumers can also contact the marketer to get their names removed, so there are options for consumers to take action themselves.

   Reducing the amount of junk mail is beneficial to direct mailers. By sending mail only to likely prospects, their mailing costs will decrease. The "irritation factor" will also be reduced as less mail will be perceived as junk mail if it is targeted to the right people. However, costs of acquiring and maintaining more precise mailing lists will be higher.

2. Explain the opt-in model. Suggest other ways for direct mailers and consumers to reduce unsolicited mail. Identify organizations that help consumers in this task. (AACSB: Communication; Reflective Thinking)

Answer:

The opt-in model is a permission-based model. Instead of mailing pieces to consumers and requiring them to indicate that they do not want further contact, opt-in starts with consumers granting permission to contact them in the first place. Other suggestions for reducing unsolicited mail are to ensure mailing lists are up-to-date to reduce wasted delivery and shifting more to digital information, such as on-line catalogs and email communications. The Direct Marketing Association's Mail Preference Service (MPS) removes consumers' names from many mailing lists, and there are other organizations that will reduce the amount of unsolicited mail for a fee. For example, www.greendimes.org and www.41pounds.org are two services that assist consumers in reducing unsolicited mail by 80 percent or more.

Great Ideas

Barriers to Effective Learning

1. The students will have grown up with the Internet, so there are few concepts in this chapter that will be totally new to them. However, the vocabulary and terminology could be new to them, so you will want to go through all the Key Terms carefully.
2. Students will largely not have thought of e-commerce as having spawned new intermediaries, largely because they will not have even heard of that term prior to this class. Therefore, spend some time talking about the differences between click-only and click-and-mortar companies. Also, explain the problems brick-and-mortar companies faced when the dot-com explosion first hit—should they develop their own Web sites and e-commerce facilities
3. Most students will know the terms and concepts B2B and B2C, but C2C and C2B may be new to them, at least in terminology. Applying the C2C concept to the rise (and fall) of Napster will drive the point home, as will the various chat rooms and other cyber-communities. For C2B, ask if anyone has ever contacted a company via email to ask a question, lodge a complaint, or send a compliment.
4. Many students will have their own Web sites, either for personal use or through their college activities. They will understand the nuances of web design, but may not understand some of the key concepts of attracting and retaining customers through effective design decisions. Discussing Web sites that they enjoy using, as well as those they think are poorly designed, will help with these concepts.

Student Projects

1. Look at the different types of online advertising. Describe each. Which form of advertising do you believe would be the most effective for you? Why? How often do you click on one of these ads?

2. You are the owner of a small hometown brick-and-mortar gourmet meats store. What, if any, advantage do you see in setting up an online presence? In what ways could this possible help your business? Or could it?
3. How does your college/university use the Internet to attract quality prospective students? Are they doing a good job? What suggestions would you make to them to improve their Net appearance?
4. Find an example of a company that appears to be doing an absolutely terrible job of connecting with customers via the Net. Make recommendations to improve their "Net appeal."
5. What do you believe to be the future of traditional catalog marketing? Find examples of companies that have discontinued their printed catalog in favor of a fully online version. Has this been successful for them?

Small Group Assignments

Form students into groups of three to five. Each group should read the opening vignette to the chapter on Dell. Each group should answer the following questions:

1. How has Dell become so successful with customers?
2. What are the advantages of Dell's business model? What are the disadvantages?
3. Why have Dell's sales stalled, particularly as some competitors are seeing rapidly increasing sales?
4. How is Dell moving to regain its sales momentum?
5. What does this experience say about the future of the direct sales model?

Each group should share its findings with the class.

Individual Assignments

Go onto to Dell's Website (www.dell.com) and that of major competitor Hewlett-Packard (www.hpshopping.com). "Build" your ideal laptop on each. Compare the competitors on product offerings, price, and Website ease of navigation, appeal, and use. Who wins? Why?

Think-Pair-Share

Consider the following questions, formulate an answer, pair with the student on your right, share your thoughts with one another, and respond to questions from the instructor.

1. How would you define direct marketing?
2. What are the benefits of direct marketing to customers? To companies?
3. What are the major forms of direct marketing?
4. What are some of the significant ethical issues raised by the use of direct marketing?
5. How are companies using online marketing to deliver greater value to consumers?

Classroom Exercise/Homework Assignment

The University of Phoenix's "online campus" was established in 1989, well before the advent of and widespread use of the World Wide Web. Since then, the University of Phoenix has exploded, and more and more adults are earning their Bachelor's, Master's and even Doctoral degrees online.

Because this model has proven so successful, traditional universities have added online options to their degree programs. Sometimes courses are only "Web enhanced," meaning that the students still gather in a traditional classroom, but some work takes place on the Internet. Many colleges and universities, however, are moving at least some of their courses completely online. This allows them to reach many non-traditional students, and students who simply cannot relocate to the city in which their campus is located.

1. How has the University of Phoenix Online affected the college experience? Be specific.
2. What are the benefits of obtaining a degree online? What are the disadvantages, if any?
3. Analyze where the University of Phoenix Online advertises. Are they reaching their target audience?
4. Visit their Web site at www.phoenix.edu. Is it an effective Web site? Defend your answer.

Classroom Management Strategies

As was noted previously, students today have grown up with the Internet and e-commerce. This chapter should not be difficult for them, although stressing the Key Terms will be important for them to be able to have intelligent business discussions about the uses of the Internet.

1. Spend 10 minutes each on the first two sections regarding the forces shaping the digital age and the strategies for responding. Figure 14.1, showing the forces that underlie the digital age, will be of great assistance in getting this topic across.
2. E-Marketing Domains and Conducting E-Commerce should each receive 15 minutes. Again, although this material may well be familiar to students, they have not considered it from a business-building perspective and may not know all of the Key Terms. The figures, tables, and Linking the Concepts will help here, as will the Marketing at Work.
3. The final section, on the promise and challenges of e-commerce, can be covered in 15 minutes.

CHAPTER 15
The Global Marketplace

Previewing the Concepts: Chapter Objectives

1. Discuss how the international trade system and the economic, political-legal, and cultural environments affect a company's international marketing decisions
2. Describe three key approaches to entering international markets
3. Explain how companies adapt their marketing mixes for international markets
4. Identify the three major forms of international marketing organization

JUST THE BASICS

Chapter Overview

This chapter examines the fundamentals of global marketing.

Advances in communication, transportation, and other technologies have made the world a much smaller place.

Today, almost every firm, large or small, faces international marketing issues.

There are several factors that draw a company into the international arena.

- Global competitors might offer better products or lower prices.
- The company might discover foreign markets that present higher profit opportunities than the domestic market does.

Most companies start with exporting, using either indirect or direct exporting, or they could go into a joint venture, through such means as licensing, contract manufacturing, management contracting, or joint ownership.

Finally, the company could make a direct investment by developing assembly or manufacturing facilities.

Each form of entry carries its own risks and rewards; the company must weigh these carefully before making final decisions.

Companies that operate in one or more foreign markets must decide how much, if at all, to adapt their marketing mixes to local conditions.

At one extreme are global companies that use a standardized marketing mix, selling largely the same products and using the same marketing approaches worldwide.

At the other extreme is an adapted marketing mix. In this case, the producer adjusts the marketing mix elements to each target market, bearing more costs but hoping for a larger market share and return.

However, global standardization is not an all-or-nothing proposition. Rather, it is a matter of degree.

Companies can manage their international marketing activities in at least three different ways.

1. They can organize an export department,
2. They can create an international division,
3. They can become a global organization.

Annotated Chapter Notes/Outline

Introduction

During the past two decades, the National Basketball Association (NBA) has become a global marketing enterprise.

Nowhere was this more apparent than in last year's NBA finals, which were televised to more than 215 countries in 41 languages.

Like many other businesses, the NBA's primary motive for going global is growth. The league now sells out most of its games, and domestic licensing revenues have flattened in recent years.

Adding to the league's global appeal is the growing presence of foreign-born players.

The NBA now has nine offices in major world cities, including Paris, Tokyo, and Hong Kong.

During last year's summer off-season, the league sponsored 132 international events, with 198 players representing all 30 NBA teams appearing in 87 cities on five continents.

NBA Europe Live does more than simply showcase team training. Each team competes in exhibition games against host teams from Euroleague basketball.

Given the bulk of the NBA's international fan base is in Europe, NBA Europe Live makes good business sense.

Basketball in China is the number one sport for youth 30 and under.

NBA.com's Mandarin language Web site accounts for over 22 percent of all the league's

Internet traffic, and 20,000 Chinese retail outlets now sell NBA merchandise.

Despite the dazzling prospects, many challenges remain.

Global Marketing Today

Since 1990, the number of multinational corporations in the world has grown from 30,000 to more than 60,000.

Since 2003, total world trade has been growing at 6 to 11 percent annually, while global gross domestic product has grown at only 2.5 to 5 percent annually.

Foreign firms are expanding aggressively into new international markets, and home markets are no longer as rich in opportunity.

Few industries are now safe from foreign competition.

A **global firm** is one that, by operating in more than one country, gains marketing, production, R&D, and financial advantages that are not available to purely domestic competitors.

Use **Discussing the Issues** 1 here.

The global company sees the world as one market.

It minimizes the importance of national boundaries and develops "transnational" brands.

The rapid move toward globalization means that all companies will have to answer basic questions:

- What market position should we try to establish in our country, in our economic region, and globally?
- Who will our global competitors be and what are their strategies and resources?
- Where should we produce or source our products?
- What strategic alliances should we form with other firms around the world?

A company faces six major decisions in international marketing. (Figure 15.1)

Use **Key Term** *Global Firm* here. Use **Figure** 15.1 here. Use **Application Question** 1 here.

Looking at the Global Marketing Environment

Use **Chapter Objective** 1 here.

The International Trade System

Tariffs are taxes on certain imported products designed to raise revenue or to protect domestic firms.

Quotas are limits on the amount of foreign imports that a country will accept in certain product categories.

The purpose of a quota is to conserve on foreign exchange and to protect local industry and employment.

Exchange controls are limits on the amount of foreign exchange and the exchange rate against other currencies.

Nontariff trade barriers are such things as biases against U.S. company bids, restrictive product standards, or excessive regulations.

Certain forces ***help*** trade between nations.

The World Trade Organization and GATT

The General Agreement on Tariffs and Trade (GATT) is a 60-year-old treaty designed to promote world trade by reducing tariffs and other international trade barriers.

Since the treaty's inception in 1947, member nations (currently numbering 150) have met in eight rounds of GATT negotiations to reassess trade barriers and set new rules for international trade.

The first seven rounds of negotiations reduced the average worldwide tariffs on manufactured goods from 45 percent to just 5 percent.

The benefits of the Uruguay Round (1994) include reducing the world's remaining merchandise tariffs by 30 percent.

The Uruguay Round set up the World Trade Organization (WTO) to enforce GATT rules.

The WTO acts as an umbrella organization, overseeing GATT, mediating global disputes, and imposing trade sanctions.

Regional Free Trade Zones

Free trade zones or ***Economic communities*** are groups of nations organized to work toward common goals in the regulation of international trade.

Use **Key Term** *Economic Community* here.

One such community is the ***European Union (EU)***.

The European Union represents one of the world's single largest markets. Currently, it has 27 member countries containing close to half a billion consumers and accounts for more than 20 percent of the world's exports.

As a result of increased unification, European companies have grown bigger and more competitive.

Widespread adoption of the euro will decrease much of the currency risk associated with doing business in Europe, making member countries with previously weak currencies more attractive markets.

However, even with the adoption of the euro, it is unlikely that the EU will ever go against 2,000 years of tradition and become the "United States of Europe."

The ***North American Free Trade Agreement (NAFTA)*** established a free trade zone among the United States, Mexico, and Canada.

The agreement created a single market of 443 million people who produce and consume over $15.4 trillion worth of goods and services annually.

NAFTA will eliminate all trade barriers and investment restrictions among the three countries.

Trade among the NAFTA nations has risen 173 percent.

U.S. merchandise exports to NAFTA partners grew 133 percent, compared with exports to the rest of the world at 77 percent.

Canada and Mexico are now the nation's first and second largest trading partners.

The ***Central American Free Trade Agreement (CAFTA)*** established a free trade zone between the United States and Costa Rica, the Dominican Republic, El Salvador, Guatemala, Honduras, and Nicaragua.

Talks have been underway since 1994 to investigate establishing a ***Free Trade Area of the Americas (FTAA).***

Mercosur links eleven Latin America and South America countries.

The ***Andean Community*** (***CAN***, for its Spanish initials) links four more countries.

In late 2004, Mercosur and CAN agreed to unite, creating ***the Union of South American Nations (Unasur)***.

Economic Environment

Two economic factors reflect the country's attractiveness as a market:

1. Industrial structure
2. Income distribution.

1. The country's ***industrial structure*** shapes its product and service needs, income levels, and employment levels.

The four types of industrial structures are as follows:

- ***Subsistence economies:*** The vast majority of people engage in simple agriculture. They consume most of their output and barter the rest for simple goods and services. They offer few market opportunities.
- ***Raw material exporting economies:*** These economies are rich in one or more natural resources but poor in other ways. These countries are good markets for large equipment, tools and supplies, and trucks.
- ***Industrializing economies:*** Manufacturing accounts for 10 to 20 percent of the country's economy. The country needs more imports of raw textile materials, steel, and heavy machinery, and fewer imports of finished textiles, paper products, and automobiles.
- ***Industrial economies:*** Major exporters of manufactured goods, services, and investment funds. They trade goods among themselves and also export them to other types of economies for raw materials and semifinished goods.

2. ***Income distribution*** is the second factor.

Industrialized nations may have **low-, medium-,** and **high-income** households.

Countries with subsistence economies may consist mostly of households with very low family incomes.

Still other countries may have households with only either very low or very high incomes.

Even poor or developing economies may be attractive markets for all kinds of goods, including luxuries.

Political-Legal Environment

Some nations are very receptive to foreign firms; others are less accommodating.

Companies must consider a country's monetary regulations.

Use **Key Term** *Countertrade* here. Use **Focus on Ethics** here.

Countertrade takes several forms:

- ***Barter*** involves the direct exchange of goods or services.
- ***Compensation*** (or ***Buyback***) is where the seller sells a plant, equipment, or technology to another country and agrees to take payment in the resulting products.
- ***Counterpurchase*** (the most common form of countertrade) is when the seller receives full payment in cash but agrees to spend some of the money in the other country.

Cultural Environment

The Impact of Culture on Marketing Strategy

The seller must understand the ways that consumers in different countries think about and use certain products before planning a marketing program.

Business norms and behavior vary from country to country.

The Impact of Marketing Strategy on Cultures

Social critics contend that large American multinationals such as McDonald's, Coca-Cola, Starbucks, Nike, Microsoft, Disney, and MTV are "Americanizing" the world's cultures.

Critics worry that, under such "McDomination," countries around the globe are losing their individual cultural identities.

Such concerns have sometimes led to a backlash against American globalization.

In the most recent *BusinessWeek*/Interbrand survey of global brands, 11 of the top 15 brands were American-owned.

Deciding Whether to Go Global

Not all companies need to venture into international markets to survive.
Any of several factors might draw a company into the international arena.

- Global competitors might attack the company's home market by offering better products or lower prices.
- The company might want to counterattack these competitors in their home markets.

- The company's home market might be stagnant or shrinking.
- Foreign markets may present higher sales and profit opportunities.
- The company's customers might be expanding abroad and require international servicing.

Before going abroad, the company must weigh several risks and answer many questions about its ability to operate globally.

- Can it learn to understand the preferences and buyer behavior of consumers in other countries?
- Can it offer competitively attractive products?
- Will it be able to adapt to other countries' business cultures and deal effectively with foreign nationals?
- Do the company's managers have the necessary international experience?
- Has management considered the impact of regulations and the political environments of other countries?

Deciding Which Markets to Enter

Before going abroad, the company should:

- Define its international ***marketing objectives and policies.***
- Decide what ***volume*** of foreign sales it wants.
- Decide ***how many*** countries it wants to market.
- Decide on the ***types*** of countries to enter.
- Evaluate each selected country.

Possible global markets should be ranked on several factors, including:

- Market size,
- Market growth,
- Cost of doing business,
- Competitive advantage, and
- Risk level.

Use **Focus on Technology** here.

Deciding How to Enter the Market (Figure 15.2)

Use **Key Term** *Exporting* here. Use **Figure** 15.2 here. Use **Chapter Objective** 2 here.

Exporting

Exporting is the simplest way to enter a foreign market.

Indirect exporting is working through independent international marketing intermediaries.

Indirect exporting involves less investment and less risk.

Direct exporting is where the company handles their own exports.

The investment and risk are somewhat greater in this strategy, but so is the potential return.

A company can conduct direct exporting in several ways:

- It can set up a domestic export department that carries out export activities.
- It can set up an overseas sales branch that handles sales, distribution, and promotion.
- It can send home-based salespeople abroad at certain times in order to find business.
- It can do its exporting either through foreign-based distributors or foreign-based agents.

Joint Venturing

Joint venturing is joining with foreign companies to produce or market products or services.

There are four types of joint ventures:

1. Licensing,
2. Contract manufacturing,
3. Management contracting, and
4. Joint ownership.

1. Licensing

Licensing is a simple way for a manufacturer to enter international marketing. The company enters into an agreement with a licensee in the foreign market.

For a fee or royalty, the licensee buys the right to use the company's manufacturing process, trademark, patent, trade secret, or other item of value.

Licensing has disadvantages:

- The firm has less control over the licensee than it would over its own operations.
- If the licensee is very successful, the firm has given up profits.
- When the contract ends, it may find it has created a competitor.

2. **Contract Manufacturing**

Contract manufacturing occurs when the company contracts with manufacturers in the foreign market to produce its product or provide its service.

The drawbacks are:

- Decreased control over the manufacturing process.
- Loss of potential profits on manufacturing.

The benefits are:

- The chance to start faster, with less risk.
- The later opportunity either to form a partnership with or to buy out the local manufacturer.

3. **Management Contracting**

Management contracting takes place when the domestic firm supplies management know-how to a foreign company that supplies the capital.

This is a low-risk method of getting into a foreign market, and it yields income from the beginning.

The arrangement is not sensible if the company can put its management talent to better uses or if it can make greater profits by undertaking the whole venture.

4. **Joint Ownership**

Joint ownership ventures consist of one company joining forces with foreign investors to create a local business in which they share joint ownership and control.

A company may buy an interest in a local firm, or the two parties may form a new business venture.
Joint ownership may be needed for economic or political reasons.

Joint ownership has drawbacks:

- The partners may disagree over policies.

- Whereas U.S. firms emphasize the role of marketing, local investors may rely on selling.

Use **Key Terms** *Direct Investment, Joint Venturing, Licensing, Contract Manufacturing, Management Contracting,* and *Joint Ownership* here.
Use **Discussing the Issues** 2 here.
Use **Application Question** 2 here.

5. Direct Investment

Direct investment is the development of foreign-based assembly or manufacturing facilities.

Advantages:

- Lower costs in the form of cheaper labor or raw materials, foreign government investment incentives, and freight savings.
- The firm may improve its image in the host country.
- Development of a deeper relationship with government, customers, local suppliers, and distributors.
- The firm keeps full control over the investment.

The main disadvantage of direct investment is that the firm faces many risks.

Use **Key Terms** *Standardized Global Marketing* and *Adapted Global Marketing* here.
Use **Chapter Objective** 3 here.
Use **Discussing the Issues** 3 here.

Deciding on the Global Marketing Program

Standardized global marketing is using largely the same marketing strategy approaches and marketing mix worldwide.

Adapted global marketing is adjusting the marketing strategy and mix elements to each target market, bearing more costs but hoping for a larger market share and return.

Use **Discussing the Issues** 5 here.

Some global marketers believe that technology is making the world a smaller place and that consumer needs around the world are becoming more similar.

This paves the way for **"global brands"** and standardized global marketing. Global branding and standardization, in turn, result in greater brand power and reduced costs from economies of scale.

However, because cultural differences are hard to change, most marketers adapt their products, prices, channels, and promotions to fit consumer desires in each country.

Product

Use **Figure** 15.3 here. Use **Discussing the Issues** 4 here.

Five strategies exist allow for adapting product and marketing communication strategies to a global market (Figure 15.3).

Straight product extension means marketing a product in a foreign market without any change.

Product adaptation involves changing the product to meet local conditions or wants.

Product invention consists of creating something new for a specific country market.

This strategy can take two forms.

1. Maintaining or reintroducing earlier product forms that happen to be well adapted to the needs of a given country.
2. Create a new product to meet a need in a given country.

Use **Key Terms** *Straight Product Extension, Product Adaptation,* and *Product Invention* here. Use **Video Case** here.

Promotion

Companies can either:

1. Adopt the same communication strategy they used in the home market or
2. Change it for each local market.

Colors are changed sometimes to avoid taboos in other countries.

Communication adaptation is fully adapting their advertising messages to local markets.

Use **Key Term** *Communication Adaptation* here.

Price

Regardless of how companies go about pricing their products, their foreign prices probably will be higher than their domestic prices for comparable products.

Why? It is a ***price escalation*** problem. It must add the cost of transportation, tariffs, importer margin, wholesaler margin, and retailer margin to its factory price.
To overcome this problem when selling to less-affluent consumers in developing countries, many companies make simpler or smaller versions of their products that can be sold at lower prices.

Dumping occurs when a company either charges less than its costs or less than it charges in its home market.

The Internet is making global price differences more obvious.

When firms sell their wares over the Internet, customers can to see how much products sell for in different countries. This is forcing companies toward more standardized international pricing.

Distribution Channels

The **whole-channel view** takes into account the entire global supply chain and marketing channel. It recognizes that to compete well internationally, the company must effectively design and manage an entire ***global value delivery network.***

Figure 15.4 shows the two major links between the seller and the final buyer.

Channels between nations move company products from points of production to the borders of countries within which they are sold.

Channels within nations moves the products from their market entry points to the final consumers.

Use **Key Term** *Whole-Channel View* here. Use **Figure** 15.4 here. Use **Linking the Concepts** here.

Deciding on the Global Marketing Organization

Use **Chapter Objective** 4 here.

A firm normally gets into international marketing by simply shipping out its goods. If its international sales expand, the company organizes an *export department.*

Many companies get involved in several international markets and ventures. An *international division* may be created to handle all its international activity.

International divisions are organized in a variety of ways.

- *Geographical organizations*: Country managers who are responsible for salespeople, sales branches, distributors, and licensees in their respective countries.
- *World product groups*: each responsible for worldwide sales of different product groups.
- *International subsidiaries*: each responsible for its own sales and profits.

Global organizations are companies that have stopped thinking of themselves as national marketers who sell abroad and have started thinking of themselves as global marketers.

Use **Discussing the Issues** 6 here.

Travel Log

Discussing the Issues

1. Explain what is meant by the term *global firm*. (AASCB: Communication)

   Answer:

   A **global firm** is one that, by operating in more than one country, gains marketing, production, R&D, and financial advantages that are not available to purely domestic competitors. The global company sees the world as one market. It minimizes the importance of national boundaries and develops "transnational" brands. It raises capital, obtains materials and components, and manufactures and markets its goods wherever it can do the best job.

2. Name and describe the various restrictions on international trade. (AACSB: Communication)

   Answer:

   When selling to another country, a firm may face restrictions on trade between nations. Foreign governments may charge **tariffs**, taxes on certain imported products designed to raise revenue or to protect domestic firms. Or they may set **quotas**, limits on the amount of foreign imports that they will accept in certain product categories. The purpose of a quota is to conserve on foreign exchange and to protect local industry and employment. Firms may also face **exchange controls**, which limit the amount of foreign exchange and the exchange rate against other currencies. The company also may face **nontariff trade barriers**, such as biases against U.S. company bids, restrictive product standards, or excessive regulations.

3. Discuss the factors that a business must consider when deciding whether to go global and factors considered in deciding which market to enter. (AACSB: Communication)

   Answer:

   Any of several factors might draw a company into the international arena. Global competitors might attack the company's home market by offering better products or lower prices. The company might want to counterattack these competitors in their home markets to tie up their resources. Or the company's home market might be stagnant or shrinking, and foreign markets may present higher sales and profit opportunities. Or the company's customers might be expanding abroad and require international servicing.

   Before going abroad, the company must weigh several risks and answer many questions about its ability to operate globally. Can the company learn to understand the preferences and buyer behavior of consumers in other countries? Can it offer competitively attractive products? Will it be able to adapt to other countries' business cultures and deal effectively with foreign nationals? Do the company's managers have the necessary international experience? Has management considered the impact of regulations and the political environments of other countries? Because of the difficulties of entering international markets, most companies do not act until some situation or event thrusts them into the global arena. Someone—a domestic exporter, a foreign importer, a foreign government—may ask the company to sell abroad. Or the company may be saddled with overcapacity and need to find additional markets for its goods.

   Before going abroad, the company should try to define its international *marketing objectives and policies*. It should decide what *volume* of foreign sales it wants. The company also needs to choose in *how many* countries it wants to market. Next, the company needs to decide on the *types* of countries to enter. A country's attractiveness depends on the product, geographical factors, income and population, political climate, and other factors. After listing possible international markets, the company must carefully evaluate each one on several factors, including market size, market growth, cost of doing business, competitive advantage, and risk level. The goal is to determine the potential of each market, using indicators such as those shown in Table 15.1. Then the marketer must decide which markets offer the greatest long-run return on investment.

4. Compare and contrast the three ways to enter foreign markets. Which is the best? (AACSB: Communication; Reflective Thinking)

Answer:

Once a business decides to go global, there are three mode of entry: exporting, joint venturing, and direct investment. Each succeeding strategy involves more commitment and risk, but also more control and potential profits. The simplest way to enter a foreign market is through **exporting**. The company may passively export its surpluses from time to time, or it may make an active commitment to expand exports to a particular market. In either case, the company produces all its goods in its home country. It may or may not modify them for the export market. Exporting involves the least change in the company's product lines, organization, investments, or mission.

A second method of entering a foreign market is **joint venturing**—joining with foreign companies to produce or market products or services. Joint venturing differs from exporting in that the company joins with a host country partner to sell or market abroad. It differs from direct investment in that an association is formed with someone in the foreign country. There are four types of joint ventures: licensing, contract manufacturing, management contracting, and joint ownership.

The biggest involvement in a foreign market comes through **direct investment**—the development of foreign-based assembly or manufacturing facilities. If a company has gained experience in exporting and if the foreign market is large enough, foreign production facilities offer many advantages. The firm may have lower costs in the form of cheaper labor or raw materials, foreign government investment incentives, and freight savings. The firm may improve its image in the host country because it creates jobs. Generally, a firm develops a deeper relationship with government, customers, local suppliers, and distributors, allowing it to adapt its products to the local market better. Finally, the firm keeps full control over the investment and therefore can develop manufacturing and marketing policies that serve its long-term international objectives. The main disadvantage of direct investment is that the firm faces many risks, such as restricted or devalued currencies, falling markets, or government changes.

No single way to enter a foreign market is "best." It depends on the situation and the business going global.

5. Define standardized global marketing and adapted global marketing and discuss the implications of each. (AACSB: Communication)

Answer:

Companies that operate in one or more foreign markets must decide how much, if at all, to adapt their marketing strategies and programs to local conditions. At one extreme are global companies that use **standardized global marketing**, using largely the same marketing strategy approaches and marketing mix worldwide. At the other extreme is an **adapted global marketing**. In this case, the producer adjusts the marketing strategy and mix elements to each target market, bearing more costs but hoping for a larger market share and return.

The question of whether to adapt or standardize is debatable. On one hand, some global marketers believe that technology is making the world a smaller place and that consumer needs around the world are becoming more similar. This paves the way for "global brands" and standardized global marketing. Global branding and standardization, in turn, result in greater brand power and reduced costs from economies of scale. On the other hand, the marketing concept holds that marketing programs will be more effective if tailored to the unique needs of each targeted customer group. If this concept applies within a country, it should apply even more in international markets. Despite global convergence, consumers in different countries still have widely varied cultural backgrounds. They still differ significantly in their needs and wants, spending power, product preferences, and shopping patterns. Because these differences are hard to change, most marketers adapt their products, prices, channels, and promotions to fit consumer desires in each country. However, global standardization is not an all-or-nothing proposition. It's a matter of degree. Most international marketers suggest that companies should "think globally but act locally"—that they should seek a balance between standardization and adaptation. The corporate level gives global strategic direction; regional or local units focus on individual consumer differences across global markets.

6. Explain the differences in organizing the international marketing function as an export department, an international division, or a global organization. What drives the evolution from one organizational form to another? (AACSB: Communication; Reflective Thinking)

   Answer:

   Companies manage their international marketing activities in at least three different ways. Most companies first organize an **export department**, then create an **international division**, and finally become a **global organization**. A firm normally gets into international marketing by simply shipping out its goods. If its international sales expand, the company organizes an export department with a sales manager and a few assistants. As sales increase, the export department can expand to include various marketing services so that it can actively go after business. If the firm moves into joint ventures or direct investment, the export department will no longer be adequate. Many companies get involved in several international markets and ventures. A company may export to one country, license to another, have a joint ownership venture in a third, and own a subsidiary in a fourth. Sooner or later it will create international divisions or subsidiaries to handle all its international activity. Many firms have passed beyond the international division stage and become truly global organizations. The global operating units report directly to the chief executive or executive committee of the organization, not to the head of an international division.

Application Questions

1. Convert $1.00 U.S. to euros and to the currencies of five other countries. One Web site that converts currencies is www.xe.com/ucc/. Is the dollar stronger or weaker than each other currency? Is a strong dollar good or bad for United States businesses doing business in other countries? (AACSB: Communication; Use of IT; Reflective Thinking)

   Answer:

   Students' answers will vary as exchange rates vary by country and by day. However, on September 24, 2007, $1.00 U.S. was equivalent to 0.71007 euros, which means the dollar was weaker than the euro. However, $1.00 U.S. was equivalent to 1,296.91 South Korean Wons, so the dollar was stronger there. Whether a strong dollar is good or bad depends on what a business is doing. If a U.S. business is buying goods from a country with a stronger currency than the dollar, these goods will be more expensive than if the dollar were stronger. However, a stronger dollar means that U.S. goods will be more expensive for buyers in countries with weaker currencies.

2. The political-legal environment in countries such as Russia and Venezuela has had a significant impact on foreign oil companies. Research these countries and write a brief report on the impact of the political-legal environment on foreign oil companies. (AACSB: Communication; Use of IT; Reflective Thinking)

   Answer:

   Students' answers will vary, but they should be able to find information on what has been happening in oil-producing countries such as Russia and Venezuela. For example, in 2007, Hugo Chavez of Venezuela nationalized the oil industry in that country. Exxon Mobile and ConocoPhillips ceased operations in that country, which will negatively impact this country's production. It will also dissuade other companies from investing in this country. Russia forced BP to sell its stake in the oil industry for a fraction of its value, which will also hinder foreign investment in the future.

3. Form teams of four students and discuss how the following products might adapt their marketing mixes when entering the Chinese market: Oreo cookies, Herbal Essences Conditioner, Ben and Jerry's ice cream, and Hummer H3 SUVs. (AACSB: Communication; Reflective Thinking)

   Answer:

   Students will probably comment most on product and communication adaptations.

   Product Issues:
   Oreo cookies/Ben & Jerry's – local tastes must be considered. Is chocolate and

vanilla still the best combination for Oreos? Is the cookie too sweet? What flavor ice cream is most popular?
Herbal Essences/Hummer H3 – how do these products fit into everyday life? Do Chinese consumers use hair conditioners at all? Do they have the space or income for a larger vehicle or must the Hummer be redesigned to be smaller?

Communication:
Messages might need to be changed. Americans know the classic fun in an Oreo is in twisting and licking it, which is commonly seen in commercials. How does this compare with Chinese cultural standards for table manners? How/when is ice cream eaten? Will the pieces of candy and nuts in Ben and Jerry's need additional explanations? Do the Hummer ads need to display less aggression than in the U.S.? In all situations, the ads might want to use local actors for slice-of-life themes, Chinese language, and local cultural symbols and music.

Price:
The price must be adapted for local competition and disposable income differences.

Distribution:
Cars may not be sold through a dealer network as in the U.S. Ice cream is difficult to move through the channel – how will distribution need to be changed?

<u>Under the Hood: Focus on Technology</u>

GMI (Global Market Insight) is a leader in global market research. It offers an online global panel of more than 5 million members in 200 countries. Panelists speak more than 37 different languages and are available in the Americas, Europe, Asia Pacific, and the Middle East. In addition to consumer markets, GMI provides access to hard-to-reach business consumers, including B2B specialty medical markets of physicians, nurses, and patients with a variety of chronic illnesses. GMI differentiates itself from competitors with claims that it has the highest standards of panel integrity.

1. What questions might a U.S. manufacturer of blood diagnostic equipment ask the members of the GMI medical panel when considering entry into a new country? (AACSB: Communication; Reflective Thinking)

   Answer:

   This manufacturer would want to find out from nurses and doctors the products that are currently used at the hospitals, testing labs, and physician offices. It would also want to know whether panelists are satisfied with existing products and suppliers. This manufacturer would also want to get some preliminary measures of interest in its products, as well as feedback on pricing, levels of demand, and key buying influences.

2. Sign up to be a GMI survey respondent at www.globaltestmarket.com. After going through the registration process, do you think that GMI has a rigid standard for its survey respondents? (AACSB: Communication; Reflective Thinking)

   Answer:

   It is not difficult to register for this service. In fact, one will observe that there is no control for the authenticity of the information survey respondents provide about themselves. A lot of information is collected—almost too much to believe that the respondents put time and care into their answers. Many applicants will be motivated purely by the cash rewards.

Focus on Ethics

Global companies face many challenges when expanding abroad. Cultural differences in particular are difficult. In several emerging markets, such as parts of Asia, Africa, the Middle East, the former Soviet Union, Eastern Europe, and South America, bribery is considered "standard operating procedure." The World Bank estimates bribery in international trade to be about $1 trillion annually.

The Foreign Corrupt Practices Act (FCPA) has existed in the United States since 1977, but the Securities and Exchange Commission and the U.S. Department of Justice have only recently stepped up enforcement. This law prohibits U.S. companies from giving corrupt payments to foreign officials to obtain favor in business transactions. To get around this law, many companies have used third parties to do their dirty deeds. However, many companies are now confessing their misdeeds rather than remaining silent and hoping to avoid detection. This is because of provisions of the 2002 Sarbanes-Oxley law regarding accounting reporting practices. Under this law, American senior executives can go to prison for violations.

For a long time, the United States was one of few leaders in battling corruption in foreign trade, but now many more countries are joining the fight. In China, bribery is punishable by death, which makes the multimillion dollar penalties levied from FCPA violations seem light. Aside from financial penalties (the largest being over $40 million so far), guilty companies may also be prohibited from doing business with the U.S. government or may be denied export licenses.

1. Is it right for U.S. companies to be penalized for going along with cultural norms in other countries? Is it right for the United States and other countries to demand that businesses in other countries follow our laws? (AACSB: Communication; Ethical Reasoning)

   Answer:

   Students' responses will vary. Some students may say that, "When in Rome, do as the Romans do" applies, meaning businesses should behave according to local customs and norms. However, others will be adamant that there is a right and a wrong in this situation and that bribery is wrong and should never be considered an acceptable practice.

2. What are the consequences for U.S. companies of not doing what foreign businesses and governments expect or what competitors foreign markets do? (AACSB: Communication; Reflective Thinking)

Answer:

The main consequence to U.S. companies is that they may lose business if they do not go along with accepted bribery demands. A company from another country that is not as vigilant in prosecuting foreign corruption as the U.S. will likely step in and get the business. However, U.S. companies can help the U.S. government in getting more countries involved to fight global corruption, leveling the competitive playing field.

GREAT IDEAS

Barriers to Effective Learning

1. Many students today have traveled internationally, and perhaps even studied abroad. However, this chapter will introduce concepts that most likely will not have crossed their minds before. Free trade agreements may be known in name, but not in what they actually do. The analytics of deciding whether to go global and if so, which countries to enter, will certainly not have been encountered before. This chapter will serve as an excellent introduction to these ideas.
2. The terms involved in the international trade system (tariff, quota, embargo, etc.) are generally unfamiliar to most students. Go through these carefully and use examples from recent press. Ask the students to express their feelings about tariffs, quotas, embargoes, etc. How does government policy affect free trade? Why would these barriers be erected? How do they feel about NAFTA? Do they think that it will be good for trade? When would trade barriers be justified?
3. The economic and political-legal environments will also most likely be unfamiliar to most students. Some students might have done some mission or humanitarian work in foreign countries with economies and political systems vastly different from our own. If you are lucky enough to have them in your class, have them relate their experiences. Economics majors, or those who enjoyed an economics class, may also be able to relate what they have learned about these issues from a different point of view.
4. On deciding whether to go international, many students will believe that it is simply a matter of the company deciding to expand. The concept of being forced to go into other countries because of customers pulling you along, or having to fight a global competitor on your home turf, will surprise some of them. Challenge them to think about how small companies grow, and why they might start selling their goods overseas. Use a local company that sells unique items. How might foreign customers find them? How would they decide that there is a

market in another country? You can break the class into teams to work on these types of issues.

5. Countertrade is almost always an issue with undergraduate students. The various types can be very confusing, and so these concepts and terms need to be described very carefully. The examples in the book are quite useful, and you can generally find additional examples in the business press. Joint venturing is slightly easier to understand, but again, using lots of examples will really help the students appreciate the complexities and how these decisions are made.

Student Projects

1. Read about the WTO (www.wto.org). What are the advantages and disadvantages of the existence of this organization? Take a stand on its effectiveness and substantiate your position.
2. Describe the three key approaches to entering international markets. Which do you believe would be the best for a company just beginning to work internationally?
3. What are "transnational" brands? Give examples of three brands you believe fall into this category and why.
4. Research the history of the North American Free Trade Agreement (NAFTA). Write a position paper stating your beliefs regarding its overall effectiveness.
5. Talk about the "Americanization" of foreign cultures. What is it? How does it happen? Is it even a real phenomenon?

Small Group Assignment

Form students into groups of three to five. Each group should read the opening vignette to the chapter on the NBA. Each group should then answer the following questions:

1. What do you see as the image of the NBA worldwide?
2. How has the NBA worked to become a powerful worldwide brand? Have they been effective?
3. What do you see as the future growth potential of this brand?
4. What is NBA Europe Live?
5. What are the major challenges facing the NBA's continued global growth?

Each group should share its findings with the class.

Individual Assignment

Read Thomas Friedman's great book, *The Lexus and the Olive Tree*. Write a 5 page summary of the major points he makes.

Think-Pair-Share

Consider the following questions, formulate an answer, pair with the student on your right, share your thoughts with one another, and respond to questions from the instructor.

1. What is the fundamental difference between a tariff and a quota?
2. What is countertrade and how does it work?
3. What is the purpose of the World Trade Organization (WTO)? Do you believe it is doing a good job?
4. Discuss NAFTA and FTAA. In the long run, which do you believe has the greatest probability of success?
5. What is meant by the term dumping? Why can it be a problem?

Classroom Exercise/Homework Assignment

Review the history of Disneyland Paris. Why was it initially such a failure? How did Disney turn it around (or have they really)? What lessons can we take away from their experiences in France?

Classroom Management Strategies

This chapter contains a lot of information that will be new to all students. Each section should be reviewed carefully.

1. The introduction and first section can be covered in 10 minutes. They provide a basis for the remaining content, and the NBA example in the opening vignette is excellent.
2. The next section has key information in it that the students must understand. Take 10 minutes with this section, paying particular attention to the international trade system and the economic environment. These two subsections cover very important material and new terminology that the students should understand before moving on.
3. Deciding whether to go global and into which markets to move can be covered together in 10 minutes. Table 15.1 should figure prominently in this discussion.
4. The global marketing program introduces for the first time the marketing mix element decisions that must be made. This should also be discussed for at least 10 minutes, and again, examples are very important here.
5. The various ways to organize the company for global marketing can be covered in 5 to 10 minutes. Again, examples of various firms and how they are organized will be very helpful here.

CHAPTER 16
Marketing Ethics and Social Responsibility

Previewing the Concepts: Chapter Objectives

1. Identify the major social criticisms of marketing
2. Define ***consumerism*** and ***environmentalism*** and explain how they affect marketing strategies
3. Describe the principles of socially responsible marketing
4. Explain the role of ethics in marketing

JUST THE BASICS

Chapter Overview

This final chapter focuses on marketing as a social institution.

First, the chapter covers at some common criticisms of marketing as it impacts individual consumers, other businesses, and society as a whole.

Next are an examination consumerism, environmentalism, and other citizen and public actions to keep marketing in check.

Lastly, the chapter looks at how companies themselves can benefit from proactively pursuing socially responsible and ethical practices that bring value not just to individual customers but to society as a whole.

Social responsibility and ethical actions are more than just the right thing to do; they're also good for business.

Annotated Chapter Notes/Outline

Introduction

Timberland's Swartz, a third-generation CEO whose grandfather founded the company in 1952, is trying to do is to use the resources, energy, and profits of a publicly traded footwear and apparel company to combat social ills, help the environment, and improve conditions for laborers around the globe.

Rather than using his company as a charity, he's using the hard financial metrics of profit, return on investment, and shareholder return to try to prove that companies actually can do well by doing good.

For Timberland, service is not something you do once a year. Although volunteer projects are always under way, many of them have been organized under the rubric of Serv-a-palooza, held in late September.

To inspire consumers to ask questions and make more informed purchase decisions, every Timberland shoebox carries a label, modeled after the nutrition labels on food products, outlining the ecological footprint created by the manufacture and distribution of the footwear inside.

Timberland is introducing a Green Index hang tag, which provides product-specific ratings on environmental factors such as climate impact, chemical usage, and the amount of sustainable or organic materials used.

Swartz's biggest challenge is getting Wall Street to buy into the doing-good side of the story.

Use **Chapter Objective** 1 here.

Social Criticisms of Marketing

Marketing's Impact on Individual Consumers

Use **Discussing the Issues** 1 here.

Consumer advocates, government agencies, and other critics have accused marketing of harming consumers through high prices, deceptive practices, high-pressure selling, shoddy or unsafe products, planned obsolescence, and poor service to disadvantaged consumers.

High Prices

Many critics charge that the American marketing system causes prices to be higher than they would be under more Asensible@ systems.

High Costs of Distribution: A long-standing charge is that greedy channel intermediaries mark up prices beyond the value of their services.

How do resellers answer these charges? They argue that intermediaries do work that would otherwise have to be done by manufacturers or consumers.

High Advertising and Promotion Costs: Modern marketing is accused of pushing up prices to finance heavy advertising and sales promotion.

Marketers respond that advertising does add to product costs. But it also adds value by informing potential buyers of the availability and merits of a brand.

Excessive Markups: Critics charge that some companies mark up goods excessively.

Marketers respond that most businesses try to deal fairly with consumers because they want to build customer relationships and repeat business.

Deceptive Practices

Deceptive practices fall into three groups:

1. Pricing,
2. Promotion,
3. Packaging.

Deceptive pricing includes practices such as falsely advertising Afactory@ or Awholesale@ prices or a large price reduction from a phony high retail list price.

Deceptive promotion includes practices such as misrepresenting the product's features or performance or luring the customers to the store for a bargain that is out of stock.

Deceptive packaging includes exaggerating package contents through subtle design, using misleading labeling, or describing size in misleading terms.

The Wheeler-Lea Act gives the Federal Trade Commission (FTC) power to regulate Aunfair or deceptive acts or practices."

A**Puffery**@ is defined as innocent exaggeration for effect.

High-Pressure Selling

Marketers have little to gain from high-pressure selling.

Such tactics may work in one-time selling situations for short-term gain. However, most selling involves building long-term relationships with valued customers.

Shoddy, Harmful, or Unsafe Products

Typical product complaints:

- Products are not made well and services are not performed well.
- Many products deliver little benefit, or that they might even be harmful.
- Product safety has been a problem for several reasons, including company indifference, increased product complexity, and poor quality control.

Use **Application Question** 1 here. Use **Focus on Technology** here.

Planned Obsolescence

Critics also have charged that some companies practice planned obsolescence, causing their products to become obsolete before they actually should need replacement.

Marketers respond that consumers *like* style changes; they get tired of the old goods and want a new look in fashion. Or they *want* the latest high-tech innovations, even if older models still work.

Poor Service to Disadvantaged Consumers

The American marketing system has been accused of serving disadvantaged consumers poorly.

Critics accuse major chain retailers of A**redlining,**@ drawing a red line around disadvantaged neighborhoods and avoiding placing stores there.

Clearly, better marketing systems must be built to service disadvantaged consumers.

In cases where marketers do not step in to fill the void, the government likely will.

Use **Linking the Concepts** here.

Marketing's Impact on Society as a Whole

False Wants and Too Much Materialism

Critics have charged that the marketing system urges too much interest in material possessions.

People are judged by what they *own* rather than by who they *are*.

These criticisms overstate the power of business to create needs.

Too Few Social Goods

Business has been accused of overselling private goods at the expense of public goods.

A way must be found to restore a balance between private and public goods.

Options:

- Make producers bear the full social costs of their operations.
- Make consumers pay the social costs.

Cultural Pollution

Critics charge the marketing system with creating ***cultural pollution.***

Marketers answer the charges of Acommercial noise@ with these arguments:

1. Because of mass-communication channels, some ads are bound to reach people who have no interest in the product and are therefore bored or annoyed.
2. Ads make much of television and radio free to users and keep down the costs of magazines and newspapers.
3. Today's consumers have alternatives.

Marketing's Impact on Other Businesses

Critics charge that a company's marketing practices can harm other companies and reduce competition.

Three problems are involved:

1. Acquisitions of competitors,
2. Marketing practices that create barriers to entry, and
3. Unfair competitive marketing practices.

Use **Chapter Objective** 2 here. Use **Application Question** 2 here.

Citizen and Public Actions to Regulate Marketing

Consumerism

Use **Key Term** *Consumerism* here.

American business firms have been the target of organized consumer movements on three occasions.

1. The first consumer movement took place in the early 1900s. It was fueled by rising prices, Upton Sinclair's writings on conditions in the meat industry, and scandals in the drug industry.
2. The second consumer movement, in the mid-1930s, was sparked by an upturn in consumer prices during the Great Depression and another drug scandal.
3. The third movement began in the 1960s. Consumers had become better educated, products had become more complex and potentially hazardous, and people were unhappy with American institutions.

Consumerism is an organized movement of citizens and government agencies to improve the rights and power of buyers in relation to sellers.

Traditional ***sellers' rights*** include:

- The right to introduce any product in any size and style, provided it is not hazardous to personal health or safety; or, if it is, to include proper warnings and controls.
- The right to charge any price for the product provided no discrimination exists among similar kinds of buyers.
- The right to spend any amount to promote the product provided it is not defined as unfair competition.
- The right to use any product message provided it is not misleading or dishonest in content or execution.
- The right to use any buying incentive programs provided they are not unfair or misleading.

Traditional ***buyers' rights*** include:

- The right not to buy a product that is offered for sale.
- The right to expect the product to be safe.
- The right to expect the product to perform as claimed.

Consumer advocates call for the following additional consumer rights:

- The right to be well informed about important aspects of the product.
- The right to be protected against questionable products and marketing practices.
- The right to influence products and marketing practices in ways that will improve the Aquality of life.@

Consumers have not only the ***right*** but also the ***responsibility*** to protect themselves instead of leaving this function to someone else.

Environmentalism

Use **Key Term** *Environmentalism* here.

Environmentalism is an organized movement of concerned citizens, businesses, and government agencies to protect and improve people's living environment.

The first wave of modern environmentalism in the United States was driven by environmental groups and concerned consumers in the 1960s and 1970s.

The second environmentalism wave was driven by government, which passed laws and regulations during the 1970s and 1980s governing industrial practices impacting the environment.

The third environmentalism wave is a merging of the first two waves in which companies are accepting more responsibility for doing no harm to the environment.

Use **Key Term** *Environmental Sustainability* here. Use **Application Question** 3 here. Use **Figure** 16.1 here.

Environmental sustainability - Environmental sustainability is about generating profits while helping to save the planet.

Figure 16.1 shows a grid that companies can use to gauge their progress toward environmental sustainability.

Pollution prevention - Eliminating or minimizing waste before it is created.

Product stewardship - Minimizing not just pollution from production and product design but all environmental impacts throughout the full product life cycle, and all the while reducing costs.

Design for environment (DFE) and ***cradle-to-cradle*** practices are practices that involve thinking ahead to design products that are easier to recover, reuse, or recycle and developing programs to reclaim products at the end of their lives.

The A**beyond greening**@ activities identified in Figure 16.1 look to the future.

New clean technology. Many organizations that have made good sustainability headway are still limited by existing technologies. To create fully sustainable strategies, they will need to develop innovative new technologies.

Sustainability vision. Serves as a guide to the future. It shows how the company's products and services, processes, and policies must evolve and what new technologies must be developed to get there.

Public Actions to Regulate Marketing (Figure 16.2)

Use **Figure** 16.2 here.

Many of the laws that affect marketing are listed in Chapter 3.

The task is to translate these laws into the language that marketing executives understand as they make decisions.

Business Actions toward Socially Responsible Marketing

Use **Chapter Objective** 3 here. Use **Discussing the Issues** 2 here. Use **Video Case** here.

Enlightened Marketing

The philosophy of **enlightened marketing** holds that a company's marketing should support the best long-run performance of the marketing system.

Enlightened marketing consists of five principles:

1. **Consumer-Oriented Marketing**

Use **Key Term** *Consumerism* here.

Consumer-oriented marketing means that the company should view and organize its marketing activities from the consumer's point of view.

Only by seeing the world through its customers' eyes can the company build lasting and profitable customer relationships.

2. **Customer-Value Marketing**

Customer-value marketing means the company should put most of its resources into customer value-building marketing investments.

By creating value *for* consumers, the company can capture value *from* consumers in return.

3. **Innovative Marketing**

Innovative marketing requires that the company continuously seek real product and marketing improvements.

4. **Sense-of-Mission Marketing**

Sense-of-mission marketing means that the company should define its mission in broad *social* terms rather than narrow ***product*** terms.

5. **Societal Marketing**

Societal marketing means an enlightened company makes marketing decisions by considering consumers' wants and interests, the company's requirements, and society's long-run interests.

Products can be classified according to their degree of immediate consumer satisfaction and long-run consumer benefit. (Figure 16.3)

- **Deficient products** have neither immediate appeal nor long-run benefits.
- **Pleasing products** give high immediate satisfaction but may hurt consumers in the long run.
- **Salutary products** have low appeal but may benefit consumers in the long run; for instance.
- **Desirable products** give both high immediate satisfaction and high long-run benefits.

Use **Key Terms** *Enlightened Marketing, Consumer-Oriented Marketing, Innovative Marketing, Sense-of-Mission Marketing, Societal Marketing, Deficient Products, Pleasing Products, Salutary Products,* and *Desirable Products* here. Use **Figure** 16.3 here. Use **Discussing the Issues** 3 and 4 here. Use **Focus on Ethics** here.

Use **Table** 16-1 here. Use **Chapter Objective** 4 here. Use **Discussing the Issues** 5 here.

Marketing Ethics (Table 16.1)

Corporate marketing ethics policies are broad guidelines that everyone in the organization must follow.

What principle should guide companies and marketing managers on issues of ethics and social responsibility?

One philosophy is that such issues are decided by the free market and legal system.

A second philosophy puts responsibility not on the system but in the hands of individual companies and managers.

Written codes and ethics programs do not ensure ethical behavior.

Ethics and social responsibility require a total corporate commitment.

Use **Discussing the Issues** 6 here.

Travel Log

Discussing the Issues

1. In what ways do consumers believe that marketers make products more expensive to the end consumer? (AASCB: Communication)

   Answer:

   By having high costs of distribution and high advertising and promotion costs which they pass on to final customers. In addition, many consumers believe that the mark-up on products and services is too high.

2. Marketing's impact on society as a whole has been criticized. Discuss the issues relevant to this impact. (AACSB: Communication)

   Answer:

   Three criticisms are discussed in the chapter: **false wants and too much materialism**, **too few social goods**, and **cultural pollution**. Critics have charged that the marketing system urges too much interest in material possessions. People are judged by what they *own* rather than by who they *are*. This drive for wealth and possessions hit new highs in the 1980s and 1990s, when phrases such as Agreed is good@ and Ashop till you drop@ seemed to characterize the times. The critics do not view this interest in material things as a natural state of mind but rather as a matter of false wants created by marketing. Businesses hire Madison Avenue to stimulate people's desires for goods, and Madison Avenue uses the mass media to create materialistic models of the good life. People work harder to earn the necessary money. Their purchases increase the output of American industry, and industry in turn uses Madison Avenue to stimulate more desire for the industrial output. Thus, marketing is seen as creating false wants that benefit industry more than they benefit consumers.

   Business has been accused of overselling private goods at the expense of public goods. As private goods increase, they require more public services that are usually not forthcoming. For example, an increase in automobile ownership (private good) requires more highways, traffic control, parking spaces, and police services (public goods). The overselling of private goods results in Asocial costs.@ For cars, some of the social costs include traffic congestion, gasoline shortages, and air pollution.

   Critics charge the marketing system with creating cultural pollution. Our senses are being constantly assaulted by marketing and advertising. Commercials interrupt serious programs; pages of ads obscure magazines; billboards mar beautiful scenery; spam fills our e-mailboxes. These interruptions continually pollute people's minds with messages of materialism, sex, power, or status.

3. Discuss the types of harmful impact that marketing practices can have on competition and the associated problems. (AACSB: Communication)

Answer:

Critics charge that a company's marketing practices can harm other companies and reduce competition. Three problems are involved: acquisitions of competitors, marketing practices that create barriers to entry, and unfair competitive marketing practices.

Critics claim that firms are harmed and competition reduced when companies expand by acquiring competitors rather than by developing their own new products. The large number of acquisitions and the rapid pace of industry consolidation over the past several decades have caused concern that vigorous young competitors will be absorbed and that competition will be reduced. In virtually every major industry the number of major competitors is shrinking. Acquisitions can sometimes be good for society. The acquiring company may gain economies of scale that lead to lower costs and lower prices. A well-managed company may take over a poorly managed company and improve its efficiency. An industry that was not very competitive might become more competitive after the acquisition. But acquisitions can also be harmful and, therefore, are closely regulated by the government.

Critics have also charged that marketing practices bar new companies from entering an industry. Large marketing companies can use patents and heavy promotion spending or tie up suppliers or dealers to keep out or drive out competitors. Those concerned with antitrust regulation recognize that some barriers are the natural result of the economic advantages of doing business on a large scale. Other barriers could be challenged by existing and new laws.

Finally, some firms have in fact used unfair competitive marketing practices with the intention of hurting or destroying other firms. They may set their prices below costs, threaten to cut off business with suppliers, or discourage the buying of a competitor's products. Various laws work to prevent such predatory competition. It is difficult, however, to prove that the intent or action was really predatory.

4. Can an organization focus on both consumerism and environmentalism at the same time? Explain. (AACSB: Communication)

Answer:

Yes, an organization can focus on both at the same time. In fact, the two often go hand in hand. Both result from outward-looking orientations. A company that respects the rights of its consumers will likely also be concerned about the quality of their environment. Examples are companies such as Timberland and Whole Foods Market.

5. Define enlightened marketing and explain the five principles associated with it. (AACSB: Communication)

   Answer:

   The philosophy of **enlightened marketing** holds that a company's marketing should support the best long-run performance of the marketing system. Enlightened marketing consists of five principles: *consumer-oriented marketing*, *customer-value marketing*, *innovative marketing*, *sense-of-mission marketing*, and *societal marketing*.

   Consumer-oriented marketing means that the company should view and organize its marketing activities from the consumer's point of view. It should work hard to sense, serve, and satisfy the needs of a defined group of customers. According to the principle of **customer-value marketing**, the company should put most of its resources into customer value-building marketing investments. Many things marketers do may raise sales in the short run but add less *value* than would actual improvements in the product's quality, features, or convenience. Enlightened marketing calls for building long-run consumer loyalty and relationships by continually improving the value consumers receive from the firm's market offering.

   By creating value *for* consumers, the company can capture value *from* consumers in return.

   The principle of **innovative marketing** requires that the company continuously seek real product and marketing improvements. The company that overlooks new and better ways to do things will eventually lose customers to another company that has found a better way. **Sense-of-mission marketing** means that the company should define its mission in broad *social* terms rather than narrow *product* terms. When a company defines a social mission, employees feel better about their work and have a clearer sense of direction. Brands linked with broader missions can serve the best long-run interests of both the brand and consumers.

   Finally, following the principle of **societal marketing**, an enlightened company makes marketing decisions by considering consumers' wants and interests, the company's requirements, and society's long-run interests. The company is aware that neglecting consumer and societal long-run interests is a disservice to consumers and society. Alert companies view societal problems as opportunities.

6. Discuss the philosophies that guide marketers facing ethical issues. (AACSB: Communication)

Answer:

One philosophy is that ethical issues are decided by the free market and legal system. Under this principle, companies and their managers are not responsible for making moral judgments. Companies can in good conscience do whatever the market and legal systems allow.

A second philosophy puts responsibility not on the system but in the hands of individual companies and managers. This more enlightened philosophy suggests that a company should have a Asocial conscience.@ Companies and managers should apply high standards of ethics and morality when making corporate decisions, regardless of Awhat the system allows.@

Application Questions

1. Consumers can contact the U.S. Consumer Product Safety Commission (CPSC) if they have a complaint about an unsafe product. Visit www.cpsc.gov to learn about this agency. Discuss a recent recall. (AACSB: Communication; Use of IT; Reflective Thinking)

   Answer:

   This Web site is very informative and lists several consumer product recalls. Interestingly, all eleven of the recent recalls listed were for children's products.

2. In a small group, discuss the pros and cons of the proposed merger between the two satellite radio companies, XM Radio and Sirius. Is the merger good or bad for competition and society as a whole? (AACSB: Communication; Reflective Thinking)

   Answer:

   Student responses will vary. Critics claim that firms are harmed and competition reduced when companies expand by acquiring competitors rather than by developing their own new products. If the market is narrowly defined as Asatellite radio,@ then there will only be one company offering service in this market. A monopoly is usually not in the best interest of consumers. However, the market can be more broadly defined in terms of radio, which means the combined company will compete with AM and FM radio. It can also be defined even more broadly than radio, such as entertainment, which then brings in competing products like MP3 players.

   Acquisitions can sometimes be good for society. The acquiring company may gain economies of scale that lead to lower costs and lower prices. A well-managed company may take over a poorly managed company and improve its efficiency. An industry that was not very competitive might become more competitive after the acquisition. But acquisitions can also be harmful and, therefore, are closely regulated by the government.

3. Identify a company you believe is environmentally responsible. Does this influence your opinion of the company? Does it increase the likelihood that you'll buy from the company? Explain. (AACSB: Communication; Reflective Thinking)

   Answer:

   Student responses will vary, but they may mention companies they've seen advertising their environmental responsiveness. Or they can search Aenvironmentally responsible companies@ in Google and find examples. For example, Sony lists its eco-products and services at www.sony.net/SonyInfo/Environment/environment/eco/index.html. Students should be able to find similar examples from other companies. Whether or not this information influences their opinion of the company or their purchases is a personal matter.

Under the Hood: Focus on Technology

We are living in a time when technological advancement causes technological obsolescence. We like technological advances but they create problems. For example, you may be too young to remember 5 2 inch floppy computer disks or even the smaller 3 2 inch disks that replaced them. USB drives now replace disks and CDs as a data storage device. Most new computers can no longer access data that were stored on disks, so what will it be like five, ten, or twenty years from now? How many people have video cameras but can no longer purchase the tapes they use to record videos? Or what about a cell phone for which you can no longer purchase a charger?

1. Think of other instances of technological obsolescence and discuss them with others in your class. (AACSB: Communication; Reflective Thinking)

   Answer:

   Student responses will vary and it will be interesting to see their perspectives. For example, they may mention VCR video tapes being replaced by DVDs but not realize that before video tapes there were video discs. They may not know about 8-track tapes and cassette tapes but they understand CDs and CD players being replaced by digital music, such as MP3 files and MP3 players.

2. Is this obsolescence just a ploy by manufacturers to force consumers to purchase new products or is it based on consumer demand for new products? Explain your position. (AACSB: Communication; Reflective Thinking)

Answer:

Student responses will vary, but most will likely agree that changes are driven by consumer demand for newer and better products. The new technologies add value for consumers and better meet their needs.

Focus on Ethics

Take a look at any advertisement in a women's fashion magazine and you'll see that thin is in. Fashion designers are criticized for their use of ultra thin models. However, the president of Italy's fashion-group, Marlo Boselli, is spearheading a drive to encourage designers and media to use Afuller-bodied models@ and several designers agree. One designer, however, might have gone too far. To bring this issue to light in a more graphic manner, Nolita, an Italian label, pictured an emaciated, naked young woman in an ad with the line, "No. Anorexia." Some critics claim that this advertisement may encourage young women to be unhealthily thin due to all the attention it is getting. Others claim that Nolita is trying to profit from a deadly disease and scream Ahypocrisy@ because, like all designers in the industry, Nolita uses thin models. The Italian government has taken this issue so seriously that it developed a set of guidelines for fashion houses and magazines for using healthier-looking models. The guidelines include models providing doctors' certificates as to their health, limiting the use of models younger than 16, and banning models with body-mass indexes of 18.5 or less, which is considered to be underweight by the World Health Organization.

1. Do fashion designers and advertisements encourage young women to be unhealthily thin? (AACSB: Communication; Ethical Reasoning)

   Answer:

   Student responses will vary. However, most will probably agree that this is a problem for young women and that marketers are adding to it.

2. Create a set of guidelines for the fashion and advertising industries that promote more ethical presentations of women. (AACSB: Communication; Reflective Thinking)

   Answer:

   The most reasonable suggestion is to use healthy-weight models in their ads. Dove ran a campaign that used "real" women in underwear to promote healthier self-images for women. However, some may argue that healthy-weight models will appear too large for the cutting-edge fashion industry as well as for how young women want to be perceived.

GREAT IDEAS

Barriers to Effective Learning

1. Most of the concepts in this chapter will be new. Some students cast an uncritical eye on the opinions of activist groups and think that not a single company can be trusted to "do the right thing." The task in this chapter is to present both sides, both good and bad, so that students can see that although problems do exist, there are solutions, and industry does tend to work toward reining in those who would create problems for consumers, society as a whole, or other businesses.
2. Unless the university is in an urban environment, most students will be surprised that many large retailers stay away from disadvantaged neighborhoods, and that banks and insurance companies might discriminate against customers living in these areas. Even at urban universities this could be cause for surprise, because most urban schools are not located in the truly disadvantaged areas. A discussion on the pros and cons of, say, a Wal-Mart or a major grocery retailer locating in an inner-city neighborhood can aid in the comprehension of the risks and rewards for the company, as well as for the consumers.
3. Consumerism and environmentalism are two important concepts for the students to be aware of. It is unlikely that either of these movements will go away any time soon, and because the Internet has made so much information available to so many, these issues will likely only become more in the forefront of consumers' minds. Product recalls have become commonplace, but it is worthwhile discussing in class any recalls the students have been affected by. Comparing the number of recalls today to the number in the 1960s and 1970s will also help. As for environmentalism, one thing that is useful is to ask how many students have traveled to cities in other countries where the pollution controls are not as stringent as in the United States. Also, discuss how your own university recycles, particularly if computers are given to the students every two years, as many business schools are now doing.
4. The concepts of enlightened marketing should not be difficult to understand, however, you should go through them carefully. Consumer-oriented marketing should certainly not be new, but the term will be.

Student Projects

1. Explain how the marketing concept is applicable to marketing ethics and social responsibility.
2. From a marketing concept point of view, is it wrong to sell cigarettes? Defend your position.
3. What is planned obsolescence? Think about the fashion industry. How (or is) planned obsolescence employed in this industry? If it is, do you believe its practice to be ethical?
4. Examine the urban area of your town. Do you find examples of what you would consider redlining? Explain.
5. Discuss the statement "Marketing creates false wants and too much materialism."

Small Group Assignments

Form students into groups of three to five. Each group should read the opening vignette to the chapter on Timberland. Each group should then answer the following questions:

1. Describe the "Timberland Culture."
2. Do you believe companies have a responsibility to combat social ills, help the environment, and improve conditions for laborers around the globe? Or is their responsibility to their shareholders? Are the two mutually exclusive?
3. Describe Timberland's belief in the importance of service.
4. Do you think that customers really care about Timberland's social responsibility beliefs? Defend your position.

Each group should share its findings with the class.

Individual Assignment

Traditional buyers' rights include the following three items.

1. The right not to buy a product that is offered for sale.
2. The right to expect the product to be safe.
3. The right to expect the product to perform as claimed.

Do you believe these rights are sufficient to adequately protect consumers? Defend your answer. If you do not believe the rights are sufficient, what additional rights would you suggest and why?

Think-Pair-Share

Consider the following questions, formulate an answer, pair with the student on your right, share your thoughts with one another, and respond the questions from the instructor.

1. How would you define consumerism?
2. What is planned obsolescence? Do you believe marketers make a habit of using this concept?
3. Do you believe marketers should be responsible to their shareholders or to environmentalists? Why?
4. Define environmentalism.
5. Explain the role of ethics in marketing.

Classroom Exercise/Homework Assignment

People for the Ethical Treatment of Animals, known as PETA, claims animals have rights, and humans have no right to eat them, use them to produce clothing (leather goods and furs, for example), or for testing purposes. They are against practices they say are cruel and barbaric, including everything from corporate animal farming to breeding dogs and cats to supply our nation's pet supply.

The organization targets high profile companies and their practices, recently targeting Perdue Farms and KFC for cruelty to chickens. Their activists have been known to break into test labs and release the animals there. Others have released dogs that were with their owners at dog shows.

Some have decried PETA as the lunatic fringe, while others praise their efforts to force us all to treat animals humanely.

Read about PETA (www.peta.org). What do you think about the organization, their goals and methods?

Classroom Management Strategies

Although there are several Key Terms in this section that should be defined for the students, this is that rare chapter that could be more easily learned in a discussion format than a lecture. Drawing out student opinions on the topics in this chapter will make the material come alive.

1. You can spend a full 30 minutes on the first section. Discussing actual situations that could cause critics to make these charges would be helpful. If Christmas is near, a good discussion can also ensue about the onslaught of advertising, both on television and in newspapers. Debate whether this is the cause of materialism, or a reaction to it. An interesting debate can also be held regarding cigarettes and alcohol - is it ethical to market these products when we know they can be harmful? Have students take sides to fully discuss the pros and cons.
2. The section on citizen and public actions should take 15 minutes. A brief history of both consumerism and environmentalism is generally helpful. If you have an activist university, and Earth Day is near, perhaps you could organize a group to participate through increasing your own recycling and studying the history of the environmental movement in the United States.
3. Finally, take 15 minutes to discuss business actions, enlightened marketing, and marketing ethics.

Company Case Notes

Chapter 1
Build-A-Bear: Build-A-Memory

Synopsis

This case illustrates the success that Build-A-Bear Workshop has achieved since its founding in 1996. A detailed description is given of the Build-A-Bear retail experience and why it is that both parents and children are drawn to this concept. Personalization, and not just customization, is the driving force.

The case also highlights how founder Maxine Clark stays in touch with the customer and the employees. For Clark, management-by-walking-around is more than just a way to supervise operations. It is a way of conducting her own market research. Clark has also embraced the networking capabilities of the Internet as a way of keeping in touch with the customer.

Future prospects for Build-A-Bear's continued success are also discussed.

Teaching Objectives

The teaching objectives for this case are to:

1. Introduce students to the concept of customer value creation and its central role in marketing.
2. Allow students to analyze Build-A-Bear's product offering in depth.
3. Introduce the concepts involved in customer relationship management.
4. Introduce the concepts of customer lifetime value and customer equity.
5. Allow students to develop specific recommendations for Build-A-Bear's future.

Discussion Questions

1. Give examples of needs, wants, and demands that Build-A-Bear customers demonstrate, differentiating each of these three concepts. What are the implications of each on Build-A-Bear's actions?

   The purpose of this question is to force students to consider whether or not it is important for a company to differentiate between needs, wants, and demands. By the textbook definition, Build-A-Bear customer needs might include:
   - *belonging—joining the Build-A-Bear "club."*
   - *affection—creating and caring for another being.*
   - *self-expression—the ability to create a product that reflects elements of the self.*

   Students should consider how wants differ from these fundamental needs. Basically, they may need to belong, but could fulfill that need through any number of outlets. Based on cultural and personality factors, they develop a specific desire to belong to the Build-A-Bear club. In the same manner, affection and self-expression can be fulfilled in various ways. Why do Build-A-Bear customers desire to fulfill these through needs with Build-A-Bear's product offering? Students should outline specific elements of Build-A-Bear's offering that fulfill each of the above-noted needs.

Demands are differentiated from wants by the buying power of the Build-A-Bear's customer base. To what extent can/do Build-A-Bear customers demand the things that they want? If they are coming to Build-A-Bear, then they have the money. Therefore, they are demanding it. But the question remains—to what extent?

It is important for a company like Build-A-Bear to distinguish between these three concepts. Core needs must be identified first. Then, every element of the product offering should be created with the intention of fulfilling one of these needs, thus generating wants and desires within the consumer base. The company must then understand what it is that customers might want that is not being offered—in essence, are they demanding something? Maxine Clark and her team have taken careful measures to understand the specifics of what customers are demanding: what is working in the stores, what isn't, and what they want that is not being supplied.

2. In detail, describe all facets of Build-A-Bear's product. What is being exchanged in a Build-A-Bear transaction?

   Students should be able to identify that Build-A-Bear's "product" is multi-faceted. It can also be analyzed on different levels, from the most concrete to the most abstract:

   - *The specifics of the tangible item. This would include the various options for the basic stuffed animal—the clothing, voice box, name, and birth certificate.*

   - *The experience. This would include the ability to customize and personalize each part of the product. It also includes being a part of the creative process and coming away with an item that is a piece of the customer. The store ambience and even waiting in line are also part of the experience.*

   That which the product is being exchanged for should also be discussed. This would definitely include the price of the bear. But it would to some extent also include other cost factors given up by the customer as identified in the response to question 4.

3. Which of the five marketing management concepts best describes Build-A-Bear Workshop?

   The marketing concept. Maxine Clark has very clearly taken Build-A-Bear to high levels of financial success by knowing and understanding the needs and wants of the customers. The goals of the organization are dependent upon that. Clearly, the business strategy displayed by Build-A-Bear fits the marketing concept better than it does the production, product, or selling concepts. Also, there is no information in the case that would lead the student to believe that Build-A-Bear is focused on the welfare of society.

4. Discuss in detail the value that Build-A-Bear creates for its customers.

   Student responses or discussion of this question should incorporate a complete list of customer benefits as well as customer costs (value being of function of benefits minus costs). By this point, the benefits should be easily identified as they have already come out in answering the previous questions. The benefits received by the customer could be identified in terms of need/want fulfillment. However, the cost factor has not been discussed. The most obvious cost is the monetary price, which ranges from $10 to upwards of $30. Other costs include time (waiting in line, that of actually going through the building process) and effort (the mental effort involved with so many choices of building this bear) expended. This should be an interesting discussion in that the very things that on the surface are considered to be costs for so many customers, in this case, are actually benefits.

   The students should consider a comparison between the value formula for Build-A-Bear and that of a substitute like Vermont Teddy Bear. One thing that may come out strongly is that Vermont customers may not view the time and effort expended as a benefit. They'd rather order one and have it sent, or step in to a store, take a bear off the shelf, and be done with it. On the other hand, why is a Vermont customer willing to pay three to five times the price of a Build-A-Bear?

5. Is Build-A-Bear likely to be successful in continuing to build customer relationships? Why or why not?

   A couple of issues should be considered here. As mentioned in the case, the toy industry is fickle. The popularity of toys comes and goes as trends and fads. In fact, it might be interesting to discuss how many top selling toys today were top sellers 10 years ago, much less 20 or 30 years ago. Very few toys make it from one generation to the next. Power Rangers are still out there, but hardly the rage they once were. Even blue chip brands like Barbie eventually show signs of age (its sales have been decreasing in recent years faced with newer "in" dolls like the Bratz line).

But the thing that should come out here is that Build-A-Bear is not just a toy company. It is an entertainment company, a theme-park-like experience. At the core of its success have been Maxine Clark's strategic vision and her uncanny ability to pay attention to the real benefits that customers are seeking. As long as she and the company can continue to successfully do that, then they should be able to evolve and adapt to the trends as they happen. The inside of a Build-A-Bear store may therefore look very different in 20 years.

Teaching Suggestions

This case will stimulate students to think about some of their own product experiences, now and in previous years. One way to begin the discussion is to ask what products students buy that involve much more than the core, functional item. As students recount their experience, it is helpful to ask them how they felt before, during, and after the experience to help bring out reasons why they purchase such a product.

This case also works well with the marketing strategy chapter (Chapter 2), the consumer behavior chapter (Chapter 5), and the product and services marketing chapter (Chapter 7).

Chapter 2
Trap-Ease America: The Big Cheese of Mousetraps

Synopsis

A group of investors has purchased from an inventor the U.S. rights to sell a patented, innovative mousetrap. The group has hired Martha House to manage the company that includes assuming responsibility for sales and marketing.

Trap-Ease America has targeted the trap to housewives, whom it believes will be attracted to the safety and cleanliness that its trap offers. The trap lures the mouse into a square tube in which it finds itself trapped alive. Thus, there is no danger in baiting and setting the trap, and there is no "mess" resulting from the trap's operation.

Martha is marketing the trap directly to large retail store chains such as Safeway and Kmart. The traps are sold in packages of two and are priced at $2.49—about five to 10 times the price of the traditional, spring-loaded trap.

Martha has been promoting the mousetrap through trade shows and personal selling. As the case opens, she has just returned from a trade show at which the mousetrap received the award as Best New Product of the Year.

Despite the innovativeness of the mousetrap and its success at gaining public attention, sales are disappointingly slow. Martha finds herself wondering why the world is not beating a path to her door, as Ralph Waldo Emerson would have predicted.

Teaching Objectives

This case was selected to accompany Chapter 2 because it does an excellent job of introducing the student to the concepts of the mission of the firm and the elements of a marketing strategy in a simple but rich case. The teaching objectives for this case are to:

1. Introduce the idea of a firm's "mission."
2. Introduce the basic elements of a marketing strategy.
3. Drive home the point that customers seldom beat a path to a firm's door.

Discussion Questions

1. Martha and the investors in Trap-Ease seem to face a "once-in-a-lifetime opportunity." What information do they need to evaluate this opportunity? What do you think the investor group would write as its "mission statement?"

   The case paints a very typical picture of a group of businesspeople who believe they have an outstanding product that will be readily accepted by the market. There is little evidence in the case that the investors have done any real thinking about customer needs or have followed the marketing concept as it is introduced in the chapter. The investors believe they have a mousetrap, which will satisfy customer needs, and, therefore, customers will buy it. Students need to realize that even though a firm may have an excellent product it needs to understand customers' needs and how they respond to those needs. There is no indication in the case that the investor group has any marketing information about its potential customers or has done any real marketing research. The investors would need to know the size of the mousetrap market in the United States. Who buys mousetraps? What kinds do they buy? What prices are charged for the various kinds of mousetraps? How are these mousetraps sold to consumers? What customer needs do existing mousetraps solve, and which needs do they fail to solve adequately? How do consumers deal with their mice and rat problems? Answers to these and other "marketing research" types of questions would give the investors a better feel for the challenges facing them in marketing the mousetrap.

Like many new, small businesses, however, the investors would write a mission statement that focused on making money for themselves. Their statement might be, "Make a lot of money by selling a patented mousetrap." Discussing this with the class will allow the instructor to raise the oft-repeated slogan, "maximize shareholder wealth." Proponents of the marketing concept might well argue that making money is not the goal of the firm. Rather, if one follows the marketing concept, the goal of the firm must be first to satisfy the firm's customers and to do that better than the competition. Only then does a firm have the opportunity to "make money."

2. Who is identified as Trap-Ease's target market? Are there other possible market segments that the firm could target?

   The case indicates that Trap-Ease is targeting housewives, and implies that housewives are reluctant to set and bait traditional spring-loaded mousetraps. They also are concerned about the safety of children and pets that may be around the home because once the spring-loaded trap has caught a mouse, one often has a mess resulting from its action. Besides being unpleasant, the mess presents health concerns due to the diseases that may be carried by mice.

   There are a number of other market segments that the firm could target. The issue of disease control suggests several other potential targets. First, the instructor might ask students where disease control concerns would be important. Any business that handles or stores food and, therefore, is attractive to rats and mice would be a potential target. Restaurants should come to mind here, both because of the presence of food and food products and also because these establishments cannot use chemicals near food. This also should suggest food wholesalers or warehouses where large quantities of food may be stored in the channel of distribution. Food manufacturers also need rodent protection.

   Another potential market is research laboratories. Here, researchers use large numbers of mice in research projects. It is not unreasonable to think that some of these mice occasionally get loose. A researcher would be interested in the ability to recapture a mouse without harming it—something that the researcher would be able to do with the Trap-Ease.

Another potential target market is exterminators. Because they must work in areas where chemicals would not be allowed and traditional traps would have the same messiness problem, these companies might be a target market. These exterminator companies might also sell the traps directly to consumers with whom they deal. This possibility will allow the instructor to talk about channels of distribution and the impact of Trap-Ease's decision to go directly to the end customer.

3. How is the product positioned relative to the selected target market in the case? Are there other ways to position the product?

As suggested in the answer to question 2, Trap-Ease has been positioned from the point of view of the customer as meeting safety and cleanliness needs. Because of its pricing and distribution, Trap-Ease is positioned for use by the individual homeowner who has these concerns.

The major alternative positioning for the product focuses on its ability to control disease. Because the mouse would be trapped in a fully enclosed device and would be captured live, there is little opportunity for disease to spread as a result of its capture. It should be noted, however, that positioning the product this way would make substantial differences in the entire marketing strategy This allows the instructor to make the point that will be reinforced throughout the semester that the full marketing mix must be coordinated to position the product properly in the customer's mind.

4. What marketing mix has Trap-Ease established? Do you see any problems with this mix?

In summary, Trap-Ease's marketing mix is as follows:

Product: As noted above, Trap-Ease is a patented mousetrap that is designed to allow consumers to avoid the safety and cleanliness problems associated with traditional mousetraps.

Perhaps by this time in the discussion someone will have already suggested one of the obvious problems with this product. That is, what does one do with a live mouse caught inside the trap? The inventor had designed the product to capture the mouse alive and to suffocate it over a period of several hours. This, however, presents a problem for the user. If the consumer discovers the trap has worked, she must pick up a trap containing a live mouse that may be squirming and squealing. Then, what does the consumer do with the mouse? It might be flushed down the toilet or let out in the woods, if one lives near woods. We might wonder, however, if the target market, housewives, will be comfortable carrying the trap containing the live mouse and then opening the door to let it out. Later market research revealed that few people felt comfortable in this situation.

On the other hand, if the consumer allows the mouse to simply suffocate in the trap, he will find that mice, like most animals, do not die quietly. You can imagine the trap bouncing around under a sink like a large Mexican jumping bean as the mouse tries to free itself. Experience indicated that the mouse also made a lot of noise prior to suffocating. The targeted housewife may find herself presented with the dilemma of how to handle a live mouse or how to put up with the noise and unpleasantness of its suffocating. Thus, although the trap works well to catch a mouse, it fails to deal with the problem of what does one do with the mouse.

Price: The price of approximately $1.25 per trap, when sold in packages of two, also creates a problem in that it is five to 10 times more expensive than traditional traps. This problem is complicated by the fact that if consumers have significant mouse problems, they would need a number of traps to address the problem. Or, if they decide to simply throw away traps that contain mice to solve the disposal problem, the cost could again become prohibitive.

Place: Martha House has made the decision to distribute the products directly to national chains. Although on one hand this decision makes sense given the company's desire to achieve rapid sales growth, it creates problems for the company due to its small size. As noted in the example, which concludes the case, the company does not have its own truck and distribution facilities. It must depend on outside firms to deliver its product. Because national chains have very strict time schedules, this makes it difficult for Trap-Ease to control its distribution.

Promotion: Trap-Ease is relying basically on appearances at trade shows and some limited advertising. In fact, it is relying on word-of-mouth. Primarily, the firm depends on point-of-purchase displays to sell its product. One might wonder, however, how quickly consumers passing point-of-purchase displays for the product will understand it. Further, the firm is dependent on whatever advertising the chains may do to generate end-customer awareness. Even early in the semester, students should understand that generating such awareness is extremely expensive and difficult. It is not clear that Trap-Ease has adequate resources to do significant advertising aimed at end customers, and it is not clear that the chains will devote sufficient resources to advertising the product.

All of these marketing mix problems should suggest that Trap-Ease has a number of significant hurdles to address if it is going to improve its performance.

5. Who is Trap-Ease's competition?

Even though Trap-Ease has a patent on its mousetrap, it does have competition. Students may tend to think that a patent protects a firm from competition. Obviously, the traditional, spring-loaded trap is competition. Although the Trap-Ease trap has significant advantages, its price means that for many low-income consumers who probably have more mice problems, Trap-Ease is too expensive.

Consumers who have better incomes and who may not be excited about dealing with dead or live mice will probably simply turn to exterminators to take care of their problems. Although exterminators are more expensive, the benefits of having someone else take care of this unpleasant problem will be attractive to many consumers. Thus, Trap-Ease finds itself with competition both above and below its relative price. This competition significantly reduces the size of the target market.

6. How would you change Trap-Ease marketing strategy? What kinds of control procedures would you establish in connection with this strategy?

   There are, of course, numerous possibilities that students might suggest. Many students will focus on trying to make specific changes to elements of the established marketing mix. For example, some students may suggest that by lowering price the Trap-Ease will become more competitive with traditional traps and be more attractive to consumers. Any attempt to manipulate the existing marketing mix, however, allows the instructor to make the point that the marketing mix should flow from the target market. At this time, having discussed previous questions, it should be clear to students that there is some question about the size and viability of the selected target market. In fact, there may not be a real market given the product's positioning—at least not a market that is big enough to support the firm and reach the investor's goals.

   To revise the firm's marketing strategy, the firm needs to begin by thinking about its target market selection. First, the student could suggest that the product has been positioned improperly. Although health and cleanliness concerns are of interest to consumers, the other aspects of the marketing mix make the product unattractive. The disease control aspects of the product, however, are important. It would be possible to reposition the product for disease control purposes and to select the industrial/institutional target market. Thus, the target market would become food manufacturers, wholesalers, and others who store quantities of food that are subject to rat infestation and also restaurants and other institutions, where food may be handled and where poisons and other rat control measures are inappropriate.

   With respect to the marketing for this new target market, the firm needs to develop larger sizes of the trap. Some of the potential customers will have larger rats with which to deal. These firms will often have maintenance employees who will not be squeamish about dealing with and disposing of rats that are caught in such traps.

   With respect to price for this new strategy, there is really no information in the case to allow the instructor to figure what the price might be. We can imagine that, in connection with the place decision, the firm might decide to deal directly with larger exterminating companies or food wholesaling chains. The company will probably find itself in a negotiation situation as it has with the large retail chains. This will make it important that the firm understand its costs and be able to figure what prices it can agree to that will allow it to make an adequate profit.

With respect to place, the firm will be required to continue to sell to a limited number of customers due to the lack of any real sales force. This would imply that it will have to sell to food wholesalers or exterminating companies themselves unless it can find a distributor who caters to these kinds of operations. Looking for distributors who could handle some or all of the sales effort would be appropriate given the firm's limited resources. This may put additional pressures on margins, but the firm will have to evaluate accepting smaller margins versus absorbing the cost of improving its own distribution system.

The new strategy would continue to imply a trade promotion strategy. Appearing at trade shows for food wholesalers or exterminators would be a first step, and one with which the firm is familiar. This strategy avoids the necessity for having to pursue expensive media options for developing end-customer retail demand. Advertising in trade magazines should help bring the product to the attention of targeted customers. Further, if the firm is successful in selling to exterminators, they will become its sales force.

As to control procedures, the process of revising the marketing strategy allows one to ask the students how they will monitor their progress. In the case, Martha has no connection with the end-customer. She is dealing with buyers for the large retail chains. She is not sure who is buying the mousetrap or why or how they are using it. A first control procedure for any strategy then is to identify the target market and establish mechanisms to monitor the target's use of and satisfaction with the product. Chapter 4, Managing Marketing Information, will introduce students to techniques, which might be used by Trap-Ease to evaluate the success of the strategy.

Teaching Suggestions

This case is an excellent early case because it deals with a product and a need with which students are familiar. Further, as the discussion unfolds, students will have little trouble spotting some of the marketing problems and marketing concerns that the firm faces. Although cases can sometimes intimidate students early in the semester, this case should begin to give them some confidence that they can deal successfully with a marketing situation even though they do not have a lot of experience.

If instructors are interested in any field research, they might ask a group of students to check local retail and hardware stores to see what devices and methods are available for helping people deal with their mice and rat problems.

If instructors do not use this case at this point in the text, it may be used in connection with the marketing research chapter (Chapter 4), the consumer behavior chapter (Chapter 5), the segmentation chapter (Chapter 6), and the new product chapter (Chapter 8).

Chapter 3
Prius: Leading a Wave of Hybrids

Synopsis

This case recounts the introduction of the Toyota Prius and compares it with the strategy that Honda has followed. Additionally, the competitive response by various other car makers is highlighted. This gives students an opportunity to compare the two strategies and debate which one seems more appropriate for the American market.

The Prius was originally introduced in 2000 with very targeted marketing aimed at techies (innovators). The second version of the Prius came out in 2004 and was a sporty, more fashionable car aimed at a wider market (early adopters). By 2007, sales of Prius models increased so much that it was the third best selling car for Toyota. Thus, Toyota is in the position that it is eying the early majority.

The case provides an excellent opportunity to compare Toyota's marketing of the introductory and follow-up models—very different campaigns, well thought out and implemented. At introduction, Toyota used the Internet very heavily, but by 2007, they were using more mass market media. Both are quite different from the strategy that GM and other companies are using and plan to use. This should stimulate good discussion in class about how automotive companies might move away from reliance on gasoline powered engines.

Teaching Objectives

The teaching objectives for this case are to:

1. Identify how microenvironmental factors can affect the introduction and marketing of an innovation.
2. Identify how macroenvironmental factors can affect the introduction and marketing of an innovation.
3. Explain how marketing can be targeted to a specific segment.
4. Evaluate the usefulness of different marketing strategies at different stages in the PLC.
5. Evaluate marketing strategies of different firms selling the same product in terms of advantages, disadvantages, and appropriateness.

Discussion Questions

1. What microenvironmental factors affect the introduction and sale of the Toyota Prius? How well has Toyota dealt with these factors?

   The Company: The company has expended plenty of money on R&D and marketing of the Prius. Why? Toyota expects the Prius to set the standard for the entry of a line of hybrids from minicompacts to luxury vehicles. Thus, the car is an important component of company strategy. To successfully introduce the Prius and build this new line of vehicles will require coordination within the company. The second generation of Prius has already caused problems within the company. Production was increased at one plant necessitating a cut in production for other lines.

Suppliers: With the successful introduction of the Prius, companies such as Panasonic may invest more in R&D to develop cheaper batteries. If they can do so, this will result in lower prices that, in turn, may further stimulate demand. Thus, it is to Toyota's advantage to work with suppliers to encourage this R&D.

Marketing Intermediaries: The most important marketing intermediaries here would be dealers. Toyota had to prepare materials for dealers and their salespeople so that they could sell the Prius. Now, they have to "teach" purchasers how to drive the cars to get maximum fuel efficiency. A shortage of cars for the second generation of Prius is causing problems with dealers who want more and could sell the additional cars. In turn, dealers marking up the cars can negatively injure relationships with the company, who does not want to see the price of the cars inflated. There is also a major issue of why more cars were allocated to Japan when the United States is the bigger market.

Customers: The case indicates that Toyota carefully studied the consumer market and adapted its marketing accordingly. It thought innovators and adapters who are likely to be techies would be the purchasers, and the evidence indicates that the company was right. With this market in mind, Toyota pushed the technology of the car, used the Internet, and promoted environmental aspects of the vehicle. Techies are highly interested in the net and may be pro-environmental. They are certainly interested in technology given the description of owners modifying their Prius described in the case.

For the second generation, Toyota broadened its market focus to include less-technical types (are these the customers who don't know how to drive the car?). They also redesigned the car to have more mass-market appeal, introduced more features and improved the performance—all aspects of the car that would be more important to a less technical market.

(Jumping ahead to adoption theory, this is a good example of marketing to the techies as innovators with targeted promotion and then marketing to early adopters with more mainstream media. The techies have gotten the car on the road and in the view of early adopters.)

Competitors: A major aspect of Toyota's strategy was to get a jump on competitors who will have to enter the market later. Again correctly guessing that American companies would be slow to introduce hybrids, Toyota and Honda entered first and that may help them in marketing hybrids in the future. They were the first may lead to they were the best. Toyota seems to have been more willing to enter this market and establish a technological lead, although American companies appear to begrudgingly plan on entering the market.

American companies are following a different strategy as they believe that gas savings are greatest on vehicles that use the most gas. Rather than small cars, they aim to introduce hybrids on bigger cars. They also point out that savings are much greater when hybrids are used in mass transit.

Publics: There is little mention of publics in the case, but Toyota did flood the media and news groups with videos and press releases on the cars. Their Earth Day promotion got them additional media coverage and may have helped their relations with environmental groups. Successful sales of the car will lead to sales of more hybrids in the future that would endear the company to financial publics such as investors. Given the general attention shown to the vehicle in the media, the general public may be favorably disposed toward a company that aims to reduce emissions and lower gas mileage. They have placed ads in more general interest magazines with the second generation vehicle.

Another public that Toyota studied was the <u>*government.*</u> *They understood correctly that American politicos will be pushing for higher gas standards and willing to supply a tax deduction for consumers purchasing more environmentally friendly cars that get higher gasoline mileage. These are helpful factors in overcoming the higher prices when selling to consumers.*

2. Outline the major macroenvironmental factors—demographic, economic, natural, technological, political, and cultural—that have affected the introduction and sale of the Toyota Prius. How has Toyota dealt with each of these factors?

   Demographic: Baby boomers are the major market in the United States and they have reached the stage where the kids are grown and gone. This means that they can pay more for cars (overcoming the higher price). They have always been known for an interest in quality and willing to try the new—both factors that might incline them toward purchase of a Prius. Younger generations may be more environmentally concerned and want a Prius, but few may be able to afford one.

   Economic: Because it does cost more, Toyota has sought tax deductions to help with the "sticker shock." The price of the car, however, is in line with what Americans are paying for cars. This is not priced as a luxury car. To be one of the first to own such a car may be worth the higher initial price. Success of selling the car should lead to an increase in supply, which would result in a lower price, and is the essences of basic economics.

   With the increase in gas prices, the Prius offers even greater savings and in the summer, some consumers shifted to smaller cars and demand for the Prius grew. Although increased gas prices alone cannot account for the increase in demand, they certainly didn't hurt Prius sales.

Natural: The Prius claim to be better for the environment has some impact on the natural world—less air pollution and less need for oil exploration and gasoline production.

Technological: This is the Prius' primary strength—its technology. Toyota has played this up in their marketing and aimed the car at the "techie" part of the market. This supports the Japanese cars in their claim to be technologically advanced. As the case indicates, the introduction of the car is likely to lead to other technological advances (such as the batteries). The second general vehicle adds more features such as the six-disc CD player and cruise control—options that the first generation, stripped-down car did not offer.

Political: Obviously Toyota took this into account. Recognizing that some senators may adopt a tougher stance toward gas emissions and mileage standards, they would be favorably inclined toward the car. Some detail on tax incentives is given in the case.

Cultural: Cultural factors are Americans' love of automobiles, our willingness to adopt technology and progress, our claim to care about the environment, and our rebellion against gasoline price increases. These are given in the first paragraph of the case and these are all factors that will favor introduction of the vehicle. Even though it may not be a cultural characteristic, we also like tax deductions.

3. Evaluate Toyota's marketing strategy so far. What has Toyota done well? How might it improve its strategy?

Toyota did a superb job of introducing the Prius. They created clever ads that highlight the car's major features and utilized the Internet well. This is all based on a careful, thorough, and accurate analysis of their market. Although they have used traditional media, they relied on the Internet that would be heavily used by this market. To overcome price differentials, they have worked on securing tax deductions while realizing that price will not be the major motivator of purchase for this car. They have secured a lot of distribution for a vehicle that will not sell at present in large numbers and has a lower margin. This indicates their recognition that access to the product is key. They have also not made the mistake of trying to sell over the Internet. That could antagonize dealers and decrease the extent of distribution.

The broadening of their marketing with the second generation is only to be expected. They are selling to a different consumer market and they are using different media appropriate to that market. Their promotion is far less targeted, but it does not need to be given the successful introduction of the car.

Where Toyota scored big was with a successful introduction that gives them a good sales base from which to expand.

4. GM's marketing director for new ventures, Ken Stewart, says, "If you want to get a lot of hybrids on the road, you put them in vehicles that people are buying now." This tends to summarize the U.S. auto makers' approach to hybrids. Would you agree with Mr. Stewart? Why or why not?

   Think back to the Arab oil embargo of the '70s. Once Americans were scared that gas could be rationed and prices rose, they bought small cars in large numbers. Since then, they have switched to buying bigger cars than they bought before the oil embargo (SUVs). Basically, most Americans love big cars. We're big people and we want room. So, Mr. Stewart has a point. Given the big share of the market that large vehicles (cars and trucks) have captured, sales of hybrids will be greater if they're put on large vehicles rather than small ones. (Large vehicles have a bigger share of the market if you add SUV, van, and truck sales together.) If the goal of the firm is to sell more hybrids in models with higher price tags (possibly creating greater profits), then his argument makes sense.

   However, SUVs and trucks are usually performance vehicles, so one has to wonder if a hybrid truck (for example) is an oxymoron. Would consumers believe that a truck or a Jeep hybrid could be a big, tough vehicle? Promotion for these vehicles tends to emphasize performance—speed, toughness, driving through rough terrain and around hairpin turns. Is that consistent with the image of a hybrid?

   Are owners of such vehicles interested in gas efficiency and environmental issues?

   Obviously, Toyota thinks that those consumers most likely to respond to these appeals are those who buy smaller cars. So far, they have been successful selling their cars, but they are still not selling them in such large numbers as to affect their bottom line. The market may not be that large at this time.

Teaching Suggestions

Ask a few students to visit auto dealers before class and interview a salesman about the Prius in terms of sales, etc. If students or you know someone who owns a Prius, it would be nifty to interview them about their purchase—motivations and satisfaction. Ask students to look for ads for Prius and bring them to class to see how marketing of the car has shifted since introduction.

Begin class with a discussion of what was learned at the dealerships. A major part of Toyota's success was their correct analysis of the target market and their astute marketing plan. Because consumers are a microenvironmental factor, this can be used to lead into a discussion of other microenvironmental factors along with Toyota's marketing strategy. For this, it is advantageous to visit the Prius Web site and discuss it in class.

Then, identify the important elements of the marketing for the second version of the Prius (these could be listed side by side on the blackboard, using target and the 4 Ps). Ask what microenvironmental and macroenvironmental factors support the increasing demand for the Prius.

Finally, highlight the different strategies being employed by competitors (again target and 4 Ps). Have students debate the advantages, disadvantages, and appropriateness of the current Prius strategy and that of competitors.

Chapter 4
Enterprise Rent-A-Car: Measuring Service Quality

Synopsis

Kevin Kirkman receives a Service Quality Survey in the mail from Enterprise Rent-A-Car. Kevin had been involved in a wreck earlier in the month and had rented a replacement car from Enterprise while his car was being repaired. Enterprise routinely surveys one of each 20 customers about seven days following completion of a rental. A case exhibit presents a copy of the Enterprise survey form. Enterprise used the survey to determine the percentage of customers who were completely satisfied, which produced the Enterprise Service Quality Index (ESQi) for both the company and for each individual branch.

Enterprise has become the largest rent-a-car company in the United States by targeting the local replacement market and maintaining a laser-like focus on customer service and satisfaction.

However, top management wanted to take its customer satisfaction program further by using the ESQi into account in promotion decisions. To do so, however, managers believed they needed to improve the response rate and timeliness of the information.

Teaching Objectives

The teaching objectives for this case are to:

1. Expose students to the decisions, problems, and issues companies face in conducting market research in consumer markets.
2. Help students consider the advantages and disadvantages of various research techniques.
3. Involve students in thinking through and planning the market research process.

Discussion Questions

1. Analyze Enterprise's Service Quality Survey (Exhibit 1). What information is it trying to gather? What are its research objectives?

   The questionnaire begins with a summary question that asks about the customer's overall satisfaction and then asks an open-ended question as to how it could have improved. Then, the questionnaire takes the respondent through the rental process on a step-by-step basis. It is important to point out to students that service quality is determined at each step in the process and Enterprise is measuring quality at each step in order to determine where any problems may have developed in that process. Note, for example, that question 8 asks how the customer rates the Enterprise employee who handled the paperwork at the <u>*beginning*</u> *and* <u>*end*</u> *of the rental process, realizing that in all probability a different employee would have been involved at each time. Notice also that only two questions at the end of question 8 (mechanical condition and cleanliness) and question 9 (did you get the type of car you wanted) deal with the car itself. The rest of the questions deal with the service aspects of the rental and with overall satisfaction.*

Question 10 asks why the customer rented the car, helping Enterprise track which market segments it is serving.

Question 11 is arguably the most important question. Question 1 addressed overall satisfaction, but the real question is how likely the customer will be to rent from you the next time. A person could be satisfied with the past rental but not willing to rent from your firm, perhaps assuming that he or she might be more satisfied with a competitor next time. Or, perhaps the customer was just trying your firm and has other experiences with which to compare the experience with your firm.

The final two questions try to determine how much experience the customer has with Enterprise and with rent-a-car companies in general. So, Enterprise's research objective is descriptive. It is trying to describe/determine customer characteristics and attitudes toward the overall service experience and specific steps in that process. Students will note question 3a that deals with whether or not the customer experienced problems with the rental process and what happened. Market research shows that many customers do not complain when they have a problem. They simply find somewhere else to do business next time. Enterprise's Service Quality Survey is an attempt to be proactive in soliciting complaints/problems/suggestions, realizing that unless a company does something like this survey, it may not find out about serious service problems.

2. What decisions has Enterprise made with regard to primary data collection—research approach, contact methods, sampling plan, and research instruments?

   Research approach: Enterprise has decided to use the survey approach that the text says is the best way to gather descriptive information. The text indicates that survey research can be flexible, quick, and can be at a lower cost than observational or experimental research.

   Contact method: Enterprise is using the mail method to contact customers as opposed to the telephone and personal methods. The text indicates that this method provides poor flexibility, speed, and response rate but excellent control of interviewer effects, good cost, quantity of information, and fair control of the sample. The instructor can use this part of the case discussion to point out the tradeoffs that companies make when they select one contact method over the others.

Sampling plan: Enterprise has decided to use a simple random probability sample with each customer having a 1-in-20 chance of selection. The customer is the sampling unit. We don't know how many customers Enterprise has, so we cannot know the sample size, but we can assume that the company has selected the 1-in-20 rule because it provides a large enough sample given predicted response rates so that it has a statistically valid and reliable sample.

Research instrument: Enterprise has selected the questionnaire with primarily closed-ended questions.

3. In addition to or instead of the mail survey, what other means could Enterprise use to gather customer satisfaction and other information about its customers and competitors?

Enterprise has decided to mail a questionnaire to selected customers about a week after the end of the rental, assuming the experience will still be fresh on the customer's mind and the customer will have time to complete the instrument.

Students may suggest a number of other possibilities. Some will suggest that Enterprise could put a survey form in each vehicle so that people experiencing a problem could record/report it while it was fresh on their minds. They could mail these in or turn them in when they return the car. Perhaps, people might be reluctant to hand the forms to someone about whom they might be complaining.

Other students will suggest that Enterprise employees could hand the customer the questionnaire upon return of the car and ask the person to complete it then or to complete it later and mail it in. Enterprise apparently thinks that customers may be too busy or rushed at this time to ask them to take the time to complete the questionnaire. This is an assumption, however, and something the company could test.

Enterprise could also have employees or an outside firm telephone customers following a rental to ask the same or similar questions. As the text suggests, there are some positive aspects to the telephone method, but it can be relatively expensive and carry interviewer effects. Furthermore, people may be reluctant to answer many questions over the phone and may not be comfortable reporting problems and complaining to another person.

Creative students can suggest that Enterprise could also use observational research. For example, it could have researchers sitting in its rental offices who watch and evaluate the rental process. If employees are aware of this, as they would have to be, however, one is not assured that one is observing "normal" behavior. To solve this problem, Enterprise could have an independent firm's employees go through the rental process and then report their findings. Such "secret shopper" programs are common in retailing. These efforts are good for evaluating the rental process, but do not get at customer satisfaction.

Students can also suggest that Enterprise consider focus groups. It could recruit focus group participants from recent customers and have a facilitator conduct focus group interviews on the rental process and customer satisfaction. The value of such groups is that they allow the facilitator to pursue topics or points that might come up during the discussion that cannot normally be pursued in a survey. The participants may raise a topic that Enterprise had not considered and thus would not include on a survey. Yet this topic might turn out to be important to customers.

Enterprise could also have a toll-free telephone number displayed in its offices and in its cars that encourages customers to call with complaints/suggestions at any time.

4. What specific recommendations would you make to Enterprise to improve the response rate and the timeliness of feedback from the process?

Given the discussions above, students will have a number of suggestions. As to the current survey, they may suggest that it is visually complex and looks like it would take a long time to complete. This may discourage customers from responding. Students may suggest that Enterprise develop shorter survey forms. One form might focus on overall satisfaction measures along with the open-ended question. Another form might focus on the rental process. Enterprise could alternate between the two forms or it could increase its sample size, developing a sample for each form.

As to speeding up the process, students should have noticed in the text that telephone surveys and online surveys are rated as excellent in terms of speed. One possibility would be to have the outside firm telephone the selected customers rather than relying on the mail. Telephone surveys produce potential interviewer effects, of course, as noted in the discussion of question 3, but they also provide an opportunity for a skilled interviewer to pursue other lines of questioning if they develop. One problem with the telephone survey is simply that there are more and more telemarketing calls. Many consumers are reluctant to talk to anyone who may be perceived as a telemarketer.

A second method of speeding up the process would be to develop a customer feedback area on the company's Web site. Customers could be given a feedback request card when they completed the rental and encouraged to go online to provide the feedback. Although being online could provide rapid feedback, this method, like the mail survey, requires that customers take the initiative to visit the site and complete the survey. It is not clear that this would help the response rate. Furthermore, students may note that the company would have no way of identifying who is really providing the feedback.

Students may also recommend that Enterprise implement some of the other ideas developed in the discussion of question number 3. In this discussion, it will be important for them to see the pros and cons of each alternative and the tradeoffs the company makes as it selects one method over another. Students must also be aware that none of these programs will be cheap. The company will have to measure the value of the information obtained against its cost.

Enterprise can test any of these proposals by applying them in a limited geographic area to see how they affect response rate and timeliness before rolling them out systemwide.

The instructor can also use the discussion to emphasize the point that a company wants to maximize the customer's opportunity to complain. Marketing research shows that dissatisfied customers tell somewhere between 10 and 15 other people. The company wants to encourage customers to complain so that it can try to fix the problem and short-circuit the complaints. This argues for Enterprise focusing on making it easy for customers to complain on the spot, at the time of a problem, while the customer may be more willing to complain.

Teaching Suggestions

Enterprise has more than 4,000 offices in the United States, and it has offices in Canada. If an office is located near the college or university, the instructor may wish to contact the manager and invite him or her to visit the class in conjunction with this case.
Some students will have had experiences with Enterprise or other replacement rent-a-car companies that they will be willing to share as a beginning of the case discussion. The instructor may wish to ask how satisfied they or their families were with the rental process and if the company involved conducted any sort of quality survey. Did they respond? Why or why not?

This case also goes well with the chapter on product and services marketing (Chapter 7).

Enterprise decided that it would develop a telephone survey. The outside company that conducts the survey selects customers at random from each branch and completes at least 30 surveys each month from each branch. The person who calls asks only three questions—those are questions 1 and 11 from Exhibit 1 and a follow-up question depending on the answers to questions 1 and 11. If the person is satisfied, or better, and will probably call Enterprise for the next rental, or better, the caller just asks if the respondent needs for someone from Enterprise to follow up. If the respondent is somewhat dissatisfied or completely dissatisfied with the rental and/or probably or definitely will not call Enterprise next time, the caller states that someone from Enterprise would like to call the respondent and tries to set up a convenient time for that call.

Enterprise decided that the two main questions were all it needed answers to and that if there were problems, it would try to get at the cause of the problems in the follow-up telephone interview.

Andy Taylor, President of Enterprise, wrote a brief article on the company's ESQi process that the instructor can find in the July 2002 edition of the *Harvard Business Review,* pages 24–25, under the title "Driving Customer Satisfaction."

Chapter 5
Victoria's Secret Pink: Keeping the Brand Hot

Synopsis

This case illustrates the general strategy employed by Victoria's Secret to acquire a new segment of customers through the introduction of its brand Pink. Pink is a line of "loungewear" (sweatpants, T-shirts, pajamas, bras and panties, pillows and bedding) targeted toward 18-30 year old females. The garments feature comfortable cuts and mostly cotton fabrics in bright colors. New garments are introduced every three or four weeks. The image is one of "cute and playful" versus the more overtly sexy image of the core brand.

The case highlights the different promotional approaches that Pink managers are taking in contrast to those of the core brand. This is a lifestyle brand. The Victoria's Secret chain has been a big driver of financial success for Limited Brands (parent company), and Pink is expected to be a big part of Victoria's Secret's sustained growth. Not only does it give the chain a new set of customers, but it brings in customers at a younger age who will then "graduate" up to the Victoria's Secret core brands. The ethics of the Pink strategy are considered in detail.

Teaching Objectives

1. Apply a specific product situation to the buyer decision process.
2. Explain how and why social, psychological, and personal factors affect the manner in which consumers solve their problem.
3. Gain practical experience by applying the concepts of attitude, self-concept, and reference groups.
4. Consider the ethical implications of employing principles of consumer behavior in marketing.

Discussion Questions

1. Analyze the buyer decision process of a typical Pink customer.

   Need recognition: This can come from internal stimuli (basic needs such as hunger, thirst, protection) or external stimuli. Considering that people do not purchase fashion brands based on such needs as, "I am cold/naked and need protective covering," this first step is likely to be based on external stimuli. Note that the factors that influence a potential Pink customer's recognition of need may also affect other phases of the buyer decision process. These include promotional information from the company itself, word-of-mouth information from friends/acquaintances, groups, lifestyle, status, and self-concept. Consumers are likely to filter some bit of information from one of these sources in recognizing that they need a clothing item that is fashionable, trendy, and hip.

Information search: Again, this can be internal or external. However, the nature of internal/external influences is different for this phase. Potential Pink customers could draw from either source. They draw from internal (i.e., experiential) sources (their own knowledge based on previous experience or exposure to product information) based on how familiar they are with the brand. For those very familiar with the brand, frequent purchasers, they may not gather information beyond internal information. However, many will draw from external sources, including friends and acquaintances or company advertising/point-of-purchase displays/sales people.

Evaluation of alternatives: Methods used for evaluating alternatives vary widely. Thus, it is difficult to illustrate what the "typical" Pink customer might do for this phase. However, one thing is consistent across individuals as they go through this phase. Consumers compare the option(s) in question to a set of criteria. Thus, if potential customers are looking for a pair of sweats that they can use for marathon training, the criteria will likely be much different than if they were looking for a pair of sweats to wear in social situations. Potential Pink customers might be looking for something that is comfortable, fashionable, casual but dressy enough to wear to class/out shopping, priced within a certain range, etc. Potential Pink customers might compare the Pink brand to one or more other brands on this set of criteria, or they might consider the Pink brand in isolation relative to the criteria. This will depend on factors already discussed in the first two steps of the buyer decision process.

Purchase decision: The potential Pink customer will choose Pink if the article under consideration meets the criteria better than any other option. There are additional considerations that may pop up at this phase, including the opinion of friends and unexpected changes to any of the factors considered during evaluation of alternatives.

Postpurchase behavior: During this phase, consumers form impressions that will have an effect on future purchase and word-of-mouth. Much of this boils down to the concept of satisfaction: How do consumers perceive the product's performance relative to their expectations prior to purchase? Pink customers' expectations could be based on things already mentioned in the previous steps of the buyer decision process. If they are confirmed or exceeded, then the consumers develop some level of satisfaction or delight. They then are more likely to spread positive word-of-mouth and purchase again. If the Pink customers' expectations are not met, they are then dissatisfied.

2. Apply the concept of aspirational groups to Victoria's Secret's Pink line. Should marketers have boundaries with regard to this concept?

   Certainly, the issue of celebrity endorses as brought up in the case are part of a potential aspirational group for consumers. In fact, that is one of the main reasons that such celebrity endorsers are used (Lindsay Lohan and Sophia Bush and a host of other celebs who receive and wear Pink products). Consumers may aspire to be like such celebrities. Other aspirational groups might include other consumers who are part of a group to which the potential Pink customer aspires, such as sorority members.

One other aspirational group should be considered in relation to the second part of this question. Young tweens view older teens as an aspirational group. This issue should spark considerable discussion. On the one hand, do all corporations have the same right to employ principles of marketing in the achievement of their objectives? On the other hand, where should lines be drawn in terms of social responsibility and ethics? This may be further considered in question 4.

3. Explain how both positive and negative consumer attitudes toward a brand like Pink develop. How might someone's attitude toward Pink change?

   Attitude describes a person's relatively consistent evaluations, feelings, and tendencies toward an object or idea. Positive and negative attitudes toward Pink might be based on general perceptions such as, "I love bright colors and soft cotton," "I really want to wear the types of things that [fill-in-the-blank] wears," or "Mall stores really turn me off." Pink attitudes might also be based on perceptions more specific to the brand, such as "I have loved everything that I have ever bought from Pink," or "A friend whose fashion sense I really value gave me these Pink boxers for my birthday." Marketers such as Victoria's Secret are constantly trying to influence consumer attitudes (persuasion) by affecting such factors as those listed here. They may have a difficult time changing such attitudinal factors as hating mall stores, but they can certainly take advantage of following popular trends (bright colors and soft cottons) or placing products with popular celebrities.

4. What role does Pink appear to be playing in the self-concept of preteens, teens, and young adults?

   In the context of the Pink brand, the concept of self-concept may very well be one of the most influential of all the factors discussed in Chapter 5. Self-concept is based on how consumers perceive themselves as well as how they think others perceive them. For fashion items, people are strongly influenced by these things in making their purchases. Even for people who do NOT want to follow current fashion trends, they are thus very influenced by the opinions of others.

   The role that Pink plays in the self-concept may vary across the three mentioned groups. For preteens who are very concerned about growing up quickly, the brand may help such consumers perceive themselves as being more mature. For teens, the issue might be much more oriented around wanting to fit in and wear what the in-crowd wears. For young adults, the self-concept may be more individualistic and self-expressive. Customers may purchase Pink as a means of self-expression.

Teaching Suggestions

You might begin the discussion by asking, "How many of you own a Pink article of clothing?" Obviously, the respondents will likely all be female. However, this is an interesting question to ask because the students in a college class are the very customers that Victoria's Secret is targeting with the Pink brand. The answer, however, might be surprising. Are college co-eds wearing Pink? Or does this group perceive the Pink brand as a "teen" brand? Some discussion on this might be pursued.

Following this discussion, the instructor should initiate a discussion based on the success of Pink and the reasons for such. After initial responses by students, the first discussion question can be used to weave in almost any of the social, personal, and psychological factors that are covered in the text. Question 3 can also be incorporated into this discussion.

After some discussion on the success of Pink and even its future outlook, the issues of ethics and social responsibility should be covered. A case such as this is designed around such issues. Discussion questions 2 and 4 should be incorporated into this discussion. But overall, students should be pushed to consider whether Victoria's Secret is doing anything wrong in their marketing of Pink.

Students will likely be split on this topic. Some may say that targeting teens and preteens is not wrong at all. Others will say that while it may not be healthy for preteens, Victoria's Secret is not responsible because they are not targeting the younger consumers. The question should then be considered, "Is a company not responsible for harmful outcomes that were unintentional?" Some comparison is likely to be made to marketers of tobacco and alcohol products. The difficult question to come to a conclusion on is, "Is there a line between marketing clearly harmful products to teens and children and marketing products that are not so easily defined as harmful?"

Chapter 6
Saturn: An Image Makeover

Synopsis

This case chronicles the successful history of Saturn as a company narrowly focused on a single line of compact cars. Some attempts the company has made to differentiate into other market segments have not exactly been successful. In most recent years, Saturn's financial performance has suffered. However, executives at GM are intent on changing that. Saturn has launched an entirely new vehicle lineup, including a compact, a mid-sized sport sedan, an eight-passenger crossover SUV, a hybrid SUV, and a two-seat roadster. A $3 billion investment in Saturn clearly illustrates the confidence that GM has in its newest division, especially given that it is one of the smallest GM brands. GM hopes to take sales from 215,000 in 2005 to 400,000 by the end of 2007.

With all the new models, there are those who question whether Saturn will maintain its image as the United States' lone "Asian" brand and a socially responsible company. Some industry insiders are confused about the segment that Saturn is trying to target.

Teaching Objectives

The teaching objectives for this case are to:

1. Allow students to apply the concepts of market segmentation, targeting, and positioning in a particular new product introduction.
2. Consider the ways to segment the consumer market for a general automobile company.
3. Allow students to develop positioning strategies.
4. Allow students to develop specific marketing strategy recommendations for GM and Saturn.

Discussion Questions

1. Using the full spectrum of segmentation variables, describe how GM has segmented the automobile market.

   Given the information in the case, this may be challenging. Students will have to call upon their external perceptions to create a more complete profile of the "old" Saturn's customer profile. They are likely to come up with general conclusions rather than specific. But a profile should emerge, nonetheless.

   Here are some suggestions:

   Demographic:
   a. *Age—younger than the average GM buyer. Most typically college age on through early 40s.*

b. *Gender—fairly evenly split.*
c. *Family life cycle—young marrieds with and without children are certainly among Saturn's early target market. However, young to middle-age singles are also prevalent. Some customers may exist in other categories (the image of an SL1 being towed behind a motor home with a retired couple at the wheel comes to mind), but are not part of Saturn's core.*
d. *Income—lower-middle income.*

Psychographic:

- *Personality—environmentally and socially responsible*

Behavioral:

- *Benefits—quality, economy, innovation, personal service, and the image of an Asian import*
- *Loyalty status—strong*

2. What segment(s) is Saturn now targeting? How is GM now positioning Saturn? How do these strategies differ from those employed with the original Saturn S-series?

This is the core of the case and the question that is posed toward the end. The case cites industry observers who question what segment Saturn is targeting, that the message they are sending is fuzzy. Yet GM proclaims that they are not creating another Chevrolet, a brand that is all things to all people. Students should give this careful consideration to see if they can identify a general profile that links the different sub-segments that Saturn will target with its broader line of specialized vehicles.

Demographic:

- *Age—A classic strategy is to grow old with your target audience while still trying to keep the young ones coming in. The Japanese Big Three have clearly done the former. They added more models to the lineups and even new luxury divisions to appeal to those who were raised on Japanese imports. So Saturn's move in this direction makes complete sense.*
- *Gender—Likely not much change here.*
- *Family life cycle—While there will still be models that will appeal to the same core customer, Saturn has recognized that its loyal customers of many years have graduated into other phases of life—married with more and older kids (bigger sedan and eight-passenger cross-over SUV), middle-aged married and unmarried (two-seat roadster).*
- *Income—Lower- to upper-middle incomes.*

Psychographic:

- *Personality—environmentally and socially responsible. This is part of the Saturn image that Saturn should make every effort to maintain.*

Behavioral:

- *Benefits—quality, innovation, personal service; again, these factors are part of the core Saturn image that has made them successful. And while the benefit of economy will still be there with some models, that is clearly not the focus of the entire new line.*

  One key change that poses a big challenge for Saturn is that its previous image has always been that of an import ... an Asian import. The new Saturn line is heavily infused with European design and engineering. GM says that it wants Saturn to continue to appeal to customers who would only consider an import, but the question is, does the new Saturn focus on the wrong type of import?

  Another key change is the added benefit of "sporty." This is something that Saturn has never really been. Will this be important to Saturn customers?

- *Loyalty status—strong*

3. Describe the role that social responsibility plays in Saturn's targeting strategy.

   Social responsibility has always played a big role, as mentioned in the previous answer. From the beginning, Saturn has proclaimed that its sole focus is people: customers, employees, and communities. While the focus on customers may not exactly be social marketing, the policies and initiatives that focus on employees and communities are. Many examples are given in Saturn's history on its own Web site at http://www.saturn.com/saturn/aboutus/ourstory/index.jsp. Social responsibility has been central in both attracting customers that GM would never have otherwise attracted as well as contributing to the strong loyalty of Saturn's customer base.

4. Do you think that GM will accomplish its goals with the "new Saturn"? Why or why not?

   Student responses will likely cover the spectrum on this question. At the same time, it is impossible to predict what is going to happen. Saturn's goals should be clearly identified by students. The main goal is increasing sales to 500,000 units. Some students may simply surmise that because Saturn is more than doubling the number of models in its lineup, then doubling its sales should not be that difficult. But they must consider that many buyers of the new models will be customers who would have bought one of the previous Saturn models anyway. The question with respect to this sales goal should be, can Saturn attract enough new customers to account for the incremental increase in projected unit sales, while at the same time retaining traditional Saturn customers? Saturn's shift in image may affect the answer to both parts of this question.

Students should also consider that many of the new models are not high-volume models. Industry wide, cross-over SUVs, roadsters, and hybrid SUVs have not demonstrated the type of sales numbers that four-door sedans typically do. Thus, Saturn is going to have to continue to post very strong numbers with its compact line and its new mid-sized sedan.

5. What segmentation, targeting, and positioning recommendations would you make to GM for future Saturn models?

   A major consideration for future models will depend on the success of the models that Saturn will have already released by the time this text goes to print, the models mentioned in the case. Another concept vehicle that Saturn is currently considering is a compact SUV called the Prevue, a cross between an SUV and a sport compact. Caution should be taken by Saturn not to get too broad too quickly. And there are likely only so many bases that a single car division will be able to cover. But one thing should be very clear in student responses: Saturn should maintain a strong focus on the characteristics that have established its success. Specifically, they should target customers who value quality, innovation, social responsibility, and a low-pressure personal sales environment.

Teaching Suggestions

The questions for this case can be used to guide a class discussion around the application of the main concepts in the chapter. One concept not directly addressed by these questions is that of competitive advantage. Thus, a discussion of this case, even prior to having students work on the discussion questions, might effectively be started by exploring the positioning of Saturn within the GM family (and without) based on its competitive advantages.

Another point of interest that might be addressed is the issue of how a company should progress from a concentrated strategy to a differentiated strategy. It is widely believed by industry observers as well as by Saturn employees and dealers that Saturn has taken too long to differentiate. The division got off to such a strong start, especially given that not a lot of resources were showered on it. So, when would it have made sense for Saturn to differentiate? In which direction? In how many directions? It took nine years before Saturn released its first non-S series model, the mid-sized L-series. While this was a logical direction, it was also later than it should have been, it was a tepid attempt, and it didn't go far enough into broadening Saturn's customer base. Some parallels could easily be drawn between Saturn and Toyota or Honda and their rollouts in the United States.

Following a discussion of these issues, students could be assigned to work on (in or out of class) the discussion questions, focusing the analysis on whether or not the current strategy can overcome Saturn's slow evolution. This case could also be used with Chapters 2 (marketing strategy).

Chapter 7
Converse: We Love You, Chuck!

Synopsis

This case is about the famous Chucks (Charles Taylor All Star Basketball Shoes) from Converse. The case chronicles the history of Chucks which were named for a Converse salesman (named Charles Taylor) and dominated basketball shoe sales into the 1970s when Nike appeared on the scene. Between the 1970s and 2000, Converse's market share dropped from over 70 percent to less than 5 percent.

Nike bought Converse in 2003. Since then, it has taken the company in two major directions. First, it has taken Converse back to the professional basketball courts with the endorsement of Miami's Dwyane Wade. Not only does this allow Converse to market a performance shoe, but it also has opened the door for retroperformance, or the reissue of the Converse Pro (originally made famous by Dr. J.).

While signing Dwyane Wade appears to have been a good move for Converse, it looks like the real success will come from the brand's second strategy. Nike is turning Converse into a fashion shoe. Chuck Taylors now come in styles ranging from the classic canvas version to a $1,800 snakeskin limited edition. High-end designer John Varvatos has been signed to create a line of Chucks and accompanying apparel. And the brand is being carried in Saks, Bloomingdales, and Barneys.

Teaching Objectives

The teaching objectives for this case are to:

1. Identify the three levels of the Converse product.
2. Evaluate the importance of those levels.
3. Appreciate the importance of a strong brand image.
4. Explain why Converse has built such a strong brand.
5. Explain how Converse lost market share without losing its brand image.
6. Position Converse in Nike's brand portfolio.

Discussion Questions

1. What are the core, actual, and augmented product benefits of the Converse Chuck?

   Level 1: The core benefit—success on the basketball court like Magic Johnson, Dr. J, Kareem Abdul Jabbar, and Larry Johnson.

   Level 2: Actual product, features, and design—the actual physical product. Rubber covered toes; canvas tops; high tops; three colors—black, white and red; "Made in the U.S.A." on the back. Highly identifiable shoe. Packaging—shoe boxes that continue the color theme (although this is not stated in the case). Quality level—not as good as the techno-shoes from Nike and Reebok. Brand name—well-known brand due to long history, being the first major basketball shoe and associations with famous players.

Level 3: Augmented product: Warranty—little to none. Delivery and credit—function of where sold, but as market share declined, it became harder and harder to find Chucks. (I know. I had to find some for my daughter.) After-sales service and installation are not major concerns here.

2. When Converse sourced production of its shoes to India, it entered into a licensing arrangement. What are the benefits and negatives of that action? Do you think it has helped or hurt the company? The brand?

   The big negative is that the company could no longer claim that Converse was a totally American product. However, such claims seem to have limited ability to stimulate purchasing. The textile and apparel industries for years tried to encourage "buy American made" with little success. Although it's a "nice" feature, it does not seem to determine purchase. Kids were looking for performance and what their friends were wearing, not where the shoes were made. Even the scandals about Nike production seemly have not hurt the company significantly.

   Licensing, however, takes production of the product out of the hands of the brand sponsor and quality can slip if the sponsor does not stay on top of the production quality. When you put many thousand miles and cultural differences between the brand sponsor and the actual producer, it is easy for quality to slip. On the other hand, Chucks are relatively simple shoes, so the licensee is not required to produce "difficult-to-make, high-tech" shoes. Perhaps licensing is more likely to be successful for Chucks than for performance shoes.

   Prospective purchasers may not even be aware of where the shoes are made. Who knows if they read "Made in India" on the inside of the shoe or the box? If being made in America doesn't determine purchase, then being made outside the United States shouldn't hurt it unless the potential buyer questions the ability of Indians to make shoes.

3. What are the sources of brand equity for both Converse and Chuck Taylor All Stars?

   Most young people probably think of them more as a fashion statement than a basketball shoe. Not fashion such as Vogue ads, but fashion such as non-preppy, non-mainstream types of people wear. Older consumers may have fond memories of Chucks from years ago when they wore them to play basketball. Both groups, however, would be buying Chucks to wear every day, not for performance. The brand has a lot of nostalgia appeal for consumers over 40.

Not only is Converse an old brand, it has strong associations with basketball and famous players (the Johnsons, Dr. J, etc.). Its dominant position in basketball for so long is still a source of brand equity. Basically, Converse invented basketball shoes.

The new ads (that seem to be working) are aimed at consumers not interested in hype and fancy features that they don't use. In a sense, they are a return to the lower price positioning that Converse chose years ago. The ads, however, are much more apt for the market. Price isn't mentioned, but all the hype and surrounding funk are and it's clear that Converse isn't part of that; they are some kind of purist brand that just focuses on the game and the ball. There is no need to have big-name, overpaid stars endorse the brand. Converse is the basics! In a sense, this promotional theme is consistent with the Converse brand.

4. Analyze the Nike-era direction of Converse. (a) Assess the benefits and risks of the fashion and performance strategies individually, and of the combined two-tiered approach. (b) What targeting and positioning would you recommend for the Converse brand in the future?

Fashion positioning: The benefits to positioning Converse as a fashion brand brings with it the tremendous opportunity to produce line and brand extensions. While initially this might seem strange, it is working. Line extensions include all the new varieties of Chuck Taylor All Stars. Thus, Nike has taken a fledgling brand with only a limited number of styles and has capitalized on its legacy and equity. The result is that there are now more than 1,000 types of Chucks alone. These line extensions also have allowed the brand to branch out into new, upscale outlets.

Brand extensions include the new line of apparel by John Varvatos. The benefit of this is that Converse has the opportunity to sell more products to the same customers, as well as appeal to new customers who otherwise might not have purchased the brand. With the new apparel line, there is instant brand recognition.

But there are risks to this strategy. One risk is that this strategy is the complete antithesis of the brand's previously antiestablishment image. Thus, the new fashion direction may do damage to the core brand. However, this issue doesn't seem to be hindering it. If Converse has lost customers because of this, it is more than making up for it in new sales. But fashion is fickle, and this poses the greatest risk. As the product and brand extensions grow, all of it rests on the image of a single brand. If at some point, that brand falls out of favor with pop culture and the fashion industry, sales will plummet.

Performance positioning: This strategy also capitalizes on the Converse brand equity. Chucks were basketball shoes; they just didn't go high tech. Eventually, however, Converse did include some performance features. This performance basis should build on Converse tradition as a comfortable, supportive shoe for everyday use and for playing use while recognizing that it's not a high performance shoe. This approach might work best with adults over forty. It fits with the current promotion of getting back to the basics with younger folks (as well as older folks). It's an updated Chuck that does not compete with more high-tech and expensive shoes.

The downside to a two-tier approach such as this is that the two elements do not seem relevant to each other.

Teaching Suggestions

This is a good case to assign to teams, with each team providing its own analysis of the brand, both past and present. Specifically, questions 3 and 4 are good ones to focus on for this exercise. Each team can make a brief 5-10 minute presentation on the equity of the Converse brand based on its history, as well as an analysis of the current Nike strategy. This exercise should help students realize that any one product could have several possible positions and that there are benefits and risks to most any strategy. During the discussion, be sure to ask how Nike's current two-tiered strategy fits with Nike's overall strategy. What advantages does each have for Nike?

Chapter 8
Sony: Betting It All on Blu-Ray

Synopsis

This case was written just after the introduction of two high definition DVD formats, Sony's Blu-Ray and the competing HD DVD. A historic parallel is given to the competition between Sony's Beta and VHS videotape formats of the 1970s and 1980s. This time around, however, there are many factors that are different. First, Blu-Ray was developed and is being supported not only by Sony, but by a strong coalition of companies. HD DVD is backed by a similar coalition. However, Sony and Toshiba appear to be the dominant players in each camp.

Similar to the battle for VCR formats, this battle finds both sides vying for superiority on image quality, disc capacity, price, and availability of content. But there are factors that may make these issues not nearly as important as they were three decades ago. First, both technologies are evolving very rapidly. Thus, the technology that initially has the advantage on any given factor could quickly find the tables turned. Second, since the early 1990s, the video-game industry has demonstrated that three competing formats can exist with each one succeeding. Third, given that both formats utilize the same size disc (unlike Beta and VHS), it may result that hardware technology will rapidly evolve to create players capable of playing both Blu-Ray and HD DVD. And fourth, many industry insiders predict that the wave of the future will be non-physical media, including online video and video-on-demand television. This may result in both formats failing as consumers bypass the concept of a disc altogether.

Teaching Objectives

The teaching objectives for this case are to:

1. Identify which stage of the product life cycle high definition DVD is in.
2. Determine whether the companies involved are using appropriate marketing strategies for their services.
3. Apply the stages of new-product development to high definition DVD.
4. Describe a typical consumer's adoption process for a new service.

Discussion Questions

1. Classify the high definition DVD market using the product life-cycle framework. Based on this analysis, what objectives and strategies should Sony and the other competitors pursue? Are any of the competitors deviating from this formula?

   The answer to this question will depend on the evolution of high definition DVD and when this case is analyzed. At the time this case was written, the technologies were just being introduced to the market. Likely, as Principles of Marketing 12e *is released, high definition DVD will still be in the introductory stage of the product life cycle. But this could change quickly over the course of 2007 and 2008. Nonetheless, this case could still be analyzed as per the written case.*

The introductory phase is characterized by a period of slow sales growth and low to non-existent profits. This should be considered, not in terms of how many units have been sold to date, but in the perspective of the potential of the product category. In other words, it may appear that both formats are selling a high number of units. But relative to the potential size of the market, when is rapid growth really taking place? Given an introductory stage, the companies involved should be doing the following:

Promotion: Each should be spending heavily on promotion and advertising. Promotion should be focused on informing consumers of the new product, rather than seeking to create brand preference through differentiation. In this case, it appears as though both formats are touting points of difference from the get-go, trying to jockey for early advantage in what should be a highly competitive market. The text (Table 9.2) indicates that sales promotion should used liberally to entice trial. However, this is a durable product, not a consumable. Thus, consumer sales promotions are not necessarily appropriate. It does not appear that either camp is using consumer sales promotions and introduction. Of course, if sales are sluggish, that would very likely change.

Distribution: In the introductory phase, companies should invest heavily in building distribution networks. It appears that this is the case for both formats. This situation is unique, given that each side is backed by a coalition of corporations that span the supply chain, even including entertainment content companies. Thus, there is a heavy emphasis on getting the players distributed as well as having a strong distribution of content that will be playable on the players.

Price: As far as pricing goes, both a skimming and a penetration strategy are appropriate. From the information in the case, Pioneer introduced the first Blu-Ray machine using a skimming strategy and a price of $1,800. While Toshiba's entry price of $499 to $799 is much lower, it could hardly be considered a penetration strategy given that it is relatively much higher than standard DVD players. But it is clear that Toshiba is committed to accelerating product adoption through its pricing strategy despite possibly selling it at a loss.

Product: In the introductory stage, the product is generally basic with few versions or options. Based on the information in the case, this is true. Toshiba, the first to market, has two models while Pioneer has only one.

2. As sales of the new DVD players increase, what will happen to the characteristics of the home video market and the strategies employed by Sony and other competitors?

The answers to this are contained in Table 9.2. Students should use this table and the accompanying text as they respond to this question. They should be encouraged to study and learn this material. Instructors should also be certain to point out the pattern in strategy as a product progresses from one stage of the product life cycle to the next. For example, sales go from low to high to highest, then decline. In parallel, profits, competitors, and customers also follow this pattern. Accordingly, the strategies for each of the four Ps progress appropriately.

A main factor that could alter the normal progression through the product life cycle is if (as predicted by one observer at the end of the case) the high definition formats go into decline before ever really getting off the ground.

3. Analyze the development of Blu-Ray and HD DVD according to the stages of new-product development process.

   While this is a very relevant question for an emerging technology, the case does not present sufficient information to be able to identify activities carried out at each stage of the new-product development process. Some suggestions are given for some of the stages here:

   Idea generation: Unlike many new products where the concept simply didn't exist, the concept of high definition DVD was almost prescribed. The basic idea is backed by years in the high-tech industry where successive generations of a given product focus on boosting data storage or data processing power. Thus, as the first standard DVD players were hitting the market in the mid 1990s, the concept of high definition DVD was already being developed. The advent of high definition televisions further begged for better content quality and players. Students might speculate that idea generation for these products was relatively simple: players and discs would remain basically the same in terms of size, usability, and function. The differences would be in the invisible technologies contained therein, many of which could not be developed until later stages.

   Marketing Strategy Development:
   - *Product positioning and target market—the product is positioned as a technology product capable of delivering home video and audio far superior to that of existing technologies. The positioning includes exclusivity and quality based on price. The initial target market would be the classic innovator – well-educated, venturesome, risk-taking individuals who crave the latest in high-tech and home cinema offerings.*
   - *Planned price—the introductory pricing strategies for each camp are made very clear in the case. Pioneer's and Blu-Ray's strategy is best illustrated in this quote: "Consumers interested in buying technology that gives them the best display or audio quality won't balk at the price. This is why our player is $1,800. We focused on getting 1080P, because that is something we knew would resonate*

with the initial target market, whereas the $499 strategy is probably going off in the wrong direction, because the folks who are really paying attention to this right now want the highest resolution." The HD DVD and Toshiba philosophy focuses on accelerating product adoption through lower pricing.

- *Long-run sales, profit, and marketing mix strategy—the case does not give sufficient information to outline this portion of the marketing strategy for either format.*

Business Analysis: This is the phase where companies involved should have been reviewing sales, costs, and profit projections for the new products to determine feasibility. What was the history of DVD sales? If the market makes the shift completely to high definition, what is the potential, therefore, of the market? The case states that the home video market is worth more than $24 billion. What isn't clear is whether that refers only to hardware players or includes the entertainment content on DVD. But companies during this phase should have examined historical figures for products, as well as sales and trends of HDTVs.

Product Development: This is the phase where each camp and the companies therein needed to determine the specifications of the products, including storage capacity, image quality, and content availability.

4. Who are the current combatants in the battle for the home video market? Who will they be in five years?

This is an interesting question because the two competing formats are represented by numerous companies. Thus, Blu-Ray is backed by a coalition of companies that includes Sony, Hitachi, Pioneer, Philips, Panasonic, Samsung, LG, Sharp, Apple, HP, and a host of other companies. HD DVD is supported by a similar coalition including Toshiba, Sanyo, Kenwood, Intel, and NEC, among others. Thus, all these companies are combatants with a vested interested in the home video market.

However, notice that the question asks about home video and not high definition DVD players and discs. The point of this question is to force students to consider the alternatives pointed out in the case. Home video is a broad market being fought over by Blu-Ray, HD DVD, and other physical formats. But it is also being fought over by online options and video-on-demand television. Thus, the cable companies are combatants. Additionally, many of the same companies who are part of either the Blu-Ray Disc Association or the HD DVD coalition are also competing either directly or indirectly with their own physical formats. For example, Apple backs Blu-Ray, but has been one of the strongest companies in developing technologies to download movie content over the Internet and store it locally on hard-drive devices. Microsoft backs HD DVD, but is also has its hand in various ventures leading down the path of online video.

Thus, the question of who the combatants will be in five years is purely speculative, but fun and challenging for students to consider.

Teaching Suggestions

Perhaps the best way to introduce this case is to talk about the PLC and where the high definition DVD market currently is. (This case was written in the summer of 2007; so again, the answers may have changed upon reading the case). Ask the class to outline the strategies companies are employing. Then, put the chart showing PLC characteristics, objectives, and strategies up and compare with company strategies to see if they are following the traditional theory. Where they aren't, ask why, which should lead into a discussion of marketplace imperfections. This could include the future issues of online video and on-demand television. As a result, some of the high definition DVD advantages may disappear. Will that hurt adopters who may later want to switch? What happens to consumer perceptions of products/services when and if some advantages are reduced?

Question 4 is a good one to finish on because it forces students to speculate over not only which of the two formats will be the more successful (if any), but whether either of them will succeed at all.

Chapter 9
Southwest Airlines: Waging War in Philly

Synopsis

This case depicts Southwest Airlines entry into the Philadelphia market in May 2004. This event was significant in Southwest's history because it marked its first head-to-head confrontation with a major airline, US Airways, in one if its core markets. The battle was also significant as US Airways, like the other "legacy" airlines, was struggling financially. As the opening paragraph in the case notes, for US Airways, this battle represented a life-or-death encounter for the airline. With Southwest's proven low-price leader strategy and superb service, the battle would be tough.

The entry into the Philadelphia market represented a major change in strategy. However, US Airways was not going to give up in its home market without a serious fight. Two years after Southwest entered the Philadelphia market, things had changed. Southwest had quadrupled its capacity in that market, and all major carriers had dropped their fares. Shortly thereafter, Southwest entered Pittsburgh, another US Airways hub. Southwest also announced that it would enter Charlotte, North Carolina, the last of US Airways' strongholds.

But the case ends by presenting information that questions whether or not Southwest will be able to continue to have the same effect on the industry that it has had in the past. Environmental factors are different. And Southwest, the long-time underdog airline, is seemingly turning into one of the airlines that it has been competing against for more than 30 years.

Teaching Objectives

The teaching objectives for this case are to:

1. Allow students to understand how a firm's marketing objectives and marketing mix strategy affect its pricing decisions.
2. Help students understand the nature of costs in the airline industry and how the relationship of fixed and variable costs affect marketing decisions.
3. Enable students to understand how the nature of a market and market demand affect pricing decisions.
4. Let students examine the pricing approaches airlines have used.
5. Allow students to make pricing and other marketing recommendations for Southwest.

Discussion Questions

1. How do Southwest Airlines' marketing objectives and its marketing mix strategy affect its pricing decisions?

Students will suggest that although Southwest is smaller than some of the major airlines, it is pursuing a market share leadership strategy. The example in the case of its success in the Oakland market versus US Airways indicates that even though it may not be the biggest overall airline, it tries to dominate any particular market it enters through its low-price strategy. This should suggest to students that even though it is entering the Philadelphia market with only 14 flights per day, US Airways should expect it to expand its number of flights quickly if it is successful in getting a foothold in the market. Southwest is not pursuing a current profit maximization strategy, as some students may suggest, even though it has been highly profitable. This should help students see that low prices do not necessarily result in lower profits.

As to the relationship with the other marketing mix variables, students should see that in order to deliver low prices, Southwest must keep the cost of the other variables low. Thus, it offers a no-frills, point-to-point, air transportation service (product) at out-of-the-way airports (places) where costs are low, with limited and low-cost promotion. Price is the only marketing mix variable that produces revenue, so with low prices the company must keep the cost of the other variables low. Southwest has done an excellent job of getting the marketing mix variables to fit with each other.

2. Discuss factors that have affected the nature of costs in the airline industry since the year 2000. How have these factors affected pricing decisions?

These are key questions for the students to understand. It is helpful to ask students to think about which costs are fixed and which are variable in the airline business. Students should quickly see that all the salaries of the pilots, flight attendants, ground crews, terminal personnel, reservations systems personnel, and corporate employees are all fixed. The costs of the planes, the gates at the airports, terminal fees, etc., are also fixed. The only variable costs are the transaction costs of issuing a ticket (very low with e-tickets), the extra fuel the plane uses because of the extra weight of the passenger and luggage, and any in-flight food or beverages. The true variable cost of flying one additional passenger is very low.

So, students should see that air transportation is a very high fixed-cost business. In such a business, volume is important. The unit price minus unit variable cost (unit contribution) is high. An airline must have a high volume of passengers to cover the high fixed costs. Operating below break-even volume results in an airline losing lots of money quickly. Operating above break-even volume results in an airline making lots of money quickly. This is why the airlines can have lots of sales promotions and discounts—they had rather have a passenger in a seat making some unit contribution than have that seat be empty and produce no unit contribution. In this type of business, a company varies its pricing to produce the volume it needs. The text discusses dynamic pricing—charging different prices depending on individual customers and situations. The airline industry is an excellent example of this practice.

Students should also see from the information in the case that the older airlines, like US Airways, have very different cost structures from the newer entrants. Not only do they have pilots, flight attendants, and ground crews that may be unionized and have higher salaries, wages, and benefits, but also they may have high-cost airplanes and infrastructure. Note in the case that Southwest has an important advantage in that it has no fixed-cost pension system. Rather, it has a profit-sharing system. This converts pension cost from a fixed cost to a variable cost, significantly reducing its break-even point.

Since the year 2000, various things have changed in the industry that have affected the nature of costs. First, the costs associated with travel agencies are dropping as Internet booking services have replaced that intermediary. While this is a factor that is improving the cost structure for the legacy airlines, it is not helping Southwest at all given that they have never worked through travel agents. Second, fuel prices have gone up considerably. The nature of the fuel contracts that many airlines have, including Southwest, are changing. In some cases they may be more favorable. In Southwest's case, they are becoming less favorable. Other things that are affecting Southwest's structure is that it is adding amenities that it previously did not offer (satellite radio) and it is starting to provide service out of the big airports that charge higher fees.

3. How do the nature of the airline market and the demand for airline service affect Southwest's decisions?

   Students will suggest that the airline market traditionally has been an example of oligopolistic competition—relatively few sellers were highly sensitive to each other's pricing and marketing strategies. Students may recall news stories about how an airline announced a price increase but then had to cancel it because other airlines did not follow.
   However, other students may suggest that the airline industry is moving toward monopolistic competition. As more airlines enter the industry and trade over a wide range of prices with differentiated offers, the market's nature is changing. The text discusses the importance of consumer perceptions. As low-fare airlines entered the market, their low prices affected the way consumers viewed airline prices. Consumers saw that they could fly from point A to point B at a much lower price if they were willing to give up some of the frills and extras that airlines traditionally offered. This affected their view of what the "right" price was for air transportation.

   The text also discusses price elasticity. Students who are more perceptive will have noticed the discussion in the case that indicated when Southwest entered the Oakland market, average one-way fares fell from $104 to $42—and traffic <u>tripled</u>. This indicates that the demand for air transportation is price elastic.

Using these numbers, we could calculate the elasticity: +300 percent divided by -60 percent = -5. One would expect that as Southwest enters the Philadelphia market, that market would expand also.

Students will also note that an important external factor in airline pricing is the price of fuel. Although the case does not discuss oil prices, students will remember that 2004 was a time of rapidly rising oil prices. These prices put much pressure on the airlines to cut costs or raise prices to reflect the increased fuel costs. However, with the low-fare airlines already having lower cost structures, the older airlines were not successful in raising prices.

4. What general pricing approaches have airlines pursued?

Students will suggest that airlines have traditionally practiced value-based pricing. They should know that airlines have often charged much more for last-minute purchases as compared with tickets purchased well in advance. This strategy charged more to the person, often a business traveler, who was willing to pay more for the availability of that seat. Airlines priced some seats high just to hold them for these last-minute travelers. Leisure travelers would not and could not pay such high prices. However, they were willing to purchase in advance and pay a lower price.

Students will also note that, as the text suggests, the airline industry, led by the low-fare airlines, is practicing value pricing. The new companies are offering just the right combination of quality and good service at a fair price. They have introduced less expensive versions of the "brand name" airlines' products.

There is also an element of competition-based pricing here. To the extent that competitors' prices establish a "going rate" for a particular route, a firm may have to offer that price also regardless of its particular costs.

5. Do you think that Southwest will be able to continue to maintain a competitive advantage based on price? What will happen if other carriers match the low-price leader?

Based on the last part of the answer to question 3, it is becoming more and more difficult for Southwest to maintain a big cost advantage. As Gary Kelly states, "I just don't see how that can be indefinitely sustained without some sacrifice." At the same time, legacy airlines are getting more cost efficient. And, the presence of low-cost upstart airlines has increased dramatically. Thus, the difference in cost structure between Southwest and all other airlines in the industry is shrinking. As a result, other airlines are more capable of matching Southwest's fares and being able to sustain those prices without incurring the damage they once did. The issues with respect to airlines matching Southwest's prices are different now than they were 10 years ago. More airlines will do this, and they will hurt less from it.

Thus, Southwest will either have to dig deeper as far as price cuts (which it likely will not be able to afford to do) or find some additional point to compete on.

Teaching Suggestions

This case provides an excellent opportunity for students to do some research to find out how Southwest has done in the Philadelphia market and what has happened to US Airways, both in that market and in general.

In addition to the questions asked, students could be engaged in a discussion of recommendations. Students may discuss how Southwest should position itself versus the other low-fare airlines. Southwest has a history of being entertaining. Its flight attendants often work to get the customers to laugh. At a time when flying has become more of a hassle due to security regulations, Southwest might want to emphasize that positioning. Helping its customer relax and have some fun in the midst of what can be a mentally and physically tiring trip could add value to flying Southwest.

A first recommendation that students may make is that Southwest should use its promotional tools not only to communicate about its low fares but also to educate customers about what Southwest is and what it offers. Although many customers may know of or have used Southwest at a neighboring airport, many potential leisure customers will not have had that experience. Southwest wants to use these customers to expand the market. These customers may not have thought about how inexpensive it might be to fly on their next vacation or family visit. Southwest wants these people to consider flying versus driving.

Southwest's strategy is about more than just low price. It has established a brand that promises a total experience that will be satisfying to its customers. It offers on-time departures and arrivals, friendly service, error-free baggage handling, the availability of low fares, an easy frequent-flyer program, and direct flights. Students can suggest any number of promotion ideas to communicate Southwest's brand promise to the leisure traveler.

For the thrift-minded businessperson, students will suggest that price may be the most important factor, but the total experience will be what keeps that customer coming back to Southwest. It may be that some businesspeople do not think about flying Southwest. So, promotions should communicate that Southwest also serves businesspeople interested in saving money. Some students may suggest that Southwest should segment the business market and target that small business owner or manager who may travel only a few times per year. There may be locally-oriented business newspapers or magazines that Southwest can use to communicate with these customers.

The case mentions that other low-fare airlines are beginning to offer some frills, such as JetBlue making Direct TV available at every seat free of additional charges. This points out the disadvantage of letting customers focus only on price. Meeting a competitor's price may be easy. However, the company has to differentiate itself. A customer who can get a low fare and free TV may well take that offer. Southwest is going to have to deal with the issue of what it is going to do as competitors, some of whom have even lower cost structures, enter its markets with enhanced product offerings. Again, the key will be to get its customers and potential customers to see the value of the entire Southwest experience, not just the price.

This case goes well with the chapters on managing customer relationships and company strategy (Chapters 1 and 2).

Chapter 10
Zara: The Technology Giant of the Fashion World

Synopsis

Zara is a company that defines what the fashion industry has termed "fast fashion." The flagship specialty chain of Spain-based clothing conglomerate, Inditex, Zara has built an information and distribution system that allows it to put the latest runway fashions in its stores in a matter of weeks at a fraction of what the big-name designers charge.

In addition to fast, Zara is prolific. In a typical year, Zara launches about 11,000 new items. Compare that to the 2,000 to 4,000 items introduced by both H&M and Gap. Zara stores receive new merchandise two to three times each week, compared to four to six times per year for most clothing retailers. More and smaller batches of items translate into fashion exclusivity. This in turn results in fewer mark-downs and higher profits.

Zara controls a true vertical marketing system. A good portion of the channel participants are centralized geographically around its corporate headquarters in a remote corner of Northeast Spain, rather than spread out around the globe. This and its IT system are what allow it to achieve the speed and responsiveness that it does.

Teaching Objectives

The teaching objectives for this case are to:

1. Illustrate a value delivery system in action.
2. Help students understand why and how companies use value delivery systems.
3. Expose students to issues of channel conflict and conflict management.
4. Illustrate how value can be added through different aspects of supply chain management.

Discussion Questions

1. As completely as possible, sketch the supply chain for Zara from raw materials to consumer purchase.

   As the case points out, finding the starting point of a product concept is hard to nail down with Zara. But the following is an attempt to do this:
   Design: The starting point is a collaborative phase that includes teams of creative professionals who carry out the design process and store managers who spot trends and feed data to corporate.

   Materials: Zara makes 40 percent of its own fabric. It is not clear from the case where the other 60 percent comes from, but given the information on the rest of the process, it is likely purchased more on a local basis than on a global basis.

Cutting: Zara produces more than half of its own clothing. It cuts all fabric in-house at its complex in Spain.

Sewing: Cut fabric and designs are sent to one of several hundred local co-operatives.

Ironing: Ironing is performed in-house by workers trained for a specific task (lapels, shoulders, etc.).

Final preparation: Clothing is wrapped in plastic and transported on conveyors to local Zara-owned warehouses. The automated warehouses sort, pack, label, and allocate clothing items to specific regions and stores.

Delivery: Stores within a 24-hour drive receive deliveries by truck. All other stores receive their goods via air parcel.

Sale: All stores are company owned.

2. Discuss the concepts of horizontal and vertical conflict as they relate to Zara.

   There is little information given in the case regarding channel conflict. But one could easily speculate as to the outcomes. Because Zara owns much of its own supply chain and exhibits an extreme amount of control over the elements that it does not own, conflict is likely minimal. With respect to horizontal conflict, the only members of the supply chain on a horizontal level would be the hundreds of local sewing co-operatives. It is difficult to imagine the type of complaints that such co-operatives might wage against each other that would affect Zara. However, horizontal issues might result in vertical conflict. Zara owns much of the supply chain. Thus, any conflict would be internal and could be handled in a much different manner than if the entities were independent. But the co-operatives are not company owned. Because there are so many of them, however, conflict should be minimized as Zara has plenty of options.

3. Which type of vertical marketing system does Zara employ? List all the benefits that Zara receives by having adopted this system.

   While Zara does not own all of the stages of the vertical marketing system, it seems to have a strong control over those that it does not own. Zara's system fits the description of a corporate VMS better than it fits the contractual or administered systems. The text provides an outtake example of Zara in the section on corporate VMS that illustrates the benefits that Zara achieves through this structure. These include control over almost every aspect of the supply chain, more items produced, faster design-to-shelf times, lower inventories, and more frequent shipments. In short, Zara is faster, more flexible, and more efficient than other fashion houses and chains because of its corporate VMS.

4. Does Zara incur disadvantages from its "fast-fashion" distribution system? Are these disadvantages offset by the advantages?

   One disadvantage that Zara incurs is possibly a higher cost on materials and labor by not sourcing globally to the cheapest source. This, however, is offset by the cost savings of not having items shipped all over the world. It is also offset by dramatically faster response time between each stage. Because Zara's competitive advantage is the "fast" part of the fashion, this is much more important than the minimal amount that Zara could save by sourcing globally.

5. How does Zara add value for the customer through major logistics functions?

   Warehousing: The only warehousing done in this system is local and brief for the component parts and the finished items. This adds value by cutting down on costs associated with warehousing and by decreasing the time-to-shelf.

   Inventory Management: The IT system and the VMS in general both contribute to Zara's ability to offer a just-in-time system. This results in lower inventories, cut costs, and faster throughput.

   Transportation: Zara's shipping system is certainly quick. That is the big advantage. Shipping by air freight to individual stores is not the cheapest way to go. But again, Zara's competitive advantage is speed.

Teaching Suggestions

This case can be used to illustrate just about every part of the chapter. This is also an interesting case for students in the United States, because most of them have never heard of Zara. Before launching a discussion based on this case, instructors might consider engaging students in a discussion of how they shop for clothes. What are the main U.S. retailers like? What patterns do they follow in shopping? Try to bring out the characteristics of major seasonal clothing releases, periodic markdowns throughout the season, and drastic closeouts at the end just as the new season's apparel is hitting the shelves. Ask students what the advantages and disadvantages of shopping like this are. Then, have them read the case. This can be used as a comparison to other retailers.

This case goes well with the segmentation chapter (Chapter 6) and with the retailing chapter (Chapter 11).

Chapter 11
Peapod: Thriving in the World of Online Groceries

Synopsis

In 1989, brothers Andrew and Thomas Parkinson started a business selling groceries online, years before the World Wide Web would take the Internet public. Their concept was to return to the full-service grocers of the early 1900s. In fact, they envisioned making grocery shopping more full service than ever before, allowing people to place orders from the comfort and convenience of their own homes, 24/7.

Headquartered in the Chicago area, Peapod has maintained a conservative growth rate that has allowed them to whether the storm of the dot.com fallout. From the beginning, they settled on the strategy of partnering with existing grocery chains. This allowed them to focus on online order fulfillment and delivery while allowing established partners to take care of purchasing and warehousing groceries.

Now a wholly owned subsidiary of Stop & Shop's parent, Royal Ahold, Peapod has delivered more than 10 million orders. In an industry characterized by single digit growth rates, Peapod has achieved an annual revenue increase of 25 percent. It has achieved this success by overcoming the most commonly sited barriers to buying groceries online.

Teaching Objectives

The teaching objectives for this case are to:

1. Gain an understanding for a little known type of retailer in a well-known industry.
2. Compose a profile for a retailer based on the classifications of retailers.
3. Understand the importance of targeting and positioning for retail organizations.
4. Gain an understanding of the Wheel of Retailing Concept through application.

Discussion Questions

1. Visit www.Peapod.com and click on the "Groceries for Your Home" link. Enter a Chicago-area zip code (say 60602), and click on the "Learn More" arrow. Compare the Peapod customer experience to a bricks-and-mortar grocery shopping experience. What benefits can a customer receive by using Peapod? What are the disadvantages?

   This is largely an experiential exercise. Instructors should go through this exercise as well. What should emerge from this is an outline of the advantages and disadvantages cited in the case. The most commonly cited disadvantages are:
   - *It takes too long to place an order.*
   - *You can't tell what you want unless you're in the store, walking the aisles.*
   - *You have no control over quality of product.*
   - *It costs too much.*

- *It's inconvenient to meet the delivery person.*

However, Peapod has overcome each of these to a pretty satisfactory extent. Thus, one of the remaining disadvantages of using Peapod is that there is a substantial startup cost in terms of time and learning for the initial account setup, creation of a master list, and getting to know the site and the procedures. The advantages are:

- *A substantial time savings for regular orders once you become accustomed to the service*
- *The convenience of ordering from home any time of day*
- *Expert advice provided by professional shoppers*
- *Browsing capabilities that exceed those of in-store shopping*

2. Using the various characteristics for classifying types of retailers, develop a profile of Peapod.

Peapod's profile includes the following classifications:

- *Full-service*
- *Supermarket/convenience store*
- *Corporate chain*

3. Who does Peapod target? How does it position itself in this market? Does its marketing mix support this targeting and positioning?

As far as end-users go, Peapod targets customers based on the following variables:

- *Geography: The current focus is on region and city size. Specifically, Peapod has focused on densely populated urban areas in and around Chicago; Washington, D.C.; Baltimore; Boston; and New York.*
- *Demographic: High-income, two-paycheck, or single parent households; people with physical disabilities.*
- *Psychographics: Upper middle through upper classes, time-pressured, Internet-savvy.*
- *Behavioral: Highly loyal customers seeking specific benefits of full-service, time savings, and anytime ordering.*

As a full-service, online supermarket, Peapod is well-positioned for this target market. Peapod's marketing mix further serves to solidify the positioning. Peapod is not a discount grocer and charges a small premium to deliver. It is an online grocer. Thus, only the Internet-savvy will likely find it and use it. The time-saving promise of value will appeal to the time-pressured individuals; this would include homes where both parents work, single-parent homes, individuals who work long hours in high-paying professional jobs, etc.

4. Apply the Wheel of Retailing Concept to the entire grocery industry, defining Peapod's role.

   The Wheel of Retailing Concept generally places low cost/low margin/low service operations at the beginning of the cycle of retail evolution. Then, such outlets add services, higher priced items, and other amenities that "fatten" them up. They become something other than they started as. As this progression continues, there opens up opportunity for a return to the original low cost/low margin/low service formula.

   The grocery industry is unique in terms of the application of the Wheel of Retailing Concept. The grocery business originated as a full-service, low volume concept that was not necessarily low cost or low margin. But then in the 1950s, supermarkets emerged applying the benefits of economies of scale. Thus, even as these retail outlets added depth and breadth of product lines to storefronts, they also cut prices and margins rather than increasing such, as the standard Wheel of Retailing progression would dictate.

   While the characteristics of each phase of the Wheel of Retailing as described in the text do not exactly apply to the case of the grocery industry, the basic concept does. That is, a given industry begins with one type of retail outlet. That outlet progresses and changes, becoming something quite different than the original concept; then, at some point, there is an opportunity for a return to the original concept.

   Peapod is the fulfillment of this cycle. It is a business that has returned to the original grocery store concept. It is not low priced or low-margin. It is full-service. To boot, it is also something different by offering round-the clock order-taking from home.

5. What does the future hold for Peapod, in both the short term and the long term?

   The final section of the case on the competitive landscape offers a great deal of perspective for this question. It would appear that for both the short term and the long term, there is no reason that Peapod cannot maintain the growth rate that it has achieved in the past. This is because it has grown slowly and there is a long way to go before the market for this type of grocery service becomes saturated. There is very little threat of competition for Peapod (or for any of the online grocers for that matter) as each of the online grocers overlaps very little in terms of geographic regions served. Peapod can continue to focus on its targeting and positioning strategies, growing by expanding into new areas. It will likely be quite some time before any of the online grocers grows enough that competitive pressures will force Peapod into altering its strategy and target new segments of customers. However, one must also consider that over the next couple of decades, consumers across the socioeconomic spectrum will be turning more and more to the Internet to make purchases of all types. It can only be assumed that this will include groceries.

Teaching Suggestions

It might be a fun and educational prelude to this case to make an assignment to specific individuals. Come up with a list of commonly purchased grocery items. Assign some individuals to go to a brick-and-mortar grocery store while assigning others to shop online at Peapods (the students do not have to make the actual purchase, just find the items and mock-shop). Instruct them to keep track of the price of each item as well as the amount of the total bill. Also, students should track their time from the point in which they begin shopping (for those going to the store, this would begin when they depart for the store) to the point in which they end it. Students could then report on their experiences. The instructor could even compile the data and provide descriptive statistics of the online versus the off-line grocer experiences as a means of comparing the two.

Students could then be assigned to read the case and answer the discussion questions on their own or in small groups. This case can also be used with the segmentation, targeting, and positioning chapter (Chapter 6) and the product, services, and branding strategy chapter (Chapter 7).

Chapter 12
Burger King: Promoting a Food Fight

Synopsis

In early 2004, Burger King's CEO Brad Blum abruptly fired its advertising agency, Young & Rubicam, and hired Miami-based Crispin Porter + Bogusky in an attempt to revive BK's slumping sales. BK's move marked the fifth time in four years that it had moved its account. CP+B had established a reputation for developing "out-of-the box" promotional campaigns that produced results.

Instead of recommending some new, sexy idea, CP+B suggested BK return to a tagline developed in 1974—"Have It Your Way." CP+B believed it could make the message relevant to customers in 2004. Uncharacteristically, CP+B began the new campaign with television commercials and a package of promotions that included everything from in-store promotions to messages on cups.

Then, CP+B took on the job of promoting BK's TenderCrisp chicken products by designing a Web site, www.subservientchicken.com. The site allowed visitors to type in commands that a man dressed like a chicken executed. In the first 10 days, more than 20 million people visited the Web site, with an average stay of more than seven minutes—demonstrating that CP+B was a master at viral marketing.

As a follow-up to the Subservient Chicken campaign, CP+B has engaged in other creative and non-traditional campaigns. These include a the creation of a faux heavy metal band called Coq Roq as an aid in launching the new Chicken Fries. It has also created various creative TV campaigns. But most recently, the www.petmoustache.com campaign has further demonstrated CP+B's talent for creative viral campaigns. The franchisees are pleased. Sales at Burger King are finally on the rise.

Teaching Objectives

The teaching objectives for this case are to:

1. Introduce students to the elements of the promotion mix.
2. Introduce the concept of integrated marketing communications.
3. Allow students to identify a target audience and see how communications objectives flow from that decision.
4. Allow students to consider the issues involved in designing a message.
5. Enable students to appreciate the power of viral or buzz marketing, especially in the Internet world.
6. Allow students to develop recommendations as to how BK can continue to integrate its promotions.

Discussion Questions

1. What are Burger King's communication objectives for its target audience?

   Students will suggest that BK can consider almost anyone as being in its target market. Everyone from young children to senior citizens are potential customers for fast-food chains. However, the instructor should help students see that some customers are core customers. The firm depends on them to drive its business. In the fast-food business, generally young males between 18 and 35 are seen as the "heavy users" the chains want to attract.

   > *The case begins by noting that BK had just fired Y&R for its failed campaign that featured the tagline "The Fire's Ready" and focused on the broiled versus fried cooking process. Students will note that this approach focused on a product feature rather than a benefit. There is an implied benefit and taste, but it is only implied. In the CP+B campaign, the focus returned to "Have It Your Way," which focuses on the customer benefit—I can have a sandwich prepared just the way I like it. In a sense, the target market becomes a market of one—we prepare each sandwich individually, just the way you like it.*

   As for the communications objectives, students will suggest that BK has achieved awareness, knowledge, and even liking. Its goal is to develop preference among fast-food customers. There are many alternatives available to these customers. How can BK get them to choose its offerings? It hopes that by using the "Have It Your Way" message, customers will develop the conviction that its sandwiches are therefore better, leading them to visit BK.

2. With its focus on the "super fan," does BK risk alienating other customers? What are the implications of this?

   BK was suffering from an image problem, or rather, a lack of image problem. What was BK? What were its points of distinction? Who was it for? Numerous companies have faced this same problem time and time again. Thus, the solution is to create a brand image that is focused and vibrant and that targets a given segment or segments of customers. In this case, CP+B took BK in the direction of focusing on "men who love beef."

   Do such strategies risk alienating customers who are not part of the target group? The issue with a question such as this should focus not on whether or not some type of customer will be alienated, but on the implications. If a company focuses on a specific customer profile, then it is obvious that it is not going to appeal to many other types of customers. But BK's previous lack of image was focused on being too little to too many. With a new focused campaign, will there be enough interest from the new target group to offset any loses of other customers? In the case of BK, the answer is yes. They became a big hit with the "super fan" when they were previously not a big hit with anyone.

One other issue is that while the "super fan" campaign may not tickle the fancy of females, the "super fans" do not always dine alone. They take their dates, girlfriends, spouses, etc., and get some Chicken Fries.

3. Why is viral or buzz marketing effective? Analyze the design of the Subservient Chicken site's message, including content, structure, and format. What can you conclude from this analysis?

   If we examine the Subservient Chicken Web site, it is easy to conclude that we are not dealing with rational appeals. "Having Chicken Your Way" by having the chicken perform various activities says nothing particular about the product in the way of cooking technique, the quality of the input ingredients, or the dietary characteristics of the product. BK is presenting an emotional appeal designed to make its point through humor. As the text notes, people like ads with humorous themes. People like to laugh—and from the point of view of driving viral marketing, people like to tell other people about funny or amusing things.

   In terms of message structure, BK is letting the visitor to the site draw his/her own conclusions. Although the message of "Having Chicken Your Way" is not very subtle here, BK leaves it to the viewer to make the connection between the message and the fact that the viewer can get a chicken sandwich made his/her way at the local BK. BK presents no arguments here. It simply supports the point that having anything your way is better than having to accept something prepared for the average customer or for the masses.

   As to format, CP+B chose delivering the message over the Internet. With the video cam format, the viewer gets the benefits of a television commercial while also seeming to communicate with the chicken in real time. Given our younger core target market, using the Internet makes sense. Many of these customers are familiar and comfortable with the Internet. They are used to sharing e-mail and popular Web sites with their friends. Furthermore, the built-in e-mail feature makes it very easy to share one's find with friends, thus jump-starting the viral process.

   Given CP+B's interest in stimulating word of mouth, the Web site with the humorous chicken seems to be an excellent way to get its main point across while stimulating word-of-mouth communication.

4. Do the TV and viral elements of the BK campaign work well together? What additional elements and media might CP+B add to the integrated marketing communications campaign?

   Although the television ads discussed in the case focused on BK's burgers, they delivered the same benefit statement—"Have It Your Way." Thus, the consistent theme does result in reinforcing the key message. The office ads appeal to the sense that office workers often work in an environment where it is hard to be an individual. The "Have It Your Way" message gives the customer a chance to be an individual. Furthermore, people, especially young men, are often competitive. Having the most unusual burger is just another appeal to that competitive nature.

   Students can be creative in suggesting additional elements and media. Radio is an obvious way to communicate with customers who may be in their cars during commuting times or at lunch and be interested in finding a place to eat. Billboards could communicate with these customers. "Tired of following everybody else? Try Burger King and Have It Your Way."

   Students may recommend a sales promotion contest that takes off on the traditional trip giveaway. Instead of giving away a trip to a specific location, like Cancun or Mexico, BK could give away a "Design It Yourself" trip where the winner has a certain amount to spend to design the trip of his/her dreams. Customers could enter the contest by buying a BK TenderCrisp sandwich and getting an entry form. Newspaper advertising could support this effort by including coupons good for a discount on BK TenderCrisp sandwiches.

   To follow up on the Web basis for the initial campaign, BK could start a Web log where people could post their favorite chicken jokes or stories with a panel of judges periodically awarding prizes for the best entries.

   The possibilities are endless. The key is to have the elements reinforce and support each other in delivering the desired message to the target consumer.

5. What other recommendations would you make to BK and CP+B to help them improve the integration of BK's promotion mix?

   First, perceptive students will suggest that all these promotional ideas are great, but BK wants to know if the campaign works—does it generate sales as well as word of mouth? Students should propose ways that BK can monitor sales results that come from the campaign.

   Next, students will probably recommend that BK and CP+B will have to develop fresh ideas and continually update the campaign. Humor works, but it gets old fast. Students may suggest that CP+B should find new places for the chicken to be when one logs onto the Web site. Instead of just being in a living room, the chicken might be out by a pool, on a beach, or on a mountainside.

CP+B could also create events. The chicken could tour the country on a "Funky Chicken" tour, visiting BKs and passing out prizes. BK's public relations operation could work to develop press coverage and other publicity around these visits.

BK also needs to involve workers in its stores in this effort. The personnel who wait on customers should understand the campaign and participate in it. It is important that they stress to customers that they have many options in placing their orders. The staff should be prepared to say things and do things that support the "Have It Your Way" theme.

One caution, however. As noted in the case, BK's sales had lagged even though Y&R was spending heavily on a new promotion campaign. Promotion won't rescue a flawed marketing strategy. BK's products have to meet or exceed customer expectations. They have to taste good. A problem with having it your way is that this slows down the production process. BK will need to monitor customer wait time to make sure that it does not turn off people who are looking for fast food made their way.

Teaching Suggestions

The instructor will want to see if www.subservientchicken.com is still in operation. If it is, the instructor may want to visit the site in class before the class works on this case. Students could also visit BKs to see what products it is offering and what promotions it is running. Is "Have It Your Way" still the promotional message? Students can also examine BK's sales and profitability since early 2004 to see how things are going. Students may want to do a search of recent business articles to find out how BK is doing and if CP+B is still its agency.

This case goes well with the advertising chapter (Chapter 12), with the direct marketing chapter (Chapter 14), and with the consumer behavior chapter (Chapter 5).

Chapter 13
Lear Corporation: Structuring the Sales Force

Synopsis

The Lear Corporation (Not Lear Jet) has been around since 1917 when it was a manufacturer of tubing assemblies for the automotive and aircraft industries. Lear went on to become a major supplier of automotive seating systems. But since 1994, the company has diversified into the production of all five major vehicle interior systems. Lear is a global leader in this industry and was ranked 130th in the 2007 Fortune 500.

One of the key elements that have allowed Lear to achieve the success that it has is its sales force. The focus of sales at Lear is teamwork, relationship building, and doing what's best for the customer. Lear understands that if its customers do not do well, then it will not do well either.

Lear has a sales force structure that is split into divisions based on specific customers (e.g., Ford, GM, etc.). Within each division, platform teams (composed of salespeople, engineers, and program managers) interface with their customers to best determine how to meet those customers' needs. Lear is involved with customer operations and is very responsive to customer needs.

Lear has focused on fewer larger customers rather than many small-contract customers. While this has allowed the company to achieve the relationships that it has, it has also lead to a downturn. Things have gone sour for the few customers that Lear has, leaving it in a tight situation.

Teaching Objectives

The teaching objectives for this case are to:

1. Allow students to consider the role of a company's salespeople in creating value for and building relationships with customers.
2. Help students understand how companies make sales force strategy decisions.
3. Help students understand how sales force structure affects organizational performance.
4. Allow students to develop specific recommendations to assist Lear.

Discussion Questions

1. Classify Lear's sales force structure. What role has this structure played in the company's successes and failures?

   Lear very clearly has a customer sales force structure. As described, the sales force is organized by division, each representing a major customer like Ford or GM. One thing that makes Lear's sales force unique is that each sales unit is a team, rather than a single representative. This has allowed each sales unit to achieve some degree of product specialization as well, a task that is often difficult for sales reps with a customer structure when the company sells a broad array of products.

One of the main strengths of a customer sales force structure is that it allows the seller to build closer relationships with the buyer. This case definitely describes that dynamic. Part of that close customer relationship includes the fact that Lear is very responsive to customer needs. Lear's structure has also allowed it to develop efficiencies from teamwork.

The downside to Lear's sales force structure is that it has all of its eggs in few baskets. With fewer larger customers, a decrease in even one customer's orders (regardless of reason) affects Lear's sales. In this case, many of Lear's customers are cutting back due to an industry downturn.

2. What role does team selling play in Lear's sales force strategy? Should Lear make any changes to this strategy?

   As mentioned in the answer to the previous question, the sales team structure is a major part of Lear's sales force strategy. In addition to the customer sales force structure, the platform teams allow for a wider set of resources, knowledge, and skills, which leads to deeper relationships and greater responsiveness.

   The question of whether or not Lear should change the platform team strategy is complex. It does not appear that there are too many downsides to the platform team structure. At least, not any that are directly contributing to the troubles that Lear is experiencing. It seems that the greater question should be whether Lear should maintain its customer sales force structure. With more major customers splitting up orders across companies, that may be a sign that it is time for Lear to consider a product sales structure or a product by customer structure.

3. What implications would selling its interior systems division have on Lear's sales force and its ability to serve its customers? What do you recommend that Lear do?

   If Lear sells one of its major divisions such as the interior systems division, this would have an impact on customer relations given the current customer sales force structure. If everything in the industry remained constant, then this alone would affect Lear's ability to meet all the needs of any given customer. One big piece of the pie would be missing.

   However, everything is not the same in the industry. As mentioned, sales patterns have shifted dramatically based on changing consumer interest in vehicle type. But more important, automotive manufacturers are spreading their orders across companies rather than giving all business to one company. Thus, regardless of whether or not Lear sells the interior systems division, it may want to change from a customer sales force structure or shifts to a product structure. But this would especially be true if Lear were to sell.

If Lear were to sell the interior systems unit, there may be less need for full platform teams as well. Fewer product lines may put less need on team structure. This, again, would be even more critical if the sales force structure is changed.

4. Make other recommendations for how Lear can reverse the difficulties that it now faces. How would you implement each recommendation?

In all of the considerations made for the previous questions, Lear must consider some very important issues. First is that there is substantial change going on in the industry with respect to the end-user and, therefore, automotive manufacturer needs. This would imply that Lear needs to be dynamic and engage in strategic changes of its own.

But this does not necessarily dictate that the sales force structure be changed. One thing to remember is that Lear has become successful because it is renowned for the depth of relationships that it develops with customers. The customer sales force structure is what has allowed it to achieve this. Changing to a product structure would definitely affect that capability.

With the dynamics that are going on in the automotive industry, particularly those that are affecting consumer tastes, Lear might consider assisting its customers with new product ideas. It has demonstrated that it can do this with the Express LT project. If people are buying fewer gas-guzzlers, then Lear could create ideas based on the modification of existing or upcoming smaller vehicles. This could include creating an Express LT-type vehicle that is smaller, lighter, and more fuel efficient (a la PT Cruiser). But it could also include something totally different. Toyota's Scion division has built its image in part on the catalog of customization options. Lear could create an even broader array of products in any of the five interior systems groups to further the nature of the products' customizability. Or better yet, why not work with Scion's competitors (Honda, Mitsubishi, Subaru) to develop similar customization products?

One other issue that Lear needs to work on is the manner in which it addresses rising material costs. Those will likely not go away anytime soon. It may be that Daimler-Chrysler overreacted to how Lear was handling the price of resin costs. But it may be that Lear framed that issue in a way that led to Daimler-Chrysler's reaction. Lear has an exceptional record with customer relationships. It should be able to use that to its advantage in communicating the need for its customers to work with them in order for a win-win situation to emerge.

Teaching Suggestions

The instructor might consider having a business-to-business sales representative visit the class as a guest speaker and comment on this case. Ideally, it would be someone from the automotive industry, but it wouldn't have to be. A sales rep could comment on the issues of sales force structure associated with this case.

Students can also carry out research on Lear to see if they can learn how the company is doing, especially in the independent marketing channel.

This case goes well with the integrated marketing communications chapter (Chapter 12).

Chapter 14
StubHub: Ticket Scalping Becomes Respectable

Synopsis

In the age of modern technology, event ticket reselling has moved into the mainstream. On average, 29 percent of all concert goers buy their tickets through a reseller of some kind. In addition to the professional ticket brokers, any consumer can also engage in flipping tickets for potential profit. The increase in ticket reselling has both created and been created by online exchange agents such as ebay, Craigslist, and newcomer StubHub.

Created by two Stanford graduate students in 2000, StubHub is now the leader and the fastest-growing agent in the reselling business. StubHub maintains no inventory of its own. It simply provides the venue for buyers and sellers to come together. Sellers post their tickets via a standardized template, buyers select the tickets they want, and StubHub guarantees the transaction. The buyer does not get charged until the seller verifies that they have shipped the tickets. The seller does not get paid until the buyer confirms receipt. StubHub makes its money by charging a fee to both the buyer and the seller.

StubHub has risen to success not only based on this model of focusing on individual buyers and sellers. Its primary model for growth is partnering with institutions such as major league and college sports organizations, musicians, and venues. By partnering with these institutions, StubHub becomes the authorized go-to link for aftermarket ticket sales in exchange for a small piece of the action.

Teaching Objectives

The teaching objectives for this case are to:

1. Allow students to analyze the evolution of StubHub's strategy.
2. Help students understand how an industry can change in response to internal and external forces.
3. Gain an understanding of online marketing domains through application.
4. Allow students to work out recommendations for StubHub's continued development.
5. Consider the ethical and legal issues for ticket-reselling Web sites.

Discussion Questions

1. Conduct a brief analysis of the marketing environment and the forces shaping the development of StubHub.
   A good place to start for this is to consider the opening vignette. Roger, the Rolling Stones fan, lives in the past. In his mind, concert tickets are purchased a certain way, by standing in a physical line at a ticket outlet (Ticketmaster or box office) and being closer to the front than other people.

In today's world, very few people buy tickets that way. One of the main forces that have changed this is the advent of the Internet in the technological environment. Like so many other industries, the Internet has provided the communication medium for buyers and sellers to come together in a way that reduces the barriers of time and space.

Beyond the Internet, however, companies and organizations had to come along to employ the technology and capabilities provided by the World Wide Web. At some point, Ticketmaster made changes by allowing people to buy tickets online. Overnight, the idea of standing in a physical line became a thing of the past. While people still have to "get in line," this now is in the form of an electronic cue. While there were previously thousands of different lines, there is now essentially one line for everyone, everywhere, who wants to buy tickets to a given event.

With this online buying capability, professional brokers became increasingly capable of buying larger quantities of tickets. This factor contributed to the difficulty of individuals getting tickets, whether in the physical line or online.

Then, companies such as eBay, Craigslist, and StubHub came along (discussed in greater detail in question 3). Accompanying these sites are the organizations such as Paypal that provide for a means of secure online payment.

2. Discuss StubHub's business model. What general benefits does it afford to buyers and sellers? Which benefits are most important in terms of creating value for buyers and sellers?

   For buyers:

   a. *More ticket-buying options. These include being able to buy any kind of ticket for a sold-out event or being able to buy a better seat than those available through the ticket originator.*
   b. *Security. StubHub guarantees the ticket transaction. Sellers never get a hold of the buyer's financial information. The buyer is guaranteed an authentic ticket for the price paid, delivered in a set amount of time.*
   c. *Comparison shopping. StubHub's model reduces all tickets to a commodity. Because sellers are not identified specifically and StubHub guarantees each purchase, buyers can browse and compare tickets easily based on event, venue, seating location, and price.*
   d. *Getting the best possible price. Whether tickets are selling for many times face value, or for less than face value, StubHub allows buyers to price-compare easily and get the best possible price.*
   e. *Convenience. No waiting in line, no hassle, no being shut out of the original ticket-buying process.*

For sellers:

f. More ticket-selling options. Previously, professional brokers had to rely on their own phone lines, local newspaper ads, and beating the streets. Individual sellers were pretty much confined to classified ads and word-of-mouth. For all types of ticket sellers, StubHub and similar venues have provided the opportunity to reach anyone in the world who might be looking for a ticket to a given event.

g. Security. The seller is guaranteed payment and does not have to hassle with conducting a transaction (exchange of payment) with every individual buyer.

h. Ease of listing. Because StubHub has a standardized listing template, information is entered quickly and easily. Pricing becomes a snap because the going rate for tickets is easily assessed based on prices indicated by other sellers.

i. Getting the best possible price. Just as this is a benefit for buyers, it is also a benefit for sellers. This does go both ways. The dynamics of a mass market may drive ticket prices up or down, depending on the nature of supply and demand. Regardless, the seller has access to a much larger audience and most often will optimize revenue.

j. Convenience. Easy access to buyers in a virtual environment, pre-paid shipping through a designated courier (Fed Ex), and all the electronic communication provide by StubHub make selling and shipping a snap.

3. Discuss StubHub as a new intermediary. What effects has this new type of intermediary had on the ticket industry?

As a more specific continuation of question 1, StubHub's entry into to the ticket reselling market as a new intermediary is an environmental occurrence. From one perspective, StubHub has added to the effects of other online reselling venues such as eBay. Such reselling agents have allowed both professional and individual ticket resellers more capabilities to engage in reselling. Thus, these resellers have certainly had the effect of shifting more original ticket sales to resellers. Without StubHub and the others, the number of resold tickets would not be as high as 29 percent and would not be growing. Not only are professionals ending up with more tickets to resell, but individual event goers are encouraged to buy more tickets than they need and resell them.

The StubHub type of intermediary has also had an effect on the price of resold tickets and tickets in general. But it is difficult to determine the exact nature of this effect. In short, the price of resold tickets is based more on supply and demand than it used to be. Thus, in markets where there is scarcity, prices go up. Given that more tickets are purchased from the ticket originator than people can use, this generally creates more scarcity in the marketplace for those who want tickets but couldn't get them through the original seller.

However, all that ticket overbuying is speculative. Thus, it comes down to demand. If more tickets are bought than the market will bear, then aftermarket ticket sales drop, in some cases to a point lower than face value.

The dynamics of aftermarket ticket pricing has in some respects had an effect on the price that ticket originators put on their tickets. Given that aftermarket ticket prices have risen in many cases, some artists have placed a higher price on their tickets than otherwise might have been the case. A clear example of this is Madonna's 2006 Confessions tour. Management of the tour clearly decided that the aftermarket resellers should not get all the spoils as they price tickets for this tour at more than double the price of contemporary tours. Ticket prices for any seat in the lower bowl of an arena were a minimum $250.

From a competitive standpoint, StubHub has entered the game after the Internet and other agents have already had a tremendous effect on ticket reselling. Thus, StubHub has had the competitive effect of taking market share away from these other companies. Also, given that it has pioneered the model of partnering with professional institutions, it can be argued that StubHub itself has magnified the effects already mentioned of this new type of ticket reselling intermediary.

4. Apply the text's e-marketing domains framework to StubHub's business model. How has each domain played a role in the company's success?

Business to consumer (B2C): From the hands of professional ticket brokers to individual consumers. Also, from the hands of organizations such as collegiate and professional sports teams and musicians to individual consumers (sometimes, these organizations sell some of their own tickets directly).

Business to business (B2B): Professional ticket brokers often scour StubHub and other sites looking for deals that they can flip. While these transactions likely account for a very small part of total transactions, they do exist.

Consumer to consumer (C2C): Many consumers buy more tickets than they need and resell them. In most cases, these tickets are purchased by other individual event goers. Even under the StubHub model of partnering with professional organizations (B2B), most often the actual transaction comes down to C2C (season ticket holder selling to an individual buyer). In such cases, the B2B involvement takes on a promotional role.

Consumer to business (C2B): Again, professional ticket brokers are looking for deals to flip. Such brokers are more likely to find such deals from individuals reselling tickets than they are from other businesses.

5. What recommendations can you make for improving StubHub's future growth and success?

   As far as original ticket sales are concerned, many in the industry believe that Ticketmaster has had a virtual monopoly for quite some time. While most venues sell tickets directly through their box offices, such sales account for a minimal amount of overall sales given that buyers have to physically visit the box office. Some venues have gone through small-time agents handling the selling of tickets over the phone or the Internet (Live Nation and Tickets.com are two up and coming threats to Ticketmaster; there are other small regional players). Artists such as Pearl Jam have boycotted Ticketmaster's hold on the industry by going through other means of selling (many believe that this hurt Pearl Jam extensively).

   A recent op-ed piece in the Wall Street Journal *by economics professor Kent Smetter (U Penn) blasts an aggressive nationwide lobby effort by Ticketmaster to severely limit aftermarket ticket selling. Essentially, Ticketmaster apparently wants to not only get a piece of the aftermarket action, but to dominate it. To ensure its future success, StubHub needs to ensure that such action by Ticketmaster does not infringe on its business activities. If legislation were passed that would prevent most individuals from reselling tickets, or would put the legal right to resell in the hands of Ticketmaster, this would severely reduce StubHub's activities.*

6. What are the legal or ethical issues, if any, for ticket-reselling Web sites?

   Some will say that ticket buying and reselling, if not illegal, is morally wrong. People should not buy more tickets than they need just so they can make a profit. This is keeping tickets out of the hands of those who want to buy them at regular prices. Obviously, some in the business agree with this. Most event performers, managers, and producers have put a limit on the number of tickets that can be purchased in any given transaction or by any given individual or business.

   However, it is more likely that the majority of students will recognize the wonders of a free enterprise market. Every small business owner in the world is engaged in selling something at a price greater than they paid. At least, that is the idea. So, why is it any different for an individual concert goer to buy 10 tickets and resell eight?

   The laws are a different issue. Many states have laws that regulate the reselling of tickets, limiting the amount of the price of a resold ticket to within a given dollar amount or percentage of the face value (often, this is a very small amount). Professional brokers get around this because such laws put an exemption on them. Many states have no such laws.

StubHub does not enforce such laws or monitor the activities of its buyers/sellers with respect to such laws. Specifically, it has stated that it puts that burden on the buyers and sellers. Obviously, such laws are ignored by many buyers and sellers and local law enforcement has little power to catch such violators.

The question that obviously arises is, Is StubHub breaking the law? If not, is it involved in unethical practices by encouraging and providing the venue for the violation of laws? A very close parallel can be drawn to the Napster case of not so long ago. Like StubHub, Napster maintained no inventory of product. It simply provided the forum for people to come together to exchange music. Is StubHub's situation different? Was Napster within legal and ethical boundaries to do what it was doing (was it shut down unfairly)?

Teaching Suggestions

The instructor may wish to begin discussion of the case by surveying the students to see how many have purchased event tickets online and from Ticketmaster, eBay, Craigslist, or StubHub. Students will be willing to discuss their experiences and the issues associated with original ticket sales versus aftermarket ticket sales.
The instructor might also wish to pre-assign students the task of "shopping" for a concert or sports event ticket.

This case goes well with Chapters 1 and 2, with the product chapter (Chapter 7), with the distribution chapter (Chapter 10), and with the retailing chapter (Chapter 11).

Chapter 15
Wal-Mart Takes On the World

Synopsis

This case describes the expansion of Wal-Mart into foreign countries, ending with possible entry into the Indian marketplace. In reading about Wal-Mart's experiences in various countries, students become acquainted with many of the factors that affect success in the global marketplace. The goal of the case is to highlight these so that students can apply them in a discussion of the proposed entry into India. Students are also asked to select an entry strategy: either buy an existing chain or work with a consulting partner. Both of these options are presented at the end of the case.

Teaching Objectives

The teaching objectives for this case are to:

Identify factors leading to the success or failure descriptions of Wal-Mart's global expansion.
Understand the need to adapt strategy to differences in consumer markets around the globe; i.e., not all consumers are alike.
Evaluate a country as an entry target using the success/failure factors identified earlier.
Evaluate entry strategies based on Wal-Mart's previous experiences.

Discussion Questions

1. In which countries has Wal-Mart done well? Can you identify any common consumer, market, retailer, or entry strategy traits across these countries that might account for Wal-Mart's success?

   Wal-Mart has done well in the United States, Canada, Mexico, Puerto Rico, Hong Kong, China, and England. The United States, Canada, Hong Kong, and England are relatively affluent markets; Mexico is in-between and China and Brazil lag behind Mexico in affluence. Thus, the first trait of Wal-Mart's success might be countries with healthy economies—at least healthy enough that customers have some disposable income. Another characteristic is that these markets may not be as demanding as the Germans and Japanese. Perhaps they are more interested in lower price (the British seem to be like the United States in this regard). Obviously price would be important in Mexico and China, where incomes are lower. Canada and the United States are considered predominantly Anglo countries, so perhaps the success of Wal-Mart in these countries along with the United Kingdom is not surprising as these consumers share a similar heritage and even a common retailing approach. In all of these countries, Wal-Mart has either had good partners (Hong Kong, Mexico, and China) or bought successful store chains (Canada and Puerto Rico). Thus, access to local market knowledge is an important factor in successful entry. This is especially true of the United Kingdom, where ASDA had already adopted and adapted the Wal-Mart philosophy for their market. Where Wal-Mart has not used existing expertise (Germany), they have not been successful.

2. In what countries has Wal-Mart done poorly? Can you identify any common consumer market, retailer traits, or entry strategies across these countries that might account for Wal-Mart's lack of success?

   Germany, Japan, Brazil, and Argentina have not been good entries for Wal-Mart. In Germany and Japan, consumers are more demanding and more quality conscious. They seem to be less interested in the type of goods that Wal-Mart sells. In both locations, real estate and market conditions stymie Wal-Mart's growth—whether this is unions or convoluted distribution systems. In both Japan and Germany, Wal-Mart bought existing chains with shabby stores and poor sales. Perhaps the lack of success of their acquired firms accounts for why Wal-Mart management did not utilize the expertise of those managers. Another possibility is that Wal-Mart had had such good success in Mexico and Canada that it was overconfident of its approach when it entered the German market. Since then, it seems to be more willing to listen to local partners.

   In Brazil and Argentina, there are many factors against success—economic factors, real estate, and crowded cities demanding different store formats. Also, Wal-Mart found it hard to compete with Carrefour, which is the second largest discount chain in the world. Although Carrefour has some stores in Mexico, Wal-Mart had not previously entered a country where Carrefour was entrenched (it stays away from the German market) and is a formidable foe. So, in these markets, Wal-Mart encountered more competition than it had had anywhere else except in the United States.

3. In your opinion, will Wal-Mart be successful in Japan? Why or why not?

   Japan will probably be like Germany. Wal-Mart would have to improve the quality of their assortment, possibly change store formats, and give themselves a more upscale look. They would also have to change their pricing strategy and promotional policies in order to cater to the Japanese consumer. Japan is difficult to market in because of their protectiveness of their markets and the closed nature of their distribution system (this is changing slowly). One thing that Wal-Mart has going for them is that they are American and the Japanese seem interested in American products. Retailers, however, in Japan have learned the hard way that they must adapt very, very carefully to the Japanese market. Given that Wal-Mart still has not cracked the market in Germany, one has to wonder about Wal-Mart's ability to do this—especially as Wal-Mart. They might consider that some countries are just not amenable to the standard Wal-Mart image and approach. In addition, their slow approach to entry is giving Japanese chains (who can be formidable competitors) time to change their strategies to counter Wal-Mart.

4. Beyond India, what countries do you think Wal-Mart should consider entering? What factors are important in making this decision? Be prepared to defend the countries that you choose.

   This could be an assignment for class discussion. Groups of students could be assigned to select countries and present them in class. Some possible choices are Australia, which has the same Anglo heritage (Australia is not mentioned in the case nor did the author find evidence that Wal-Mart operates there); other Southeast Asian countries such as Thailand; other European countries such as France, Italy, and Spain (a very likely market); the Scandinavian countries; Holland; Belgium, etc. Most of the Middle Eastern and African countries are not viable candidates at the time, with the exception of South Africa (which is not particularly large or rich). Neither are the South American countries, with the exception of Chile. Most of them have economies and governments that are highly volatile and are in the economic doldrums. If countries are not large or do not have a significant population, Wal-Mart's bottom line will be better enriched by opening another store in the United States. It takes a lot of population to justify the high costs of entry by Wal-Mart.

Teaching Suggestions

This case could be taught over two class periods. Near the end of the first class period, hold a discussion in which key success or failure factors are identified along with where Wal-Mart has been successful. For the second class, assign students to compare India and a country of their own choosing with these factors.

Begin the second class with a discussion about India. Ask whether Wal-Mart should go there, and if so, how? Then ask students to present some of the countries they choose and why Wal-Mart should enter those countries. Probably many students will have the same countries. The goal is to impress students with the seriousness and difficulty of making entry decisions.

Chapter 16
Vitango: Fighting Malnutrition

Synopsis

This case discusses the development of a micronutrient drink, Vitango, developed by Coca-Cola. Vitango is intended for poor people in developing countries. The case begins with statistics about the number of deaths, diseases, and physical defects caused globally each year because of the loss of simple nutrients such as iodine. The statistics are staggering and sickening—especially because the solution, which would be decent food, would seem to be so simple.

The problem with Vitango is its price—far too much for the poverty-stricken in spite of the benefits of the product. Development costs are very high and the product is currently in powdered form that might be mixed with questionable quality water in many countries.

The case also describes the experience of P&G with a similar product, GrowthPlus, which failed because of high prices and has been reformulated and introduced as NutriStar in another country.

A nonprofit group, GAIN, is introduced as interested in promoting and advertising these types of products. GAIN is funded by the Bill and Melissa Gates charitable foundation. Although some see GAIN as a potential partner in getting nutrient-enriched foods to poor people, some observers are highly critical. Instead they claim that the actions of GAIN or Coca-Cola do not attack the root problem of poverty and might mislead people to substitute supplements for nutritious foods.

The point of the case is to stimulate student thought about how difficult it is for a for-profit corporation to attack a problem like nutrient deficiency without being misjudged and criticized. Coca-Cola may be genuinely interested in helping poor people, but it is always possible for their actions to be misinterpreted that Vitango is just a way for Coca-Cola to sell more of its products. Unfortunately for Coca-Cola, their leading product is not nutritious and the promotion of Coca-Cola in poor countries is frequently criticized as leading poor people to spend their money poorly.

Teaching Objectives

The teaching objectives for this case are to:

1. Stimulate student thinking about the many ways that corporation actions could be considered unethical and illegal.
2. Illustrate the difficulties for-profit firms face when attempting to solve social problems.
3. Emphasize that sometimes corporate actions can help build goodwill toward the United States.

Discussion Questions

1. Which of the textbook's criticisms of marketing's impact on consumers, if any, are found in the cases of Vitango and NutriStar?

High Prices: Clearly the prices for these products are high from the point of view of the intended market—even though these prices may be low from the company's point of view. One issue with pricing is that it must be considered from the point of view of the beholder. The poverty stricken of the world have what are unbelievably low incomes and sometimes virtually no income at all. Some workers in very depressed countries make 13 cents an hour for working 12 hours per day for six days per week. In a year, they earn less than $500. Clearly anyone with a family could not afford luxuries such as powdered drinks.

High Costs of Distribution: The case does not provide enough information to assess this.

High Advertising and Promotion Costs: There will have to be advertising and promotion for these products. Although those costs might not be high, they will increase the price of the product. This is where GAIN can help by shouldering the advertising and promotion, especially through government channels. This could help hold down the price of the products.

Excessive Markups: Wherever prices cannot be controlled, this is a possibility. In most developing countries, the government does not attempt to control price and items can be sold at varying prices. This creates the opportunity for middlemen or retailers to set a high price reflecting high markups.
Deceptive Practices: There is no evidence in the case that the companies or GAIN will engage in deceptive pricing, advertising, or packaging. However, there is always the possibility that the market may use the products in preference to nutritious meats and vegetables—to assume that the enriched foods are more powerful and nutritious than they are.

High-Pressure Selling: Could be a possibility if any reseller actually sells these products personally, but it seems somewhat unlikely.

Shoddy or Unsafe Products: Let's hope not.

Planned Obsolescence: No evidence of this, but it could happen if companies have plans to penetrate the market with low-priced products and follow them with higher-priced substitutes.

Poor Service to Disadvantaged Consumers: The point of Coca-Cola's and P&G's efforts would seem to be good service to disadvantaged consumers. Poor service might be more likely to occur at the retail level. Some retailers could mix the product inappropriately to sell on their own as a sort of fountain drink.

2. Which of the criticisms of marketing's impact on society are found in the Vitango and NutriStar case?

   False Wants and Too Much Materialism: This is the essence of the critics' criticism—that Coca-Cola and P&G are teaching consumers to replace healthy foods with chemical substitutes. Those would be false wants.

   Too Few Social Goods: Remember the poor quality water? One could argue that this product loses much of its value when mixed with poor water; thus government should improve water quality. One would hope that governments would want to improve water quality, but in desperately poor nations, there could be greater needs than improving the quality of the water. Medical care and the supply of basic foodstuffs might be such needs unless the water is undrinkable.

   Too Much Political Power: If Coca-Cola and P&G were to attempt to wield threats to force the introduction of their products, this could be a legitimate criticism. Given the low margins likely on such products, it would seem ridiculous for Coca-Cola and P&G to do so.

3. Could Vitango and NutriStar be considered enlightened marketing? Why or why not?

   To answer this, one must consider the five principles of enlightened marketing.

   Consumer-Oriented Marketing: On the surface, this would seem to be consumer-oriented. Many, many people need supplemental vitamins and minerals. But Coca-Cola and P&G hope to make a profit and have seemingly overestimated the market's ability to pay. Is it consumer-oriented to produce products that the market cannot afford? Demand is defined as the want and the ability to pay. In this case, it seems that Coca-Cola and P&G have not paid enough attention to the ability to pay.

   Innovative Marketing: There is no evidence that these companies' actions are new and better ways of marketing. Selling through McDonald's is not innovative. GAIN may be innovative marketing, but it is not the same as the companies involved. Some cynics might say it's excess wealth from a corporate endeavor (Microsoft) used to encourage other for-profit products.

   Value Marketing: The case would suggest that companies are interested in a long-run relationship with consumers in the countries involved. The question is, Does the product provide enough positive benefits given the high cost (cost as a function of the household's income)?

   Sense-of-Mission Marketing: We don't have the Coca-Cola and P&G mission statements, but producing these kinds of products would seem to have the interests of the world's peoples at heart—that there is an attempt to combat a very serious problem.

Societal Marketing: Certainly the company has considered society's needs here. There isn't enough evidence to decide whether this is in society's long-run interests. A healthier population is always in society's long-run interests. It isn't clear that Vitango and NutriStar are the appropriate means of reaching a healthier population.

4. Are the development and marketing of such products as fortified foods and beverages ethical and socially responsible?

   Rose Kennedy once got into a lot of trouble by saying, "If it's legal, it's ethical" (referring to the heavy campaign funds that Robert Kennedy had spent in the Indiana primary). There is nothing to suggest that what Coca-Cola or P&G is doing is illegal. There is no evidence of bribery, corruption, or scandal. But is it ethical to promote and sell products that are tantalizing to poorly educated people on poverty-level incomes? Would these people be better off spending their money on a little meat or vegetables? Would they have the nutritional knowledge to make good choices? Or would they spend their money on poorer quality foods?

   Given educational levels in most of these countries, it is questionable that people make the best nutritional choices. Citizens of the United States are among the best educated in the world, but obesity (which is poor choices and too many poor choices) is a very dangerous problem here. Far more so than in Europe, where educational levels are also high (and sometimes higher). If U.S. citizens choose to make poor choices, why wouldn't uneducated consumers who may not be able to read labels or understand what a vitamin is? Might they not attribute powers to these products that are not there?

   Students will have to make their own choices here, but it seems to this writer that companies and/or GAIN will push these products for their nutritional value, which could raise both ethical and social issues.

5. How should Coca-Cola proceed with the marketing of Vitango?

   Until they can get the cost down, the company is going to be subject to criticism and even with lower prices, it will probably be criticized. It might only be able to avoid this by giving Vitango away. They might even consider selling it at a low cost to educational systems for distribution. It really doesn't seem that this is going to be a profitable venture for a long time, so Coca-Cola might do well to give it away and reap positive publicity.

Teaching Suggestions

When assigning this case, ask students to look for enriched "micronutrients" in products at the grocery store. Perhaps different groups of students could be given different sections (such as breakfast cereal, dog food, canned vegetables, dairy, etc.) of the store. The goal is to discover how many of these products are on the American market. There are far more than we realize. Americans are probably taking in an excess of micronutrients.

In class begin by asking for a report and then ask if the students think purchase is predicated on the addition of the micronutrients. Probably to most Americans, it is not, and most of us are not concerned about getting adequate nutrition.

Then, shift the discussion to poverty-stricken countries and the need for micronutrients. Students cannot really appreciate the position of the poor in these countries, so I would avoid asking, "Would you buy Vitango if you were in their situation?" We just can't imagine being so poor.

If Coca-Cola has their way, they will advertise this product (either themselves or through GAIN) to make people aware of it. What would it be like to know that there are products that exist that could help children and adults, but they would be unable to buy them? Is the consumer better off without that knowledge? Does distributing products that people cannot afford bring home their inability to take care of themselves or their children? This is not a dimension mentioned in the questions for discussion, but it is an important part of understanding the ethical and social implications for marketing. These are not luxury goods. Should they be available to everyone? Or is it better not to have them? The example of NutriStar in Venezuela is enlightening. The drink is in McDonald's, but many Venezuelans can't afford McDonald's, so what good does the product do them?

From this point, work through the discussion questions and at the end of the discussion, ask how the members of the class feel. They might have started out thinking that Vitango is a good idea and it seems to be well-intended. The end result on the consumer market might not be so positive in the students' opinion after participating in the discussion.

Video Case Notes

Chapter 1
Harley Davidson

Executive Summary

Few brands engender such intense loyalty as that found in the hearts of Harley-Davidson owners. Why? Because the company's marketers spend a great deal of time thinking about customers. They want to know who customers are, how they think and feel, and why they buy a Harley. That attention to detail has helped build Harley-Davidson into a $5 billion company with more than 900,000 Harley Owners Group (HOG) members, the largest company-sponsored owner's group in the world. Harley sells much more than motorcycles. The company sells a feeling of independence, individualism, and freedom. These strong emotional connections have made Harley-Davidson ownership much more of a lifestyle than only a product consumption experience. To support that lifestyle, Harley-Davidson recognizes that its most important marketing tool is the network of individuals that ride Harleys. For this reason, Harley-Davidson engages its customer base through company-sponsored travel adventures, events, and other things such as clothes and accessories both for riders and for those who simply like to associate with the brand.

Questions and Answers

1. How does Harley-Davidson build long-term customer relationships?
   As noted in the text, there are two major building blocks for customer relationships. One is customer satisfaction, the other is customer value. Both of these can be discussed (however, customer value is treated more fully in question 2). But students should also be prompted to identify specific tools or programs that HD employs to help build customer relationships. Among these are HD's sponsorship of the Harley Owner's Group (H.O.G) which includes events, publications, and other means of facilitating customer-to-customer interaction.

2. What is Harley-Davidson's value proposition?
   The text defines customer perceived value as the difference between all the benefits and all the costs of a market offering relative to those of competing offers. This video case does not really focus on the costs of owning a Harley, but that can certainly be discussed with students. The price tag is high. Non-monetary costs like storing the bike and not being able to use it during cold and rainy seasons might also be considered.

   However, the bigger focus here should be on, "What benefits does a Harley customer receive?" Early in the video clip, Joanne Bischmann, VP of Marketing, seems to summarize this element of the value proposition. Harley-Davidson stands for independence, freedom, individuality, expressing one's self, adventure on the open road, and experiencing life to its fullest. This is what people are buying when they buy a Harley.

3. Relate the concept of customer equity to Harley-Davidson. How does Harley-Davidson's strategy focus on the right relationships with the right customers? *The case does not overtly treat these topics, but there should be enough information that students can make some sound observations. Two things need to be considered in discussing customer equity: loyalty and profitability. Figure 1.5 in the text illustrates the concept of building the right relationships with the right customers. While HD might generate revenues and profits through some Butterflies, their main focus seems to be on the True Friends, the long-term customers who are also profitable. Harley's core products (the motorcycles) are high-dollar and high-margin products. A customer buying one such product contributes a certain amount to HD's bottom line and is therefore "worth" a certain amount. But customer equity grows dramatically when such customers buy consecutive bikes either for themselves or for spouses or other family members. Add to all this the opportunities for further transactions through the purchase of accessories, clothing, and other HD licensed items, and the potential for building customer equity with such a loyal core of customers is tremendous.*

Teaching Ideas

1. Ask students to list the characteristics of the typical Harley owner. Then ask them how Harley's marketing efforts target those and other consumers.
2. Use this case to walk students through the model of the marketing process in Figure 1.1.

Chapter 2
Mayo Clinic

Executive Summary

The Mayo Clinic was started in a 1880s by a father and his two sons and grew from a frontier doctor's office into a healthcare giant on the frontiers of medicine. The clinic pioneered many advances in medicine in the arenas of new treatments, new approaches to organizing doctors, new medical records, education for doctors, research, and publication of medical research. Along the way, Mayo earned an enviable reputation through the strength of its performance in the eyes of physicians and patients alike.

As the Mayo Clinic became famous, it realized that it must nurture the brand that it created. That meant investing in marketing and strategic thought about marketing, even as the organization thrived on word-of-mouth. In particular, the clinic needed to think about prospective partners, ensuring that each new partner adds something to Mayo while not creating a risk to Mayo's good name.

Questions and Answers

1. What is the Mayo Clinic's mission? Who are its target customers and what is its relationship with these customers?

   While Mayo Clinic's mission is not overtly specified in the video case, students should be able to effectively create a mission statement or at least various bullet points that seem to be part of Mayo's mission. These include:

   a. *Collaboration and collective wisdom in giving the most effective patient care.*
   b. *Providing an atmosphere that contributes to patient comfort and healing.*
   c. *Conducting world-class research to facilitate greater knowledge.*
   d. *To serve as a reliable source of health information.*

   Mayo has many different "customers." In Mayo's patient-care role, the patients range from the worried-well (seeking trustworthy health information or proactive changes in diet and exercise) to sick patients with known treatable diseases, to special-case patients seeking experimental treatment or treatment for unusual or complex conditions. The relationship with the worried-well may be more tenuous than with a cancer patient, but the relationship with the worried well might be for the long-term or establish Mayo as the preferred provider in the event of a serious medical conditions.

Influencers also play a major role -- the doctor that recommends the Mayo Clinic to a very sick patient affects the relationship with Mayo. Mayo's educational, services, medical publications, and graduate studies programs predispose doctors to send patients to Mayo.

2. What is Mayo's marketing mix? Discuss how the organization manages its marketing mix within its marketing strategy.

   Product *-- a discussion of Mayo's services would include not just the patient-care services but also Mayo's services in medical research and medical education. Options might include other NetJet-like partnerships that reach other target audiences.*
   Price *-- Students might discuss how Mayo gets paid by affluent consumers, those with insurance, and those with Medicaid.*
   Place *-- Mayo has expanded both physically from Rochester and virtually through publications and the Internet.*
   Promotion *-- Mayo seems to take a low profile because it doesn't want a brand that is too flashy. Yet its partnerships do promote the brand by putting it in front of others.*

3. How are the Mayo Clinic's partnering activities helping it to achieve its mission and strategy?

   The narrator mentions that preserving the belief that Mayo Clinic exists for patient well-being, and not for making profits, is fundamental to Mayo's mission. It is for this reason that partnerships can be challenging. There is a need to negotiate a common image with other companies who would like to use Mayo's strong name and image. Therefore, Mayo uses caution in partnering and in allowing other organizations to promote Mayo in a way that is counter to its mission and brand image.

Teaching Ideas

Ask students what impression they have of the Mayo Clinic. Most of them likely no have no direct experience with the clinic, but they have likely heard of it and hold a favorable impression. Then, ask "Who are Mayo's 'customers' and how does it create value for them? In what other ways might it provide value?" This should lead to a discussion of Mayo's mission statement, opportunities for growth, and marketing plan and mix issues.

Chapter 3
American Express

Executive Summary

Understanding consumers and their needs can be a challenge. As the American population diversifies, and as consumers redefine their values and preferences, marketers work to provide relevant products and services that meet consumers' changing needs and wants. For American Express, keeping up with environmental shifts translates into creating new marketing offers. American Express issued its first charge card in 1958. Within five years, it had more than 1 million cards in use. The company now offers more than 20 consumer cards, 14 small business cards, and customizable corporate cards. Some cards target very specific consumers. For example, the IN:CHICAGO, IN:NYC, and IN:LA cards offer cardholders special perks for local shopping, dining, and entertainment. By targeting such specific consumers, American Express builds strong relationships with the right customers.

Questions and Answers

1. Visit the American Express Web site (www.americanexpress.com) to learn more about the different cards that American Express offers. Select three of the macroenvironmental forces discussed in the chapter. How do the different card options reflect the changes in those forces?

   Student responses will vary based on the different cards selected as well as the events that are occurring in any given part of the macroenvironment at the time the case is discussed.

   This question could also be modified to address how some general changes in the macroenvironmental forces could affect AmEx's future. ***Technology forces*** *play a major role in future payment systems. Payment technologies based on cell phones, RFID, and biometrics could radically change how people make payments.* ***Economic forces*** *could impact consumer debt, interest rates, default rates, and overall spending.* ***Political forces*** *could mean legislation regarding bankruptcy, fair lending practices, and privacy.* ***Demographic forces*** *could change spending patterns as Baby Boomers age or as new generations reach maturity.* ***Natural forces*** *could impact consumer buying habits or change economic development patterns. Even* ***cultural forces*** *could effect the company if credit card usage becomes more (or less) acceptable or if people seek affinity cards tied to a favorite group.*

2. How does American Express deal with the various publics in its microenvironment?

Figure 3.1 in the text identifies six different actors in the microenvironment. The video case specifically treats customers and competitors:

- *Customers – this is one of the biggest areas of focus in this case. A great deal of discussion is given to how American Express is constantly evaluating the changes in the macroenvironment and how they are affecting customer preferences. The marketing team at AmEx spends a great deal of time and effort studying what customers are doing, how they are spending their time, where they are accessing their information, and how they can be engaged. The recognition of customers wanting to be treated as individuals led to the development of multiple cards. AmEx realized that they had to cater to more than one kind of customer.*
- *Competitors – for many years, AmEx was the preferred card. But as times changed, competition intensified. One way that AmEx responded was by realizing that one card simply was not enough to meet customer needs and maintain a competitive advantage.*

It may be of further help to draw again from the company website to identify ways that the company is focusing on other areas of the microenvironment. For example, there is a section which focuses on building relationships with ***suppliers*** *and* ***marketing intermediaries****. On a page entitled "giving back," American Express address some of its various* ***publics****.*

3. Is American Express taking a proactive approach to managing its marketing environment? How?

Through the years, the company has consistently reached consumers by keeping in step with the changing needs of the population. They've also acknowledged that it is the consumer who really decides what American Express stands for. But as the population grew up and customers' needs started to change the company realized that offering one card was not enough. In response they offered a variety of cards based on customer needs and spending levels. The company launched the blue card to capture the business of young consumers and target the entire family with a variety of cards.

Teaching Ideas

The video mentions the challenges of reaching consumers, especially younger consumers who are just starting their financial lives. Ask if students have received credit card offers. Did they apply for the card? Students could also discuss or keep an informal log of all the financial services brand impressions they experience in the average day -- from a credit card statement in the mail to the card they see in the wallet to the logo at the ATM machine.

The video also describes changes in how people use credit cards as one of many modes of payment. Ask students about their payment preferences (cash, credit card, debit card, checks, online-payment, parents, etc.) and how those payment preferences differ from their parents. This can spark a discussion of future potential AmEx products, new features on existing products, or changing messages for marketing efforts. Students might describe how they use which types of payments (for food, clothing, rent, textbooks, tuition, etc.) with discussions of the frequency, size of payment, and how they manage money. If some students have an AmEx card or other credit card, they might explain why the use it or don't use it in particular situations. The key is to think about what people want in a payment system, how it differs across generations, or what might sway them to use a particular payment system.

This case can also be used to illustrate the use of marketing to guide or change the behavior of existing customers, not just to recruit new customers.

Chapter 4
Burke

Executive Summary

For more than 75 years, Burke has been helping marketers to understand the marketplace and build stronger relationships with customers. As a full-service, custom marketing research firm, the company helps its clients better understand everything from how consumers make purchase decisions to what drives customer loyalty. The company uses a rich array of avenues to reach consumers, including telephone and Web interviewing, direct mail, and online surveys.

Burke helps marketers discover information about customers, competitors, products, and marketing programs. But more than just gathering information, Burke's services help clients use the information to gain customer insights. With sophisticated computer analysis, Burke offers the right information, in the right form, at the right time to help them make better marketing decisions.

Questions and Answers

1. What process does Burke use to define the research question?
   Burke works with the client to determine the actual research questions, often broadening the issue explored. The account executive sits down with the client to try to determine if the client has a clear understanding of the problem. Often, Burke helps the client to discover that it may have been focusing on the wrong problem by having focused on an issue that is too narrow. Burke helps clients employ critical thinking to properly define the problem.

2. How does Burke's process for marketing research compare to the steps outlined in the chapter?
   As defined in the video, Burke roughly follows the process outlined in the text. The company starts by defining the research question, then determining the research process. Next Burke defines the sample group. The company then identifies the research objectives and begins field research. Finally, the company interprets the research findings and delivers an "answer" to the client.

3. How does marketing research, the Burke way, help clients build strong relationships with customers?
   Burke helps marketers discover information about customers, competitors, products, and marketing programs. But more than just gathering information, Burke's services help clients use the information. With sophisticated computer analysis, Burke offers the right information, in the right form, at the right time to help them make better marketing decisions.

Teaching Ideas

1. Ask students to identify a variety consumer groups. Then have groups of students list possible ways to get to know those consumers preferences, interests, and buying habits.

2. Have students reflect on their own experiences with marketing research. How have they been involved, either as subjects or as researchers? What form did the research take? What was the goal of the research?

Chapter 5
Wild Planet

Executive Summary

Wild Planet markets high quality, nonsexist, nonviolent toys that encourage kids to be imaginative and creative and to explore the world around them. But Wild Planet sells more than just toys. It sells positive play experiences. To better understand those experiences, the company conducts a tremendous amount of consumer research to delve into consumer buyer behavior. Wild Planet even created a Toy Opinion Panel to evaluate current products and develop new product ideas. The panel helps Wild Planet to understand why parents and kids buy the toys they buy.

Questions and Answers

1. Explain how each of the four sets of factors affecting consumer behavior affects the consumer purchase process as it relates to toys from Wild Planet.
   This is a very broad question and student responses will certainly vary. Students should identify the four broad categories of factors affecting consumer behavior as found in figure 5.2. Below are some examples of how each factor could affect the consumer purchase process for Wild Planet toys:

   Cultural. *Today's kids are growing up in an entirely different culture than did children 25 years ago. Kids today are savvier and more sophisticated. They have always been in a world where the Internet exists. They value being asked about their opinions.*
   Social. *The case discusses the role of peer pressure (reference groups) in the buying decision of toys. But more importantly, it is recognized that even at young ages, many kids want to be the first to have the latest and greatest toy. Reference is made to the "trendsetters" (roles and status).*
   Personal. *Obviously, age and lifecycle are going to affect how people buy toys. This is true for the primary customer (the child) as well as the secondary customer (the parent). Also, the case discusses the role of gender and gender perceptions at length. This can be explained by the impact of self-concept.*
   Psychological. *Beliefs and attitudes play a major role in buying toys. Wild Planet is built around the idea that toys should be not only fun, they should be quality learning tools and help children develop various skills. Parents who agree are more likely to be drawn to Wild Planet products. Also, the case highlights how the beliefs and attitudes of girls (that their rooms should be decorated and accessorized) are different than those of boys (that toys should be for playing with).*

2. What demographic segment of consumers is Wild Planet targeting?
   Student responses may vary. This is a good case to show the complexities of defining the customer. There are two very clear customer segments that Wild Planet is targeting: children and parents. Within those broad segments, Wild Planet certainly segments in more detail. Other demographic characteristics include gender and opinion leadership.

3. Visit the Wild Planet Web site at www.wildplanet.com to learn more about the company. How does the Web site help consumers through the buyer decision process?
   Students should be able to identify something from this website in at least the first four steps of the buyer decision process:
   Need recognition*. Assisting in this phase is subtle at best. Browsing customer may be struck with how Wild Planet toys are designed to help foster relationships with certain toys (e.g. Dino-Mites or Purse Pals). This may spark a need in the consumer's mind if they do not have those types of toys.*
   Information search. *Websites such as the Wild Planet site are loaded with product information, thus taking advantage of the strengths of the Internet. Customers can easily gather information on any product of choice.*
   Evaluation of alternatives. *The Wild Planet site is not set up for comparison of toys for other brands. Even within the Wild Planet portfolio, the site does not seem to facilitate easy comparisons of different products, enabling potential customers to compare features.*
   Purchase decision. *Each product sub-site has a link to the Wild Planet online toy store where purchases can be made. The toy store can also be accessed from the home page.*

<u>Teaching Ideas</u>

1. Have students list the characteristics they possess that make them more or less likely to shop at Wild Planet. Then have them consider how those characteristics will change over the next ten years. Are they more likely to patronize the company in ten years? Fifty years?

2. Have the students think about a hypothetical new toy: How might they come up with an idea for the new toy? How will they know if the product will sink or swim? Use this discussion as a lead-in to understanding Wild Planet's research program—what it does well and how it might improve.

Chapter 6
Meredith

Executive Summary

The Meredith Corporation has developed an expertise in building customer relationships through segmentation, targeting, and positioning. But the amazing thing is that they have done this by focusing on only half of the population...the female half. That's right, Meredith has become one of the most successful magazine and specialty book publishers in the world by focusing on the specific needs and desires of women.

Meredith is known for leading titles such as *Better Homes and Gardens, Family Circle,* and *Ladies' Home Journal*. But that list has grown to a portfolio of 14 magazines and more than 200 special interest publications. Through these magazines alone, Meredith regularly reaches approximately 30 million readers. By focusing on core categories of home, family, and personal development, Meredith has developed a product mix designed to meet various needs of women.

Questions and Answers

1. What are the main variables that Meredith has focused on to segment its markets?
Gender. *Clearly, this is the greatest area of focus. But to say that this drives Meredith's segmentation strategy would be far too broad. This factor is more like the starting point for cutting out half the market.*
Life stage/Life events *– this one really stands out as a factor that breaks the female market down into groups that are specific enough to have their own product or product line. The case mentions life events like having a baby, sending kids off to college, or getting ready for retirement. Other possibilities include getting married or buying a first home.*
Passions *– this could be considered an extension of interests and hobbies. The case specifically discusses Meredith's ingenious method (Passion Points) of gauging a customer's level of interest in a given area such as cooking.*
Geographic/Demographic *– The case describes how Meredith creates different versions of their bigger magazines (e.g., "Better Homes and Gardens") across different demographic and geographic segments. For example, a special version of BHG has been offered in the past to subscribers of a particular income range.*

2. Which target marketing strategy do you think best describes Meredith's efforts? Support your choice.
Of the four main targeting strategies covered in the text (undifferentiated, differentiated, concentrated, and micromarketing), Meredith clearly pursues a differentiated strategy. Meredith clearly targets several market segments and designs separate offers for each. For its print magazines alone, Meredith

publishes hundreds of titles. Each of these is crafted to appeal to a certain kind of customer.

3. How does Meredith use its variety of products to build relationships with the right customers?
Meredith's efforts to build relationships with customers are very closely tied to its segmentation activities. Overall, Meredith's extensive database gathers as much information as possible about a customer so that various customer needs can be met. The idea is not just to sell a person one magazine, but to create a link with a customer and then become the go-to source for multiple interest areas. For example, one person may be looking at remodeling their home, love to cook, and have diabetes. There is a Meredith magazine for each and every one of those characteristics. Also, Meredith's deep portfolio allows for adapting with customers as their needs change within a given interest area. For example, "American Baby" (prenatal), "Parents" (postnatal), and "Family Circle" (teens and tweens) are all designed to appeal to parents, but meet different needs depending upon life stage. Thus, a prospective parent might become a Meredith customer by subscribing to "American Baby," and then progress through the other publications, remaining a Meredith customer for life.

Teaching Ideas

1. Have students visit the Meredith website. In conjunction with the first discussion question, have students categorize the various magazine titles according to segmentation variables.

2. Lead the class in a discussion about the future of print magazines. Have them comment and speculate on the future of this industry. Small groups could generate recommendations for a company like Meredith and how it might adapt to the changes in culture and technology. For further supplements, instructors might research the Meredith publication websites to discover what Meredith is already doing in that area.

Chapter 7
Swiss Army

Executive Summary

Victorinox created a widely known brand with its Swiss Army knives. High brand awareness prompted the company to extend its brand to other products such as watches, luggage, and apparel. Although the company tries to maintain a cross-cutting ethos of Swiss precision and multifunctional products, its expansion into more fashion-oriented apparel raises the question of brand dilution.

Questions and Answers

1. What additional products and lines might Swiss Army consider?
Here are just a few ideas. Swiss Army could extend its "travel" line with multifunctional travel kits, such a personal grooming kits, clothing repair kits, and first-aid kits. It could also extend into travel services ranging from adventure travel to tours of Switzerland. In addition, Swiss Army could extend its "tool" line with cordless drill/screwdriver sets, car-repair tool kits, etc. The company could also expand into camping gear with a line of hikers' backpacks, tents, camp cookware, etc.

2. How do brand extensions affect a company such as Swiss Army in both positive and negative ways?
Positive aspects include:
    - *adds revenue from sales of new lines of products*
    - *leverages relationships with retailers or distribution partners*
    - *provides economies of scale for brand marketing efforts*
    - *recruits new customers as they buy the new lines, learn to like the brand, and buy further products from other lines.*

    Negative aspects include:
    - *potentially offends loyal "purist" customers*
    - *diverts management attention from the core product*
    - *dilutes marketing messages or brand identify with tangential, off-message products*
    - *presents product quality risks if the company partners with a third-party maker of the new product line.*

3. Why did Swiss Army open a retail store? How does the store help the company build its brand?
Swiss Army created an "experience store" to help introduce its consumers to the broader line of products now available under the brand name. The store enables customers to preview all of Swiss Army's products and product categories in one

place, introducing them to products which the customers may not have known the company makes. The store draws in the young and the curious, drawing a younger consumers segment and thus raising the level of awareness of Swiss Army Brands to that group. Finally, the store helps to create a relationship between the brand and the customer. Retail store employees are trained to sell the brand, which makes the brand stronger.

Teaching Ideas

This video case illustrates the challenge of associating multiple product lines under a single brand -- are all the products and categories compatible in the minds of prospective customers? One way to understand this problem is to consider pairs of actual or prospective products.

Have students list alternative products that the company might make or license as part of an on-going brand expansion strategy (discussion question 1). For each idea, discuss the possible opportunities and risks of expanding the brand in different directions. Then, think about how pairs of product lines interrelate -- e.g., knives vs. watches, knives vs. luggage, watches vs. luggage, etc. The class could create a matrix listing the existing and proposed products on both the rows and columns and discuss the compatibility of different pairs of products. With a matrix, the class might discover how products in one set are mutually consistent or compatible with each other, whereas other products either don't extend naturally or create a risk of dilution or incompatible brand messages. For example, would Swiss chocolates go well with Swiss Army knives? Throughout the discussion, try to highlight the tension between wanting to leverage the brand and leveraging it too far.

Chapter 8
Ziba

Executive Summary

ZIBA is one of a new breed of consultancies whose soul purpose is to help corporations better understand customer needs and to turn that understanding into ground-breaking new products. ZIBA's novel process for developing successful new products begins with the customer. The firm's novel approach to market research utilizes the likes of social anthropologists and cultural ethnographers get to the heart of what makes consumers tick. ZIBA's unique approach has earned it contracts with major corporations ranging from P&G and KitchenAid to Logitech, Microsoft, and Intel, as well as a variety of small start-up companies.

Questions and Answers

1. Describe ZIBA's product design process. Is this process consistent with the one detailed in the chapter?
   Figure 8.1 of the text establishes the major stages in new-product development. These include idea generation, idea screening, concept development and testing, marketing strategy development, business analysis, product development, test marketing, and commercialization.

   It is very clear from the video case that ZIBA is not the type of design firm that operates by convention. The following are some of the steps that ZIBA follows in arriving at new product designs. Students might be challenged once they arrive at such steps to compare them with those in the book. It should be noted that ZIBA's process may not necessarily follow a prescribed order (referred to as a linear process in the case). Some of the following steps may occur in an order different than indicated.
   - *Research – this is emphasized as the first step in ZIBA's process. The company places a heavy weight on understanding the customer. By this, it is not just referring to knowing customer needs and wants. It is talking about gaining a deep understanding of values and emotions; of understanding what makes customers tick. To get at this, ZIBA not only follows standard research methods. It employs more qualitative methods by cultural anthropologists.*
   - *Establish customer insights – conducting research helps to arrive at the "aha" touch points that have the potential to establish customer-product relationships. This step is all about finding insights that can establish a meaningful emotional connection with the consumer.*
   - *Refining and testing – even before design begins, ideas are refined and tested. One example of this from the case is the "gravity method" through which the good ideas rise to the top and the not-so-good ideas sink to the bottom and are discarded.*

- *Examine the market and competition – this is the part of ZIBA's process that can be closely aligned with scanning the environment. This creates the context for a ZIBA design. Trends (through trend analysis) are discovered and tracked. Activity of competition is monitored. Information gathered from this phase is important in establishing the timing of new product releases.*
- *Journey to create a meaningful customer experience – there is not a great deal mentioned about this phase. The implication is that this phase is where product development and launch take place. It is not clear how much of a role ZIBA plays in this phase. It could be that ZIBA's more critical role is getting to this phase, then letting the company handle the remainder of the process.*

2. Discuss the various ways that ZIBA's process focuses on customer relationships in its design process.
   In trying to arrive at the means of connecting on a deep, meaningful level, ZIBA considers the many ways that customers relate to any given product. One of the better examples of creating customer relationships is noted through the ZIBA project for the City of Portland in creating a planned community. ZIBA had the challenge of having people experience what life would be like in such a community. This was an extreme challenge given that the community did not exist. Thus, ZIBA created multiple methods of helping to establish a consumer-product relationship. The community concept of "bright green living" was communicated through a website experience, a showroom experience, and a site experience.

3. Discuss the relevancy of the product life-cycle to ZIBA's design efforts. Do ZIBA's activities focus on any particular phase of the life-cycle?

   No information is given in this case that indicates any particular attention to the product life cycle. However, students could be given the challenge of considering some of ZIBA's products (squeegee, satellite radio interface, planned waterfront community) and discussing how the product life cycle might have affected ZIBA's planning activities.

Teaching Ideas

Visit the ZIBA website at www.ziba.com to create a more complete portfolio of examples of ZIBA design. Incorporate images and descriptions of such examples in to the video case presentation and the students' involvement in the discussion questions. Particular attention should be given to ZIBAs unorthodox approach and the outcomes that result from such.

Chapter 9
General Electric

Executive Summary

GE recently applied its considerable marketing muscle to revamp, rebrand, and reprice its entire appliances line. Rather than accepting lower prices, GE invested heavily in new product innovation to add more customer value that would support higher prices and margins. In addition to its core mass-market GE appliance brand, the company added the GE Monogram and GE Profile lines.

Questions and Answers

1. Does GE use a cost-based or value-based pricing approach? Support your response.
   A cost-based pricing strategy would be one in which the foundation for price is the cost of goods sold. There are various types of cost-based strategies (e.g., cost-plus, break-even). However, there is very little mentioned in this case about the cost of GE's appliance products.

   Rather, the entire focus is on positioning the Profile and Monogram lines around innovation and emotion. The whole idea is to raise the perception of value for customers in a manner that they are willing to pay a higher price. Certainly, product quality (material, feature, etc.) are important. But this is definitely a value-based approach.

2. Which of the product mix pricing strategies discussed in the book most closely describes GE's approach?
   GE employs product line pricing, taking into account cost differences between the products in the line, customer evaluations of their different features, and competitors' prices. In many industries, sellers use well-established price points for the products in their line.

3. How did the new positioning statements for the Monogram and Profile lines affect pricing decisions?
   GE Profile targeted the upper quartile of the market, offering "the marriage of style and innovation" with "the best in contemporary design matched with the latest kitchen technologies." GE Monogram targeted the ultrahigh end of the market, offering built-in products with "depth and breadth of design choices that allow you to customize your home and make it your own." The new positioning allowed GE to increase its prices to match the high end positioning of its products.

Teaching Ideas

In small groups, have students list the characteristics of a consumer considering purchasing a GE Profile appliance. Then have the groups list the characteristics of a consumer considering purchasing a GE Monogram appliance. Compare the descriptions to those discussed in the video. Ask students how the pricing of each line reflects the characteristics they listed.

Chapter 10
Progressive

Executive Summary

Progressive has grown into the third-largest auto insurance group in the country. Progressive attained its status by not only focusing on growth but by focusing on innovation. Some of Progressive's most innovative moves have involved its channels of distribution. Whereas most insurance companies distribute their products to consumers via intermediary agents or direct-to-consumer methods, Progressive was one of the first companies to recognize the value in doing both.

In 1995, Progressive moved into the future by becoming the first major insurer in the world to launch a Web site. In 1997, customers could buy auto insurance policies online in real time. Today, customers can do everything from managing their own account information to reporting claims directly through Progressive's Web site.

Questions and Answers

1. Apply the concept of the supply chain to Progressive.
   As per chapter 10, the concept of supply chain management deals with "managing upstream and downstream value-added flows of materials, final goods, and related information among suppliers, the company, resellers, and final consumers." This concept is probably much more easily applied to examples involving tangible products. In this case, Progressive is creating and distributing an intangible service.

   One approach that students might take for this is to list out the possible participants in the supply chain, then discuss the extent to which each applies to Progressive. For example, there really are no suppliers for Progressive's insurance products (at least, none that are mentioned in this case). The company manages the flow of "product" and related information with its agents as well as directly to its customers. With respect to its agent channel, Progressive has nurtured these relationships for over 40 years. Progressive supplies these resellers with training, product information, financial incentives (commissions), and flexible pricing for products. For Progressive's direct channel, the company communicates to customers through mass-media advertising (this has also had an incidental effect on increasing brand awareness for customers shopping through agents). It also communicates through its website. Various features are given through this medium for customers to become educated about Progressive's products. Direct customers can then interact with the company and purchase product in two ways, by telephone or through the Internet.

2. Using the model of consumer and business channels found in the chapter, sketch out as many channels for Progressive as you can. How does each of these channels meet distinct customer needs?
   As discussed in the first question, Progressive distributes through two main channels:

   Progressive ☛ *Agents* ☛ *Consumer segment 1*

   The customers in this segment need more hands on help from someone in determining the type of policy and coverage that they might need. This customer may not be Internet savvy. They also may want to go to a source that has multiple options in terms of companies to choose from.

   Progressive ☛ *Consumer segment 2*

   Customers in this segment are looking for benefits of control and convenience. The customer is in control of the process from start to finish. If they choose, they never have to talk to a representative of the company. Such customers can also access the company and even make purchases any time of day from any location. Cross-shopping customers also may be even more attracted to this channel as cross-company comparisons are made readily available as clearly and easily as if shopping for a consumer good through a shopping engine.

   note: some students may include more than one channel for direct to consumer. 800-call centers are one channel with the customers calling in, and the Internet is another channel.

3. Discuss the various ways that Progressive has had an impact on the insurance industry.
   Responses here should focus on the innovations that Progressive has pioneered in this industry. Progressive was the first insurance company to:
   - *start a website.*
   - *sell an insurance product on the Internet.*
   - *provide an easy comparison to competing company's products.*
   - *offer online claims services.*
   - *include a "call me" button on the website to speak with a representative.*
   - *provide text messaging bill reminders.*
   - *provide concierge claim processing.*
   - *put response vehicles on the road.*

Teaching Ideas

In addition to the concepts covered in the discussion questions, a good class discussion may focus around the concept of channel conflict. Lead a discussion that centers on the synergy achieved through promoting the direct-to-consumer channels with mass-media advertising. How did this benefit the agency channel? One point that should be brought out is that even after selling online for over 10 years, the agency channel still comprises 65% of Progressive's business and is much larger than it was pre-Internet. Be sure that the discussion touches upon how choosing to go with a dual-channel strategy could produce significant channel conflict. How might Progressive's direct strategy have clashed with the agency network?

Chapter 11
Wellbeing

Executive Summary

In 2003, Dan Wales and Matt Lennox opened their first Wellbeing restaurant. Their goal was to offer consumers a healthy alternative to typical fast food options. Working with fresh ingredients, bright and open stores, and a well-crafted, healthy menu, the new chain offered something new. "There are few truly healthy fast food chains," says Wales. "People have been desperate for healthy options." So it came as no surprise that customers responded with enthusiasm to Wellbeing's new choices as they gobbled up sandwiches, salads, soups, juices, smoothies, and fruit salads. In only a few years, the chain has expanded to 18 stores and expects to nearly double that number in the next two years.

Questions and Answers

1. Categorize Wellbeing according to the four characteristics of retailers discussed in the chapter.
   Amount of Service – *At Wellbeing, customers perform their own "locate-compare-select" process with little to no assistance from any sales staff. By the text book definition, this would classify Wellbeing as a self-service operation. But clearly, the fact that the customer cannot prepare their own food changes things. A customer cannot go in to a Wellbeing store and serve themselves without any assistance from store personnel.*

   As a service operation, the application of such classifications is a bit different than that of a tangible good retailer. Consider stores where customers select their own items off the shelf and then simply pay for them (e.g., a convenience store). In many respects, a quick-service food operation like Wellbeing is no different than that. At the convenience store, the tangible good was not made by the customer. It was manufactured by a company and placed on a shelf. At an operation like Wellbeing, the food is being made on the spot, then essentially placed on the "shelf" for the customer to retrieve it.

   The difference is that at a fast-food operation, while a customer can get their own condiments, their own drink, and choose what they want to have, a customer cannot make their own food. Thus, it would seem that Wellbeing is more readily classified as a limited-service operation.

   Product line – *Wellbing is a specialty store. It carries a narrow line of products with a fairly deep assortment. It is focused on a specific segment of the quick-service food market.*

Relative prices – *A quick-service food store like Wellbeing does not fit neatly into any of the relative price classifications given in the text. It certainly is not a warehouse club, factory outlet, or any other kind of off-price retailer. It also could not be classified as a discount store as it is not offering food products cheaper than its competition. It also does not demonstrate the other characteristics of discount stores. Thus, this classification is not really relevant to Wellbeing.*

Organizational approach – *As a retail organization with more than two outlets (it is mentioned that Wellbeing has 16 stores), Wellbeing is a chain store. There is brief mention of Wellbeing's relationship with franchisees, thus, it is also a franchise operation.*

2. How is Wellbeing positioned in the marketplace? Which consumers does the chain target? Are its product assortment, pricing, promotion, and place decisions consistent with this targeting and positioning?
Positioning - *Wellbeing offers dining experience for consumers who want convenient, healthy alternatives to traditional fast food. To support this positioning, the company offers healthful products that can be eaten on the go at reasonably low prices in convenient locations.*

Targeting - *Wellbeing is targeting consumers with a fast-paced lifestyle (time poor consumers) who value health and wellbeing. Such consumers are likely working professionals with little time on their hands. The wellbeing consumer is also likely the type of person who exercises more than the average consumer. Consumers who are environmentally conscious may also be attracted to Wellbeing's offerings.*

Marketing mix – *Product. Wellbeing worked with a dietician to develop healthy and tasty menu items. Fresh fruits and vegetables are selected and delivered to stores daily. The focus is on a core of lesser offerings rather than 20 to 30 different sandwiches. This makes it possible for the items to be made fresh daily, and to be made quickly.*
Place. Store locations are selected to maximize traffic flow. Store design is oriented around creating an efficient flow so that service times are minimized.
Promotion. As a young, growing company, Wellbeing does not have a lot of external promotion. Their focus is inward on the customer experience. They utilize a great deal of signage that promotes to customers once they are near or in the stores.
Price. Wellbeing has done research that shows that customers are willing to pay a premium for healthy food. However, products are also priced within a range that is not outside the expectation for fast food.

3. Which trend affecting the future of retailing do you think will most impact Wellbeing in the coming years?
   Trends include new retail forms and shortening retail life cycles, growth of nonstore retailing, retail convergence, the rise of megaretailers, growing importance of retail technology, global expansion of major retailers, and retail stores as "communities" or "hangouts." Probably the greatest trend is mentioned during the "opportunity" section of the video when it is mentioned that more and more consumers are being educated about healthy eating. Thus, Wellbeing is focusing on a trend that is growing.

Teaching Ideas

1. Have students list companies targeting similar consumers in the United States. Next have students compare the positioning statements of those companies to that of Wellbeing.

2. Ask students to consider how altering the price decisions that Wellbeing has implemented might impact the company's product and positioning decisions.

Chapter 12
Crispin Porter +Bogusky

Executive Summary

Crispin Porter + Bogusky has been working over time to prove that it is the most innovative firm at truly integrating marketing promotions. Crispin has worked miracles for companies like Virgin Atlantic Airways and BMW's MINI by executing non-traditional campaigns designed to work within limited budgets. Crispin's unique capability to balance strategy with creativity is what produced such ground breaking efforts as the "Truth" campaign. Crisping landed this campaign in the late 1990s after the state of Florida successfully sued tobacco companies and set up a foundation to fund anti-tobacco advertising targeted toward youth. What followed was a campaign that shaped the agency and changed the nature of social advertising forever.

Questions and Answers

1. Alex Bogusky once said, "Anything and everything is an ad." What does this means? How is Crispin putting this idea into practice?
   When most people think of an "ad", they think of the traditional media such as broadcast, print, and outdoor (e.g., billboards). But because CP+B has become so adept at thinking outside the box, it employs various non-traditional media. CP+B's philosophy is that any message communicated through a medium of any kind can be an ad. Thus, they have defined events, rallies, video games, apparel, and websites as ads.

2. In what ways has Crispin differentiated itself from other advertising agencies?
   While this case does not discuss other agencies specifically, it does point out various things that make CP+B unique and therefore differentiate it from others. These include:
   a. *the culture – people who work at CP+B are workaholics. Not for the common workaholic reasons, but because they feel that they are part of something truly unique, truly different.*
   b. *non-traditional approach – many agencies are focusing on integrating marketing communications across different media. But CP+B has a knack for employing things that are totally out of the norm.*
   c. *size – it is a big agency that thinks and functions like a small one.*
   d. *taking on the impossible – CP+B is at its best when signing up for something that others in the industry say can not be done.*

3. Give some examples of how Crispin balances strategy with creativity to develop truly integrated marketing communications campaigns.
   The "Truth" campaign is the only basis for example in this case. In examining this campaign, it is apparent that the strategy was to create a message that would

communicate the idea of rebelling against the "man," or, Big Tobacco. This strategy also involved creating a brand with which the target market could identify. This portion of the process could be considered CP+B's definition of the problem.

After having defined the problem, CP+B used this strategy as an umbrella. It then employed one of its greatest strengths...creating ideas. As stated in the case, those ideas can come from anywhere...a creative director, an intern, or a secretary. This is what takes CP+B into employing tradition (ads and PR) as well as non-traditional (events, rallies, gear, apparel, websites) methods. The key is that the company doesn't just throw darts and do something zany because it is zany. It looks for ways to communicate a message that fall in line with the established strategy. Thus, everything from the apparel to the ad "Body Bags" communicated the strategic message of rebelling against Big Tobacco.

Teaching Ideas

Crisping Porter + Bogusky has created some really ground breaking campaigns. The "Truth" campaign is only one of them. Gather information, print, and broadcast ads from other campaigns such as CP+B's efforts with Burger King over the past few years. Presenting this material in class along side the video case will combine to make a truly informative as well as entertaining presentation.

Chapter 13
Nudie

Executive Summary

All across the globe, consumers are seeking all-natural, wholesome foods. Even Wal-Mart, a low-price leader, carries organic and all-natural foods. Nudie, a quirky little company in Australia, makes its own contribution to the fast-growing natural foods market—all-natural fruit juices, fruit crushes, and smoothies that provide a day's fruit in every bottle. Amidst a sea of all natural products, how did Nudie reach customers and encourage them to try its new products? Through a carefully designed program of personal selling and sales promotion.

Nudie uses well-crafted point-of-purchase displays and a devoted, motivated sales force to work with resellers to reach consumers. As a result, Nudie is the fastest growing juice maker in Australia, attracting an ever-increasing number of highly devoted customers who love Nudie's products. Says one Nudie customer, "love and happiness are overrated. But nudies make living worthwhile!"

Questions and Answers

1. How does Nudie's process for selecting sales representatives compare to the process described in the text?
   With respect to recruiting and selecting salespeople, the text highlights the importance of attaining top performers rather than relative-to-low performers. Four characteristics of top performing sales people are intrinsic motivation, disciplined work style, the ability to close a sale, and the ability to build relationships with customers.

   Nudie's prospective sales representatives often seek out positions with the company because of their passion for the product. As a result, Nudie's selection process may differ from that of many companies. Nudie primarily assesses applicant's personality and work ethic to insure a good fit with the company. Thus, it would seem that Nudie puts more weight on intrinsic motivation and disciplined work style as characteristics.

2. What sales promotion tools does Nudie employ to reach consumers and encourage sales?
   Nudie uses point of purchase displays, concert sponsorships, rallies, contests, samples, premiums for distributors and sellers, and advertising specialties.

3. Select a sales promotion tool not listed in your previous response. How could Nudie use that tool to further promote its products?
   Student responses will vary.

Teaching Ideas

Have students reflect on their personal experiences with salespeople and list the characteristics of the typical salesperson. Compare student responses. Are the images general positive or negative? How do they compare to the description in the text of a successful salesperson?

Chapter 14
Google

Executive Summary

Fourteen years ago, Google didn't even exist as a concept. Yet the advent of the World Wide Web set the foundation for what would become Google's mission: to organize the world's information and make it universally accessible and useful. Google was not the first Web search engine. But soon after founders Larry Page and Sergey Brin introduced their service based on a unique search technology, Google became *the* go-to way to search for information on the Internet. Google now has dozens of free services, including foreign language translation, stock quotes, maps, phone book listings, images, videos, and news headlines.

But perhaps Google's most revolutionary impact on the dot.com environment is the manner in which it has turned Internet advertising upside down. Today, services such as AdWords (keyword search advertising) and AdSense (a method that generates only the most relevant ads for client Web sites) are breaking new ground because they result in ads that actually help consumers.

Questions and Answers

1. Brainstorm the many benefits that Google provides for consumers.
   The case illustrates many consumer and business benefits. However, students may also come up with things that are not mentioned in the case. Hal Varian, Chief Economist for Google, makes a statement in the case that illustrates benefits to both consumer and business. He says that Google matches up people who have information with people who are seeking information; and matches people who want to sell things with people who want to buy things. Clearly, there are benefits here for both sides.

   More specifically, the case highlights one single major benefit for consumers: free stuff. Searching, Google Maps, Gmail, and YouTube are all major features of Google's vast web-presence. Each of these can be analyzed in terms of the benefits that customers receive. For example, benefits of Google Maps include being able to attain point-by-point directions between any two points, being directed to points of interest like restaurants, hotels, airports, etc., and saving time by not having to drive around or ask for directions.

2. Brainstorm the many benefits that Google provides for online marketers.
   matches people who want to sell things with people who want to buy things.
   The main benefits for marketers are in the area of promotions. The video highlights Google's evolution from text-only ads at the top of the page to where it

is today. Student responses should recognize the two main Google ad programs and the benefits provided by each:

AdWords – advertisers could reach more consumers more efficiently by purchasing keywords that would produce the company website if the word were used in a keyword query. This tool helps advertisers by directing ads that are more relevant to users. The auction-based system incorporates both the price that a company is willing to pay for keywords plus the user's interests. This utilizes click-through rates. Thus, advertisers aren't just paying an upfront cost to be "on top" of the query, but they are paying on a "per-click" basis that links actual ad effectiveness to advertising cost.
AdSense – This ad tool allows Website owners to generate revenue on their sites by inserting ads for other companies that are relevant to their website. They do not have to know where to look for advertisers or worry about making sales. Google takes care of all of that and allows for a simple plug-and-play format.

Other benefits to businesses are that Google's ad products allow them to set up their own ads in minutes, measure advertising effectiveness immediately, and generate revenue on their own sites by inserting relevant advertising.

3. Visit www.google.com. Based on what you find there, discuss Google's presence in each of the four major e-marketing domains.
   There are an endless number of items that may result in Google's vast array of features. Here are a few examples:
   ***B2C** – The most obvious example of this is when consumers use keyword searches to find company websites. Specifically, Google's Product Search function only provides lists of online retailers. Gmail also provides a venue for this.*
   ***B2B** – Examples of true B2B may be harder to find. Clearly, keyword searches will turn up companies that are suppliers or purchasers of industrial products. Also, pages like Google Finance are set up for both individuals and companies to gather data. And Google itself caters to the business community with its ad products.*
   ***C2B** – In this domain, consumers communicate with companies. Given that most websites offer such options, Google's keyword searches will clearly lead to C2B opportunities. However, Gmail, Blogger, and Groups are Google features that also allow consumers to interact with companies.*
   ***C2C** – Examples for this should be easy: Blogger, Gmail, Groups, YouTube and Google Video, Orkut, etc.*

<u>Teaching Ideas</u>

This is a case that students should be able to relate to very well because in many respects, Google is the Internet. In addition to the discussion questions and activities that may revolve around them, one interesting approach to this case would be to lead students in a discussion surrounding the "Promises and Challenges of E-Commerce" section. Some discussion points might be:

- The extent to which the Internet has, is, or will replace traditional sources of commerce and information.
- The disadvantages that the Internet brings with its advantages (e.g., it makes information much more accessible to individuals, but at the same time inundates us with information overload).
- The privacy and security issues associated with Internet commerce.

Chapter 15
NIVEA

Executive Summary

In 1911, German company Nivea introduced the revolutionary Nivea Crème in a simple blue tin. Today, that Crème is the centerpiece of a wide range of personal care products. The product line includes everything from soap, shampoo, and shaving products, to baby care products, deodorant, and sunscreen. From small beginnings, the company's products are sold today in more than 150 countries worldwide.

But despite this global presence, most Nivea consumers believe that the products they buy are produced and marketed locally. Why? Although Nivea looks for commonalities between consumers around the globe, the company's marketers also recognize the differences between consumers in different markets. So Nivea adapts its marketing mix to reach local consumers while keeping its message consistent everywhere products are sold. This globally consistent, locally customized marketing strategy has sold more than 11 billion tins of the traditional Nivea Crème.

Questions and Answers

1. Which of the five strategies for adapting products and promotion for the global market does Nivea employ?
   Ms. Peters, VP of International Brand Management for Nivea, clearly states the company strategy. She says that the main challenge is to not look for differences between countries, but for commonalities. She goes on to say that only products should be varied to reflect local cultural preferences, but that promotions should be kept as consistent as possible. This philosophy best illustrates the product adaptation strategy of the five global and communications strategies.

2. Visit Nivea's Website, www.nivea.com, and tour the sites for several different countries. How does Nivea market its products differently in different countries? How does the company maintain the consistency of its brand?
   Student responses will vary based on the sites they visit. Students should look beyond the language differences on sites and focus on other aspects that they can observe without knowledge of foreign languages. They should find that Nivea changes small details on each site to cater to local consumers. For example, the models on each site vary to reflect the local culture and heritage. Additionally, the site sections vary as do things like the product line. Nivea does not offer every product in every country (Netherlands identifies eight different product lines while the U.S. has only five. Saudi Arabia has ten!). But when there is overlap, the products are essentially the same.

Something else that might be noted is the degree of "sensuality" that is communicated on various country sites. The U.S. site has a section where customers can send e-card invitations that are quite suggestive. The same type of feature on the Saudi Arabia site is set up only to send Valentine's Day cards that are not framed as overt sexual invitations. One other thing that is pretty consistent is that each country site appears to offer the same basic information about Nivea and consistently tells the Nivea story, communicating the brand's history and positioning. It should be noted that this is not necessarily in conflict with the standardized promotional strategy that Ms. Peters discusses in the video case.

Teaching Ideas

1. Have students list other hair and skin care products and identify each product's manufacturer. Are most of the products manufactured in the US or abroad?
2. In small groups, have students debate the pros and cons of standardized versus adapted marketing mixes.

Chapter 16
NFL

Executive Summary

The NFL offers fans much more than Sunday afternoons full of football. Players and teams alike consider football and community involvement to be the twin pillars of the NFL. Through more than twenty separate community programs, the NFL focuses considerable human efforts to give back to the community and encourage others to do the same.

One of the NFL's biggest efforts to engage in socially responsible behavior is its partnership with the United Way that has been ongoing for more than 30 years. This partnership is exhibited through various types of team and player support as well as through public service ads. With help from the NFL, United Way fundraising has skyrocketed from $800 million in 1974 to nearly $4 billion today. And the NFL benefits by building stronger relationships with fans through its community involvement.

Questions and Answers

1. Why does the NFL partner with United Way? How, if at all, does that partnership impact your opinion of the League? How does it impact your interest in volunteering?
   Student responses will vary. The NFL partners with United Way to build deeper relationships with fans and create a better image of the league in the communities in which it operates. It also partners to benefit the United Way, creating publicity and encouraging donations and volunteerism.

2. Make a list of social criticisms of the NFL. Then visit JoinTheTeam.com and read more about the NFL's outreach programs. Do these efforts alleviate any concerns you have about the League's negative impact on society?
   Student responses will vary based on impressions of the NFL and its activities in the community.

3. By the text's definition, does the NHL practice "enlightened marketing"?
   The philosophy of enlightened marketing holds that a company's marketing should support the best long-run performance of the marketing system. Enlightened marketing consists of five principles: consumer-oriented marketing, customer-value marketing, innovative marketing, sense-of-mission marketing, and societal marketing. Student opinions will vary as to the extent that the NFL practices enlightened marketing. However, the company does make efforts to follow each of the five principles.

Teaching Ideas

1. Have students make a list of the socially responsibly activities of the businesses they patronize. Do those activities influence the students' choice to buy the company's products and services?
2. In small groups, have students discuss the pros and cons of trying to balance the double bottom line. Is it truly possible to run a mission centered business and still make a profit?